SUPER DUPER EXTRA DELUXE
ESSENTIAL HANDBOOK

STATS ON MORE THAN
1,000 CHARACTERS!

SCHOLASTIC INC.

All rights reserved. Published by Scholastic Inc., *Publishers since 1920*. SCHOLASTIC and associated logos are trademarks and/or registered trademarks of Scholastic Inc.

The publisher does not have any control over and does not assume any responsibility for author or third-party websites or their content.

ISBN 978-1-339-02801-9

10 9 8 7 6 5 4 3 2 1   24 25 26 27 28

Printed in China   62

First printing 2024

Interior design by Kay Petronio
Cover design by Cheung Tai

WELCOME TO THE WORLD OF POKÉMON!

Kanto . . . Johto . . . Hoenn . . .
Sinnoh . . . Unova . . . Kalos . . .
Alola . . . Galar . . . and now Paldea!

There are nine known Pokémon regions bursting with fascinating Pokémon—creatures that come in all shapes, sizes, and personalities. They live in oceans, caves, old towers, rivers, tall grass, and many other areas.

Trainers can find, capture, train, trade, collect, and use Pokémon in battle against their rivals in the quest to become the best.

The key to success with Pokémon is staying informed. Information about each Pokémon's type, category, height, and weight can make all the difference in catching, raising, battling, and evolving your Pokémon.

In this book, you'll get all the stats and facts you need about more than 1,000 Pokémon. You'll discover how each Pokémon evolves and which Abilities it has.

So get ready, Trainers: With this *Super Duper Extra Deluxe Essential Handbook*, you'll be prepared to master almost any Pokémon challenge!

3

GHOLDENGO

Coin Entity Pokémon

#1000

TYPE: STEEL-GHOST

Its body seems to be made up of 1,000 coins. This Pokémon gets along well with others and is quick to make friends with anybody.

It has a sturdy body made up of stacked coins. Gholdengo overwhelms its enemies by firing coin after coin at them in quick succession.

HOW TO SAY IT: GOHL-den-goh
IMPERIAL HEIGHT: 3'11"
IMPERIAL WEIGHT: 66.1 lbs.
METRIC HEIGHT: 1.2 m
METRIC WEIGHT: 30.0 kg
GENDER: Unknown
ABILITIES: Good as Gold
WEAKNESSES: Fire, Ghost, Dark, Ground

GIMMIGHOUL

GHOLDENGO

211

HOW TO USE THIS BOOK

This book provides the basic stats and facts you need to know to start your Pokémon journey. Here's what you'll discover about each Pokémon:

NAME

NUMBER: National Pokédex Number

TYPE: Each Pokémon has a type, and some even have two. (Pokémon with two types are called dual-type Pokémon.) Every Pokémon type comes with advantages and disadvantages.

CATEGORY: All Pokémon belong to a certain category.

DESCRIPTION: Knowledge is power. Pokémon Trainers have to know their stuff. Find out everything you need to know about your Pokémon here.

HOW TO SAY IT: When it comes to Pokémon pronunciation, it's easy to get tongue-tied! There are many Pokémon with unusual names, so we'll help you sound them out. Soon you'll be saying Pokémon names so perfectly, you'll sound like a professor.

HEIGHT AND WEIGHT: How does each Pokémon measure up? Find out by checking its height and weight stats. And remember, good things come in all shapes and sizes. It's up to every Trainer to work with their Pokémon and play up its strengths.

GENDER: Most Pokémon are both male (♂) and female (♀), but some are exclusively one gender or have an Unknown gender.

ABILITIES: Most Pokémon have one Ability that can help them in battle. A Pokémon's Ability usually relates back to its type in one way or another. Some Pokémon have one of two possible Abilities.

WEAKNESSES: In a battle, the effectiveness of a Pokémon's moves depends on the type of its opponent. A Pokémon's weaknesses show what other Pokémon types will most successfully be able to damage it in an attack!

EVOLUTION: If your Pokémon has an evolved form or pre-evolved form, we'll show you its place in the chain and how it evolves.

GUIDE TO POKÉMON TYPES

A Pokémon's type can tell you a lot about it—from where to find it in the wild to the moves it'll be able to use on the battlefield. Type is the key to unlocking a Pokémon's power.

A clever Trainer should always consider type when picking a Pokémon for a match, because each type shows a Pokémon's strengths and weaknesses. For example, a Fire type may melt an Ice type, but against a Water type, it might find it's the one in hot water. And while a Water type usually has the upper hand in battle with a Fire type, a Water type move would act like a sprinkler on a Grass-type Pokémon. But when that same Grass type is battling a Fire type, it just might get scorched.

HERE ARE THE EIGHTEEN KNOWN POKÉMON TYPES:

FIRE

GRASS

WATER

NORMAL

ELECTRIC

BUG

GHOST

FLYING

FIGHTING

PSYCHIC

STEEL

ROCK

GROUND

ICE

POISON

DARK

DRAGON

FAIRY

BATTLE BASICS

WHY BATTLE?

There are two basic reasons for a Pokémon to battle. One is for sport. You can battle another Trainer in a friendly competition. Your Pokémon do the fighting, but you decide which Pokémon and which moves to use.

The second reason is to catch wild Pokémon. Wild Pokémon have no training and no owners. They can be found pretty much anywhere. Battle is one of the main ways to catch a Pokémon. But other Trainers' Pokémon are off-limits. You can't capture their Pokémon, even if you win a competition.

CHOOSING THE BEST POKEMON FOR THE JOB

As you prepare for your first battle, you may have several Pokémon to choose from. Use the resources in this book to help you decide which Pokémon would be best. If you're facing a Fire-type Pokémon, like Fuecoco, you can put out its flames with a Water-type Pokémon, like Quaxly.

THE FACE-OFF

You and your Pokémon will have to face, and hopefully defeat, each and every Pokémon on the other Trainer's team. You win when your Pokémon have defeated all the other Trainer's Pokémon. But Pokémon do not get seriously hurt in battle. If they are defeated, they faint and then return to their Poké Balls to rest and be healed. An important part of a Trainer's job is to take good care of their Pokémon.

MEGA EVOLUTION

A select group of Pokémon possesses the ability to Mega Evolve. A Pokémon can only Mega Evolve during battle, and Mega Evolution increases its strength in ways no Trainer could imagine.

But Mega Evolution requires more than just capturing a Pokémon of a specific species. First, there must be an incredibly strong bond of trust and friendship between the Trainer and Pokémon. They must be unified on and off the battlefield.

Second, the Trainer must possess both a Key Stone and the right Mega Stone. Each Pokémon species has a specific Mega Stone. A Trainer must quest for the perfect one and prove themself worthy of its power.

LUCARIO   **MEGA LUCARIO**

GIGANTAMAX POKÉMON

In the Galar region, some Pokémon have a Gigantamax form. It's a special kind of Dynamax that both increases their size and changes their appearance! Gigantamax Pokémon are extremely rare—not every Pokémon of a given species can Gigantamax—and each has access to a special G-Max Move.

REGIONAL FORMS

In Alola, Galar, and Paldea, some Pokémon have a unique form that can differ in many ways from their previously discovered form. These Alolan, Galarian, and Paldean form Pokémon may look different, have a different height and weight, be a different type, and use different moves. Each form of Pokémon has its own strengths and weaknesses. A Pokémon and its regional form can seem like two totally different creatures!

These regional variations develop because of differences in the environments between regions where the Pokémon live. For example, the reason Alolan Exeggutor have grown taller is Alola's warm and sunny climate. It's perfect for Exeggcute and Exeggutor to thrive. Some believe that Alolan Exeggutor is actually the "true" form of the Pokémon!

Some regional forms also evolve into a totally new Pokémon than their previously discovered form does. For example, only Galarian Farfetch'd evolves into Sirfetch'd.

11

ULTRA BEASTS

Ultra Beasts possess mighty powers. These mysterious creatures come from Ultra Wormholes.

LEGENDARY AND MYTHICAL POKÉMON

These extremely rare and powerful Pokémon are a bit of a mystery. They are unusually strong, and many have had incredible influence. Some have used their power to shape history and the world. And they are so rare that few people ever glimpse them. Trainers who have spotted a Legendary or Mythical Pokémon count themselves among the lucky.

PARADOX POKÉMON

Paradox Pokémon are Pokémon from out of time. Some are from the past, and some are from the future.

POKÉMON STATS AND FACTS

Ready to discover more about every Pokémon?
Turn the page and begin!

ABOMASNOW

Frost Tree Pokémon

#0460

TYPE: GRASS-ICE

It lives a quiet life on mountains that are perpetually covered in snow. It hides itself by whipping up blizzards.

They appear when the snow flowers bloom. When the petals fall, they retreat to places unknown again.

HOW TO SAY IT: ah-BOM-ah-snow
IMPERIAL HEIGHT: 7'03"
IMPERIAL WEIGHT: 298.7 lbs.
METRIC HEIGHT: 2.2 m
METRIC WEIGHT: 135.5 kg
GENDER: ♂ ♀
ABILITIES: Snow Warning
WEAKNESSES: Steel, Fire, Flying, Poison, Fighting, Rock, Bug

MEGA ABOMASNOW

TYPE: GRASS-ICE

It blankets wide areas in snow by whipping up blizzards. It is also known as "The Ice Monster."

It lives a quiet life on mountains that are perpetually covered in snow. It hides itself by whipping up blizzards.

IMPERIAL HEIGHT: 8'10"
IMPERIAL WEIGHT: 407.9 lbs.
METRIC HEIGHT: 2.7 m
METRIC WEIGHT: 185.0 kg

SNOVER

ABOMASNOW

MEGA ABOMASNOW

TYPE: PSYCHIC

ABRA
Psi Pokémon

This Pokémon uses its psychic powers while it sleeps. The contents of Abra's dreams affect the powers that the Pokémon wields.

Abra can teleport in its sleep. Apparently the more deeply Abra sleeps, the farther its teleportations go.

HOW TO SAY IT: AB-ra
IMPERIAL HEIGHT: 2'11"
IMPERIAL WEIGHT: 43.0 lbs.
METRIC HEIGHT: 0.9 m
METRIC WEIGHT: 19.5 kg
GENDER: ♂ ♀
ABILITIES: Inner Focus, Synchronize
WEAKNESSES: Ghost, Dark, Bug

ABRA

KADABRA

ALAKAZAM

MEGA ALAKAZAM

ABSOL

Disaster Pokémon

#0359

TYPE: DARK

Swift as the wind, Absol races through fields and mountains. Its curved, bow-like horn is acutely sensitive to the warning signs of natural disasters.

Because of this Pokémon's ability to detect danger, people mistook Absol as a bringer of doom.

HOW TO SAY IT: AB-sahl
IMPERIAL HEIGHT: 3'11"
IMPERIAL WEIGHT: 103.6 lbs.
METRIC HEIGHT: 1.2 m
METRIC WEIGHT: 47.0 kg
GENDER: ♂ ♀
ABILITIES: Pressure, Super Luck
WEAKNESSES: Fairy, Bug, Fighting

MEGA ABSOL

TYPE: DARK

Normally, it dislikes fighting, so it really hates changing to this form for battles.

It converts the energy from Mega Evolution into an intimidating aura. Fainthearted people expire from shock at the sight of it.

IMPERIAL HEIGHT: 3'11"
IMPERIAL WEIGHT: 108.0 lbs.
METRIC HEIGHT: 1.2 m
METRIC WEIGHT: 49.0 kg

ABSOL   **MEGA ABSOL**

#0617 ACCELGOR
Shell Out Pokémon

TYPE: BUG

It moves with blinding speed and lobs poison at foes. Featuring Accelgor as a main character is a surefire way to make a movie or comic popular.

Discarding its shell made it nimble. To keep itself from dehydrating, it wraps its body in bands of membrane.

HOW TO SAY IT: ak-SELL-gohr
IMPERIAL HEIGHT: 2'07"
IMPERIAL WEIGHT: 55.8 lbs.
METRIC HEIGHT: 0.8 m
METRIC WEIGHT: 25.3 kg
GENDER: ♂ ♀
ABILITIES: Hydration, Sticky Hold
WEAKNESSES: Fire, Flying, Rock

SHELMET **ACCELGOR**

#0681 AEGISLASH
Royal Sword Pokémon

TYPE: STEEL-GHOST

In this defensive stance, Aegislash uses its steel body and a force field of spectral power to reduce the damage of any attack.

Its potent spectral powers allow it to manipulate others. It once used its powers to force people and Pokémon to build a kingdom to its liking.

SHIELD FORME

BLADE FORME

HOW TO SAY IT: EE-jih-SLASH
IMPERIAL HEIGHT: 5'07"
IMPERIAL WEIGHT: 116.8 lbs.
METRIC HEIGHT: 1.7 m
METRIC WEIGHT: 53.0 kg
GENDER: ♂ ♀
ABILITIES: Stance Change
WEAKNESSES: Fire, Ghost, Dark, Ground

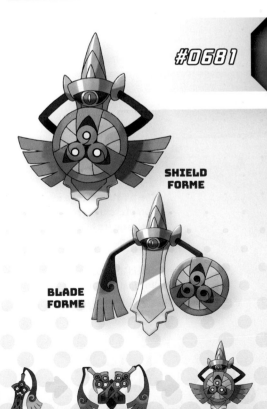

HONEDGE **DOUBLADE** **AEGISLASH**

AERODACTYL

Fossil Pokémon

TYPE: ROCK-FLYING

This is a ferocious Pokémon from ancient times. Apparently even modern technology is incapable of producing a perfectly restored specimen.

Aerodactyl's sawlike fangs can shred skin to tatters—even the skin of Steel-type Pokémon.

HOW TO SAY IT: AIR-row-DACK-tull
IMPERIAL HEIGHT: 5'11"
IMPERIAL WEIGHT: 130.1 lbs.
METRIC HEIGHT: 1.8 m
METRIC WEIGHT: 59.0 kg
GENDER: ♂ ♀
ABILITIES: Rock Head, Pressure
WEAKNESSES: Steel, Water, Electric, Ice, Rock

MEGA AERODACTYL

TYPE: ROCK-FLYING

The power of Mega Evolution has completely restored its genes. The rocks on its body are harder than diamond.

IMPERIAL HEIGHT: 6'11"
IMPERIAL WEIGHT: 174.2 lbs.
METRIC HEIGHT: 2.1 m
METRIC WEIGHT: 79.0 kg

AERODACTYL　　**MEGA AERODACTYL**

AGGRON
Iron Armor Pokémon

TYPE: STEEL-ROCK

Aggron has a horn sharp enough to perforate thick iron sheets. It brings down its opponents by ramming into them horn first.

Long ago, there was a king who wore a helmet meant to resemble the head of an Aggron. He was trying to channel the Pokémon's strength.

HOW TO SAY IT: AGG-ron
IMPERIAL HEIGHT: 6'11"
IMPERIAL WEIGHT: 793.7 lbs.
METRIC HEIGHT: 2.1 m
METRIC WEIGHT: 360.0 kg
GENDER: ♂ ♀
ABILITIES: Sturdy, Rock Head
WEAKNESSES: Water, Fighting, Ground

MEGA AGGRON

TYPE: STEEL

Aggron claims an entire mountain as its own territory. It mercilessly beats up anything that violates its environment. This Pokémon vigilantly patrols its territory at all times.

Aggron is protective of its environment. If its mountain is ravaged by a landslide or a fire, this Pokémon will haul topsoil to the area, plant trees, and beautifully restore its own territory.

IMPERIAL HEIGHT: 7'03"
IMPERIAL WEIGHT: 870.8 lbs.
METRIC HEIGHT: 2.2 m
METRIC WEIGHT: 395.0 kg

ARON **LAIRON** **AGGRON** **MEGA AGGRON**

AIPOM

Long Tail Pokémon

#0190

TYPE: NORMAL

As it did more and more with its tail, its hands became clumsy. It makes its nest high in the treetops.

It searches for prey from the tops of trees. When it spots its favorite food, Bounsweet, Aipom gets excited and pounces.

HOW TO SAY IT: AY-pom
IMPERIAL HEIGHT: 2'07"
IMPERIAL WEIGHT: 25.4 lbs.
METRIC HEIGHT: 0.8 m
METRIC WEIGHT: 11.5 kg
GENDER: ♂ ♀
ABILITIES: Run Away, Pickup
WEAKNESSES: Fighting

AIPOM   AMBIPOM

ALAKAZAM

Psi Pokémon

TYPE: PSYCHIC

It has an incredibly high level of intelligence. Some say that Alakazam remembers everything that ever happens to it, from birth till death.

Alakazam wields potent psychic powers. It's said that this Pokémon used these powers to create the spoons it holds.

HOW TO SAY IT: AL-a-kuh-ZAM
IMPERIAL HEIGHT: 4'11"
IMPERIAL WEIGHT: 105.8 lbs.
METRIC HEIGHT: 1.5 m
METRIC WEIGHT: 48.0 kg
GENDER: ♂ ♀
ABILITIES: Synchronize, Inner Focus
WEAKNESSES: Ghost, Dark, Bug

MEGA ALAKAZAM

TYPE: PSYCHIC

It's adept at precognition. When attacks completely miss Alakazam, that's because it's seeing the future.

IMPERIAL HEIGHT: 3'11"
IMPERIAL WEIGHT: 105.8 lbs.
METRIC HEIGHT: 1.2 m
METRIC WEIGHT: 48.0 kg

ABRA

KADABRA

ALAKAZAM

MEGA ALAKAZAM

ALCREMIE
Cream Pokémon

#0869

TYPE: FAIRY

When it trusts a Trainer, it will treat them to berries it's decorated with cream.

When Alcremie is content, the cream it secretes from its hands becomes sweeter and richer.

HOW TO SAY IT: AL-kruh-mee
IMPERIAL HEIGHT: 1'00"
IMPERIAL WEIGHT: 1.1 lbs.
METRIC HEIGHT: 0.3 m
METRIC WEIGHT: 0.5 kg
GENDER: ♀
ABILITIES: Sweet Veil
WEAKNESSES: Steel, Poison

MILCERY → **ALCREMIE**

GIGANTAMAX ALCREMIE

Cream pours endlessly from this Pokémon's body. The cream stiffens when compressed by an impact. A harder impact results in harder cream.

It launches swarms of missiles, each made of cream and loaded with 100,000 calories. Get hit by one of these, and your head will swim.

IMPERIAL HEIGHT: 98'05"+
IMPERIAL WEIGHT: ????.? lbs.
METRIC HEIGHT: 30.0+ m
METRIC WEIGHT: ???.? kg

ALOMOMOLA
Caring Pokémon

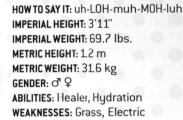

TYPE: WATER

It gently holds injured and weak Pokémon in its fins. Its special membrane heals their wounds.

They float upon the open sea. Many water Pokémon gather in the area around Alomomola.

HOW TO SAY IT: uh-LOH-muh-MOH-luh
IMPERIAL HEIGHT: 3'11"
IMPERIAL WEIGHT: 69.7 lbs.
METRIC HEIGHT: 1.2 m
METRIC WEIGHT: 31.6 kg
GENDER: ♂ ♀
ABILITIES: Healer, Hydration
WEAKNESSES: Grass, Electric

DOES NOT EVOLVE

ALTARIA

Humming Pokémon

#0334

TYPE: DRAGON-FLYING

If it bonds with a person, it will gently envelop the friend with its soft wings, then hum.

On sunny days, it flies freely through the sky and blends into the clouds. It sings in a beautiful soprano.

HOW TO SAY IT: ahl-TAR-ee-uh
IMPERIAL HEIGHT: 3'07"
IMPERIAL WEIGHT: 45.4 lbs.
METRIC HEIGHT: 1.1 m
METRIC WEIGHT: 20.6 kg
GENDER: ♂ ♀
ABILITIES: Natural Cure
WEAKNESSES: Fairy, Dragon, Ice, Rock

MEGA ALTARIA

TYPE: DRAGON-FAIRY

Altaria dances and wheels through the sky among billowing, cotton-like clouds. By singing melodies in its crystal-clear voice, this Pokémon makes its listeners experience dreamy wonderment.

Altaria sings in a gorgeous soprano. Its wings are like cotton clouds. This Pokémon catches updrafts with its buoyant wings and soars way up into the wild blue yonder.

IMPERIAL HEIGHT: 4'11"
IMPERIAL WEIGHT: 45.4 lbs.
METRIC HEIGHT: 1.5 m
METRIC WEIGHT: 20.6 kg

 SWABLU   **ALTARIA**   **MEGA ALTARIA**

#0698

AMAURA
Tundra Pokémon

TYPE: ROCK-ICE

This Pokémon was successfully restored from a fossil. In the past, it lived with others of its kind in cold lands where there were fewer predators.

Amaura is an ancient Pokémon that has gone extinct. Specimens of this species can sometimes be found frozen in ice.

HOW TO SAY IT: ah-MORE-uh
IMPERIAL HEIGHT: 4'03"
IMPERIAL WEIGHT: 55.6 lbs.
METRIC HEIGHT: 1.3 m
METRIC WEIGHT: 25.2 kg
GENDER: ♂ ♀
ABILITIES: Refrigerate
WEAKNESSES: Steel, Fighting, Water, Rock, Grass, Ground

AMAURA **AURORUS**

#0424

AMBIPOM
Long Tail Pokémon

TYPE: NORMAL

In their search for comfortable trees, they get into territorial disputes with groups of Passimian. They win about half the time.

It uses its tails for everything. If it wraps both of its tails around you and gives you a squeeze, that's proof it really likes you.

HOW TO SAY IT: AM-bee-pom
IMPERIAL HEIGHT: 3'11"
IMPERIAL WEIGHT: 44.8 lbs.
METRIC HEIGHT: 1.2 m
METRIC WEIGHT: 20.3 kg
GENDER: ♂ ♀
ABILITIES: Technician, Pickup
WEAKNESSES: Fighting

AIPOM **AMBIPOM**

AMOONGUSS

Mushroom Pokémon

#0591

TYPE: GRASS-POISON

Be wary of the poisonous spores it releases. Mushrooms resembling Amoonguss's caps will grow out of anywhere the spores touch.

Amoonguss mimics Poké Balls. It is not yet clear whether this mimicry is effective against other Pokémon.

HOW TO SAY IT: uh-MOON-gus
IMPERIAL HEIGHT: 2'00"
IMPERIAL WEIGHT: 23.1 lbs.
METRIC HEIGHT: 0.6 m
METRIC WEIGHT: 10.5 kg
GENDER: ♂ ♀
ABILITIES: Effect Spore
WEAKNESSES: Fire, Psychic, Flying, Ice

 FOONGUS → **AMOONGUSS**

AMPHAROS
Light Pokémon

TYPE: ELECTRIC

The bright light on its tail can be seen far away. It has been treasured since ancient times as a beacon.

When it gets dark, the light from its bright, shiny tail can be seen from far away on the ocean's surface.

HOW TO SAY IT: AMF-fah-rahs
IMPERIAL HEIGHT: 4'07"
IMPERIAL WEIGHT: 135.6 lbs.
METRIC HEIGHT: 1.4 m
METRIC WEIGHT: 61.5 kg
GENDER: ♂ ♀
ABILITIES: Static
WEAKNESSES: Ground

MEGA AMPHAROS

TYPE: ELECTRIC-DRAGON

Excess energy from Mega Evolution stimulates its genes, and the wool it had lost grows in again.

Massive amounts of energy intensely stimulated Ampharos's cells, apparently awakening its long-sleeping dragon's blood.

IMPERIAL HEIGHT: 4'07"
IMPERIAL WEIGHT: 135.6 lbs.
METRIC HEIGHT: 1.4 m
METRIC WEIGHT: 61.5 kg

MAREEP **FLAAFFY** **AMPHAROS** **MEGA AMPHAROS**

ANNIHILAPE

Rage Monkey Pokémon

#0979

TYPE: FIGHTING-GHOST

When its anger rose beyond a critical point, this Pokémon gained power that is unfettered by the limits of its physical body.

It imbues its fists with the power of the rage that it kept hidden in its heart. Opponents struck by these imbued fists will be shattered to their core.

HOW TO SAY IT: uh-NEYE-uh-layp
IMPERIAL HEIGHT: 3'11"
IMPERIAL WEIGHT: 123.5 lbs.
METRIC HEIGHT: 1.2 m
METRIC WEIGHT: 56.0 kg
GENDER: ♂ ♀
ABILITIES: Vital Spirit, Inner Focus
WEAKNESSES: Ghost, Psychic, Flying, Fairy

MANKEY   PRIMEAPE   ANNIHILAPE

ANORITH

Old Shrimp Pokémon

#0347

TYPE: ROCK-BUG

This Pokémon was restored from a fossil. Anorith lived in the ocean about 100,000,000 years ago, hunting with its pair of claws.

Anorith can swim swiftly by pulling its eight wings through the water like oars on a boat. This Pokémon is an ancestor of modern bug Pokémon.

HOW TO SAY IT: AN-no-rith
IMPERIAL HEIGHT: 2'04"
IMPERIAL WEIGHT: 27.6 lbs.
METRIC HEIGHT: 0.7 m
METRIC WEIGHT: 12.5 kg
GENDER: ♂ ♀
ABILITIES: Battle Armor
WEAKNESSES: Steel, Water, Rock

ANORITH   ARMALDO

APPLETUN
Apple Nectar Pokémon

TYPE: GRASS-DRAGON

It feeds mainly on sweet apples. It will also eat small bug Pokémon that are attracted by its sweet nectar.

When some Lechonk come along to lick the sweet nectar on Appletun's back, Appletun will spew sticky nectar at them to drive them away.

HOW TO SAY IT: AP-pel-tun
IMPERIAL HEIGHT: 1'04"
IMPERIAL WEIGHT: 28.7 lbs.
METRIC HEIGHT: 0.4 m
METRIC WEIGHT: 13.0 kg
GENDER: ♂ ♀
ABILITIES: Ripen, Gluttony
WEAKNESSES: Flying, Ice, Dragon, Poison, Fairy, Bug

APPLIN **APPLETUN**

GIGANTAMAX APPLETUN

It blasts its opponents with massive amounts of sweet, sticky nectar, drowning them under the deluge.

Due to Gigantamax energy, this Pokémon's nectar has thickened. The increased viscosity lets the nectar absorb more damage than before.

IMPERIAL HEIGHT: 78'09"+
IMPERIAL WEIGHT: ????.? lbs.
METRIC HEIGHT: 24.0+ m
METRIC WEIGHT: ???.? kg

APPLIN
Apple Core Pokémon
#0840

TYPE: GRASS-DRAGON

It grows by eating the flesh of an apple. Applin uses its own body fluid to strengthen the apple's skin and prevent it from rotting.

Applin lives inside an apple. When an Applin is separated from its apple, its body loses moisture and the Pokémon grows weak.

HOW TO SAY IT: AP-lin
IMPERIAL HEIGHT: 0'08"
IMPERIAL WEIGHT: 1.1 lbs.
METRIC HEIGHT: 0.2 m
METRIC WEIGHT: 0.5 kg
GENDER: ♂ ♀
ABILITIES: Ripen, Gluttony
WEAKNESSES: Flying, Ice, Dragon, Poison, Fairy, Bug

APPLETUN

APPLIN

FLAPPLE

ARAQUANID
Water Bubble Pokémon
#0752

TYPE: WATER-BUG

It launches water bubbles with its legs, drowning prey within the bubbles. This Pokémon can then take its time to savor its meal.

It acts as a caretaker for Dewpider, putting them inside its bubble and letting them eat any leftover food.

HOW TO SAY IT: uh-RACK-wuh-nid
IMPERIAL HEIGHT: 5'11"
IMPERIAL WEIGHT: 180.8 lbs.
METRIC HEIGHT: 1.8 m
METRIC WEIGHT: 82.0 kg
GENDER: ♂ ♀
ABILITIES: Water Bubble
WEAKNESSES: Flying, Electric, Rock

DEWPIDER

ARAQUANID

#0024

ARBOK
Cobra Pokémon

TYPE: POISON

The frightening patterns on its belly have been studied. Six variations have been confirmed.

HOW TO SAY IT: ARE-bock
IMPERIAL HEIGHT: 11'06"
IMPERIAL WEIGHT: 143.3 lbs.
METRIC HEIGHT: 3.5 m
METRIC WEIGHT: 65.0 kg
GENDER: ♂ ♀
ABILITIES: Intimidate, Shed Skin
WEAKNESSES: Psychic, Ground

EKANS → ARBOK

#0930

ARBOLIVA
Olive Pokémon

TYPE: GRASS-NORMAL

This calm Pokémon is very compassionate. It will share its delicious, nutrient-rich oil with weakened Pokémon.

This Pokémon drives back enemies by launching its rich, aromatic oil at them with enough force to smash a boulder.

HOW TO SAY IT: ar-bowl-EE-vuh
IMPERIAL HEIGHT: 4'07"
IMPERIAL WEIGHT: 106.3 lbs.
METRIC HEIGHT: 1.4 m
METRIC WEIGHT: 48.2 kg
GENDER: ♂ ♀
ABILITIES: Seed Sower
WEAKNESSES: Ice, Fire, Flying, Poison, Fighting, Bug

SMOLIV → DOLLIV → ARBOLIVA

ARCANINE
Legendary Pokémon

#0059

TYPE: FIRE

An ancient picture scroll shows that people were captivated by its movement as it ran through prairies.

Its magnificent bark conveys a sense of majesty. Anyone hearing it can't help but grovel before it.

HOW TO SAY IT: ARE-ka-nine
IMPERIAL HEIGHT: 6'03"
IMPERIAL WEIGHT: 341.7 lbs.
METRIC HEIGHT: 1.9 m
METRIC WEIGHT: 155.0 kg
GENDER: ♂ ♀
ABILITIES: Intimidate, Flash Fire
WEAKNESSES: Water, Ground, Rock

GROWLITHE   ARCANINE

HISUIAN ARCANINE
Legendary Pokémon

#0059

TYPE: FIRE-ROCK

Snaps at its foes with fangs cloaked in blazing flame. Despite its bulk, it deftly feints every which way, leading opponents on a deceptively merry chase as it all but dances around them.

HOW TO SAY IT: ARE-ka-nine
IMPERIAL HEIGHT: 6'07"
IMPERIAL WEIGHT: 370.4 lbs.
METRIC WEIGHT: 168.0 kg
METRIC HEIGHT: 2.0 m
GENDER: ♂ ♀
ABILITIES: N/A
WEAKNESSES: Water, Ground, Fighting, Rock

HISUIAN GROWLITHE   HISUIAN ARCANINE

MYTHICAL POKÉMON

#0493

ARCEUS
Alpha Pokémon

TYPE: NORMAL

According to the legends of Sinnoh, this Pokémon emerged from an egg and shaped all there is in this world.

It is told in mythology that this Pokémon was born before the universe even existed.

HOW TO SAY IT: ARK-ee-us
IMPERIAL HEIGHT: 10'06"
IMPERIAL WEIGHT: 705.5 lbs.
METRIC HEIGHT: 3.2 m
METRIC WEIGHT: 320.0 kg
GENDER: Unknown
ABILITIES: Multitype
WEAKNESSES: Fighting

DOES NOT EVOLVE

ARCHEN
First Bird Pokémon

#0566

TYPE: ROCK-FLYING

This Pokémon was successfully restored from a fossil. As research suggested, Archen is unable to fly. But it's very good at jumping.

Archen is said to be the ancestor of bird Pokémon. It lived in treetops, eating berries and bug Pokémon.

HOW TO SAY IT: AR-ken
IMPERIAL HEIGHT: 1'08"
IMPERIAL WEIGHT: 20.9 lbs.
METRIC HEIGHT: 0.5 m
METRIC WEIGHT: 9.5 kg
GENDER: ♂ ♀
ABILITIES: Defeatist
WEAKNESSES: Steel, Water, Electric, Ice, Rock

ARCHEN   ARCHEOPS

#0567

ARCHEOPS
First Bird Pokémon

TYPE: ROCK-FLYING

It needs a running start to take off. If Archeops wants to fly, it first needs to run nearly 25 mph, building speed over a course of about 2.5 miles.

Though capable of flight, Archeops is apparently better at hunting on the ground.

HOW TO SAY IT: AR-kee-ops
IMPERIAL HEIGHT: 4'07"
IMPERIAL WEIGHT: 70.5 lbs.
METRIC HEIGHT: 1.4 m
METRIC WEIGHT: 32.0 kg
GENDER: ♂ ♀
ABILITIES: Defeatist
WEAKNESSES: Steel, Water, Electric, Ice, Rock

ARCHEN ➡ **ARCHEOPS**

ARCTIBAX
Ice Fin Pokémon

#0997

TYPE: DRAGON-ICE

Arctibax freezes the air around it, protecting its face with an ice mask and turning its dorsal fin into a blade of ice.

It attacks with the blade of its frozen dorsal fin by doing a front flip in the air. Arctibax's strong back and legs allow it to pull off this technique.

HOW TO SAY IT: ARK-tuh-baks
IMPERIAL HEIGHT: 2'07"
IMPERIAL WEIGHT: 66.1 lbs.
METRIC HEIGHT: 0.8 m
METRIC WEIGHT: 30.0 kg
GENDER: ♂ ♀
ABILITIES: Thermal Exchange
WEAKNESSES: Steel, Fairy, Rock, Fighting, Dragon

FRIGIBAX ➡ **ARCTIBAX** ➡ **BAXCALIBUR**

#0883 ARCTOVISH
Fossil Pokémon

TYPE: WATER-ICE

Though it's able to capture prey by freezing its surroundings, it has trouble eating the prey afterward because its mouth is on top of its head.

The skin on its face is impervious to attack, but breathing difficulties made this Pokémon go extinct anyway.

HOW TO SAY IT: ARK-toh-vish
IMPERIAL HEIGHT: 6'07"
IMPERIAL WEIGHT: 385.8 lbs.
METRIC HEIGHT: 2.0 m
METRIC WEIGHT: 175.0 kg
GENDER: Unknown
ABILITIES: Water Absorb, Ice Body
WEAKNESSES: Grass, Electric, Fighting, Rock

DOES NOT EVOLVE

ARCTOZOLT #0881
Fossil Pokémon

TYPE: ELECTRIC-ICE

The shaking of its freezing upper half is what generates its electricity. It has a hard time walking around.

This Pokémon lived on prehistoric seashores and was able to preserve food with the ice on its body. It went extinct because it moved so slowly.

HOW TO SAY IT: ARK-toh-zohlt
IMPERIAL HEIGHT: 7'07"
IMPERIAL WEIGHT: 330.7 lbs.
METRIC HEIGHT: 2.3 m
METRIC WEIGHT: 150.0 kg
GENDER: Unknown
ABILITIES: Volt Absorb, Static
WEAKNESSES: Fire, Ground, Fighting, Rock

DOES NOT EVOLVE

ARIADOS

Long Leg Pokémon

#0168

TYPE: BUG-POISON

Every night, it wanders around in search of prey, whose movements it restrains by spewing threads before it bites into them with its fangs.

It spews threads from its mouth to catch its prey. When night falls, it leaves its web to go hunt aggressively.

HOW TO SAY IT: AIR-ree-uh-dose
IMPERIAL HEIGHT: 3'07"
IMPERIAL WEIGHT: 73.9 lbs.
METRIC HEIGHT: 1.1 m
METRIC WEIGHT: 33.5 kg
GENDER: ♂ ♀
ABILITIES: Swarm, Insomnia
WEAKNESSES: Fire, Psychic, Flying, Rock

SPINARAK → ARIADOS

ARMALDO

#0348

Plate Pokémon

TYPE: ROCK-BUG

After evolution, this Pokémon emerged onto land. Its lower body has become stronger, and blows from its tail are devastating.

Though it lives on land, it's also a good swimmer. It dives into the ocean in search of prey, using its sharp claws to take down its quarry.

HOW TO SAY IT: ar-MAL-do
IMPERIAL HEIGHT: 4'11"
IMPERIAL WEIGHT: 150.4 lbs.
METRIC HEIGHT: 1.5 m
METRIC WEIGHT: 68.2 kg
GENDER: ♂ ♀
ABILITIES: Battle Armor
WEAKNESSES: Steel, Water, Rock

ANORITH   ARMALDO

ARMAROUGE

Fire Warrior Pokémon

#0936

TYPE: FIRE-PSYCHIC

Armarouge evolved through the use of a set of armor that belonged to a distinguished warrior. This Pokémon is incredibly loyal.

This Pokémon clads itself in armor that has been fortified by psychic and fire energy, and it shoots blazing fireballs.

HOW TO SAY IT: ARM-uh-roozh
IMPERIAL HEIGHT: 4'11"
IMPERIAL WEIGHT: 187.4 lbs.
METRIC HEIGHT: 1.5 m
METRIC WEIGHT: 85.0 kg
GENDER: ♂ ♀
ABILITIES: Flash Fire
WEAKNESSES: Ghost, Dark, Ground, Water, Rock

CHARCADET

ARMAROUGE

AROMATISSE

Fragrance Pokémon

#0683

TYPE: FAIRY

The scent that constantly emits from its fur is so powerful that this Pokémon's companions will eventually lose their sense of smell.

The scents Aromatisse can produce range from sweet smells that bolster allies to foul smells that sap an opponent's will to fight.

HOW TO SAY IT: uh-ROME-uh-teece
IMPERIAL HEIGHT: 2'07"
IMPERIAL WEIGHT: 34.2 lbs.
METRIC HEIGHT: 0.8 m
METRIC WEIGHT: 15.5 kg
GENDER: ♂ ♀
ABILITIES: Healer
WEAKNESSES: Steel, Poison

SPRITZEE

AROMATISSE

ARON

Iron Armor Pokémon

#0304

TYPE: STEEL-ROCK

It eats iron ore—and sometimes railroad tracks—to build up the steel armor that protects its body.

When Aron evolves, its steel armor peels off. In ancient times, people would collect Aron's shed armor and make good use of it in their daily lives.

HOW TO SAY IT: AIR-ron
IMPERIAL HEIGHT: 1'04"
IMPERIAL WEIGHT: 132.3 lbs.
METRIC HEIGHT: 0.4 m
METRIC WEIGHT: 60.0 kg
GENDER: ♂♀
ABILITIES: Sturdy, Rock Head
WEAKNESSES: Water, Fighting, Ground

ARON   LAIRON   AGGRON   MEGA AGGRON

ARROKUDA

Rush Pokémon

#0846

TYPE: WATER

Arrokuda can swim quickly only in a straight line. The ones that become sluggish from overeating are the first to be targeted by flocks of Wattrel.

It takes down prey by charging into them with its hard, pointed jaw. But Arrokuda's eyesight is poor, so this tactic has a low success rate.

HOW TO SAY IT: AIR-oh-KOO-duh
IMPERIAL HEIGHT: 1'08"
IMPERIAL WEIGHT: 2.2 lbs.
METRIC HEIGHT: 0.5 m
METRIC WEIGHT: 1.0 kg
GENDER: ♂♀
ABILITIES: Swift Swim
WEAKNESSES: Grass, Electric

ARROKUDA   BARRASKEWDA

LEGENDARY POKÉMON

ARTICUNO
Freeze Pokémon

TYPE: ICE-FLYING

This legendary bird Pokémon can create blizzards by freezing moisture in the air.

HOW TO SAY IT: ART-tick-COO-no
IMPERIAL HEIGHT: 5'07"
IMPERIAL WEIGHT: 122.1 lbs.
METRIC HEIGHT: 1.7 m
METRIC WEIGHT: 55.4 kg
GENDER: Unknown
ABILITIES: Pressure
WEAKNESSES: Steel, Fire, Electric, Rock

DOES NOT EVOLVE

LEGENDARY POKÉMON

GALARIAN ARTICUNO
Cruel Pokémon

TYPE: PSYCHIC-FLYING

Its feather-like blades are composed of psychic energy and can shear through thick iron sheets as if they were paper.

Known as Articuno, this Pokémon fires beams that can immobilize opponents as if they had been frozen solid.

HOW TO SAY IT: ART-tick-COO-no
IMPERIAL HEIGHT: 5'07"
IMPERIAL WEIGHT: 112.2 lbs.
METRIC HEIGHT: 1.7 m
METRIC WEIGHT: 50.9 kg
GENDER: Unknown
ABILITIES: Competitive
WEAKNESSES: Ghost, Dark, Electric, Ice, Rock

DOES NOT EVOLVE

AUDINO
Hearing Pokémon

#0531

TYPE: NORMAL

Audino's sense of hearing is superb. Not even a pebble rolling along over a mile away will escape Audino's ears.

This Pokémon has a kind heart. By touching with its feelers, Audino can gauge other creatures' feelings and physical conditions.

HOW TO SAY IT: AW-dih-noh
IMPERIAL HEIGHT: 3'07"
IMPERIAL WEIGHT: 68.3 lbs.
METRIC HEIGHT: 1.1 m
METRIC WEIGHT: 31.0 kg
GENDER: ♂ ♀
ABILITIES: Healer, Regenerator
WEAKNESSES: Fighting

MEGA AUDINO

TYPE: NORMAL-FAIRY

Using the feelers on its ears, it can tell how someone is feeling or when an egg might hatch.

It touches others with the feelers on its ears, using the sound of their heartbeats to tell how they are feeling.

IMPERIAL HEIGHT: 4'11"
IMPERIAL WEIGHT: 70.5 lbs.
METRIC HEIGHT: 1.5 m
METRIC WEIGHT: 32.0 kg

AUDINO

MEGA AUDINO

TYPE: ROCK-ICE

#0699

AURORUS
Tundra Pokémon

Aurorus was restored from a fossil. It's said that when this Pokémon howls, auroras appear in the night sky.

When gripped by rage, Aurorus will emanate freezing air, covering everything around it in ice.

HOW TO SAY IT: ah-ROAR-us
IMPERIAL HEIGHT: 8'10"
IMPERIAL WEIGHT: 496.0 lbs.
METRIC HEIGHT: 2.7 m
METRIC WEIGHT: 225.0 kg
GENDER: ♂ ♀
ABILITIES: Refrigerate
WEAKNESSES: Steel, Fighting, Water, Rock, Grass, Ground

AMAURA

AURORUS

AVALUGG

Iceberg Pokémon

#0713

TYPE: ICE

As Avalugg walks along with Bergmite on its back, it comes across pods of Cetitan. It lets them pass to avoid conflict.

This Pokémon uses its massive icy body to flatten anything that gets in its way. When it's floating out on the ocean, it looks exactly like drift ice.

HOW TO SAY IT: AV-uh-lug
IMPERIAL HEIGHT: 6'07"
IMPERIAL WEIGHT: 1,113.3 lbs.
METRIC HEIGHT: 2.0 m
METRIC WEIGHT: 505.0 kg
GENDER: ♂ ♀
ABILITIES: Own Tempo, Ice Body
WEAKNESSES: Fire, Steel, Fighting, Rock

BERGMITE ➡ AVALUGG

#0713 **HISUIAN AVALUGG**

Iceberg Pokémon

TYPE: ICE-ROCK

The armor of ice covering its lower jaw puts steel to shame and can shatter rocks with ease. This Pokémon barrels along steep mountain paths, cleaving through the deep snow.

HOW TO SAY IT: AV-uh-lug
IMPERIAL HEIGHT: 4'07"
IMPERIAL WEIGHT: 578.5 lbs.
METRIC HEIGHT: 1.4 m
METRIC WEIGHT: 262.4 kg
GENDER: ♂ ♀
ABILITIES: N/A
WEAKNESSES: Steel, Fighting, Water, Rock, Grass, Ground

BERGMITE ➡ HISUIAN AVALUGG

AXEW

Tusk Pokémon

#0610

TYPE: DRAGON

This Pokémon lives in nests that are made in the ground. People in ancient times used its tusks as cooking knives.

If you see peculiar teeth marks on boulders or trees, it means an Axew is likely living nearby.

HOW TO SAY IT: AKS-yoo
IMPERIAL HEIGHT: 2'00"
IMPERIAL WEIGHT: 39.7 lbs.
METRIC HEIGHT: 0.6 m
METRIC WEIGHT: 18.0 kg
GENDER: ♂ ♀
ABILITIES: Rivalry, Mold Breaker
WEAKNESSES: Fairy, Ice, Dragon

AXEW   FRAXURE   HAXORUS

LEGENDARY POKÉMON

#0482

AZELF

Willpower Pokémon

TYPE: PSYCHIC

Known as "The Being of Willpower." It sleeps at the bottom of a lake to keep the world in balance.

It is thought that Uxie, Mesprit, and Azelf all came from the same egg.

HOW TO SAY IT: AZ-zelf
IMPERIAL HEIGHT: 1'00"
IMPERIAL WEIGHT: 0.7 lbs.
METRIC HEIGHT: 0.3 m
METRIC WEIGHT: 0.3 kg
GENDER: Unknown
ABILITIES: Levitate
WEAKNESSES: Ghost, Dark, Bug

DOES NOT EVOLVE

AZUMARILL

Aqua Rabbit Pokémon

#0184

TYPE: WATER-FAIRY

Its long ears are superb sensors. It can distinguish the movements of things in water and tell what they are.

By keeping still and listening intently, it can eventell what is in wild, fast-moving rivers.

HOW TO SAY IT: ah-ZU-mare-rill
IMPERIAL HEIGHT: 2'07"
IMPERIAL WEIGHT: 62.8 lbs.
METRIC HEIGHT: 0.8 m
METRIC WEIGHT: 28.5 kg
GENDER: ♂♀
ABILITIES: Thick Fat, Huge Power
WEAKNESSES: Grass, Electric, Poison

AZURILL ➡ MARILL ➡ AZUMARILL

#0298

AZURILL

Polka Dot Pokémon

TYPE: NORMAL-FAIRY

Its tail bounces like a rubber ball. It flings that tail around to fight opponents bigger than itself.

Its tail is packed full of the nutrients it needs to grow.

HOW TO SAY IT: uh-ZOO-rill
IMPERIAL HEIGHT: 0'08"
IMPERIAL WEIGHT: 4.4 lbs.
METRIC HEIGHT: 0.2 m
METRIC WEIGHT: 2.0 kg
GENDER: ♂♀
ABILITIES: Thick Fat, Huge Power
WEAKNESSES: Steel, Poison

AZURILL ➡ MARILL ➡ AZUMARILL

BAGON #0371
Rock Head Pokémon

TYPE: DRAGON

Its steel-hard head can shatter boulders. It longingly hopes for wings to grow so it can fly.

Its belief that it will be able to fly one day is apparently the influence of information carried in its genes.

HOW TO SAY IT: BAY-gon
IMPERIAL HEIGHT: 2'00"   **METRIC HEIGHT:** 0.6 m
IMPERIAL WEIGHT: 92.8 lbs.   **METRIC WEIGHT:** 42.1 kg
GENDER: ♂♀
ABILITIES: Rock Head
WEAKNESSES: Fairy, Ice, Dragon

BAGON ➡ **SHELGON** ➡ **SALAMENCE** ➡ **MEGA SALAMENCE**

#0343
BALTOY
Clay Doll Pokémon

TYPE: GROUND-PSYCHIC

It moves while spinning around on its single foot. Some Baltoy have been seen spinning on their heads.

It was discovered in ancient ruins. While moving, it constantly spins. It stands on one foot even when asleep.

HOW TO SAY IT: BAL-toy
IMPERIAL HEIGHT: 1'08"
IMPERIAL WEIGHT: 47.4 lbs.
METRIC HEIGHT: 0.5 m
METRIC WEIGHT: 21.5 kg
GENDER: Unknown
ABILITIES: Levitate
WEAKNESSES: Ghost, Water, Ice, Dark, Grass, Bug

BALTOY ➡ **CLAYDOL**

BANETTE

Marionette Pokémon

#0354

TYPE: GHOST

This Pokémon developed from an abandoned doll that amassed a grudge. It is seen in dark alleys.

Strong feelings of hatred turned a puppet into a Pokémon. If it opens its mouth, its cursed energy escapes.

HOW TO SAY IT: bane-NETT
IMPERIAL HEIGHT: 3'07"
IMPERIAL WEIGHT: 27.6 lbs.
METRIC HEIGHT: 1.1 m
METRIC WEIGHT: 12.5 kg
GENDER: ♂ ♀
ABILITIES: Insomnia, Frisk
WEAKNESSES: Ghost, Dark

MEGA BANETTE

TYPE: GHOST

Extraordinary energy amplifies its cursing power to such an extent that it can't help but curse its own Trainer.

Mega Evolution increases its vindictiveness, and the cursing power that was held back by its zipper comes spilling out.

IMPERIAL HEIGHT: 3'11"
IMPERIAL WEIGHT: 28.7 lbs.
METRIC HEIGHT: 1.2 m
METRIC WEIGHT: 13.0 kg

SHUPPET   BANETTE   MEGA BANETTE

BARBARACLE

Collective Pokémon

#0689

TYPE: ROCK-WATER

Seven Binacle come together to form one Barbaracle. The Binacle that serves as the head gives orders to those serving as the limbs.

Having an eye on each palm allows it to keep watch in all directions. In a pinch, its limbs start to act on their own to ensure the enemy's defeat.

HOW TO SAY IT: bar-BARE-uh-kull
IMPERIAL HEIGHT: 4'03"
IMPERIAL WEIGHT: 211.6 lbs.
METRIC HEIGHT: 1.3 m
METRIC WEIGHT: 96.0 kg
GENDER: ♂ ♀
ABILITIES: Tough Claws, Sniper
WEAKNESSES: Grass, Electric, Fighting, Ground

BINACLE　　**BARBARACLE**

BARBOACH

Whiskers Pokémon

#0339

TYPE: WATER-GROUND

Its two whiskers provide a sensitive radar. Even in muddy waters, it can detect its prey's location.

It probes muddy riverbeds with its two long whiskers. A slimy film protects its body.

HOW TO SAY IT: bar-BOACH
IMPERIAL HEIGHT: 1'04"
IMPERIAL WEIGHT: 4.2 lbs.
METRIC HEIGHT: 0.4 m
METRIC WEIGHT: 1.9 kg
GENDER: ♂ ♀
ABILITIES: Oblivious, Anticipation
WEAKNESSES: Grass

BARBOACH

WHISCASH

BARRASKEWDA

Skewer Pokémon

#0847

TYPE: WATER

It spins its tail fins to leap from the water, then viciously bites down on Wingull flying close to the water's surface.

It swims at speeds of over 100 knots and battles fiercely with pods of Finizen over prey.

HOW TO SAY IT: BAIR-uh-SKYOO-duh
IMPERIAL HEIGHT: 4'03"
IMPERIAL WEIGHT: 66.1 lbs.
METRIC HEIGHT: 1.3 m
METRIC WEIGHT: 30.0 kg
GENDER: ♂ ♀
ABILITIES: Swift Swim
WEAKNESSES: Grass, Electric

ARROKUDA → BARRASKEWDA

BASCULEGION

Big Fish Pokémon

#0902

TYPE: WATER-GHOST

Clads itself in the souls of comrades that perished before fulfilling their goals of journeying upstream. No other species throughout all Hisui's rivers is Basculegion's equal.

HOW TO SAY IT: BASS-kyoo-lee-jihn
IMPERIAL HEIGHT: 9'10"
IMPERIAL WEIGHT: 242.5 lbs.
METRIC HEIGHT: 3.0 m
METRIC WEIGHT: 110.0 kg
GENDER: ♂ ♀
ABILITIES: N/A
WEAKNESSES: Ghost, Dark, Grass, Electric

MALE

FEMALE

BASCULIN
(WHITE-STRIPED FORM)

BASCULEGION

RED
STRIPE

BLUE
STRIPE

WHITE
STRIPE

#0550

BASCULIN
Hostile Pokémon

TYPE: WATER

Its temperament is vicious and aggressive. This Pokémon is also full of vitality and can multiply rapidly before anyone notices.

It's so vicious that it's called the Thug of the River. Yet Basculin is still targeted by predators, such as Dondozo and Bombirdier.

HOW TO SAY IT: BASS-kyoo-lin
IMPERIAL HEIGHT: 3'03"
IMPERIAL WEIGHT: 39.7 lbs.
METRIC HEIGHT: 1.0 m
METRIC WEIGHT: 18.0 kg
GENDER: ♂ ♀
ABILITIES: Reckless, Adaptability
WEAKNESSES: Grass, Electric

BASCULIN
(WHITE-STRIPED FORM)

BASCULEGION

BASTIODON
Shield Pokémon

#0411

TYPE: ROCK-STEEL

The bones of its face are huge and hard, so they were mistaken for its spine until after this Pokémon was successfully restored.

This Pokémon is from roughly 100 million years ago. Its terrifyingly tough face is harder than steel.

HOW TO SAY IT: BAS-tee-oh-DON
IMPERIAL HEIGHT: 4'03"
IMPERIAL WEIGHT: 329.6 lbs.
METRIC HEIGHT: 1.3 m
METRIC WEIGHT: 149.5 kg
GENDER: ♂ ♀
ABILITIES: Sturdy
WEAKNESSES: Water, Fighting, Ground

SHIELDON

BASTIODON

BAXCALIBUR

#0998

Ice Dragon Pokémon

TYPE: DRAGON-ICE

This Pokémon blasts cryogenic air out from its mouth. This air can instantly freeze even liquid-hot lava.

It launches itself into battle by flipping upside down and spewing frigid air from its mouth. It finishes opponents off with its dorsal blade.

HOW TO SAY IT: bak-SKA-leh-burr
IMPERIAL HEIGHT: 6'11"
IMPERIAL WEIGHT: 463.0 lbs.
METRIC HEIGHT: 2.1 m
METRIC WEIGHT: 210.0 kg
GENDER: ♂♀
ABILITIES: Thermal Exchange
WEAKNESSES: Steel, Fairy, Rock, Fighting, Dragon

FRIGIBAX ➡ **ARCTIBAX** ➡ **BAXCALIBUR**

BAYLEEF

#0153

Leaf Pokémon

TYPE: GRASS

Bayleef's neck is ringed by curled-up leaves. Inside each tubular leaf is a small shoot of a tree. The fragrance of this shoot makes people peppy.

HOW TO SAY IT: BAY-leaf
IMPERIAL HEIGHT: 3'11"
IMPERIAL WEIGHT: 34.8 lbs.
METRIC HEIGHT: 1.2 m
METRIC WEIGHT: 15.8 kg
GENDER: ♂♀
ABILITIES: Overgrow
WEAKNESSES: Fire, Flying, Ice, Poison, Bug

CHIKORITA **BAYLEEF** **MEGANIUM**

BEARTIC
Freezing Pokémon

TYPE: ICE

It is a ferocious, carnivorous Pokémon. Once it captures its prey, it will breathe cold air onto the prey to freeze and preserve it.

Feared as the Snow-White Demon in northern lands, Beartic uses its frosty claws and fangs to attack prey.

HOW TO SAY IT: BAIR-tick
IMPERIAL HEIGHT: 8'06"
IMPERIAL WEIGHT: 573.2 lbs.
METRIC HEIGHT: 2.6 m
METRIC WEIGHT: 260.0 kg
GENDER: ♂ ♀
ABILITIES: Snow Cloak, Slush Rush
WEAKNESSES: Fire, Steel, Fighting, Rock

CUBCHOO   BEARTIC

BEAUTIFLY
Butterfly Pokémon

TYPE: BUG-FLYING

Beautifly's favorite food is the sweet pollen of flowers. If you want to see this Pokémon, just leave a potted flower by an open window. Beautifly is sure to come looking for pollen.

Beautifly has a long mouth like a coiled needle, which is very convenient for collecting pollen from flowers. This Pokémon rides the spring winds as it flits around gathering pollen.

HOW TO SAY IT: BUE-tee-fly
IMPERIAL HEIGHT: 3'03"
IMPERIAL WEIGHT: 62.6 lbs.
METRIC HEIGHT: 1.0 m
METRIC WEIGHT: 28.4 kg
GENDER: ♂ ♀
ABILITIES: Swarm
WEAKNESSES: Fire, Flying, Electric, Ice, Rock

WURMPLE

SILCOON

BEAUTIFLY

BEEDRILL

Poison Bee Pokémon

#0015

TYPE: BUG-POISON

It has three poisonous stingers on its forelegs and its tail. They are used to jab its enemy repeatedly.

HOW TO SAY IT: BEE-dril
IMPERIAL HEIGHT: 3'03"
IMPERIAL WEIGHT: 65.0 lbs.
METRIC HEIGHT: 1.0 m
METRIC WEIGHT: 29.5 kg
GENDER: ♂ ♀
ABILITIES: Swarm
WEAKNESSES: Fire, Psychic, Flying, Rock

MEGA BEEDRILL

TYPE: BUG-POISON

Its legs have become poison stingers. It stabs its prey repeatedly with the stingers on its limbs, dealing the final blow with the stinger on its rear.

IMPERIAL HEIGHT: 4'07"
IMPERIAL WEIGHT: 89.3 lbs.
METRIC HEIGHT: 1.4 m
METRIC WEIGHT: 40.5 kg

WEEDLE   KAKUNA   BEEDRILL   MEGA BEEDRILL

BEHEEYEM

Cerebral Pokémon

#0606

TYPE: PSYCHIC

Whenever a Beheeyem visits a farm, a Dubwool mysteriously disappears.

Sometimes found drifting above wheat fields, this Pokémon can control the memories of its opponents.

HOW TO SAY IT: BEE-hee-ehm
IMPERIAL HEIGHT: 3'03"
IMPERIAL WEIGHT: 76.1 lbs.
METRIC HEIGHT: 1.0 m
METRIC WEIGHT: 34.5 kg
GENDER: ♂ ♀
ABILITIES: Telepathy, Synchronize
WEAKNESSES: Ghost, Dark, Bug

ELGYEM **BEHEEYEM**

TYPE: STEEL-PSYCHIC

#0374

BELDUM

Iron Ball Pokémon

From its rear, Beldum emits a magnetic force that rapidly pulls opponents in. They get skewered on Beldum's sharp claws.

The cells in this Pokémon's body are composed of magnetic material. Instead of blood, magnetic forces flow through Beldum's body.

HOW TO SAY IT: BELL-dum
IMPERIAL HEIGHT: 2'00"
IMPERIAL WEIGHT: 209.9 lbs.
METRIC HEIGHT: 0.6 m
METRIC WEIGHT: 95.2 kg
GENDER: Unknown
ABILITIES: Clear Body
WEAKNESSES: Ghost, Fire, Dark, Ground

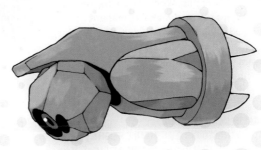

BELDUM **METANG** **METAGROSS** **MEGA METAGROSS**

BELLIBOLT

EleFrog Pokémon

#0939

TYPE: ELECTRIC

When this Pokémon expands and contracts its wobbly body, the belly-button dynamo in its stomach produces a huge amount of electricity.

What appear to be eyeballs are actually organs for discharging the electricity generated by Bellibolt's belly-button dynamo.

HOW TO SAY IT: BELL-ee-bolt
IMPERIAL HEIGHT: 3'11"
IMPERIAL WEIGHT: 249.1 lbs.
METRIC WEIGHT: 113.0 kg
METRIC HEIGHT: 1.2 m
GENDER: ♂ ♀
ABILITIES: Electromorphosis, Static
WEAKNESSES: Ground

TADBULB   BELLIBOLT

BELLOSSOM

Flower Pokémon

#0182

TYPE: GRASS

Plentiful in the tropics. When it dances, its petals rub together and make a pleasant ringing sound.

Bellossom gather at times and appear to dance. They say that the dance is a ritual to summon the sun.

HOW TO SAY IT: bell-LAHS-um
IMPERIAL HEIGHT: 1'04"   **METRIC HEIGHT:** 0.4 m
IMPERIAL WEIGHT: 12.8 lbs.   **METRIC WEIGHT:** 5.8 kg
GENDER: ♂ ♀
ABILITIES: Chlorophyll
WEAKNESSES: Fire, Flying, Ice, Poison, Bug

ODDISH   GLOOM   BELLOSSOM

BELLSPROUT
Flower Pokémon

#0069

TYPE: GRASS-POISON

Prefers hot and humid places. It ensnares tiny bugs with its vines and devours them.

HOW TO SAY IT: BELL-sprout
IMPERIAL HEIGHT: 2'04"
IMPERIAL WEIGHT: 8.8 lbs.
METRIC HEIGHT: 0.7 m
METRIC WEIGHT: 4.0 kg
GENDER: ♂ ♀
ABILITIES: Chlorophyll
WEAKNESSES: Fire, Psychic, Flying, Ice

BELLSPROUT ➡ **WEEPINBELL** ➡ **VICTREEBEL**

TYPE: ICE

#0712

BERGMITE
Ice Chunk Pokémon

They live in mountainous regions of frigid cold. On rare occasions, they ride on the back of an Avalugg to cross seas and move to new habitats.

Bergmite protects itself by coating its body in ice formed by frigid air of −148 degrees Fahrenheit. It fights with Frigibax whenever they meet.

HOW TO SAY IT: BERG-mite
IMPERIAL HEIGHT: 3'03"
IMPERIAL WEIGHT: 219.4 lbs.
METRIC HEIGHT: 1.0 m
METRIC WEIGHT: 99.5 kg
GENDER: ♂ ♀
ABILITIES: Own Tempo, Ice Body
WEAKNESSES: Fire, Steel, Fighting, Rock

BERGMITE

AVALUGG

HISUIAN AVALUGG

#0760

BEWEAR
Strong Arm Pokémon

TYPE: NORMAL-FIGHTING

Once it accepts you as a friend, it tries to show its affection with a hug. Letting it do that is dangerous—it could easily shatter your bones.

The moves it uses to take down its prey would make a martial artist jealous. It tucks subdued prey under its arms to carry them to its nest.

HOW TO SAY IT: beh-WARE
IMPERIAL HEIGHT: 6'11"
IMPERIAL WEIGHT: 297.6 lbs.
METRIC HEIGHT: 2.1 m
METRIC WEIGHT: 135.0 kg
GENDER: ♂ ♀
ABILITIES: Fluffy, Klutz
WEAKNESSES: Psychic, Flying, Fairy, Fighting

STUFFUL ➤ BEWEAR

BIBAREL
#0400
Beaver Pokémon

TYPE: NORMAL-WATER

It busily makes its nest with stacks of branches and roots it has cut up with its sharp incisors.

It makes its nest by damming streams with bark and mud. It is known as an industrious worker.

HOW TO SAY IT: bee-BAIR-rel
IMPERIAL HEIGHT: 3'03"
IMPERIAL WEIGHT: 69.4 lbs.
METRIC HEIGHT: 1.0 m
METRIC WEIGHT: 31.5 kg
GENDER: ♂ ♀
ABILITIES: Simple, Unaware
WEAKNESSES: Grass, Electric, Fighting

BIDOOF ➤ BIBAREL

#0399 BIDOOF
Plump Mouse Pokémon

TYPE: NORMAL

With nerves of steel, nothing can perturb it. It is more agile and active than it appears.

It constantly gnaws on logs and rocks to whittle down its front teeth. It nests alongside water.

HOW TO SAY IT: BEE-doof
IMPERIAL HEIGHT: 1'08"
IMPERIAL WEIGHT: 44.1 lbs.
METRIC HEIGHT: 0.5 m
METRIC WEIGHT: 20.0 kg
GENDER: ♂ ♀
ABILITIES: Simple, Unaware
WEAKNESSES: Fighting

BIDOOF → **BIBAREL**

TYPE: ROCK-WATER

#0688 BINACLE
Two-Handed Pokémon

After two Binacle find a suitably sized rock, they adhere themselves to it and live together. They cooperate to gather food during high tide.

If the two don't work well together, both their offense and defense fall apart. Without good teamwork, they won't survive.

HOW TO SAY IT: BY-nuh-kull
IMPERIAL HEIGHT: 1'08"
IMPERIAL WEIGHT: 68.3 lbs.
METRIC HEIGHT: 0.5 m
METRIC WEIGHT: 31.0 kg
GENDER: ♂ ♀
ABILITIES: Tough Claws, Sniper
WEAKNESSES: Grass, Electric, Fighting, Ground

BINACLE → **BARBARACLE**

BISHARP

Sword Blade Pokémon

#0625

TYPE: DARK-STEEL

This Pokémon commands a group of several Pawniard. Groups that are defeated in territorial disputes are absorbed by the winning side.

Bisharp mercilessly cuts its opponents to pieces with the sharp blades covering its body. It will do anything to win.

HOW TO SAY IT: BIH-sharp
IMPERIAL HEIGHT: 5'03"
IMPERIAL WEIGHT: 154.3 lbs.
METRIC HEIGHT: 1.6 m
METRIC WEIGHT: 70.0 kg
GENDER: ♂ ♀
ABILITIES: Defiant, Inner Focus
WEAKNESSES: Fire, Fighting, Ground

PAWNIARD → BISHARP → KINGAMBIT

ULTRA BEAST

#0806

BLACEPHALON

Fireworks Pokémon

TYPE: FIRE-GHOST

It slithers toward people. Then, without warning, it triggers the explosion of its own head. It's apparently one kind of Ultra Beast.

A UB that appeared from an Ultra Wormhole, it causes explosions, then takes advantage of opponents' surprise to rob them of their vitality.

HOW TO SAY IT: blass-SEF-uh-lawn
IMPERIAL HEIGHT: 5'11"
IMPERIAL WEIGHT: 28.7 lbs.
METRIC HEIGHT: 1.8 m
METRIC WEIGHT: 13.0 kg
GENDER: Unknown
ABILITIES: Beast Boost
WEAKNESSES: Water, Ghost, Ground, Dark, Rock

DOES NOT EVOLVE

BLASTOISE
Shellfish Pokémon

TYPE: WATER

It crushes its foe under its heavy body to cause fainting. In a pinch, it will withdraw inside its shell.

The rocket cannons on its shell fire jets of water capable of punching holes through thick steel.

HOW TO SAY IT: BLAS-toyce
IMPERIAL HEIGHT: 5'03"
IMPERIAL WEIGHT: 188.5 lbs.
METRIC HEIGHT: 1.6 m
METRIC WEIGHT: 85.5 kg
GENDER: ♂ ♀
ABILITIES: Torrent
WEAKNESSES: Grass, Electric

MEGA BLASTOISE

TYPE: WATER

The cannon on its back is as powerful as a tank gun. Its tough legs and back enable it to withstand the recoil from firing the cannon.

IMPERIAL HEIGHT: 5'03"
IMPERIAL WEIGHT: 222.9 lbs.
METRIC HEIGHT: 1.6 m
METRIC WEIGHT: 101.1 kg

SQUIRTLE

WARTORTLE

BLASTOISE

MEGA BLASTOISE

GIGANTAMAX BLASTOISE

It's not very good at precision shooting. When attacking, it just fires its thirty-one cannons over and over and over.

Water fired from this Pokémon's central main cannon has enough power to blast a hole into a mountain.

IMPERIAL HEIGHT: 82'00"+
IMPERIAL WEIGHT: ????.? lbs.
METRIC HEIGHT: 25.0+ m
METRIC WEIGHT: ???.? kg

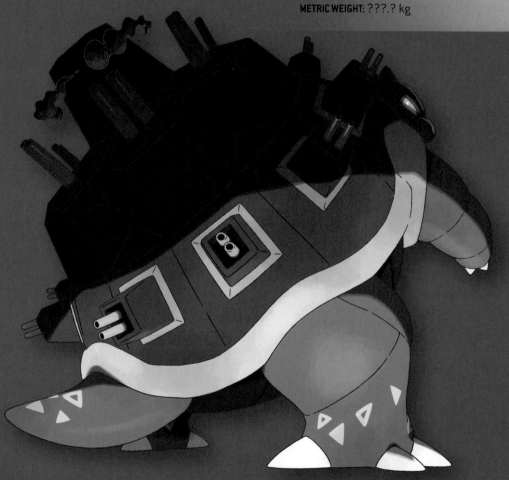

BLAZIKEN

Blaze Pokémon

TYPE: FIRE-FIGHTING

In battle, Blaziken blows out intense flames from its wrists and attacks foes courageously. The stronger the foe, the more intensely this Pokémon's wrists burn.

Blaziken has incredibly strong legs—it can easily clear a thirty-story building in one leap. This Pokémon's blazing punches leave its foes scorched and blackened.

HOW TO SAY IT: BLAZE-uh-ken
IMPERIAL HEIGHT: 6'03"   **METRIC HEIGHT:** 1.9 m
IMPERIAL WEIGHT: 114.6 lbs.   **METRIC WEIGHT:** 52.0 kg
GENDER: ♂ ♀
ABILITIES: Blaze
WEAKNESSES: Water, Psychic, Flying, Ground

MEGA BLAZIKEN

TYPE: FIRE-FIGHTING

IMPERIAL HEIGHT: 6'03"
IMPERIAL WEIGHT: 114.6 lbs.
METRIC HEIGHT: 1.9 m
METRIC WEIGHT: 52.0 kg

TORCHIC → **COMBUSKEN** → **BLAZIKEN** → **MEGA BLAZIKEN**

#0824

BLIPBUG
Larva Pokémon

TYPE: BUG

A constant collector of information, this Pokémon is very smart. Very strong is what it isn't.

Often found in gardens, this Pokémon has hairs on its body that it uses to assess its surroundings.

HOW TO SAY IT: BLIP-bug
IMPERIAL HEIGHT: 1'04"
IMPERIAL WEIGHT: 17.6 lbs.
METRIC HEIGHT: 0.4 m
METRIC WEIGHT: 8.0 kg
GENDER: ♂ ♀
ABILITIES: Swarm, Compound Eyes
WEAKNESSES: Fire, Flying, Rock

BLIPBUG → **DOTTLER** → **ORBEETLE**

TYPE: NORMAL

Anyone who takes even one taste of Blissey's egg becomes unfailingly caring and pleasant to everyone.

The eggs it lays are filled with happiness. Eating even one bite will bring a smile to anyone.

HOW TO SAY IT: BLISS-sey
IMPERIAL HEIGHT: 4'11"
IMPERIAL WEIGHT: 103.2 lbs.
METRIC HEIGHT: 1.5 m
METRIC WEIGHT: 46.8 kg
GENDER: ♀
ABILITIES: Natural Cure, Serene Grace
WEAKNESSES: Fighting

#0242

BLISSEY
Happiness Pokémon

HAPPINY → **CHANSEY** → **BLISSEY**

BLITZLE

Electrified Pokémon

#0522

TYPE: ELECTRIC

When thunderclouds cover the sky, it will appear. It can catch lightning with its mane and store the electricity.

Its mane shines when it discharges electricity. It uses the frequency and rhythm of these flashes to communicate.

HOW TO SAY IT: BLIT-zul
IMPERIAL HEIGHT: 2'07"
IMPERIAL WEIGHT: 65.7 lbs.
METRIC HEIGHT: 0.8 m
METRIC WEIGHT: 29.8 kg
GENDER: ♂ ♀
ABILITIES: Lightning Rod, Motor Drive
WEAKNESSES: Ground

BLITZLE **ZEBSTRIKA**

BOLDORE

Ore Pokémon

#0525

TYPE: ROCK

If you see its orange crystals start to glow, be wary. It's about to fire off bursts of energy.

It relies on sound in order to monitor what's in its vicinity. When angered, it will attack without ever changing the direction it's facing.

HOW TO SAY IT: BOHL-dohr
IMPERIAL HEIGHT: 2'11"
IMPERIAL WEIGHT: 224.9 lbs.
METRIC HEIGHT: 0.9 m
METRIC WEIGHT: 102.0 kg
GENDER: ♂ ♀
ABILITIES: Sturdy, Weak Armor
WEAKNESSES: Water, Steel, Grass, Fighting, Ground

ROGGENROLA **BOLDORE** **GIGALITH**

BOLTUND
Dog Pokémon

#0836

TYPE: ELECTRIC

This Pokémon generates electricity and channels it into its legs to keep them going strong. Boltund can run nonstop for three full days.

It sends electricity through its legs to boost their strength. Running at top speed, it easily breaks 50 mph.

HOW TO SAY IT: BOHL-tund
IMPERIAL HEIGHT: 3'03"
IMPERIAL WEIGHT: 75.0 lbs.
METRIC HEIGHT: 1.0 m
METRIC WEIGHT: 34.0 kg
GENDER: ♂ ♀
ABILITIES: Strong Jaw
WEAKNESSES: Ground

YAMPER → BOLTUND

BOMBIRDIER
Item Drop Pokémon

#0962

TYPE: FLYING-DARK

It gathers things up in an apron made from shed feathers added to the Pokémon's chest feathers, then drops those things from high places for fun.

Bombirdier uses the apron on its chest to bundle up food, which it carries back to its nest. It enjoys dropping things that make loud noises.

HOW TO SAY IT: BAHM-burr-deer
IMPERIAL HEIGHT: 4'11"
IMPERIAL WEIGHT: 94.6 lbs.
METRIC HEIGHT: 1.5 m
METRIC WEIGHT: 42.9 kg
GENDER: ♂ ♀
ABILITIES: Big Pecks, Keen Eye
WEAKNESSES: Fairy, Electric, Ice, Rock

64

DOES NOT EVOLVE

#0438 BONSLY
Bonsai Pokémon

TYPE: ROCK

In order to adjust the level of fluids in its body, it exudes water from its eyes. This makes it appear to be crying.

From its eyes, it can expel excess moisture from its body. This liquid is similar in composition to human sweat.

HOW TO SAY IT: BON-slye
IMPERIAL HEIGHT: 1'08"
IMPERIAL WEIGHT: 33.1 lbs.
METRIC HEIGHT: 0.5 m
METRIC WEIGHT: 15.0 kg
GENDER: ♂ ♀
ABILITIES: Sturdy, Rock Head
WEAKNESSES: Water, Steel, Grass, Fighting, Ground

BONSLY → **SUDOWOODO**

BOUFFALANT #0626
Bash Buffalo Pokémon

TYPE: NORMAL

These Pokémon can crush a car with no more than a headbutt. Bouffalant with more hair on their heads hold higher positions within the herd.

These Pokémon live in herds of about twenty individuals. Bouffalant that betray the herd will lose the hair on their heads for some reason.

HOW TO SAY IT: BOO-fuh-lahnt
IMPERIAL HEIGHT: 5'03"
IMPERIAL WEIGHT: 208.6 lbs.
METRIC HEIGHT: 1.6 m
METRIC WEIGHT: 94.6 kg
GENDER: ♂ ♀
ABILITIES: Reckless, Sap Sipper
WEAKNESSES: Fighting

DOES NOT EVOLVE

BOUNSWEET
Fruit Pokémon

#0761

TYPE: GRASS

Its sweat is sweet, like syrup made from boiled-down fruit. Because of this, Bounsweet was highly valued in the past, when sweeteners were scarce.

A Greedent drawn in by the sweet scent of these Pokémon will tuck the Bounsweet in among the berries in its tail and carry them all away.

HOW TO SAY IT: BOWN-sweet
IMPERIAL HEIGHT: 1'00"
IMPERIAL WEIGHT: 7.1 lbs.
METRIC HEIGHT: 0.3 m
METRIC WEIGHT: 3.2 kg
GENDER: ♀
ABILITIES: Leaf Guard, Oblivious
WEAKNESSES: Fire, Flying, Ice, Poison, Bug

BOUNSWEET   **STEENEE**   **TSAREENA**

#0654

BRAIXEN
Fox Pokémon

TYPE: FIRE

It has a twig stuck in its tail. With friction from its tail fur, it sets the twig on fire and launches into battle.

When the twig is plucked from its tail, friction sets the twig alight. The flame is used to send signals to its allies.

HOW TO SAY IT: BRAKE-sen
IMPERIAL HEIGHT: 3'03"
IMPERIAL WEIGHT: 32.0 lbs.
METRIC HEIGHT: 1.0 m
METRIC WEIGHT: 14.5 kg
GENDER: ♂ ♀
ABILITIES: Blaze
WEAKNESSES: Water, Ground, Rock

FENNEKIN   **BRAIXEN**   **DELPHOX**

BRAMBLEGHAST
Tumbleweed Pokémon

TYPE: GRASS-GHOST

It will open the branches of its head to envelop its prey. Once it absorbs all the life energy it needs, it expels the prey and discards it.

Brambleghast wanders around arid regions. On rare occasions, mass outbreaks of these Pokémon will bury an entire town.

HOW TO SAY IT: BRAM-bull-gast
IMPERIAL HEIGHT: 3'11"
IMPERIAL WEIGHT: 13.2
METRIC HEIGHT: 1.2 m
METRIC WEIGHT: 6.0 kg
GENDER: ♂ ♀
ABILITIES: Wind Rider
WEAKNESSES: Ghost, Fire, Flying, Dark, Ice

BRAMBLIN → BRAMBLEGHAST

BRAMBLIN
Tumbleweed Pokémon

TYPE: GRASS-GHOST

A soul unable to move on to the afterlife was blown around by the wind until it got tangled up with dried grass and became a Pokémon.

Not even Bramblin knows where it is headed as it tumbles across the wilderness, blown by the wind. It loathes getting wet.

HOW TO SAY IT: BRAM-bah-lihn
IMPERIAL HEIGHT: 2'00"
IMPERIAL WEIGHT: 1.3 lbs.
METRIC WEIGHT: 0.6 kg
METRIC HEIGHT: 0.6 m
GENDER: ♂ ♀
ABILITIES: Wind Rider
WEAKNESSES: Ghost, Fire, Flying, Dark, Ice

BRAMBLIN → BRAMBLEGHAST

BRAVIARY

Valiant Pokémon

#0628

TYPE: NORMAL-FLYING

The more scars they have, the more respect these brave soldiers of the sky get from their peers.

For the sake of its friends, this brave warrior of the sky will not stop battling, even if injured.

HOW TO SAY IT: BRAY-vee-air-ee
IMPERIAL HEIGHT: 4'11"
IMPERIAL WEIGHT: 90.4 lbs.
METRIC HEIGHT: 1.5 m
METRIC WEIGHT: 41.0 kg
GENDER: ♂
ABILITIES: Keen Eye, Sheer Force
WEAKNESSES: Electric, Ice, Rock

RUFFLET ➡ BRAVIARY

HISUIAN BRAVIARY

Battle Cry Pokémon

#0628

TYPE: PSYCHIC-FLYING

Screaming a bloodcurdling battle cry, this huge and ferocious bird Pokémon goes out on the hunt. It blasts lakes with shock waves, then scoops up any prey that float to the water's surface.

HOW TO SAY IT: BRAY-vee-air-ee
IMPERIAL HEIGHT: 5'07"
IMPERIAL WEIGHT: 95.7 lbs.
METRIC HEIGHT: 1.7 m
METRIC WEIGHT: 43.4 kg
GENDER: ♂
ABILITIES: N/A
WEAKNESSES: Ghost, Dark, Electric, Ice, Rock

RUFFLET ➡ BRAVIARY HISUIAN

BRELOOM

Mushroom Pokémon

#0286

TYPE: GRASS-FIGHTING

It scatters poisonous spores and throws powerful punches while its foe is hampered by inhaled spores.

The seeds on its tail are made of toxic spores. It knocks out foes with quick, virtually invisible punches.

HOW TO SAY IT: brell-LOOM
IMPERIAL HEIGHT: 3'11"
IMPERIAL WEIGHT: 86.4 lbs.
METRIC HEIGHT: 1.2 m
METRIC WEIGHT: 39.2 kg
GENDER: ♂ ♀
ABILITIES: Effect Spore, Poison Heal
WEAKNESSES: Fire, Psychic, Flying, Ice, Poison, Fairy

SHROOMISH   BRELOOM

BRIONNE

Pop Star Pokémon

#0729

TYPE: WATER

It gets excited when it sees a dance it doesn't know. This hard worker practices diligently until it can learn that dance.

It attacks by smacking its enemies with the exploding water balloons that it creates.

HOW TO SAY IT: bree-AHN
IMPERIAL HEIGHT: 2'00"
IMPERIAL WEIGHT: 38.6 lbs.
METRIC HEIGHT: 0.6 m
METRIC WEIGHT: 17.5 kg
GENDER: ♂ ♀
ABILITIES: Torrent
WEAKNESSES: Grass, Electric

POPPLIO   BRIONNE   PRIMARINA

TYPE: STEEL-PSYCHIC

In ages past, this Pokémon was revered as a bringer of rain. It was found buried in the ground.

It brought rains by opening portals to another world. It was revered as a bringer of plentiful harvests.

HOW TO SAY IT: brawn-ZONG
IMPERIAL HEIGHT: 4'03"
IMPERIAL WEIGHT: 412.3 lbs.
METRIC HEIGHT: 1.3 m
METRIC WEIGHT: 187.0 kg
GENDER: Unknown
ABILITIES: Levitate, Heatproof
WEAKNESSES: Ghost, Fire, Dark, Ground

#0437

BRONZONG
Bronze Bell Pokémon

BRONZOR → BRONZONG

#0436

BRONZOR
Bronze Pokémon

TYPE: STEEL-PSYCHIC

Ancient people believed that the pattern on Bronzor's back contained a mysterious power.

They are found in ancient tombs. The patterns on their backs are said to be imbued with mysterious power.

HOW TO SAY IT: BRAWN-zor
IMPERIAL HEIGHT: 1'08"
IMPERIAL WEIGHT: 133.4 lbs.
METRIC HEIGHT: 0.5 m
METRIC WEIGHT: 60.5 kg
GENDER: Unknown
ABILITIES: Levitate, Heatproof
WEAKNESSES: Ghost, Fire, Dark, Ground

BRONZOR → BRONZONG

BRUTE BONNET

Paradox Pokémon

#0986

TYPE: GRASS-DARK

It is possible that the creature listed as Brute Bonnet in a certain book could actually be this Pokémon.

It bears a slight resemblance to a Pokémon described in a dubious magazine as a cross between a dinosaur and a mushroom.

HOW TO SAY IT: BRUTE BAW-net
IMPERIAL HEIGHT: 3'11"
IMPERIAL WEIGHT: 46.3 lbs.
METRIC HEIGHT: 1.2 m
METRIC WEIGHT: 21.0 kg
GENDER: Unknown
ABILITIES: Protosynthesis
WEAKNESSES: Ice, Fire, Flying, Poison, Fighting, Fairy, Bug

DOES NOT EVOLVE

BRUXISH

Gnash Teeth Pokémon

#0779

TYPE: WATER-PSYCHIC

It grinds its teeth with great force to stimulate its brain. It fires the psychic energy created by this process from the protuberance on its head.

When sunlight reflects on the ripples created by a Bruxish grinding its teeth, the water all around sparkles brilliantly.

HOW TO SAY IT: BRUCK-sish
IMPERIAL HEIGHT: 2'11"
IMPERIAL WEIGHT: 41.9 lbs.
METRIC HEIGHT: 0.9 m
METRIC WEIGHT: 19.0 kg
GENDER: ♂ ♀
ABILITIES: Dazzling, Strong Jaw
WEAKNESSES: Ghost, Dark, Grass, Electric, Bug

DOES NOT EVOLVE

BUDEW

Bud Pokémon

#0406

TYPE: GRASS-POISON

The pollen it releases contains poison. If this Pokémon is raised on clean water, the poison's toxicity is increased.

This Pokémon is highly sensitive to temperature changes. When its bud starts to open, that means spring is right around the corner.

HOW TO SAY IT: buh-DOO
IMPERIAL HEIGHT: 0'08"
IMPERIAL WEIGHT: 2.6 lbs.
METRIC HEIGHT: 0.2 m
METRIC WEIGHT: 1.2 kg
GENDER: ♂ ♀
ABILITIES: Natural Cure, Poison Point
WEAKNESSES: Fire, Psychic, Flying, Ice

BUDEW   ROSELIA   ROSERADE

#0418

BUIZEL

Sea Weasel Pokémon

TYPE: WATER

It spins its two tails like a screw to propel itself through water. The tails also slice clinging seaweed.

It inflates its flotation sac, keeping its face above water in order to watch for prey movement.

HOW TO SAY IT: BWEE-zul
IMPERIAL HEIGHT: 2'04"
IMPERIAL WEIGHT: 65.0 lbs.
METRIC HEIGHT: 0.7 m
METRIC WEIGHT: 29.5 kg
GENDER: ♂ ♀
ABILITIES: Swift Swim
WEAKNESSES: Grass, Electric

BUIZEL   FLOATZEL

#0001 BULBASAUR
Seed Pokémon

TYPE: GRASS-POISON

There is a plant seed on its back right from the day this Pokémon is born. The seed slowly grows larger.

While it is young, it uses the nutrients that are stored in the seed on its back in order to grow.

HOW TO SAY IT: BUL-ba-sore
IMPERIAL HEIGHT: 2'04" **METRIC HEIGHT:** 0.7 m
IMPERIAL WEIGHT: 15.2 lbs. **METRIC WEIGHT:** 6.9 kg
GENDER: ♂ ♀
ABILITIES: Overgrow
WEAKNESSES: Fire, Psychic, Flying, Ice

BULBASAUR **IVYSAUR** **VENUSAUR** **MEGA VENUSAUR**

BUNEARY #0427
Rabbit Pokémon

TYPE: NORMAL

If both of Buneary's ears are rolled up, something is wrong with its body or mind. It's a sure sign the Pokémon is in need of care.

Buneary can attack by rolling up their ears and then striking with the force created by unrolling them. This attack becomes stronger with training.

HOW TO SAY IT: buh-NEAR-ee
IMPERIAL HEIGHT: 1'04"
IMPERIAL WEIGHT: 12.1 lbs.
METRIC HEIGHT: 0.4 m
METRIC WEIGHT: 5.5 kg
GENDER: ♂ ♀
ABILITIES: Run Away, Klutz
WEAKNESSES: Fighting

BUNEARY **LOPUNNY** **MEGA LOPUNNY**

BUNNELBY
Digging Pokémon
#0659

TYPE: NORMAL

It excels at digging holes. Using its ears, it can dig a nest 33 feet deep in one night.

It's very sensitive to danger. The sound of Corviknight's flapping will have Bunnelby digging a hole to hide underground in moments.

HOW TO SAY IT: BUN-ell-bee
IMPERIAL HEIGHT: 1'04"
IMPERIAL WEIGHT: 11.0 lbs.
METRIC HEIGHT: 0.4 m
METRIC WEIGHT: 5.0 kg
GENDER: ♂♀
ABILITIES: Pickup, Cheek Pouch
WEAKNESSES: Fighting

BUNNELBY   DIGGERSBY

#0412

BURMY
Bagworm Pokémon

PLANT
CLOAK

TYPE: BUG

To shelter itself from cold, wintry winds, it covers itself with a cloak made of twigs and leaves.

If its cloak is broken in battle, it quickly remakes the cloak with materials nearby.

HOW TO SAY IT: BURR-mee
IMPERIAL HEIGHT: 0'08"
IMPERIAL WEIGHT: 7.5 lbs.
METRIC HEIGHT: 0.2 m
METRIC WEIGHT: 3.4 kg
GENDER: ♂♀
ABILITIES: Shed Skin
WEAKNESSES: Fire, Flying Rock

SANDY
CLOAK

TRASH
CLOAK

BURMY

WORMADAM

MOTHIM

BUTTERFREE

Butterfly Pokémon

#0012

TYPE: BUG-FLYING

It loves the nectar of flowers and can locate flower patches that have even tiny amounts of pollen.

HOW TO SAY IT: BUT-er-free
IMPERIAL HEIGHT: 3'07"
IMPERIAL WEIGHT: 70.5 lbs.
METRIC HEIGHT: 1.1 m
METRIC WEIGHT: 32.0 kg
GENDER: ♂ ♀
ABILITIES: Compound Eyes
WEAKNESSES: Fire, Flying, Electric, Ice, Rock

CATERPIE → **METAPOD** → **BUTTERFREE**

GIGANTAMAX BUTTERFREE

Crystallized Gigantamax energy makes up this Pokémon's blindingly bright and highly toxic scales.

Once it has opponents trapped in a tornado that could blow away a 10-ton truck, it finishes them off with its poisonous scales.

IMPERIAL HEIGHT: 55'09"+
IMPERIAL WEIGHT: ????.? lbs.
METRIC HEIGHT: 17.0+ m
METRIC WEIGHT: ???.? kg

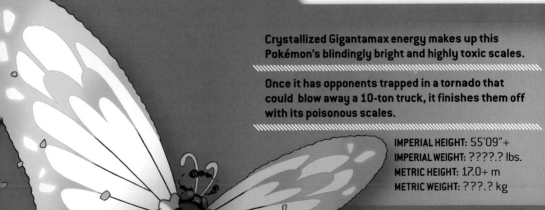

BUZZWOLE

Swollen Pokémon

#0794

TYPE: BUG-FIGHTING

Although it's alien to this world and a danger here, it's apparently a common organism in the world where it normally lives.

Buzzwole goes around showing off its abnormally swollen muscles. It is one kind of Ultra Beast.

HOW TO SAY IT: BUZZ-wole
IMPERIAL HEIGHT: 7'10"
IMPERIAL WEIGHT: 735.5 lbs.
METRIC HEIGHT: 2.4 m
METRIC WEIGHT: 333.6 kg
GENDER: Unknown
ABILITIES: Beast Boost
WEAKNESSES: Fire, Psychic, Flying, Fairy

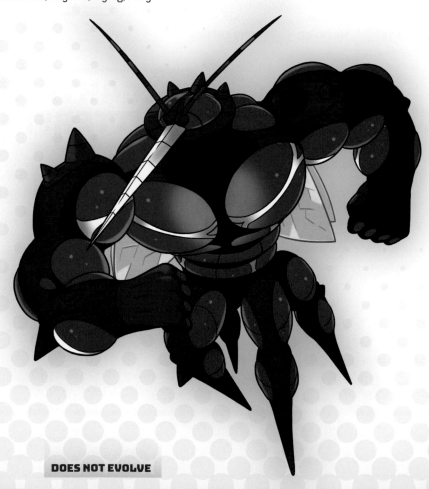

DOES NOT EVOLVE

CACNEA

Cactus Pokémon

#0331

TYPE: GRASS

It prefers harsh environments, such as deserts. It can survive for 30 days on water stored in its body.

It lives in arid locations. Its yellow flowers bloom once a year.

HOW TO SAY IT: CACK-nee-uh
IMPERIAL HEIGHT: 1'04"
IMPERIAL WEIGHT: 113.1 lbs.
METRIC HEIGHT: 0.4 m
METRIC WEIGHT: 51.3 kg
GENDER: ♂ ♀
ABILITIES: Sand Veil
WEAKNESSES: Fire, Flying, Ice, Poison, Bug

CACNEA   CACTURNE

#0332

CACTURNE

Scarecrow Pokémon

TYPE: GRASS-DARK

Packs of them follow travelers through the desert until the travelers can no longer move.

It lives in deserts. It becomes active at night when it hunts for prey exhausted from the desert's heat.

HOW TO SAY IT: CACK-turn
IMPERIAL HEIGHT: 4'03"
IMPERIAL WEIGHT: 170.6 lbs.
METRIC HEIGHT: 1.3 m
METRIC WEIGHT: 77.4 kg
GENDER: ♂ ♀
ABILITIES: Sand Veil
WEAKNESSES: Ice, Fire, Flying, Poison, Fighting, Fairy, Bug

CACNEA   CACTURNE

TYPE: PSYCHIC-GRASS

Calyrex is a merciful Pokémon, capable of providing healing and blessings. It reigned over the Galar region in times of yore.

Calyrex is known in legend as a king that ruled over Galar in ancient times. It has the power to cause hearts to mend and plants to spring forth.

HOW TO SAY IT: KAL-ih-reks
IMPERIAL HEIGHT: 3'07"
IMPERIAL WEIGHT: 17.0 lbs.
METRIC HEIGHT: 1.1 m
METRIC WEIGHT: 7.7 kg
GENDER: Unknown
ABILITIES: Unnerve
WEAKNESSES: Ghost, Fire, Flying, Ice, Dark, Poison, Bug

ICE RIDER

SHADOW RIDER

DOES NOT EVOLVE

CAMERUPT
Eruption Pokémon

TYPE: FIRE-GROUND

It lives in the crater of a volcano. It is well known that the humps on its back erupt every 10 years.

If angered, the humps on its back erupt in a shower of molten lava. It lives in the craters of volcanoes.

HOW TO SAY IT: CAM-err-rupt
IMPERIAL HEIGHT: 6'03"
IMPERIAL WEIGHT: 485.0 lbs.
METRIC HEIGHT: 1.9 m
METRIC WEIGHT: 220.0 kg
GENDER: ♂ ♀
ABILITIES: Magma Armor, Solid Rock
WEAKNESSES: Water, Ground

MEGA CAMERUPT

TYPE: FIRE-GROUND

Camerupt has a volcano inside its body. Magma of 18,000 degrees Fahrenheit courses through its body. Occasionally, the humps on this Pokémon's back erupt, spewing the superheated magma.

The humps on Camerupt's back are formed by a transformation of its bones. They sometimes blast out molten magma. This Pokémon apparently erupts often when it is enraged.

IMPERIAL HEIGHT: 8'02"
IMPERIAL WEIGHT: 706.6 lbs.
METRIC HEIGHT: 2.5 m
METRIC WEIGHT: 320.5 kg

NUMEL

CAMERUPT

MEGA CAMERUPT

CAPSAKID

Spicy Pepper Pokémon

#0951

TYPE: GRASS

The more sunlight this Pokémon bathes in, the more spicy chemicals are produced by its body, and thus the spicier its moves become.

Traditional Paldean dishes can be extremely spicy because they include the shed front teeth of Capsakid among their ingredients.

HOW TO SAY IT: KAP-suh-KID
IMPERIAL HEIGHT: 1'00"
IMPERIAL WEIGHT: 6.6 lbs.
METRIC HEIGHT: 0.3 m
METRIC WEIGHT: 3.0 kg
GENDER: ♂ ♀
ABILITIES: Chlorophyll, Insomnia
WEAKNESSES: Fire, Flying, Ice, Poison, Bug

CAPSAKID   SCOVILLAIN

CARBINK

Jewel Pokémon

#0703

TYPE: ROCK-FAIRY

When beset by attackers, Carbink wipes them all out by firing high-energy beams from the gems embedded in its body.

It's said that somewhere in the world, there's a mineral vein housing a large pack of slumbering Carbink. It's also said that this pack has a queen.

HOW TO SAY IT: CAR-bink
IMPERIAL HEIGHT: 1'00"
IMPERIAL WEIGHT: 12.6 lbs.
METRIC HEIGHT: 0.3 m
METRIC WEIGHT: 5.7 kg
GENDER: Unknown
ABILITIES: Clear Body
WEAKNESSES: Steel, Water, Grass, Ground

DOES NOT EVOLVE

CARKOL
Coal Pokémon

TYPE: ROCK-FIRE

The temperature inside its body increases when it experiences strong emotions. It rolls around frantically while spewing flames.

Due to the coal tar created inside it, the heap of coal on Carkol's back never falls apart, even when the Pokémon rolls around at high speeds.

HOW TO SAY IT: KAR-kohl
IMPERIAL HEIGHT: 3'07"
IMPERIAL WEIGHT: 172.0 lbs.
METRIC HEIGHT: 1.1 m
METRIC WEIGHT: 78.0 kg
GENDER: ♂ ♀
ABILITIES: Steam Engine, Flame Body
WEAKNESSES: Water, Ground, Fighting, Rock

ROLYCOLY → **CARKOL** → **COALOSSAL**

CARNIVINE
Bug Catcher Pokémon

TYPE: GRASS

It attracts prey with its sweet-smelling saliva, then chomps down. It takes a whole day to eat prey.

It binds itself to trees in marshes. It attracts prey with its sweet-smelling drool and gulps them down.

HOW TO SAY IT: CAR-neh-vine
IMPERIAL HEIGHT: 4'07"
IMPERIAL WEIGHT: 59.5 lbs.
METRIC HEIGHT: 1.4 m
METRIC WEIGHT: 27.0 kg
GENDER: ♂ ♀
ABILITIES: Levitate
WEAKNESSES: Fire, Flying, Ice, Poison, Bug

DOES NOT EVOLVE

CARRACOSTA

Prototurtle Pokémon

#0565

TYPE: WATER-ROCK

Carracosta completely devours its prey—bones, shells, and all. Because of this, Carracosta's own shell grows thick and sturdy.

This Pokémon emerges from the water in search of prey despite the fact that it moves more slowly on land.

HOW TO SAY IT: kah-ruh-KAHS-tuh
IMPERIAL HEIGHT: 3'11"
IMPERIAL WEIGHT: 178.6 lbs.
METRIC HEIGHT: 1.2 m
METRIC WEIGHT: 81.0 kg
GENDER: ♂ ♀
ABILITIES: Solid Rock, Sturdy
WEAKNESSES: Grass, Electric, Fighting, Ground

TIRTOUGA   CARRACOSTA

#0318

CARVANHA

Savage Pokémon

TYPE: WATER-DARK

It won't attack while it's alone—not even if it spots prey. Instead, it waits for other Carvanha to join it, and then the Pokémon attack as a group.

These Pokémon have sharp fangs and powerful jaws. Sailors avoid Carvanha dens at all costs.

HOW TO SAY IT: car-VAH-na
IMPERIAL HEIGHT: 2'07"
IMPERIAL WEIGHT: 45.9 lbs.
METRIC HEIGHT: 0.8 m
METRIC WEIGHT: 20.8 kg
GENDER: ♂ ♀
ABILITIES: Rough Skin
WEAKNESSES: Fairy, Grass, Electric, Fighting, Bug

CARVANHA   SHARPEDO   MEGA SHARPEDO

#0268 CASCOON
Cocoon Pokémon

TYPE: BUG

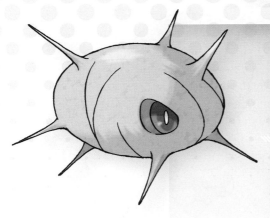

Cascoon makes its protective cocoon by wrapping its body entirely with a fine silk from its mouth. Once the silk goes around its body, it hardens. This Pokémon prepares for its evolution inside the cocoon.

If it is attacked, Cascoon remains motionless however badly it may be hurt. It does so because if it were to move, its body would be weak upon evolution. This Pokémon will also not forget the pain it endured.

WURMPLE ➡ **CASCOON** ➡ **DUSTOX**

HOW TO SAY IT: CAS-koon
IMPERIAL HEIGHT: 2'04" **METRIC HEIGHT:** 0.7 m
IMPERIAL WEIGHT: 25.4 lbs. **METRIC WEIGHT:** 11.5 kg
GENDER: ♂ ♀
ABILITIES: Shed Skin
WEAKNESSES: Fire, Flying, Rock

CASTFORM #0351
Weather Pokémon

TYPE: NORMAL

Although its form changes with the weather, that is apparently the result of a chemical reaction and not the result of its own free will.

Its form changes depending on the weather. The rougher conditions get, the rougher Castform's disposition!

HOW TO SAY IT: CAST-form
IMPERIAL HEIGHT: 1'00"
IMPERIAL WEIGHT: 1.8 lbs.
METRIC HEIGHT: 0.3 m
METRIC WEIGHT: 0.8 kg
GENDER: ♂ ♀
ABILITIES: Forecast
WEAKNESSES: Fighting

DOES NOT EVOLVE

CATERPIE
Worm Pokémon

#0010

TYPE: BUG

For protection, it releases a horrible stench from the antenna on its head to drive away enemies.

Its short feet are tipped with suction pads that enable it to tirelessly climb slopes and walls.

HOW TO SAY IT: CAT-ur-pee
IMPERIAL HEIGHT: 1'00"
IMPERIAL WEIGHT: 6.4 lbs.
METRIC HEIGHT: 0.3 m
METRIC WEIGHT: 2.9 kg
GENDER: ♂ ♀
ABILITIES: Shield Dust
WEAKNESSES: Fire, Flying, Rock

CATERPIE   **METAPOD**   **BUTTERFREE**

MYTHICAL POKÉMON

#0251

CELEBI
Time Travel Pokémon

TYPE: PSYCHIC-GRASS

This Pokémon came from the future by crossing over time. It is thought that so long as Celebi appears, a bright and shining future awaits us.

HOW TO SAY IT: SEL-ih-bee
IMPERIAL HEIGHT: 2'00"
IMPERIAL WEIGHT: 11.0 lbs.
METRIC HEIGHT: 0.6 m
METRIC WEIGHT: 5.0 kg
GENDER: Unknown
ABILITIES: Natural Cure
WEAKNESSES: Ghost, Fire, Flying, Ice, Dark, Poison, Bug

DOES NOT EVOLVE

CELESTEELA

Launch Pokémon

TYPE: STEEL-FLYING

One of the dangerous UBs, high energy readings can be detected coming from both of its huge arms.

Although it's alien to this world and a danger here, it's apparently a common organism in the world where it normally lives.

HOW TO SAY IT: sell-uh-STEEL-uh
IMPERIAL HEIGHT: 30'02"
IMPERIAL WEIGHT: 2,204.4 lbs.
METRIC HEIGHT: 9.2 m
METRIC WEIGHT: 999.9 kg
GENDER: Unknown
ABILITIES: Beast Boost
WEAKNESSES: Fire, Electric

DOES NOT EVOLVE

CENTISKORCH

Radiator Pokémon

#0851

TYPE: FIRE-BUG

When it heats up, its body temperature reaches about 1,500 degrees Fahrenheit. It lashes its body like a whip and launches itself at enemies.

While its burning body is already dangerous on its own, this excessively hostile Pokémon also has large and very sharp fangs.

HOW TO SAY IT: SEN-tih-scorch
IMPERIAL HEIGHT: 9'10"
IMPERIAL WEIGHT: 264.6 lbs.
METRIC HEIGHT: 3.0 m
METRIC WEIGHT: 120.0 kg
GENDER: ♂ ♀
ABILITIES: Flash Fire, White Smoke
WEAKNESSES: Water, Flying, Rock

SIZZLIPEDE   CENTISKORCH

GIGANTAMAX CENTISKORCH

Gigantamax energy has evoked a rise in its body temperature, now reaching over 1,800 degrees Fahrenheit. Its heat waves incinerate its enemies.

The heat that comes off a Gigantamax Centiskorch may destabilize air currents. Sometimes it can even cause storms.

IMPERIAL HEIGHT: 246'01"+
IMPERIAL WEIGHT: ????.? lbs.
METRIC HEIGHT: 75.0+ m
METRIC WEIGHT: ???.? kg

CERULEDGE

#0937

Fire Blades Pokémon

TYPE: FIRE-GHOST

The fiery blades on its arms burn fiercely with the lingering resentment of a sword wielder who fell before accomplishing their goal.

An old set of armor steeped in grudges caused this Pokémon's evolution. Ceruledge cuts its enemies to pieces without mercy.

HOW TO SAY IT: suh-ROOL-ehj
IMPERIAL HEIGHT: 5'03"
IMPERIAL WEIGHT: 136.7 lbs.
METRIC HEIGHT: 1.6 m
METRIC WEIGHT: 62.0 kg
GENDER: ♂ ♀
ABILITIES: Flash Fire
WEAKNESSES: Water, Ghost, Ground, Dark, Rock

CHARCADET → **CERULEDGE**

CETITAN

#0975

Terra Whale Pokémon

TYPE: ICE

This Pokémon wanders around snowy, icy areas. It protects its body with powerful muscles and a thick layer of fat under its skin.

Ice energy builds up in the horn on its upper jaw, causing the horn to reach cryogenic temperatures that freeze its surroundings.

HOW TO SAY IT: sih-TYE-tun
IMPERIAL HEIGHT: 14'09"
IMPERIAL WEIGHT: 1,543.2 lbs.
METRIC HEIGHT: 4.5 m
METRIC WEIGHT: 700.0 kg
GENDER: ♂ ♀
ABILITIES: Thick Fat, Slush Rush
WEAKNESSES: Fire, Steel, Fighting, Rock

CETODDLE **CETITAN**

CETODDLE

Terra Whale Pokémon

#0974

TYPE: ICE

This species left the ocean and began living on land a very long time ago. It seems to be closely related to Wailmer.

It lives in frigid regions in pods of five or so individuals. It loves the minerals found in snow and ice.

HOW TO SAY IT: sih-TAH-dul
IMPERIAL HEIGHT: 3'11"
IMPERIAL WEIGHT: 99.2 lbs.
METRIC HEIGHT: 1.2 m
METRIC WEIGHT: 45.0 kg
GENDER: ♂ ♀
ABILITIES: Thick Fat, Snow Cloak
WEAKNESSES: Fire, Steel, Fighting, Rock

CETODDLE → CETITAN

CHANDELURE

Luring Pokémon

#0609

TYPE: GHOST-FIRE

This Pokémon haunts dilapidated mansions. It sways its arms to hypnotize opponents with the ominous dancing of its flames.

In homes illuminated by Chandelure instead of lights, funerals were a constant occurrence—or so it's said.

HOW TO SAY IT: shan-duh-LOOR
IMPERIAL HEIGHT: 3'03"
IMPERIAL WEIGHT: 75.6 lbs.
METRIC HEIGHT: 1.0 m
METRIC WEIGHT: 34.3 kg
GENDER: ♂ ♀
ABILITIES: Flash Fire, Flame Body
WEAKNESSES: Ghost, Dark, Ground, Water, Rock

LITWICK   LAMPENT   CHANDELURE

#0113

CHANSEY
Egg Pokémon

TYPE: NORMAL

This kindly Pokémon lays highly nutritious eggs and shares them with injured Pokémon or people.

It walks carefully to prevent its egg from breaking. However, it is extremely fast at running away.

HOW TO SAY IT: CHAN-see
IMPERIAL HEIGHT: 3'07"
IMPERIAL WEIGHT: 76.3 lbs.
METRIC HEIGHT: 1.1 m
METRIC WEIGHT: 34.6 kg
GENDER: ♀
ABILITIES: Natural Cure, Serene Grace
WEAKNESSES: Fighting

HAPPINY → **CHANSEY** → **BLISSEY**

#0935

CHARCADET
Fire Child Pokémon

TYPE: FIRE

Burnt charcoal came to life and became a Pokémon. Possessing a fiery fighting spirit, Charcadet will battle even tough opponents.

Its firepower increases when it fights, reaching over 1,800 degrees Fahrenheit. It likes berries that are rich in fat.

HOW TO SAY IT: CHAR-kuh-deht
IMPERIAL HEIGHT: 2'00"
IMPERIAL WEIGHT: 23.1 lbs.
METRIC HEIGHT: 0.6 m
METRIC WEIGHT: 10.5 kg
GENDER: ♂ ♀
ABILITIES: Flash Fire
WEAKNESSES: Water, Ground, Rock

ARMAROUGE

 CHARCADET

 **CERULEDGE**

CHARIZARD

Flame Pokémon

#0006

TYPE: FIRE-FLYING

It is said that Charizard's fire burns hotter if it has experienced harsh battles.

HOW TO SAY IT: CHAR-iz-ard
IMPERIAL HEIGHT: 5'07"
IMPERIAL WEIGHT: 199.5 lbs.
METRIC HEIGHT: 1.7 m
METRIC WEIGHT: 90.5 kg
GENDER: ♂ ♀
ABILITIES: Blaze
WEAKNESSES: Water, Electric, Rock

GIGANTAMAX CHARIZARD

This colossal, flame-winged figure of a Charizard was brought about by Gigantamax energy.

The flame inside its body burns hotter than 3,600 degrees Fahrenheit. When Charizard roars, that temperature climbs even higher.

IMPERIAL HEIGHT: 91'10"+
IMPERIAL WEIGHT: ????.? lbs.
METRIC HEIGHT: 28.0+ m
METRIC WEIGHT: ???.? kg

MEGA CHARIZARD X

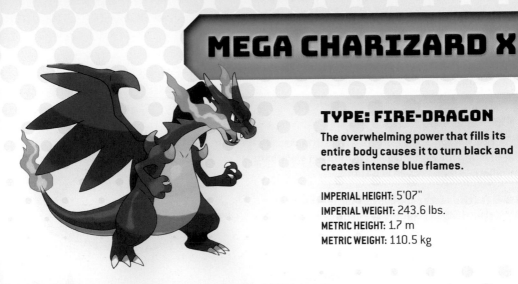

TYPE: FIRE-DRAGON

The overwhelming power that fills its entire body causes it to turn black and creates intense blue flames.

IMPERIAL HEIGHT: 5'07"
IMPERIAL WEIGHT: 243.6 lbs.
METRIC HEIGHT: 1.7 m
METRIC WEIGHT: 110.5 kg

MEGA CHARIZARD Y

TYPE: FIRE-FLYING

Its bond with its Trainer is the source of its power. It boasts speed and maneuverability greater than that of a jet fighter.

IMPERIAL HEIGHT: 5'07"
IMPERIAL WEIGHT: 221.6 lbs.
METRIC HEIGHT: 1.7 m
METRIC WEIGHT: 100.5 kg

CHARMANDER

CHARMELEON

CHARIZARD

MEGA CHARIZARD X

MEGA CHARIZARD Y

CHARJABUG #0737
Battery Pokémon

TYPE: BUG-ELECTRIC

While its durable shell protects it from attacks, Charjabug strikes at enemies with jolts of electricity discharged from the tips of its jaws.

Its digestive processes convert the leaves it eats into electricity. An electric sac in its belly stores the electricity for later use.

HOW TO SAY IT: CHAR-juh-bug
IMPERIAL HEIGHT: 1'08"
IMPERIAL WEIGHT: 23.1 lbs.
METRIC HEIGHT: 0.5 m
METRIC WEIGHT: 10.5 kg
GENDER: ♂ ♀
ABILITIES: Battery
WEAKNESSES: Fire, Rock

GRUBBIN **CHARJABUG** **VIKAVOLT**

CHARMANDER #0004
Lizard Pokémon

TYPE: FIRE

It has a preference for hot things. When it rains, steam is said to spout from the tip of its tail.

From the time it is born, a flame burns at the tip of its tail. Its life would end if the flame were to go out.

HOW TO SAY IT: CHAR-man-der
IMPERIAL HEIGHT: 2'00"
IMPERIAL WEIGHT: 18.7 lbs.
METRIC HEIGHT: 0.6 m
METRIC WEIGHT: 8.5 kg
GENDER: ♂ ♀
ABILITIES: Blaze
WEAKNESSES: Water, Ground, Rock

MEGA CHARIZARD X

MEGA CHARIZARD Y

CHARMANDER **CHARMELEON** **CHARIZARD**

#0005

CHARMELEON
Flame Pokémon

TYPE: FIRE

It has a barbaric nature. In battle, it whips its fiery tail around and slashes away with sharp claws.

If it becomes agitated during battle, it spouts intense flames, incinerating its surroundings.

HOW TO SAY IT: char-MEE-lee-un
IMPERIAL HEIGHT: 3'07"
IMPERIAL WEIGHT: 41.9 lbs.
METRIC HEIGHT: 1.1 m
METRIC WEIGHT: 19.0 kg
GENDER: ♂ ♀
ABILITIES: Blaze
WEAKNESSES: Water, Ground, Rock

CHARMANDER → CHARMELEON → CHARIZARD

MEGA CHARIZARD X

MEGA CHARIZARD Y

#0441

CHATOT
Music Note Pokémon

TYPE: NORMAL-FLYING

It mimics the cries of other Pokémon to trick them into thinking it's one of them. This way they won't attack it.

It can learn and speak human words. If they gather, they all learn the same saying.

HOW TO SAY IT: CHAT-tot
IMPERIAL HEIGHT: 1'08"
IMPERIAL WEIGHT: 4.2 lbs.
METRIC HEIGHT: 0.5 m
METRIC WEIGHT: 1.9 kg
GENDER: ♂ ♀
ABILITIES: Keen Eye, Tangled Feet
WEAKNESSES: Electric, Ice, Rock

DOES NOT EVOLVE

CHERRIM

Blossom Pokémon

#0421

OVERCAST FORM

SUNSHINE FORM

TYPE: GRASS

As a bud, it barely moves. It sits still, placidly waiting for sunlight to appear.

Its folded petals are pretty tough. Bird Pokémon can peck at them all they want, and Cherrim won't be bothered at all.

HOW TO SAY IT: chuh-RIM
IMPERIAL HEIGHT: 1'08"
IMPERIAL WEIGHT: 20.5 lbs.
METRIC HEIGHT: 0.5 m
METRIC WEIGHT: 9.3 kg
GENDER: ♂ ♀
ABILITIES: Flower Gift
WEAKNESSES: Fire, Flying, Ice, Poison, Bug

CHERUBI ➡ CHERRIM

TYPE: GRASS

#0420

CHERUBI

Cherry Pokémon

It nimbly dashes about to avoid getting pecked by bird Pokémon that would love to make off with its small, nutrient-rich storage ball.

The deeper a Cherubi's red, the more nutrients it has stockpiled in its body. And the sweeter and tastier its small ball!

HOW TO SAY IT: chuh-ROO-bee
IMPERIAL HEIGHT: 1'04"
IMPERIAL WEIGHT: 7.3 lbs.
METRIC HEIGHT: 0.4 m
METRIC WEIGHT: 3.3 kg
GENDER: ♂ ♀
ABILITIES: Chlorophyll
WEAKNESSES: Fire, Flying, Ice, Poison, Bug

CHERUBI ➡ CHERRIM

CHESNAUGHT
#0652
Spiny Armor Pokémon

TYPE: GRASS-FIGHTING

Its Tackle is forceful enough to flip a 50-ton tank. It shields its allies from danger with its own body.

When it takes a defensive posture with its fists guarding its face, it could withstand a bomb blast.

HOW TO SAY IT: CHESS-nawt
IMPERIAL HEIGHT: 5'03"
IMPERIAL WEIGHT: 198.4 lbs.
METRIC HEIGHT: 1.6 m
METRIC WEIGHT: 90.0 kg
GENDER: ♂ ♀
ABILITIES: Overgrow
WEAKNESSES: Fire, Psychic, Flying, Ice, Poison, Fairy

CHESPIN   QUILLADIN   CHESNAUGHT

CHESPIN
#0650
Spiny Nut Pokémon

TYPE: GRASS

The quills on its head are usually soft. When it flexes them, the points become so hard and sharp that they can pierce rock.

Such a thick shell of wood covers its head and back that even a direct hit from a truck wouldn't faze it.

HOW TO SAY IT: CHESS-pin
IMPERIAL HEIGHT: 1'04"
IMPERIAL WEIGHT: 19.8 lbs.
METRIC HEIGHT: 0.4 m
METRIC WEIGHT: 9.0 kg
GENDER: ♂ ♀
ABILITIES: Overgrow
WEAKNESSES: Fire, Flying, Ice, Poison, Bug

CHESPIN   QUILLADIN   CHESNAUGHT

CHEWTLE

Snapping Pokémon

#0833

TYPE: WATER

Its large front tooth is still growing in. When the tooth itches, this Pokémon will bite another Chewtle's horn, and the two Pokémon will tussle.

A popular game among children is to lift up sticks that Chewtle have bitten onto to see whose Chewtle can hang on the longest.

HOW TO SAY IT: CHOO-tull
IMPERIAL HEIGHT: 1'00"
IMPERIAL WEIGHT: 18.7 lbs.
METRIC HEIGHT: 0.3 m
METRIC WEIGHT: 8.5 kg
GENDER: ♂♀
ABILITIES: Strong Jaw, Shell Armor
WEAKNESSES: Grass, Electric

CHEWTLE → DREDNAW

LEGENDARY POKÉMON

#1004

CHI-YU

Ruinous Pokémon

TYPE: DARK-FIRE

It controls flames burning at over 5,400 degrees Fahrenheit. It casually swims through the sea of lava it creates by melting rock and sand.

The envy accumulated within curved beads that sparked multiple conflicts has clad itself in fire and become a Pokémon.

HOW TO SAY IT: CHEE-yoo
IMPERIAL HEIGHT: 1'04"
IMPERIAL WEIGHT: 10.8 lbs.
METRIC HEIGHT: 0.4 m
METRIC WEIGHT: 4.9 kg
GENDER: Unknown
ABILITIES: Beads of Ruin
WEAKNESSES: Water, Ground, Fighting, Rock

DOES NOT EVOLVE

CHIEN-PAO

Ruinous Pokémon

LEGENDARY POKÉMON

TYPE: DARK-ICE

This Pokémon can control 100 tons of fallen snow. It plays around innocently by leaping in and out of avalanches it has caused.

The hatred of those who perished by the sword long ago has clad itself in snow and become a Pokémon.

HOW TO SAY IT: CHYEHN-pow
IMPERIAL HEIGHT: 6'03"
IMPERIAL WEIGHT: 335.5 lbs.
METRIC HEIGHT: 1.9 m
METRIC WEIGHT: 152.2 kg
GENDER: Unknown
ABILITIES: Sword of Ruin
WEAKNESSES: Steel, Fire, Fighting, Rock, Fairy, Bug

DOES NOT EVOLVE

TYPE: GRASS

In battle, Chikorita waves its leaf around to keep the foe at bay. However, a sweet fragrance also wafts from the leaf, becalming the battling Pokémon and creating a cozy, friendly atmosphere all around.

#0152

CHIKORITA
Leaf Pokémon

HOW TO SAY IT: CHICK-oh-REE-ta
IMPERIAL HEIGHT: 2'11"
IMPERIAL WEIGHT: 14.1 lbs.
METRIC HEIGHT: 0.9 m
METRIC WEIGHT: 6.4 kg
GENDER: ♂ ♀
ABILITIES: Overgrow
WEAKNESSES: Fire, Flying, Ice, Poison, Bug

CHIKORITA **BAYLEEF** **MEGANIUM**

#0390

CHIMCHAR
Chimp Pokémon

TYPE: FIRE

Its fiery rear end is fueled by gas made in its belly. Even rain can't extinguish the fire.

The gas made in its belly burns from its rear end. The fire burns weakly when it feels sick.

HOW TO SAY IT: CHIM-char
IMPERIAL HEIGHT: 1'08"
IMPERIAL WEIGHT: 13.7 lbs.
METRIC HEIGHT: 0.5 m
METRIC WEIGHT: 6.2 kg
GENDER: ♂ ♀
ABILITIES: Blaze
WEAKNESSES: Water, Ground, Rock

CHIMCHAR **MONFERNO** **INFERNAPE**

CHIMECHO
Wind Chime Pokémon

#0358

TYPE: PSYCHIC

Chimecho makes its cries echo inside its hollow body. When this Pokémon becomes enraged, its cries result in ultrasonic waves that have the power to knock foes flying.

In high winds, Chimecho cries as it hangs from a tree branch or the eaves of a building using a suction cup on its head. This Pokémon plucks berries with its long tail and eats them.

HOW TO SAY IT: chime-ECK-ko
IMPERIAL HEIGHT: 2'00"
IMPERIAL WEIGHT: 2.2 lbs.
METRIC HEIGHT: 0.6 m
METRIC WEIGHT: 1.0 kg
GENDER: ♂ ♀
ABILITIES: Levitate
WEAKNESSES: Ghost, Dark, Bug

CHINGLING → CHIMECHO

TYPE: WATER-ELECTRIC

CHINCHOU
Angler Pokémon

#0170

Its antennae, which evolved from a fin, have both positive and negative charges flowing through them.

On the dark ocean floor, its only means of communication is its constantly flashing lights.

HOW TO SAY IT: CHIN-chow
IMPERIAL HEIGHT: 1'08"
IMPERIAL WEIGHT: 26.5 lbs.
METRIC HEIGHT: 0.5 m
METRIC WEIGHT: 12.0 kg
GENDER: ♂ ♀
ABILITIES: Volt Absorb, Illuminate
WEAKNESSES: Grass, Ground

 CHINCHOU → LANTURN

CHINGLING
Bell Pokémon

TYPE: PSYCHIC

Each time it hops, it makes a ringing sound. It deafens foes by emitting high-frequency cries.

There is an orb inside its mouth. When it hops, the orb bounces all over and makes a ringing sound.

HOW TO SAY IT: CHING-ling
IMPERIAL HEIGHT: 0'08"
IMPERIAL WEIGHT: 1.3 lbs.
METRIC HEIGHT: 0.2 m
METRIC WEIGHT: 0.6 kg
GENDER: ♂ ♀
ABILITIES: Levitate
WEAKNESSES: Ghost, Dark, Bug

CHINGLING ➤ CHIMECHO

CINCCINO
Scarf Pokémon

TYPE: NORMAL

Its body secretes oil that this Pokémon spreads over its nest as a coating to protect it from dust. Cinccino won't tolerate even a speck of the stuff.

A special oil that seeps through their fur helps them avoid attacks. The oil fetches a high price at market.

HOW TO SAY IT: chin-CHEE-noh
IMPERIAL HEIGHT: 1'08"
IMPERIAL WEIGHT: 16.5 lbs.
METRIC HEIGHT: 0.5 m
METRIC WEIGHT: 7.5 kg
GENDER: ♂ ♀
ABILITIES: Cute Charm, Technician
WEAKNESSES: Fighting

MINCCINO   CINCCINO

CINDERACE

Striker Pokémon

#0815

TYPE: FIRE

It juggles a pebble with its feet, turning it into a burning soccer ball. Its shots strike opponents hard and leave them scorched.

It's skilled at both offense and defense, and it gets pumped up when cheered on. But if it starts showboating, it could put itself in a tough spot.

HOW TO SAY IT: SIN-deh-race
IMPERIAL HEIGHT: 4'07"
IMPERIAL WEIGHT: 72.8 lbs.
METRIC HEIGHT: 1.4 m
METRIC WEIGHT: 33.0 kg
GENDER: ♂ ♀
ABILITIES: Blaze
WEAKNESSES: Water, Ground, Rock

SCORBUNNY → **RABOOT** → **CINDERACE**

GIGANTAMAX CINDERACE

Infused with Cinderace's fighting spirit, the gigantic Pyro Ball never misses its targets and completely roasts opponents.

Gigantamax energy can sometimes cause the diameter of this Pokémon's fireball to exceed 300 feet.

IMPERIAL HEIGHT: 88'07"+
IMPERIAL WEIGHT: ????.? lbs.
METRIC HEIGHT: 27.0+ m
METRIC WEIGHT: ???.? kg

CLAMPERL

Bivalve Pokémon

#0366

TYPE: WATER

Despite its appearance, it's carnivorous. It clamps down on its prey with both sides of its shell and doesn't let go until they stop moving.

Clamperl's pearls are exceedingly precious. They can be more than ten times as costly as Shellder's pearls.

HOW TO SAY IT: CLAM-perl
IMPERIAL HEIGHT: 1'04"
IMPERIAL WEIGHT: 115.7 lbs.
METRIC HEIGHT: 0.4 m
METRIC WEIGHT: 52.5 kg
GENDER: ♂ ♀
ABILITIES: Shell Armor
WEAKNESSES: Grass, Electric

CLAMPERL   HUNTAIL   GOREBYSS

CLAUNCHER

Water Gun Pokémon

#0692

TYPE: WATER

This Pokémon launches water by detonating gas inside its right claw. It snipes flying Pokémon.

Clauncher's claws will regrow if they fall off. The meat inside the claws is edible, but it has a distinct flavor that doesn't appeal to all tastes.

HOW TO SAY IT: CLAWN-chur
IMPERIAL HEIGHT: 1'08"
IMPERIAL WEIGHT: 18.3 lbs.
METRIC HEIGHT: 0.5 m
METRIC WEIGHT: 8.3 kg
GENDER: ♂ ♀
ABILITIES: Mega Launcher
WEAKNESSES: Grass, Electric

CLAUNCHER   CLAWITZER

CLAWITZER

#0693

Howitzer Pokémon

TYPE: WATER

Clawitzer can move through the water at a speed of 60 knots by using gas inside its body to expel water from the back of its claw.

The cannonballs of seawater that Clawitzer launches from its claw are powerful enough to punch through tanker hulls.

HOW TO SAY IT: CLOW-wit-zur
IMPERIAL HEIGHT: 4'03"
IMPERIAL WEIGHT: 77.8 lbs.
METRIC HEIGHT: 1.3 m
METRIC WEIGHT: 35.3 kg
GENDER: ♂ ♀
ABILITIES: Mega Launcher
WEAKNESSES: Grass, Electric

CLAUNCHER   CLAWITZER

CLAYDOL

#0344

Clay Doll Pokémon

TYPE: GROUND-PSYCHIC

This mysterious Pokémon started life as an ancient clay figurine made over 20,000 years ago.

It appears to have been born from clay dolls made by ancient people. It uses telekinesis to float and move.

HOW TO SAY IT: CLAY-doll
IMPERIAL HEIGHT: 4'11"
IMPERIAL WEIGHT: 238.1 lbs.
METRIC HEIGHT: 1.5 m
METRIC WEIGHT: 108.0 kg
GENDER: Unknown
ABILITIES: Levitate
WEAKNESSES: Ghost, Water, Ice, Dark, Grass, Bug

BALTOY   CLAYDOL

CLEFABLE
Fairy Pokémon

#0036

TYPE: FAIRY

A timid fairy Pokémon that is rarely seen, it will run and hide the moment it senses people.

Their ears are sensitive enough to hear a pin drop from over a mile away, so they're usually found in quiet places.

HOW TO SAY IT: kleh-FAY-bull
IMPERIAL HEIGHT: 4'03"
IMPERIAL WEIGHT: 88.2 lbs.
METRIC HEIGHT: 1.3 m
METRIC WEIGHT: 40.0 kg
GENDER: ♂ ♀
ABILITIES: Cute Charm, Magic Guard
WEAKNESSES: Steel, Poison

CLEFFA **CLEFAIRY** **CLEFABLE**

CLEFAIRY
Fairy Pokémon

#0035

TYPE: FAIRY

It is said that happiness will come to those who see a gathering of Clefairy dancing under a full moon.

Its adorable behavior and cry make it highly popular. However, this cute Pokémon is rarely found.

HOW TO SAY IT: kleh-FAIR-ee
IMPERIAL HEIGHT: 2'00"
IMPERIAL WEIGHT: 16.5 lbs.
METRIC HEIGHT: 0.6 m
METRIC WEIGHT: 7.5 kg
GENDER: ♂ ♀
ABILITIES: Cute Charm, Magic Guard
WEAKNESSES: Steel, Poison

CLEFFA **CLEFAIRY** **CLEFABLE**

CLEFFA

Star Shape Pokémon

TYPE: FAIRY

According to local rumors, Cleffa are often seen in places where shooting stars have fallen.

Because of its unusual, starlike silhouette, people believe that it came here on a meteor.

HOW TO SAY IT: CLEFF-uh
IMPERIAL HEIGHT: 1'00"
IMPERIAL WEIGHT: 6.6 lbs.
METRIC HEIGHT: 0.3 m
METRIC WEIGHT: 3.0 kg
GENDER: ♂ ♀
ABILITIES: Cute Charm, Magic Guard
WEAKNESSES: Steel, Poison

CLEFFA **CLEFAIRY** **CLEFABLE**

#0852

CLOBBOPUS

Tantrum Pokémon

TYPE: FIGHTING

It's very curious, but its means of investigating things is to try to punch them with its tentacles. The search for food is what brings it onto land.

Its tentacles tear off easily, but it isn't alarmed when that happens—it knows they'll grow back. It's about as smart as a three-year-old.

HOW TO SAY IT: KLAH-buh-puss
IMPERIAL HEIGHT: 2'00"
IMPERIAL WEIGHT: 8.8 lbs.
METRIC HEIGHT: 0.6 m
METRIC WEIGHT: 4.0 kg
GENDER: ♂ ♀
ABILITIES: Limber
WEAKNESSES: Psychic, Flying, Fairy

CLOBBOPUS **GRAPPLOCT**

CLODSIRE

Spiny Fish Pokémon

#0980

TYPE: POISON-GROUND

When attacked, this Pokémon will retaliate by sticking thick spines out from its body. It's a risky move that puts everything on the line.

It lives at the bottom of ponds and swamps. It will carry Wooper on its back and ferry them across water from one shore to the other.

HOW TO SAY IT: KLAWD-seye-er
IMPERIAL HEIGHT: 5'11"
IMPERIAL WEIGHT: 491.6 lbs.
METRIC HEIGHT: 1.8 m
METRIC WEIGHT: 223.0 kg
GENDER: ♂ ♀
ABILITIES: Poison Point, Water Absorb
WEAKNESSES: Water, Psychic, Ice, Ground

PALDEAN WOOPER

CLODSIRE

CLOYSTER

Bivalve Pokémon .

#0091

TYPE: WATER-ICE

Cloyster that live in seas with harsh tidal currents grow large, sharp spikes on their shells.

When attacked, it launches its spikes in quick volleys. Its innards have never been seen.

HOW TO SAY IT: CLOY-stur
IMPERIAL HEIGHT: 4'11"
IMPERIAL WEIGHT: 292.1 lbs.
METRIC HEIGHT: 1.5 m
METRIC WEIGHT: 132.5 kg
GENDER: ♂ ♀
ABILITIES: Shell Armor, Skill Link
WEAKNESSES: Grass, Electric, Fighting, Rock

SHELLDER　　**CLOYSTER**

COALOSSAL
Coal Pokémon

#0839

TYPE: ROCK-FIRE

To intimidate its opponents, Coalossal will vigorously shake its body, scattering coal from its smoldering back.

It's gentle usually but fearsome when angered. With a body that burns at over 2,700 degrees Fahrenheit, it crushes foes and turns them to ash.

HOW TO SAY IT: koh-LAHS-ull
IMPERIAL HEIGHT: 9'02"   **METRIC HEIGHT:** 2.8 m
IMPERIAL WEIGHT: 684.5 lbs.   **METRIC WEIGHT:** 310.5 kg
GENDER: ♂ ♀
ABILITIES: Steam Engine, Flame Body
WEAKNESSES: Water, Ground, Fighting, Rock

ROLYCOLY → CARKOL → COALOSSAL

GIGANTAMAX COALOSSAL

Its body is a colossal stove. With Gigantamax energy stoking the fire, this Pokémon's flame burns hotter than 3,600 degrees Fahrenheit.

When Galar was hit by a harsh cold wave, this Pokémon served as a giant heating stove and saved many lives.

IMPERIAL HEIGHT: 137'10"+
IMPERIAL WEIGHT: ????.? lbs.
METRIC HEIGHT: 42.0+ m
METRIC WEIGHT: ???.? kg

COBALION
Iron Will Pokémon

TYPE: STEEL-FIGHTING

This Pokémon appears in a legend alongside Terrakion and Virizion, fighting against humans in defense of the Unova region's Pokémon.

From the moment it's born, this Pokémon radiates the air of a leader. Its presence will calm even vicious foes.

HOW TO SAY IT: koh-BAY-lee-un
IMPERIAL HEIGHT: 6'11"
IMPERIAL WEIGHT: 551.2 lbs.
METRIC HEIGHT: 2.1 m
METRIC WEIGHT: 250.0 kg
GENDER: Unknown
ABILITIES: Justified
WEAKNESSES: Fire, Fighting, Ground

DOES NOT EVOLVE

COFAGRIGUS
Coffin Pokémon

#0563

TYPE: GHOST

This Pokémon has a body of sparkling gold. People say it no longer remembers that it was once human.

There are many depictions of Cofagrigus decorating ancient tombs. They're symbols of the wealth that kings of bygone eras had.

HOW TO SAY IT: kof-uh-GREE-guss
IMPERIAL HEIGHT: 5'07"
IMPERIAL WEIGHT: 168.7 lbs.
METRIC HEIGHT: 1.7 m
METRIC WEIGHT: 76.5 kg
GENDER: ♂ ♀
ABILITIES: Mummy
WEAKNESSES: Ghost, Dark

YAMASK

COFAGRIGUS

COMBEE
Tiny Bee Pokémon

TYPE: BUG-FLYING

At night, Combee sleep in a group of about a hundred, packed closely together in a lump.

The trio is together from birth. It constantly gathers nectar from flowers to please Vespiquen.

HOW TO SAY IT: COMB-bee
IMPERIAL HEIGHT: 1'00"
IMPERIAL WEIGHT: 12.1 lbs.
METRIC HEIGHT: 0.3 m
METRIC WEIGHT: 5.5 kg
GENDER: ♂ ♀
ABILITIES: Honey Gather
WEAKNESSES: Fire, Flying, Electric, Ice, Rock

COMBEE

VESPIQUEN

COMBUSKEN
Young Fowl Pokémon

#0256

TYPE: FIRE-FIGHTING

Combusken toughens up its legs and thighs by running through fields and mountains. This Pokémon's legs possess both speed and power, enabling it to dole out 10 kicks in one second.

Combusken battles with the intensely hot flames it spews from its beak and with outstandingly destructive kicks. This Pokémon's cry is very loud and distracting.

HOW TO SAY IT: com-BUS-ken
IMPERIAL HEIGHT: 2'11"
IMPERIAL WEIGHT: 43.0 lbs.
METRIC HEIGHT: 0.9 m
METRIC WEIGHT: 19.5 kg
GENDER: ♂ ♀
ABILITIES: Blaze
WEAKNESSES: Water, Psychic, Flying, Ground

TORCHIC

COMBUSKEN

BLAZIKEN

MEGA BLAZIKEN

COMFEY

#0764

Posy Picker Pokémon

TYPE: FAIRY

Comfey picks flowers with its vine and decorates itself with them. For some reason, flowers won't wither once they're attached to a Comfey.

These Pokémon smell very nice. All Comfey wear different flowers, so each of these Pokémon has its own individual scent.

HOW TO SAY IT: KUM-fay
IMPERIAL HEIGHT: 0'04"
IMPERIAL WEIGHT: 0.7 lbs.
METRIC HEIGHT: 0.1 m
METRIC WEIGHT: 0.3 kg
GENDER: ♂ ♀
ABILITIES: Flower Veil, Triage
WEAKNESSES: Steel, Poison

DOES NOT EVOLVE

CONKELDURR

#0534

Muscular Pokémon

TYPE: FIGHTING

Concrete mixed by Conkeldurr is much more durable than normal concrete, even when the compositions of the two materials are the same.

When going all out, this Pokémon throws aside its concrete pillars and leaps at opponents to pummel them with its fists.

HOW TO SAY IT: kon-KELL-dur
IMPERIAL HEIGHT: 4'07"
IMPERIAL WEIGHT: 191.8 lbs.
METRIC HEIGHT: 1.4 m
METRIC WEIGHT: 87.0 kg
GENDER: ♂ ♀
ABILITIES: Guts, Sheer Force
WEAKNESSES: Psychic, Flying, Fairy

TIMBURR

GURDURR

CONKELDURR

COPPERAJAH
Copperderm Pokémon

TYPE: STEEL

This Pokémon was brought to Paldea long ago by people from a faraway land. It's so strong that it can easily pull an airplane.

Copperajah are prideful, cantankerous Pokémon. Specimens with vibrant green skin command the respect of others of their kind.

HOW TO SAY IT: KAH-peh-RAH-zhah
IMPERIAL HEIGHT: 9'10"
METRIC HEIGHT: 3.0 m
IMPERIAL WEIGHT: 1,433.0 lbs.
METRIC WEIGHT: 650.0 kg
GENDER: ♂ ♀
ABILITIES: Sheer Force
WEAKNESSES: Fire, Fighting, Ground

CUFANT → **COPPERAJAH**

GIGANTAMAX COPPERAJAH

So much power is packed within its trunk that if it were to unleash that power, the resulting blast could level mountains and change the landscape.

After this Pokémon has Gigantamaxed, its massive nose can utterly demolish large structures with a single smashing blow.

IMPERIAL HEIGHT: 75'06"+
IMPERIAL WEIGHT: ????.? lbs.
METRIC HEIGHT: 23.0+ m
METRIC WEIGHT: ???.? kg

CORPHISH

Ruffian Pokémon

#0341

TYPE: WATER

No matter how dirty the water in the river, it will adapt and thrive. It has a strong will to survive.

It was originally a Pokémon from afar that escaped to the wild. It can adapt to the dirtiest river.

HOW TO SAY IT: COR-fish
IMPERIAL HEIGHT: 2'00"
IMPERIAL WEIGHT: 25.4 lbs.
METRIC HEIGHT: 0.6 m
METRIC WEIGHT: 11.5 kg
GENDER: ♂ ♀
ABILITIES: Hyper Cutter, Shell Armor
WEAKNESSES: Grass, Electric

CORPHISH   CRAWDAUNT

CORSOLA
Coral Pokémon

TYPE: WATER-ROCK

Many live in the clean seas of the south. They apparently can't live in polluted waters.

HOW TO SAY IT: COR-soh-la
IMPERIAL HEIGHT: 2'00"
IMPERIAL WEIGHT: 11.0 lbs.
METRIC HEIGHT: 0.6 m
METRIC WEIGHT: 5.0 kg
GENDER: ♂ ♀
ABILITIES: Hustle, Natural Cure
WEAKNESSES: Grass, Electric, Fighting, Ground

DOES NOT EVOLVE

GALARIAN CORSOLA
Coral Pokémon

TYPE: GHOST

Watch your step when wandering areas oceans once covered. What looks like a stone could be this Pokémon, and it will curse you if you kick it.

Sudden climate change wiped out this ancient kind of Corsola. This Pokémon absorbs others' life force through its branches.

HOW TO SAY IT: COR-soh-la
IMPERIAL HEIGHT: 2'00"
IMPERIAL WEIGHT: 1.1 lbs.
METRIC HEIGHT: 0.6 m
METRIC WEIGHT: 0.5 kg
GENDER: ♂ ♀
ABILITIES: Weak Armor
WEAKNESSES: Ghost, Dark

GALARIAN CORSOLA　　**CURSOLA**

CORVIKNIGHT

Raven Pokémon

TYPE: FLYING-STEEL

Corviknight can't serve as a taxi service in Paldea because the Pokémon's natural predators will attack it while it flies, endangering the customer.

Although its wings have partly turned to steel and become heavy as a result, this Pokémon flies through the skies with ease.

HOW TO SAY IT: KOR-vih-nyte
IMPERIAL HEIGHT: 7'3"
IMPERIAL WEIGHT: 165.3 lbs.
METRIC HEIGHT: 2.2 m
METRIC WEIGHT: 75.0 kg
GENDER: ♂ ♀
ABILITIES: Pressure, Unnerve
WEAKNESSES: Fire, Electric

ROOKIDEE   **CORVISQUIRE**   **CORVIKNIGHT**

GIGANTAMAX CORVIKNIGHT

Imbued with Gigantamax energy, its wings can whip up winds more forceful than any a hurricane could muster. The gusts blow everything away.

The eight feathers on its back are called blade birds, and they can launch off its body to attack foes independently.

IMPERIAL HEIGHT: 45'11"+
IMPERIAL WEIGHT: ?????.? lbs.
METRIC HEIGHT: 14.0+ m
METRIC WEIGHT: ???.? kg

CORVISQUIRE

Raven Pokémon

#0822

TYPE: FLYING

It's said that the reason behind Corvisquire's high level of intelligence is the large size of its brain relative to those of other bird Pokémon.

This intelligent Pokémon will quickly learn how to use any tool it can hold in its beak or its talons.

HOW TO SAY IT: KOR-vih-skwyre
IMPERIAL HEIGHT: 2'07"
IMPERIAL WEIGHT: 35.3 lbs.
METRIC HEIGHT: 0.8 m
METRIC WEIGHT: 16.0 kg
GENDER: ♂ ♀
ABILITIES: Keen Eye, Unnerve
WEAKNESSES: Electric, Ice, Rock

ROOKIDEE   CORVISQUIRE   CORVIKNIGHT

COSMOEM

Protostar Pokémon

#0790

LEGENDARY POKÉMON

TYPE: PSYCHIC

The king who ruled Alola in times of antiquity called it the "cocoon of the stars" and built an altar to worship it.

As it absorbs light, Cosmoem continues to grow. Its golden shell is surprisingly solid.

HOW TO SAY IT: KOZ-mo-em
IMPERIAL HEIGHT: 0'04"
IMPERIAL WEIGHT: 2,204.4 lbs.
METRIC HEIGHT: 0.1 m
METRIC WEIGHT: 999.9 kg
GENDER: Unknown
ABILITIES: Sturdy
WEAKNESSES: Ghost, Dark, Bug

COSMOG   COSMOEM   SOLGALEO   LUNALA

COSMOG
Nebula Pokémon

TYPE: PSYCHIC

Even though its helpless, gaseous body can be blown away by the slightest breeze, it doesn't seem to care.

Whether or not it's a Pokémon from this world is a mystery. When it's in a jam, it warps away to a safe place to hide.

HOW TO SAY IT: KOZ-mog
IMPERIAL HEIGHT: 0'08"
IMPERIAL WEIGHT: 0.2 lbs.
METRIC HEIGHT: 0.2 m
METRIC WEIGHT: 0.1 kg
GENDER: Unknown
ABILITIES: Unaware
WEAKNESSES: Ghost, Dark, Bug

COSMOG → COSMOEM → SOLGALEO / LUNALA

COTTONEE
Cotton Puff Pokémon

#0546

TYPE: GRASS-FAIRY

It shoots cotton from its body to protect itself. If it gets caught up in hurricane-strength winds, it can get sent to the other side of the Earth.

Weaving together the cotton of both Cottonee and Eldegoss produces exquisite cloth that's highly prized by many luxury brands.

HOW TO SAY IT: KAHT-ton-ee
IMPERIAL HEIGHT: 1'00"
IMPERIAL WEIGHT: 1.3 lbs.
METRIC HEIGHT: 0.3 m
METRIC WEIGHT: 0.6 kg
GENDER: ♂ ♀
ABILITIES: Prankster, Infiltrator
WEAKNESSES: Steel, Fire, Flying, Ice, Poison

COTTONEE → WHIMSICOTT

CRABOMINABLE

Woolly Crab Pokémon

#0740

TYPE: FIGHTING-ICE

The detached pincers of these Pokémon are delicious. Some Trainers bring Lechonk into the mountains just to search for them.

Though its punches are powerful, this Pokémon's movements are sluggish. It blows icy bubbles from its mouth to immobilize its opponents.

HOW TO SAY IT: crab-BAH-min-uh-bull
IMPERIAL HEIGHT: 5'07"
IMPERIAL WEIGHT: 396.8 lbs.
METRIC HEIGHT: 1.7 m
METRIC WEIGHT: 180.0 kg
GENDER: ♂ ♀
ABILITIES: Hyper Cutter, Iron Fist
WEAKNESSES: Steel, Fire, Psychic, Flying, Fighting, Fairy

CRABRAWLER   CRABOMINABLE

#0739

CRABRAWLER

Boxing Pokémon

TYPE: FIGHTING

This Pokémon punches trees and eats the berries that drop down, training itself and getting food at the same time.

If it loses its pincers, they'll quickly regrow. The pincers are popular ingredients in paella since their shells produce a tasty soup stock.

HOW TO SAY IT: crab-BRAW-ler
IMPERIAL HEIGHT: 2'00"
IMPERIAL WEIGHT: 15.4 lbs.
METRIC HEIGHT: 0.6 m
METRIC WEIGHT: 7.0 kg
GENDER: ♂ ♀
ABILITIES: Hyper Cutter, Iron Fist
WEAKNESSES: Psychic, Flying, Fairy

CRABRAWLER   CRABOMINABLE

#0346

CRADILY
Barnacle Pokémon

TYPE: ROCK-GRASS

It has short legs and can't walk very fast, but its neck and tentacles can extend to over three times their usual length to nab distant prey.

Once Cradily catches prey in its tentacles, it digests them whole and absorbs their nutrients.

HOW TO SAY IT: cray-DILLY
IMPERIAL HEIGHT: 4'11"
IMPERIAL WEIGHT: 133.2 lbs.
METRIC HEIGHT: 1.5 m
METRIC WEIGHT: 60.4 kg
GENDER: ♂ ♀
ABILITIES: Suction Cups
WEAKNESSES: Steel, Ice, Fighting, Bug

LILEEP → CRADILY

CRAMORANT
Gulp Pokémon

#0845

TYPE: FLYING-WATER

It's so strong that it can knock out some opponents in a single hit, but it also may forget what it's battling midfight.

This hungry Pokémon swallows Arrokuda whole. Occasionally, it makes a mistake and tries to swallow a Pokémon other than its preferred prey.

HOW TO SAY IT: KRAM-uh-rihnt
IMPERIAL HEIGHT: 2'07"
IMPERIAL WEIGHT: 39.7 lbs.
METRIC HEIGHT: 0.8 m
METRIC WEIGHT: 18.0 kg
GENDER: ♂ ♀
ABILITIES: Gulp Missile
WEAKNESSES: Electric, Rock

DOES NOT EVOLVE

CRANIDOS

Head Butt Pokémon

#0408

TYPE: ROCK

A primeval Pokémon, it possesses a hard and sturdy skull, lacking any intelligence within.

Its hard skull is its distinguishing feature. It snapped trees by headbutting them, and then it fed on their ripe berries.

HOW TO SAY IT: CRANE-ee-dose
IMPERIAL HEIGHT: 2'11"
IMPERIAL WEIGHT: 69.4 lbs.
METRIC HEIGHT: 0.9 m
METRIC WEIGHT: 31.5 kg
GENDER: ♂ ♀
ABILITIES: Mold Breaker
WEAKNESSES: Water, Steel, Grass, Fighting, Ground

CRANIDOS   RAMPARDOS

#0342

CRAWDAUNT

Rogue Pokémon

TYPE: WATER-DARK

A rough customer that wildly flails its giant claws. It is said to be extremely hard to raise.

A brutish Pokémon that loves to battle. It will crash itself into any foe that approaches its nest.

HOW TO SAY IT: CRAW-daunt
IMPERIAL HEIGHT: 3'07"
IMPERIAL WEIGHT: 72.3 lbs.
METRIC HEIGHT: 1.1 m
METRIC WEIGHT: 32.8 kg
GENDER: ♂ ♀
ABILITIES: Hyper Cutter, Shell Armor
WEAKNESSES: Fairy, Grass, Electric, Fighting, Bug

CORPHISH   CRAWDAUNT

CRESSELIA
Lunar Pokémon

TYPE: PSYCHIC

When it flies, it releases shiny particles from its veil-like wings. It is said to represent the crescent moon.

HOW TO SAY IT: creh-SELL-ee-ah
IMPERIAL HEIGHT: 4'11"
IMPERIAL WEIGHT: 188.7 lbs.
METRIC HEIGHT: 1.5 m
METRIC WEIGHT: 85.6 kg
GENDER: ♀
ABILITIES: Levitate
WEAKNESSES: Ghost, Dark, Bug

DOES NOT EVOLVE

CROAGUNK
Toxic Mouth Pokémon

#0453

TYPE: POISON-FIGHTING

Inflating its poison sacs, it fills the area with an odd sound and hits flinching opponents with a poison jab.

It rarely fights fairly, but that is strictly to ensure survival. It is popular as a mascot.

HOW TO SAY IT: CROW-gunk
IMPERIAL HEIGHT: 2'04"
IMPERIAL WEIGHT: 50.7 lbs.
METRIC HEIGHT: 0.7 m
METRIC WEIGHT: 23.0 kg
GENDER: ♂ ♀
ABILITIES: Anticipation, Dry Skin
WEAKNESSES: Psychic, Flying, Ground

CROAGUNK   TOXICROAK

#0169 CROBAT

Bat Pokémon

TYPE: POISON-FLYING

Both of its legs have turned into wings. Without a sound, Crobat flies swiftly toward its prey and sinks its fangs into the nape of its target's neck.

This Pokémon flaps its four wings skillfully. Crobat can fly through cramped caves without needing to slow down.

HOW TO SAY IT: CROW-bat
IMPERIAL HEIGHT: 5'11"
IMPERIAL WEIGHT: 165.3 lbs.
METRIC HEIGHT: 1.8 m
METRIC WEIGHT: 75.0 kg
GENDER: ♂ ♀
ABILITIES: Inner Focus
WEAKNESSES: Psychic, Electric, Ice, Rock

ZUBAT → GOLBAT → CROBAT

CROCALOR #0910

Fire Croc Pokémon

TYPE: FIRE

The combination of Crocalor's fire energy and overflowing vitality has caused an egg-shaped fireball to appear on the Pokémon's head.

The valve in Crocalor's flame sac is closely connected to its vocal cords. This Pokémon utters a guttural cry as it spews flames every which way.

HOW TO SAY IT: KROCK-uh-lor
IMPERIAL HEIGHT: 3'03"
IMPERIAL WEIGHT: 67.7 lbs.
METRIC HEIGHT: 1.0 m
METRIC WEIGHT: 30.7 kg
GENDER: ♂ ♀
ABILITIES: Blaze
WEAKNESSES: Water, Ground, Rock

FUECOCO CROCALOR SKELEDIRGE

#0159 CROCONAW
Big Jaw Pokémon

TYPE: WATER

Once Croconaw has clamped its jaws on its foe, it will absolutely not let go. Because the tips of its fangs are forked back like barbed fishhooks, they become impossible to remove when they have sunk in.

HOW TO SAY IT: CROCK-oh-naw
IMPERIAL HEIGHT: 3'07"
IMPERIAL WEIGHT: 55.1 lbs.
METRIC HEIGHT: 1.1 m
METRIC WEIGHT: 25.0 kg
GENDER: ♂ ♀
ABILITIES: Torrent
WEAKNESSES: Grass, Electric

TOTODILE **CROCONAW** **FERALIGATR**

TYPE: BUG-ROCK

This highly territorial Pokémon prefers dry climates. It won't come out of its boulder on rainy days.

Its thick claws are its greatest weapons. They're mighty enough to crack Rhyperior's carapace.

#0558 CRUSTLE
Stone Home Pokémon

HOW TO SAY IT: KRUS-tul
IMPERIAL HEIGHT: 4'07"
IMPERIAL WEIGHT: 440.9 lbs.
METRIC HEIGHT: 1.4 m
METRIC WEIGHT: 200.0 kg
GENDER: ♂ ♀
ABILITIES: Sturdy, Shell Armor
WEAKNESSES: Steel, Water, Rock

DWEBBLE **CRUSTLE**

CRYOGONAL
Crystallizing Pokémon

TYPE: ICE

Cryogonal appear during cold seasons. It is said that people and Pokémon who die on snowy mountains are reborn into these Pokémon.

Cryogonal uses its chains of ice to constrict its opponents and then flash-freezes them where they stand.

HOW TO SAY IT: kry-AH-guh-nul
IMPERIAL HEIGHT: 3'07"
IMPERIAL WEIGHT: 326.3 lbs.
METRIC HEIGHT: 1.1 m
METRIC WEIGHT: 148.0 kg
GENDER: Unknown
ABILITIES: Levitate
WEAKNESSES: Fire, Steel, Fighting, Rock

DOES NOT EVOLVE

#0613

CUBCHOO
Chill Pokémon

TYPE: ICE

Many of this species can be found along the shorelines of cold regions. If a Cubchoo lacks dangling snot, there's a chance it is sick.

When Cubchoo starts sneezing, watch out! If it spatters you with its frosty snot, you'll get frostbite.

HOW TO SAY IT: cub-CHOO
IMPERIAL HEIGHT: 1'08"
IMPERIAL WEIGHT: 18.7 lbs.
METRIC HEIGHT: 0.5 m
METRIC WEIGHT: 8.5 kg
GENDER: ♂ ♀
ABILITIES: Snow Cloak, Slush Rush
WEAKNESSES: Fire, Steel, Fighting, Rock

CUBCHOO → **BEARTIC**

CUBONE

Lonely Pokémon

#0104

TYPE: GROUND

When the memory of its departed mother brings it to tears, its cries echo mournfully within the skull it wears on its head.

This Pokémon wears the skull of its deceased mother. Sometimes Cubone's dreams make it cry, but each tear Cubone sheds makes it stronger.

HOW TO SAY IT: CUE-bone
IMPERIAL HEIGHT: 1'04"
IMPERIAL WEIGHT: 14.3 lbs.
METRIC HEIGHT: 0.4 m
METRIC WEIGHT: 6.5 kg
GENDER: ♂ ♀
ABILITIES: Rock Head, Lightning Rod
WEAKNESSES: Water, Grass, Ice

MAROWAK

CUBONE

ALOLAN MAROWAK

CUFANT

#0878

Copperderm Pokémon

TYPE: STEEL

Using the pointy tip of its trunk, it carves off chunks of hard rocks to eat. It is very docile and helps people with physical labor.

Cufant can lift loads weighing five tons. In the mornings, it heads into caves with its herd, in search of the ore on which these Pokémon feed.

HOW TO SAY IT: KYOO-funt
IMPERIAL HEIGHT: 3'11"
IMPERIAL WEIGHT: 220.5 lbs.
METRIC HEIGHT: 1.2 m
METRIC WEIGHT: 100.0 kg
GENDER: ♂ ♀
ABILITIES: Sheer Force
WEAKNESSES: Fire, Fighting, Ground

CUFANT

COPPERAJAH

CURSOLA

Coral Pokémon

#0864

TYPE: GHOST

Its shell is overflowing with its heightened otherworldly energy. The ectoplasm serves as protection for this Pokémon's core spirit.

Be cautious of the ectoplasmic body surrounding its soul. You'll become stiff as stone if you touch it.

HOW TO SAY IT: KURR-suh-luh
IMPERIAL HEIGHT: 3'03"
IMPERIAL WEIGHT: 0.9 lbs.
METRIC HEIGHT: 1.0 m
METRIC WEIGHT: 0.4 kg
GENDER: ♂ ♀
ABILITIES: Weak Armor
WEAKNESSES: Ghost, Dark

GALARIAN CORSOLA **CURSOLA**

#0742

CUTIEFLY

Bee Fly Pokémon

TYPE: BUG-FAIRY

Nectar and pollen are its favorite fare. You can find Cutiefly hovering around Gossifleur, trying to get some of Gossifleur's pollen.

An opponent's aura can tell Cutiefly what that opponent's next move will be. Then Cutiefly can glide around the attack and strike back.

HOW TO SAY IT: KYOO-tee-fly
IMPERIAL HEIGHT: 0'04"
IMPERIAL WEIGHT: 0.4 lbs.
METRIC HEIGHT: 0.1 m
METRIC WEIGHT: 0.2 kg
GENDER: ♂ ♀
ABILITIES: Honey Gather, Shield Dust
WEAKNESSES: Fire, Steel, Flying, Poison, Rock

CUTIEFLY

RIBOMBEE

CYCLIZAR

Mount Pokémon

#0967

TYPE: DRAGON-NORMAL

Apparently Cyclizar has been allowing people to ride on its back since ancient times. Depictions of this have been found in 10,000-year-old murals.

It can sprint at over 70 mph while carrying a human. The rider's body heat warms Cyclizar's back and lifts the Pokémon's spirit.

HOW TO SAY IT: SYE-clih-zahr
IMPERIAL HEIGHT: 5'03"
IMPERIAL WEIGHT: 138.9 lbs.
METRIC HEIGHT: 1.6 m
METRIC WEIGHT: 63.0 kg
GENDER: ♂ ♀
ABILITIES: Shed Skin
WEAKNESSES: Fairy, Ice, Fighting, Dragon

DOES NOT EVOLVE

CYNDAQUIL

Fire Mouse Pokémon

#0155

TYPE: FIRE

Cyndaquil protects itself by flaring up the flames on its back. The flames are vigorous if the Pokémon is angry. However, if it is tired, the flames splutter fitfully with incomplete combustion.

HOW TO SAY IT: SIN-da-kwill
IMPERIAL HEIGHT: 1'08"
IMPERIAL WEIGHT: 17.4 lbs.
METRIC HEIGHT: 0.5 m
METRIC WEIGHT: 7.9 kg
GENDER: ♂ ♀
ABILITIES: Blaze
WEAKNESSES: Water, Ground, Rock

TYPHLOSION

CYNDAQUIL **QUILAVA**

HISUIAN TYPHLOSION

DACHSBUN
Dog Pokémon

TYPE: FAIRY

The pleasant aroma that emanates from this Pokémon's body helps wheat grow, so Dachsbun has been treasured by farming villages.

The surface of this Pokémon's skin hardens when exposed to intense heat, and its body has an appetizing aroma.

HOW TO SAY IT: DAHKS-buhn
IMPERIAL HEIGHT: 1'08"
IMPERIAL WEIGHT: 32.8 lbs.
METRIC HEIGHT: 0.5 m
METRIC WEIGHT: 14.9 kg
GENDER: ♂ ♀
ABILITIES: Well-Baked Body
WEAKNESSES: Steel, Poison

FIDOUGH **DACHSBUN**

MYTHICAL POKÉMON

DARKRAI
Pitch-Black Pokémon

TYPE: DARK

It chases people and Pokémon from its territory by causing them to experience deep, nightmarish slumbers.

It can lull people to sleep and make them dream. It is active during nights of the new moon.

HOW TO SAY IT: DARK-rye
IMPERIAL HEIGHT: 4'11"
IMPERIAL WEIGHT: 111.3 lbs.
METRIC HEIGHT: 1.5 m
METRIC WEIGHT: 50.5 kg
GENDER: Unknown
ABILITIES: Bad Dreams
WEAKNESSES: Fairy, Bug, Fighting

DOES NOT EVOLVE

DARMANITAN

Blazing Pokémon

#0555

TYPE: FIRE

When one is injured in a fierce battle, it hardens into a stone-like form. Then it meditates and sharpens its mind.

Its internal fire burns at 2,500 degrees Fahrenheit, making enough power that it can destroy a dump truck with one punch.

HOW TO SAY IT: dar-MAN-ih-tan
IMPERIAL HEIGHT: 4'03"
IMPERIAL WEIGHT: 204.8 lbs.
METRIC HEIGHT: 1.3 m
METRIC WEIGHT: 92.9 kg
GENDER: ♂ ♀
ABILITIES: Sheer Force
WEAKNESSES: Water, Ground, Rock

DARUMAKA → DARMANITAN

GALARIAN DARMANITAN

Zen Charm Pokémon

#0555

TYPE: ICE

On days when blizzards blow through, it comes down to where people live. It stashes food in the snowball on its head, taking it home for later.

Though it has a gentle disposition, it's also very strong. It will quickly freeze the snowball on its head before going for a headbutt.

HOW TO SAY IT: dar-MAN-ih-tan
IMPERIAL HEIGHT: 5'07"
IMPERIAL WEIGHT: 264.6 lbs.
METRIC HEIGHT: 1.7 m
METRIC WEIGHT: 120.0 kg
GENDER: ♂ ♀
ABILITIES: Gorilla, Tactics
WEAKNESSES: Fire, Steel, Fighting, Rock

GALARIAN DARUMAKA

GALARIAN DARMANITAN

TYPE: GRASS-FLYING

This narcissistic Pokémon is a clean freak. If you don't groom it diligently, it will stop listening to you.

Supremely sensitive to the presence of others, it can detect opponents standing behind it, flinging its sharp feathers to take them out.

HOW TO SAY IT: DAR-trix
IMPERIAL HEIGHT: 2'04"
IMPERIAL WEIGHT: 35.3 lbs.
METRIC HEIGHT: 0.7 m
METRIC WEIGHT: 16.0 kg
GENDER: ♂ ♀
ABILITIES: Overgrow
WEAKNESSES: Fire, Flying, Ice, Poison, Rock

DECIDUEYE

ROWLET

DARTRIX

HISUIAN DECIDUEYE

DARUMAKA
Zen Charm Pokémon

#0554

TYPE: FIRE

Darumaka's droppings are hot, so people used to put them in their clothes to keep themselves warm.

When it sleeps, it pulls its limbs into its body and its internal fire goes down to 1,100 degrees Fahrenheit.

HOW TO SAY IT: dah-roo-MAH-kuh
IMPERIAL HEIGHT: 2'00"
IMPERIAL WEIGHT: 82.7 lbs.
METRIC HEIGHT: 0.6 m
METRIC WEIGHT: 37.5 kg
GENDER: ♂ ♀
ABILITIES: Hustle
WEAKNESSES: Water, Ground, Rock

DARUMAKA   DARMANITAN

GALARIAN DARUMAKA
Zen Charm Pokémon

#0554

TYPE: ICE

It lived in snowy areas for so long that its fire sac cooled off and atrophied. It now has an organ that generates cold instead.

The colder they get, the more energetic they are. They freeze their breath to make snowballs, using them as ammo for playful snowball fights.

HOW TO SAY IT: dah-roo-MAH-kuh
IMPERIAL HEIGHT: 2'04"
IMPERIAL WEIGHT: 88.2 lbs.
METRIC HEIGHT: 0.7 m
METRIC WEIGHT: 40.0 kg
GENDER: ♂ ♀
ABILITIES: Hustle
WEAKNESSES: Fire, Steel, Fighting, Rock

GALARIAN DARUMAKA   GALARIAN DARMANITAN

TYPE: GRASS-GHOST

It fires arrow quills from its wings with such precision, they can pierce a pebble at distances over a hundred yards.

Although basically cool and cautious, when it's caught by surprise, it's seized by panic.

DECIDUEYE
Arrow Quill Pokémon

#0724

HOW TO SAY IT: deh-SIH-joo-eye
IMPERIAL HEIGHT: 5'03"
IMPERIAL WEIGHT: 80.7 lbs.
METRIC HEIGHT: 1.6 m
METRIC WEIGHT: 36.6 kg
GENDER: ♂ ♀
ABILITIES: Overgrow
WEAKNESSES: Ghost, Fire, Flying, Dark, Ice

ROWLET ➡ DARTRIX ➡ DECIDUEYE

#0724

HISUIAN DECIDUEYE
Arrow Quill Pokémon

TYPE: GRASS-FIGHTING

The air stored inside the rachises of Decidueye's feathers insulates the Pokémon against Hisui's extreme cold. This is firm proof that evolution can be influenced by environment.

HOW TO SAY IT: deh-SIH-joo-eye
IMPERIAL HEIGHT: 5'03"
IMPERIAL WEIGHT: 81.6 lbs.
METRIC HEIGHT: 1.6 m
METRIC WEIGHT: 37.0 kg
GENDER: ♂ ♀
ABILITIES: N/A
WEAKNESSES: Fire, Psychic, Flying, Ice, Poison, Fairy

ROWLET   DARTRIX   HISUIAN DECIDUEYE

DEDENNE

Antenna Pokémon

#0702

TYPE: ELECTRIC-FAIRY

It's small and its electricity-generating organ is not fully developed, so it uses its tail to absorb electricity from people's homes and charge itself.

Dedenne emit electrical waves from the whiskers on their cheeks to communicate with each other. When low on electricity, they curl up and sleep.

HOW TO SAY IT: deh-DEN-nay
IMPERIAL HEIGHT: 0'08"
IMPERIAL WEIGHT: 4.9 lbs.
METRIC HEIGHT: 0.2 m
METRIC WEIGHT: 2.2 kg
GENDER: ♂ ♀
ABILITIES: Cheek Pouch, Pickup
WEAKNESSES: Poison, Ground

DOES NOT EVOLVE

DEERLING

Season Pokémon

#0585

TYPE: NORMAL-GRASS

Deerling have different scents depending on the season. In early spring, these Pokémon give off a delicate, sweet, and calming scent.

Despite Deerling's adorable appearance, farmers consider it a nuisance since it loves plant shoots and will eat them all up.

HOW TO SAY IT: DEER-ling
IMPERIAL HEIGHT: 2'00"
IMPERIAL WEIGHT: 43.0 lbs.
METRIC HEIGHT: 0.6 m
METRIC WEIGHT: 19.5 kg
GENDER: ♂ ♀
ABILITIES: Chlorophyll, Sap Sipper
WEAKNESSES: Fire, Flying, Fighting, Ice, Poison, Bug

SPRING FORM

SUMMER FORM

WINTER FORM

AUTUMN FORM

DEERLING → SAWSBUCK

TYPE: DARK-DRAGON

It can't see, so its first approach to examining things is to bite them. You will be covered in wounds until a Deino warms up to you.

It nests deep inside a cave. Food there is scarce, so Deino will sink its teeth into anything that moves and attempt to eat it.

HOW TO SAY IT: DY-noh
IMPERIAL HEIGHT: 2'07"
IMPERIAL WEIGHT: 38.1 lbs.
METRIC HEIGHT: 0.8 m
METRIC WEIGHT: 17.3 kg
GENDER: ♂ ♀
ABILITIES: Hustle
WEAKNESSES: Fairy, Fighting, Bug, Ice, Dragon

#0633

DEINO
Irate Pokémon

DEINO ➡ **ZWEILOUS** ➡ **HYDREIGON**

#0301

DELCATTY
Prim Pokémon

TYPE: NORMAL

Delcatty prefers to live an unfettered existence in which it can do as it pleases at its own pace. Because this Pokémon eats and sleeps whenever it decides, its daily routines are completely random.

Delcatty sleeps anywhere it wants without keeping a permanent nest. If other Pokémon approach it as it sleeps, this Pokémon will never fight—it will just move away somewhere else.

HOW TO SAY IT: dell-CAT-tee
IMPERIAL HEIGHT: 3'07"   **METRIC HEIGHT:** 1.1 m
IMPERIAL WEIGHT: 71.9 lbs. **METRIC WEIGHT:** 32.6 kg
GENDER: ♂ ♀
ABILITIES: Cute Charm, Normalize
WEAKNESSES: Fighting

SKITTY   **DELCATTY**

DELIBIRD

Delivery Pokémon

#0225

TYPE: ICE-FLYING

It carries food all day long. There are tales about lost people who were saved by the food it had.

It always carries its food with it, wherever it goes. If attacked, it throws its food at the opponent.

HOW TO SAY IT: DELL-ee-bird
IMPERIAL HEIGHT: 2'11"
IMPERIAL WEIGHT: 35.3 lbs.
METRIC HEIGHT: 0.9 m
METRIC WEIGHT: 16.0 kg
GENDER: ♂ ♀
ABILITIES: Vital Spirit, Hustle
WEAKNESSES: Steel, Fire, Electric, Rock

DOES NOT EVOLVE

DELPHOX

Fox Pokémon

#0655

TYPE: FIRE-PSYCHIC

It gazes into the flame at the tip of its branch to achieve a focused state, which allows it to see into the future.

Using psychic power, it generates a fiery vortex of 5,400 degrees Fahrenheit, incinerating foes swept into this whirl of flame.

HOW TO SAY IT: DELL-fox
IMPERIAL HEIGHT: 4'11"
IMPERIAL WEIGHT: 86.0 lbs.
METRIC HEIGHT: 1.5 m
METRIC WEIGHT: 39.0 kg
GENDER: ♂ ♀
ABILITIES: Blaze
WEAKNESSES: Ghost, Dark, Ground, Water, Rock

FENNEKIN

BRAIXEN

DELPHOX

MYTHICAL POKÉMON

DEOXYS
DNA Pokémon

TYPE: PSYCHIC

The DNA of a space virus underwent a sudden mutation upon exposure to a laser beam and resulted in Deoxys. The crystalline organ on this Pokémon's chest appears to be its brain.

Deoxys emerged from a virus that came from space. It is highly intelligent and wields psychokinetic powers. This Pokémon shoots lasers from the crystalline organ on its chest.

HOW TO SAY IT: dee-OCKS-iss
IMPERIAL HEIGHT: 5'07"
IMPERIAL WEIGHT: 134.0 lbs.
METRIC HEIGHT: 1.7 m
METRIC WEIGHT: 60.8 kg
GENDER: Unknown
ABILITIES: Pressure
WEAKNESSES: Ghost, Dark Bug

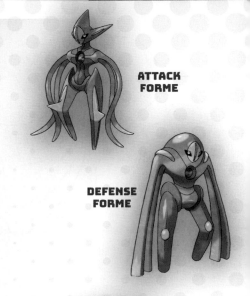

ATTACK FORME

DEFENSE FORME

SPEED FORME

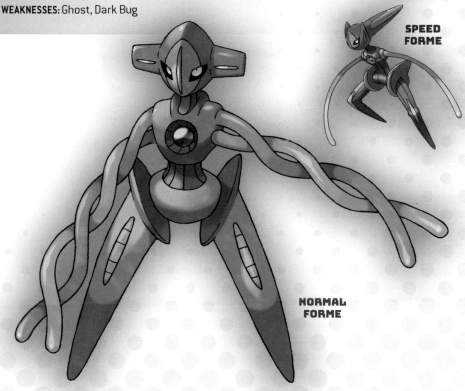

NORMAL FORME

DOES NOT EVOLVE

DEWGONG

Sea Lion Pokémon

#0087

TYPE: WATER-ICE

Its entire body is a snowy white. Unharmed by even intense cold, it swims powerfully in icy waters.

HOW TO SAY IT: DOO-gong
IMPERIAL HEIGHT: 5'07"
IMPERIAL WEIGHT: 264.6 lbs.
METRIC HEIGHT: 1.7 m
METRIC WEIGHT: 120.0 kg
GENDER: ♂ ♀
ABILITIES: Thick Fat, Hydration
WEAKNESSES: Grass, Electric, Fighting, Rock

SEEL   DEWGONG

DEWOTT

Discipline Pokémon

#0502

TYPE: WATER

Strict training is how it learns its flowing double-scalchop technique.

As a result of strict training, each Dewott learns different forms for using the scalchops.

HOW TO SAY IT: DOO-waht
IMPERIAL HEIGHT: 2'07"
IMPERIAL WEIGHT: 54.0 lbs.
METRIC HEIGHT: 0.8 m
METRIC WEIGHT: 24.5 kg
GENDER: ♂ ♀
ABILITIES: Torrent
WEAKNESSES: Grass, Electric

SAMUROTT

OSHAWOTT   DEWOTT

HISUIAN
SAMUROTT

#0751 DEWPIDER
Water Bubble Pokémon

TYPE: WATER-BUG

It forms a water bubble at the rear of its body and then covers its head with it. Meeting another Dewpider means comparing water-bubble sizes.

Dewpider normally lives underwater. When it comes onto land in search of food, it takes water with it in the form of a bubble on its head.

HOW TO SAY IT: DOO-pih-der
IMPERIAL HEIGHT: 1'00"
IMPERIAL WEIGHT: 8.8 lbs.
METRIC HEIGHT: 0.3 m
METRIC WEIGHT: 4.0 kg
GENDER: ♂ ♀
ABILITIES: Water Bubble
WEAKNESSES: Flying, Electric, Rock

DEWPIDER → ARAQUANID

#0781 DHELMISE
Sea Creeper Pokémon

TYPE: GHOST-GRASS

After a piece of seaweed merged with debris from a sunken ship, it was reborn as this ghost Pokémon.

After lowering its anchor, it waits for its prey. It catches large Wailord and drains their life force.

HOW TO SAY IT: dell-MIZE
IMPERIAL HEIGHT: 12'10"
IMPERIAL WEIGHT: 463.0 lbs.
METRIC HEIGHT: 3.9 m
METRIC WEIGHT: 210.0 kg
GENDER: Unknown
ABILITIES: Steelworker
WEAKNESSES: Ghost, Fire, Flying, Dark, Ice

DOES NOT EVOLVE

DIALGA
Temporal Pokémon

 #0483

TYPE: STEEL-DRAGON

It has the power to control time. It appears in Sinnoh-region myths as an ancient deity.

This Pokémon is spoken of in legend. It is said that time began moving when Dialga was born.

HOW TO SAY IT: dee-AWL-gah
IMPERIAL HEIGHT: 17'09"
IMPERIAL WEIGHT: 1,505.8 lbs.
METRIC HEIGHT: 5.4 m
METRIC WEIGHT: 683.0 kg
GENDER: Unknown
ABILITIES: Pressure
WEAKNESSES: Fighting, Ground

DIALGA ORIGIN FORME

Radiant light caused Dialga to take on a form bearing a striking resemblance to the creator Pokémon. Dialga now wields such colossal strength that one must conclude this is its true form.

IMPERIAL HEIGHT: 23'00"
IMPERIAL WEIGHT: 1,873.9 lbs.
METRIC HEIGHT: 7.0 m
METRIC WEIGHT: 850.0 kg

DOES NOT EVOLVE

DIANCIE
Jewel Pokémon

TYPE: ROCK-FAIRY

A sudden transformation of Carbink, its pink, glimmering body is said to be the loveliest sight in the whole world.

It can instantly create many diamonds by compressing the carbon in the air between its hands.

HOW TO SAY IT: die-AHN-see
IMPERIAL HEIGHT: 2'04"
IMPERIAL WEIGHT: 19.4 lbs.
METRIC HEIGHT: 0.7 m
METRIC WEIGHT: 8.8 kg
GENDER: Unknown
ABILITIES: Clear Body
WEAKNESSES: Steel, Water, Grass, Ground

MEGA DIANCIE

TYPE: ROCK-FAIRY

A sudden transformation of Carbink, its pink, glimmering body is said to be the loveliest sight in the whole world.

It can instantly create many diamonds by compressing the carbon in the air between its hands.

IMPERIAL HEIGHT: 3'07"
IMPERIAL WEIGHT: 61.3 lbs.
METRIC HEIGHT: 1.1 m
METRIC WEIGHT: 27.8 kg

DIANCIE   MEGA DIANCIE

DIGGERSBY

Digging Pokémon

#0660

TYPE: NORMAL-GROUND

With power equal to an excavator, it can dig through dense bedrock. It's a huge help during tunnel construction.

The fur on its belly retains heat exceptionally well. People used to make heavy winter clothing from fur shed by this Pokémon.

HOW TO SAY IT: DIH-gurz-bee
IMPERIAL HEIGHT: 3'03"
IMPERIAL WEIGHT: 93.5 lbs.
METRIC HEIGHT: 1.0 m
METRIC WEIGHT: 42.4 kg
GENDER: ♂ ♀
ABILITIES: Pickup, Cheek Pouch
WEAKNESSES: Water, Grass, Fighting, Ice

BUNNELBY **DIGGERSBY**

DIGLETT
Mole Pokémon

TYPE: GROUND

It lives about one yard underground, where it feeds on plant roots. It sometimes appears aboveground.

Its skin is very thin. If it is exposed to light, its blood heats up, causing it to grow weak.

HOW TO SAY IT: DIG-let
IMPERIAL HEIGHT: 0'08"
IMPERIAL WEIGHT: 1.8 lbs.
METRIC HEIGHT: 0.2 m
METRIC WEIGHT: 0.8 kg
GENDER: ♂ ♀
ABILITIES: Sand Veil, Arena Trap
WEAKNESSES: Water, Grass, Ice

DIGLETT   DUGTRIO

ALOLAN DIGLETT
Mole Pokémon

TYPE: GROUND-STEEL

The metal-rich geology of this Pokémon's habitat caused it to develop steel whiskers on its head.

Its three hairs change shape depending on Diglett's mood. They're a useful communication tool among these Pokémon.

HOW TO SAY IT: DIG-let
IMPERIAL HEIGHT: 0'08"
IMPERIAL WEIGHT: 2.2 lbs.
METRIC HEIGHT: 0.2 m
METRIC WEIGHT: 1.0 kg
GENDER: ♂ ♀
ABILITIES: Sand Veil, Tangling Hair
WEAKNESSES: Fire, Water, Fighting, Ground

ALOLAN DIGLETT   ALOLAN DUGTRIO

DITTO

Transform Pokémon

#0132

TYPE: NORMAL

Its transformation ability is perfect. However, if made to laugh, it can't maintain its disguise.

It can freely recombine its own cellular structure to transform into other life-forms.

HOW TO SAY IT: DIT-toe
IMPERIAL HEIGHT: 1'00"
IMPERIAL WEIGHT: 8.8 lbs.
METRIC HEIGHT: 0.3 m
METRIC WEIGHT: 4.0 kg
GENDER: Unknown
ABILITIES: Limber
WEAKNESSES: Fighting

DOES NOT EVOLVE

DODRIO

Triple Bird Pokémon

#0085

TYPE: NORMAL-FLYING

One of Doduo's two heads splits to form a unique species. It runs close to 40 mph in prairies.

HOW TO SAY IT: doe-DREE-oh
IMPERIAL HEIGHT: 5'11"
IMPERIAL WEIGHT: 187.8 lbs.
METRIC HEIGHT: 1.8 m
METRIC WEIGHT: 85.2 kg
GENDER: ♂ ♀
ABILITIES: Run Away, Early Bird
WEAKNESSES: Electric, Ice, Rock

DODUO   DODRIO

DODUO
Twin Bird Pokémon

TYPE: NORMAL-FLYING

Its short wings make flying difficult. Instead, this
Pokémon runs at high speed on developed legs.

HOW TO SAY IT: doe-DOO-oh
IMPERIAL HEIGHT: 4'07"   **METRIC HEIGHT:** 1.4 m
IMPERIAL WEIGHT: 86.4 lbs.   **METRIC WEIGHT:** 39.2 kg
GENDER: ♂ ♀
ABILITIES: Run Away, Early Bird
WEAKNESSES: Electric, Ice, Rock

DODUO ➡ DODRIO

#0929

DOLLIV
Olive Pokémon

TYPE: GRASS-NORMAL

Dolliv shares its tasty, fresh-scented oil with
others. This species has coexisted with humans
since times long gone.

It basks in the sun to its heart's content until the
fruits on its head ripen. After that, Dolliv departs
from human settlements and goes on a journey.

HOW TO SAY IT: DAH-liv
IMPERIAL HEIGHT: 2'00"
IMPERIAL WEIGHT: 26.2 lbs.
METRIC HEIGHT: 0.6 m
METRIC WEIGHT: 11.9 kg
GENDER: ♂ ♀
ABILITIES: Early Bird
WEAKNESSES: Ice, Fire, Flying, Poison, Fighting, Bug

SMOLIV   DOLLIV   ARBOLIVA

DONDOZO

Big Catfish Pokémon

#0977

TYPE: WATER

This Pokémon is a glutton, but it's bad at getting food. It teams up with a Tatsugiri to catch prey.

It treats Tatsugiri like its boss and follows it loyally. Though powerful, Dondozo is apparently not very smart.

HOW TO SAY IT: DAHN-DOH-zoh
IMPERIAL HEIGHT: 39'04"
IMPERIAL WEIGHT: 485.0 lbs.
METRIC HEIGHT: 12.0 m
METRIC WEIGHT: 220.0 kg
GENDER: ♂ ♀
ABILITIES: Unaware, Oblivious
WEAKNESSES: Grass, Electric

DOES NOT EVOLVE

DONPHAN

Armor Pokémon

#0232

TYPE: GROUND

Donphan is covered in tough hide, so even being hit by a car won't faze this Pokémon. However, it is extremely susceptible to rain.

Donphan is normally a calm Pokémon, but once it is enraged, it will curl its body into a ball and charge at you while rolling.

HOW TO SAY IT: DON-fan
IMPERIAL HEIGHT: 3'07"
IMPERIAL WEIGHT: 264.6 lbs.
METRIC HEIGHT: 1.1 m
METRIC WEIGHT: 120.0 kg
GENDER: ♂ ♀
ABILITIES: Sturdy
WEAKNESSES: Water, Grass, Ice

PHANPY

DONPHAN

DOTTLER

Radome Pokémon

#0825

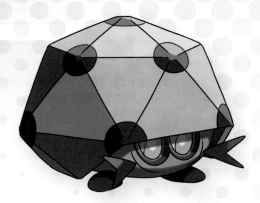

TYPE: BUG-PSYCHIC

It barely moves, but it's still alive. Hiding in its shell without food or water seems to have awakened its psychic powers.

As it grows inside its shell, it uses its psychic abilities to monitor the outside world and prepare for evolution.

HOW TO SAY IT: DOT-ler
IMPERIAL HEIGHT: 1'04" **METRIC HEIGHT:** 0.4 m
IMPERIAL WEIGHT: 43.0 lbs. **METRIC WEIGHT:** 19.5 kg
GENDER: ♂ ♀
ABILITIES: Swarm, Compound Eyes
WEAKNESSES: Ghost, Fire, Flying, Dark, Rock, Bug

BLIPBUG **DOTTLER** **ORBEETLE**

DOUBLADE

Sword Pokémon

#0680

TYPE: STEEL-GHOST

Honedge evolves into twins. The two blades rub together to emit a metallic sound that unnerves opponents.

The two swords employ a strategy of rapidly alternating between offense and defense to bring down their prey.

HOW TO SAY IT: DUH-blade
IMPERIAL HEIGHT: 2'07"
IMPERIAL WEIGHT: 9.9 lbs.
METRIC HEIGHT: 0.8 m
METRIC WEIGHT: 4.5 kg
GENDER: ♂ ♀
ABILITIES: No Guard
WEAKNESSES: Fire, Ghost, Dark, Ground

HONEDGE **DOUBLADE** **AEGISLASH**

DRACOVISH

Fossil Pokémon

#0882

TYPE: WATER-DRAGON

Powerful legs and jaws made it the apex predator of its time. Its own overhunting of its prey was what drove it to extinction.

Its mighty legs are capable of running at speeds exceeding 40 mph, but this Pokémon can't breathe unless it's underwater.

HOW TO SAY IT: DRAK-oh-vish
IMPERIAL HEIGHT: 7'07"
IMPERIAL WEIGHT: 474.0 lbs.
METRIC HEIGHT: 2.3 m
METRIC WEIGHT: 215.0 kg
GENDER: Unknown
ABILITIES: Water Absorb, Strong Jaw
WEAKNESSES: Fairy, Dragon

DOES NOT EVOLVE

DRACOZOLT

Fossil Pokémon

#0880

TYPE: ELECTRIC-DRAGON

In ancient times, it was unbeatable thanks to its powerful lower body, but it went extinct anyway after it depleted all its plant-based food sources.

The powerful muscles in its tail generate its electricity. Compared to its lower body, its upper half is entirely too small.

HOW TO SAY IT: DRAK-oh-zohlt
IMPERIAL HEIGHT: 5'11"
IMPERIAL WEIGHT: 418.9 lbs.
METRIC HEIGHT: 1.8 m
METRIC WEIGHT: 190.0 kg
GENDER: Unknown
ABILITIES: Volt Absorb, Hustle
WEAKNESSES: Fairy, Ground, Ice, Dragon

DOES NOT EVOLVE

DRAGALGE

Mock Kelp Pokémon

#0691

TYPE: POISON-DRAGON

Using a liquid poison, Dragalge indiscriminately attacks anything that wanders into its territory. This poison can corrode the undersides of boats.

Since Finizen is the better swimmer, Dragalge will approach it under the cover of seaweed, then immobilize it with a poisonous attack.

HOW TO SAY IT: druh-GAL-jee
IMPERIAL HEIGHT: 5'11"　　**METRIC HEIGHT:** 1.8 m
IMPERIAL WEIGHT: 179.7 lbs.　　**METRIC WEIGHT:** 81.5 kg
GENDER: ♂ ♀
ABILITIES: Poison Point, Poison Touch
WEAKNESSES: Psychic, Ground, Ice, Dragon

SKRELP　　**DRAGALGE**

DRAGAPULT

Stealth Pokémon

#0887

TYPE: DRAGON-GHOST

Dragapult can make its whole body transparent by clearing its mind and focusing. Even the Dreepy in Dragapult's horns become invisible.

The fastest Dragapult of the group is always surrounded by Dreepy that want to fly at sonic speed.

HOW TO SAY IT: DRAG-uh-pult
IMPERIAL HEIGHT: 9'10"
IMPERIAL WEIGHT: 110.2 lbs.
METRIC HEIGHT: 3.0 m
METRIC WEIGHT: 50.0 kg
GENDER: ♂ ♀
ABILITIES: Clear Body, Infiltrator
WEAKNESSES: Ghost, Dark, Fairy, Ice, Dragon

DREEPY　　**DRAKLOAK**　　**DRAGAPULT**

DRAGONAIR

Dragon Pokémon

#0148

TYPE: DRAGON

They say that if it emits an aura from its whole body, the weather will begin to change

It is called the divine Pokémon. When its entire body brightens slightly, the weather changes.

HOW TO SAY IT: DRAG-gon-AIR
IMPERIAL HEIGHT: 13'01"
IMPERIAL WEIGHT: 36.4 lbs.
METRIC HEIGHT: 4.0 m
METRIC WEIGHT: 16.5 kg
GENDER: ♂ ♀
ABILITIES: Shed Skin
WEAKNESSES: Fairy, Ice, Dragon

DRATINI **DRAGONAIR** **DRAGONITE**

DRAGONITE

Dragon Pokémon

#0149

TYPE: DRAGON-FLYING

It is said that somewhere in the ocean lies an island where these gather. Only they live there.

It can fly in spite of its big and bulky physique. It circles the globe in just 16 hours.

HOW TO SAY IT: DRAG-gon-ite
IMPERIAL HEIGHT: 7'03"
IMPERIAL WEIGHT: 463.0 lbs.
METRIC HEIGHT: 2.2 m
METRIC WEIGHT: 210.0 kg
GENDER: ♂ ♀
ABILITIES: Inner Focus
WEAKNESSES: Fairy, Dragon, Ice, Rock

DRATINI **DRAGONAIR** **DRAGONITE**

DRAKLOAK

Caretaker Pokémon

#0886

TYPE: DRAGON-GHOST

This Pokémon flies around at over 120 miles per hour. If a Drakloak is defeated in a battle, its Dreepy will wander off without a second thought.

This Pokémon stores up energy in its lungs, then shoots it out. It takes care of Dreepy and battles alongside them until they're all grown up.

HOW TO SAY IT: DRAK-klohk
IMPERIAL HEIGHT: 4'7"
IMPERIAL WEIGHT: 24.3 lbs.
METRIC HEIGHT: 1.4 m
METRIC WEIGHT: 11.0 kg
GENDER: ♂ ♀
ABILITIES: Clear Body, Infiltrator
WEAKNESSES: Ghost, Dark, Fairy, Ice, Dragon

DREEPY   **DRAKLOAK**   **DRAGAPULT**

DRAMPA

#0780

Placid Pokémon

TYPE: NORMAL-DRAGON

The mountains it calls home are nearly two miles in height. On rare occasions, it descends to play with the children living in the towns below.

Drampa is a kind and friendly Pokémon—until it's angered. When that happens, it stirs up a gale and flattens everything around.

HOW TO SAY IT: DRAM-puh
IMPERIAL HEIGHT: 9'10"
IMPERIAL WEIGHT: 407.9 lbs.
METRIC HEIGHT: 3.0 m
METRIC WEIGHT: 185.0 kg
GENDER: ♂ ♀
ABILITIES: Berserk, Sap Sipper
WEAKNESSES: Fairy, Fighting, Ice, Dragon

DOES NOT EVOLVE

TYPE: POISON-DARK

Its poison is potent, but it rarely sees use. This Pokémon prefers to use physical force instead, going on rampages with its car-crushing strength.

It's so vicious that it's called the Sand Demon. Yet when confronted by Hippowdon, Drapion keeps a low profile and will never pick a fight.

HOW TO SAY IT: DRAP-ee-on
IMPERIAL HEIGHT: 4'03"
IMPERIAL WEIGHT: 135.6 lbs.
METRIC HEIGHT: 1.3 m
METRIC WEIGHT: 61.5 kg
GENDER: ♂ ♀
ABILITIES: Battle Armor, Sniper
WEAKNESSES: Ground

DRAPION
Ogre Scorpion Pokémon

SKORUPI → DRAPION

#0147

DRATINI
Dragon Pokémon

TYPE: DRAGON

It sheds many layers of skin as it grows larger. During this process, it is protected by a rapid waterfall.

It is born large to start with. It repeatedly sheds its skin as it steadily grows longer.

HOW TO SAY IT: dra-TEE-nee
IMPERIAL HEIGHT: 5'11"
IMPERIAL WEIGHT: 7.3 lbs.
METRIC HEIGHT: 1.8 m
METRIC WEIGHT: 3.3 kg
GENDER: ♂ ♀
ABILITIES: Shed Skin
WEAKNESSES: Fairy, Ice, Dragon

DRATINI   DRAGONAIR   DRAGONITE

#0834

DREDNAW
Bite Pokémon

TYPE: WATER-ROCK

Its massive, jagged teeth can crush a boulder in a single bite. This Pokémon has an extremely vicious disposition.

Drednaw lurks along the shoreline. When prey come to drink water, Drednaw stretches its neck out and chomps down on them.

HOW TO SAY IT: DRED-naw
IMPERIAL HEIGHT: 3'03"   **METRIC HEIGHT:** 1.0 m
IMPERIAL WEIGHT: 254.6 lbs.   **METRIC WEIGHT:** 115.5 kg
GENDER: ♂ ♀
ABILITIES: Strong Jaw, Shell Armor
WEAKNESSES: Grass, Electric, Fighting, Ground

CHEWTLE   DREDNAW

GIGANTAMAX
DREDNAW

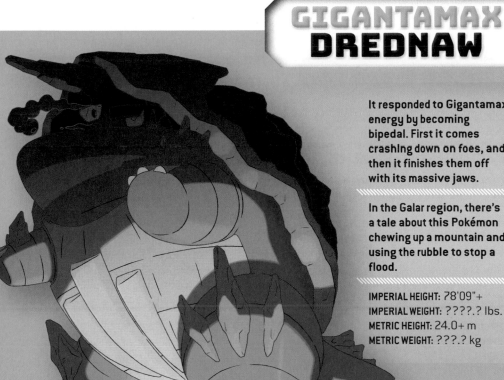

It responded to Gigantamax energy by becoming bipedal. First it comes crashing down on foes, and then it finishes them off with its massive jaws.

In the Galar region, there's a tale about this Pokémon chewing up a mountain and using the rubble to stop a flood.

IMPERIAL HEIGHT: 78'09"+
IMPERIAL WEIGHT: ????.? lbs.
METRIC HEIGHT: 24.0+ m
METRIC WEIGHT: ???.? kg

DREEPY #0885

Lingering Pokémon

TYPE: DRAGON-GHOST

In the evening, groups of Dreepy will fly at high speeds over the ocean and poke at Pokémon in the water for fun.

It has a habit of biting at Clauncher even though it doesn't feed on them. This is said to be vestigial behavior from when Dreepy was alive.

HOW TO SAY IT: DREE-pee
IMPERIAL HEIGHT: 1'08"
IMPERIAL WEIGHT: 4.4 lbs.
METRIC HEIGHT: 0.5 m
METRIC WEIGHT: 2.0 kg
GENDER: ♂♀
ABILITIES: Clear Body, Infiltrator
WEAKNESSES: Ghost, Dark, Fairy, Ice, Dragon

DREEPY   DRAKLOAK   DRAGAPULT

DRIFBLIM #0426

Blimp Pokémon

TYPE: GHOST-FLYING

It can generate and release gas within its body. That's how it can control the altitude of its drift.

They carry people and Pokémon, but the wind can catch them, so there can't be a fixed destination.

HOW TO SAY IT: DRIFF-blim
IMPERIAL HEIGHT: 3'11"
IMPERIAL WEIGHT: 33.1 lbs.
METRIC HEIGHT: 1.2 m
METRIC WEIGHT: 15.0 kg
GENDER: ♂♀
ABILITIES: Aftermath, Unburden
WEAKNESSES: Ghost, Dark, Electric, Ice, Rock

DRIFLOON   DRIFBLIM

DRIFLOON

Balloon Pokémon

#0425

TYPE: GHOST-FLYING

It is whispered that any child who mistakes Drifloon for a balloon and holds on to it could wind up missing.

Because of the way it floats aimlessly, an old folktale calls it a "signpost for wandering spirits."

HOW TO SAY IT: DRIFF-loon
IMPERIAL HEIGHT: 1'04"
IMPERIAL WEIGHT: 2.6 lbs.
METRIC HEIGHT: 0.4 m
METRIC WEIGHT: 1.2 kg
GENDER: ♂ ♀
ABILITIES: Aftermath, Unburden
WEAKNESSES: Ghost, Dark, Electric, Ice, Rock

DRIFLOON ▶ DRIFBLIM

DRILBUR

Mole Pokémon

#0529

TYPE: GROUND

It brings its claws together and whirls around at high speed before rushing toward its prey.

It's a digger, using its claws to burrow through the ground. It causes damage to vegetable crops, so many farmers have little love for it.

HOW TO SAY IT: DRIL-bur
IMPERIAL HEIGHT: 1'00"
IMPERIAL WEIGHT: 18.7 lbs.
METRIC HEIGHT: 0.3 m
METRIC WEIGHT: 8.5 kg
GENDER: ♂ ♀
ABILITIES: Sand Rush, Sand Force
WEAKNESSES: Water, Grass, Ice

DRILBUR ▶ EXCADRILL

DRIZZILE
Water Lizard Pokémon
#0817

TYPE: WATER

A clever combatant, this Pokémon battles using water balloons created with moisture secreted from its palms.

Highly intelligent but also very lazy, it keeps enemies out of its territory by laying traps everywhere.

HOW TO SAY IT: DRIZ-zyle
IMPERIAL HEIGHT: 2'04"
IMPERIAL WEIGHT: 25.4 lbs.
METRIC HEIGHT: 0.7 m
METRIC WEIGHT: 11.5 kg
GENDER: ♂♀
ABILITIES: Torrent
WEAKNESSES: Grass, Electric

SOBBLE ➡ DRIZZILE ➡ INTELEON

DROWZEE
Hypnosis Pokémon
#0096

TYPE: PSYCHIC

It remembers every dream it eats. It rarely eats the dreams of adults because children's are much tastier.

When it twitches its nose, it can tell where someone is sleeping and what that person is dreaming about.

HOW TO SAY IT: DROW-zee
IMPERIAL HEIGHT: 3'03"
IMPERIAL WEIGHT: 71.4 lbs.
METRIC HEIGHT: 1.0 m
METRIC WEIGHT: 32.4 kg
GENDER: ♂♀
ABILITIES: Insomnia, Forewarn
WEAKNESSES: Ghost, Dark, Bug

DROWZEE HYPNO

DRUDDIGON

#0621

Cave Pokémon

TYPE: DRAGON

Druddigon lives in caves, but it never skips sunbathing—it won't be able to move if its body gets too cold.

Druddigon are vicious and cunning. They take up residence in nests dug out by other Pokémon, treating the stolen nests as their own lairs.

HOW TO SAY IT: DRUD-dih-guhn
IMPERIAL HEIGHT: 5'03"
IMPERIAL WEIGHT: 306.4 lbs.
METRIC HEIGHT: 1.6 m
METRIC WEIGHT: 139.0 kg
GENDER: ♂ ♀
ABILITIES: Rough Skin, Sheer Force
WEAKNESSES: Fairy, Ice, Dragon

DOES NOT EVOLVE

DUBWOOL

#0832

Sheep Pokémon

TYPE: NORMAL

Weave a carpet from its springy wool, and you end up with something closer to a trampoline. You'll start to bounce the moment you set foot on it.

Its majestic horns are meant only to impress the opposite gender. They never see use in battle.

HOW TO SAY IT: DUB-wool
IMPERIAL HEIGHT: 4'03"
IMPERIAL WEIGHT: 94.8 lbs.
METRIC HEIGHT: 1.3 m
METRIC WEIGHT: 43.0 kg
GENDER: ♂ ♀
ABILITIES: Fluffy, Steadfast
WEAKNESSES: Fighting

WOOLOO   DUBWOOL

DUCKLETT #0580
Water Bird Pokémon

TYPE: WATER-FLYING

When attacked, it uses its feathers to splash water, escaping under cover of the spray.

They are better at swimming than flying, and they happily eat their favorite food, peat moss, as they dive underwater.

HOW TO SAY IT: DUK-lit
IMPERIAL HEIGHT: 1'08"
IMPERIAL WEIGHT: 12.1 lbs.
METRIC HEIGHT: 0.5 m
METRIC WEIGHT: 5.5 kg
GENDER: ♂ ♀
ABILITIES: Keen Eye, Big Pecks
WEAKNESSES: Electric, Rock

DUCKLETT   SWANNA

DUDUNSPARCE #0982
Land Snake Pokémon

TYPE: NORMAL

This Pokémon uses its hard tail to make its nest by boring holes into bedrock deep underground. The nest can reach lengths of over six miles.

It drives enemies out of its nest by sucking in enough air to fill its long, narrow lungs, then releasing the air in an intense blast.

HOW TO SAY IT: duh-DUHN-sparse
IMPERIAL HEIGHT: 11'10"
IMPERIAL WEIGHT: 86.4 lbs.
METRIC HEIGHT: 3.6 m
METRIC WEIGHT: 39.2 kg
GENDER: ♂ ♀
ABILITIES: Serene Grace, Run Away
WEAKNESSES: Fighting

DUNSPARCE   DUDUNSPARCE

DUGTRIO
Mole Pokémon

#0051

TYPE: GROUND

Its three heads bob separately up and down to loosen the soil nearby, making it easier for it to burrow.

In battle, it digs through the ground and strikes the unsuspecting foe from an unexpected direction.

HOW TO SAY IT: DUG-TREE-oh
IMPERIAL HEIGHT: 2'04"
IMPERIAL WEIGHT: 73.4 lbs.
METRIC HEIGHT: 0.7 m
METRIC WEIGHT: 33.3 kg
GENDER: ♂ ♀
ABILITIES: Sand Veil, Arena Trap
WEAKNESSES: Water, Grass, Ice

DIGLETT **DUGTRIO**

#0051

ALOLAN DUGTRIO
Mole Pokémon

TYPE: GROUND-STEEL

Their beautiful, metallic whiskers create a sort of protective helmet on their heads, and they also function as highly precise sensors.

The three of them get along very well. Through their formidable teamwork, they defeat powerful opponents.

HOW TO SAY IT: DUG-TREE-oh
IMPERIAL HEIGHT: 2'04"
IMPERIAL WEIGHT: 146.8 lbs.
METRIC HEIGHT: 0.7 m
METRIC WEIGHT: 66.6 kg
GENDER: ♂ ♀
ABILITIES: Sand Veil, Tangling Hair
WEAKNESSES: Fire, Water, Fighting, Ground

ALOLAN DIGLETT **ALOLAN DUGTRIO**

TYPE: NORMAL

It creates mazes in dark locations. When spotted, it flees into the ground by digging with its tail.

If spotted, it escapes by burrowing with its tail. It can float just slightly using its wings.

HOW TO SAY IT: DUN-sparce
IMPERIAL HEIGHT: 4'11"
IMPERIAL WEIGHT: 30.9 lbs.
METRIC HEIGHT: 1.5 m
METRIC WEIGHT: 14.0 kg
GENDER: ♂ ♀
ABILITIES: Serene Grace, Run Away
WEAKNESSES: Fighting

#0206

DUNSPARCE
Land Snake Pokémon

DUNSPARCE ➡ **DUDUNSPARCE**

#0578

DUOSION
Mitosis Pokémon

TYPE: PSYCHIC

Its psychic power can supposedly cover a range of more than half a mile—but only if its two brains can agree with each other.

Its brain has split into two, and the two halves rarely think alike. Its actions are utterly unpredictable.

HOW TO SAY IT: doo-OH-zhun
IMPERIAL HEIGHT: 2'00"
IMPERIAL WEIGHT: 17.6 lbs.
METRIC HEIGHT: 0.6 m
METRIC WEIGHT: 8.0 kg
GENDER: ♂ ♀
ABILITIES: Overcoat, Magic Guard
WEAKNESSES: Ghost, Dark, Bug

 SOLOSIS ➡ **DUOSION** ➡ **REUNICLUS**

DOES NOT EVOLVE

DURALUDON
Alloy Pokémon

TYPE: STEEL-DRAGON

Its body resembles polished metal, and it's both lightweight and strong. The only drawback is that it rusts easily.

The special metal that composes its body is very light, so this Pokémon has considerable agility. It lives in caves because it dislikes the rain.

HOW TO SAY IT: duh-RAL-uh-dahn
IMPERIAL HEIGHT: 5'11"   **METRIC HEIGHT:** 1.8 m
IMPERIAL WEIGHT: 88.2 lbs.   **METRIC WEIGHT:** 40.0 kg
GENDER: ♂ ♀
ABILITIES: Light Metal, Heavy Metal
WEAKNESSES: Fighting, Ground

GIGANTAMAX DURALUDON

It's grown to resemble a skyscraper. Parts of its towering body glow due to a profusion of energy.

The hardness of its cells is exceptional, even among Steel types. It also has a body structure that's resistant to earthquakes.

IMPERIAL HEIGHT: 141'01"+
IMPERIAL WEIGHT: ????.? lbs.
METRIC HEIGHT: 43.0+ m
METRIC WEIGHT: ???.? kg

TYPE: BUG-STEEL

DURANT
Iron Ant Pokémon

They lay their eggs deep inside their nests. When attacked by Heatmor, they retaliate using their massive mandibles.

With their large mandibles, these Pokémon can crunch their way through rock. They work together to protect their eggs from Sandaconda.

HOW TO SAY IT: dur-ANT
IMPERIAL HEIGHT: 1'00"
IMPERIAL WEIGHT: 72.8 lbs.
METRIC HEIGHT: 0.3 m
METRIC WEIGHT: 33.0 kg
GENDER: ♂ ♀
ABILITIES: Swarm, Hustle
WEAKNESSES: Fire

DOES NOT EVOLVE

TYPE: GHOST

DUSCLOPS
Beckon Pokémon

Its body is entirely hollow. When it opens its mouth, it sucks everything in as if it were a black hole.

It seeks drifting will-o'-the-wisps and sucks them into its empty body. What happens inside is a mystery.

HOW TO SAY IT: DUS-klops
IMPERIAL HEIGHT: 5'03"
IMPERIAL WEIGHT: 67.5 lbs.
METRIC HEIGHT: 1.6 m
METRIC WEIGHT: 30.6 kg
GENDER: ♂ ♀
ABILITIES: Pressure
WEAKNESSES: Ghost, Dark

DUSKULL   DUSCLOPS   DUSKNOIR

DUSKNOIR

#0477

Gripper Pokémon

TYPE: GHOST

At the bidding of transmissions from the spirit world, it steals people and Pokémon away. No one knows whether it has a will of its own.

With the mouth on its belly, Dusknoir swallows its target whole. The soul is the only thing eaten—Dusknoir disgorges the body before departing.

HOW TO SAY IT: DUSK-nwar
IMPERIAL HEIGHT: 7'03"
IMPERIAL WEIGHT: 235.0 lbs.
METRIC HEIGHT: 2.2 m
METRIC WEIGHT: 106.6 kg
GENDER: ♂ ♀
ABILITIES: Pressure
WEAKNESSES: Ghost, Dark

DUSKULL   DUSCLOPS   DUSKNOIR

DUSKULL

#0355

Requiem Pokémon

TYPE: GHOST

If it finds bad children who won't listen to their parents, it will spirit them away—or so it's said.

Making itself invisible, it silently sneaks up to prey. It has the ability to slip through thick walls.

HOW TO SAY IT: DUS-kull
IMPERIAL HEIGHT: 2'07"
IMPERIAL WEIGHT: 33.1 lbs.
METRIC HEIGHT: 0.8 m
METRIC WEIGHT: 15.0 kg
GENDER: ♂ ♀
ABILITIES: Levitate
WEAKNESSES: Ghost, Dark

DUSKULL   DUSCLOPS   DUSKNOIR

TYPE: BUG-POISON

Dustox is instinctively drawn to light. Swarms of this Pokémon are attracted by the bright lights of cities, where they wreak havoc by stripping the leaves off roadside trees for food.

When Dustox flaps its wings, a fine dust is scattered all over. This dust is actually a powerful poison that will even make a pro wrestler sick. This Pokémon searches for food using its antennae-like radar.

HOW TO SAY IT: DUS-tocks
IMPERIAL HEIGHT: 3'11"
IMPERIAL WEIGHT: 69.7 lbs.
METRIC HEIGHT: 1.2 m
METRIC WEIGHT: 31.6 kg
GENDER: ♂ ♀
ABILITIES: Shield Dust
WEAKNESSES: Fire, Psychic, Flying, Rock

#0269

DUSTOX
Poison Moth Pokémon

WURMPLE CASCOON DUSTOX

#0557

DWEBBLE
Rock Inn Pokémon

TYPE: BUG-ROCK

When it finds a stone appealing, it creates a hole inside it and uses it as its home. This Pokémon is the natural enemy of Roggenrola and Rolycoly.

It first tries to find a rock to live in, but if there are no suitable rocks to be found, Dwebble may move in to the ports of a Hippowdon.

HOW TO SAY IT: DWEHB-bul
IMPERIAL HEIGHT: 1'00"
IMPERIAL WEIGHT: 32.0 lbs.
METRIC HEIGHT: 0.3 m
METRIC WEIGHT: 14.5 kg
GENDER: ♂ ♀
ABILITIES: Sturdy, Shell Armor
WEAKNESSES: Steel, Water, Rock

DWEBBLE CRUSTLE

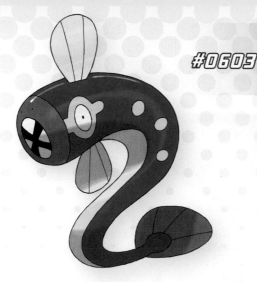

EELEKTRIK
EleFish Pokémon

TYPE: ELECTRIC

They coil around foes and shock them with electricity-generating organs that seem simply to be circular patterns.

These Pokémon have a big appetite. When they spot their prey, they attack it and paralyze it with electricity.

HOW TO SAY IT: ee-LEK-trik
IMPERIAL HEIGHT: 3'11"
IMPERIAL WEIGHT: 48.5 lbs.
METRIC HEIGHT: 1.2 m
METRIC WEIGHT: 22.0 kg
GENDER: ♂ ♀
ABILITIES: Levitate
WEAKNESSES: Ground

TYNAMO   EELEKTRIK   EELEKTROSS

EELEKTROSS
EleFish Pokémon

#0604

TYPE: ELECTRIC

They crawl out of the ocean using their arms. They will attack prey on shore and immediately drag it into the ocean.

It latches on to prey with its sucker mouth, sinking in its fangs and shocking the prey with powerful electricity.

HOW TO SAY IT: ee-LEK-trahs
IMPERIAL HEIGHT: 6'11"
IMPERIAL WEIGHT: 177.5 lbs.
METRIC HEIGHT: 2.1 m
METRIC WEIGHT: 80.5 kg
GENDER: ♂ ♀
ABILITIES: Levitate
WEAKNESSES: Ground

TYNAMO   EELEKTRIK   EELEKTROSS

EEVEE

Evolution Pokémon

#0133

TYPE: NORMAL

Its ability to evolve into many forms allows it to adapt smoothly and perfectly to any environment.

Its genetic code is irregular. It may mutate if it is exposed to radiation from element stones.

HOW TO SAY IT: EE-vee
IMPERIAL HEIGHT: 1'00"
IMPERIAL WEIGHT: 14.3 lbs.
METRIC HEIGHT: 0.3 m
METRIC WEIGHT: 6.5 kg
GENDER: ♂ ♀
ABILITIES: Run Away, Adaptability
WEAKNESSES: Fighting

JOLTEON

FLAREON

GLACEON

VAPOREON

EEVEE

ESPEON

UMBREON

LEAFEON

SYLVEON

GIGANTAMAX EEVEE

Gigantamax energy upped the fluffiness of the fur around Eevee's neck. The fur will envelop a foe, capturing its body and captivating its mind.

Having gotten even friendlier and more innocent, Eevee tries to play with anyone around, only to end up crushing them with its immense body.

IMPERIAL HEIGHT: 59'01"+
IMPERIAL WEIGHT: ????.? lbs.
METRIC HEIGHT: 18.0+ m
METRIC WEIGHT: ???.? kg

EISCUE
Penguin Pokémon
#0875

TYPE: ICE

On hot days, these Pokémon press their ice cube heads together and pass the time cooling each other down.

If you lick the ice covering its face, you'll find it has a faintly salty taste. This species rode here on ocean currents from a cold, faraway land.

HOW TO SAY IT: ICE-kyoo
IMPERIAL HEIGHT: 4'07"
IMPERIAL WEIGHT: 196.2 lbs.
METRIC HEIGHT: 1.4 m
METRIC WEIGHT: 89.0 kg
GENDER: ♂ ♀
ABILITIES: Ice Face
WEAKNESSES: Fire, Steel, Fighting, Rock

DOES NOT EVOLVE

EKANS
Snake Pokémon
#0023

TYPE: POISON

The older it gets, the longer it grows. At night, it wraps its long body around tree branches to rest.

HOW TO SAY IT: ECK-kins
IMPERIAL HEIGHT: 6'07"
IMPERIAL WEIGHT: 15.2 lbs.
METRIC HEIGHT: 2.0 m
METRIC WEIGHT: 6.9 kg
GENDER: ♂ ♀
ABILITIES: Intimidate, Shed Skin
WEAKNESSES: Psychic, Ground

EKANS → ARBOK

#0830 ELDEGOSS
Cotton Bloom Pokémon

TYPE: GRASS

The seeds attached to its cotton fluff are full of nutrients. It spreads them on the wind so that plants and other Pokémon can benefit from them.

The cotton on the head of this Pokémon can be spun into a glossy, gorgeous yarn—a Galar regional specialty.

HOW TO SAY IT: EL-duh-gahs
IMPERIAL HEIGHT: 1'08"
IMPERIAL WEIGHT: 5.5 lbs.
METRIC HEIGHT: 0.5 m
METRIC WEIGHT: 2.5 kg
GENDER: ♂ ♀
ABILITIES: Cotton Down, Regenerator
WEAKNESSES: Fire, Flying, Ice, Poison, Bug

GOSSIFLEUR   ELDEGOSS

ELECTABUZZ
Electric Pokémon
#0125

TYPE: ELECTRIC

Many power plants keep Ground-type Pokémon around as a defense against Electabuzz that come seeking electricity.

With the coming of a storm, many of these Pokémon will gather under tall trees and sit there waiting for lightning to strike.

HOW TO SAY IT: eh-LECK-ta-buzz
IMPERIAL HEIGHT: 3'07"
IMPERIAL WEIGHT: 66.1 lbs.
METRIC HEIGHT: 1.1 m
METRIC WEIGHT: 30.0 kg
GENDER: ♂ ♀
ABILITIES: Static
WEAKNESSES: Ground

ELEKID   ELECTABUZZ   ELECTIVIRE

ELECTIVIRE #0466
Thunderbolt Pokémon

TYPE: ELECTRIC

The amount of electrical energy this Pokémon produces is proportional to the rate of its pulse. The voltage jumps while Electivire is battling.

In terms of electrical-energy output, Electivire is one of the best among all Electric Pokémon. It discharges high-voltage currents from its tails.

HOW TO SAY IT: el-LECT-uh-vire
IMPERIAL HEIGHT: 5'11"
IMPERIAL WEIGHT: 305.6 lbs.
METRIC HEIGHT: 1.8 m
METRIC WEIGHT: 138.6 kg
GENDER: ♂ ♀
ABILITIES: Motor Drive
WEAKNESSES: Ground

ELEKID → ELECTABUZZ → ELECTIVIRE

TYPE: ELECTRIC

ELECTRIKE #0309
Lightning Pokémon

It stores static electricity in its fur for discharging. It gives off sparks if a storm approaches.

It stores electricity in its fur. It gives off sparks from all over its body in seasons when the air is dry.

HOW TO SAY IT: eh-LEK-trike
IMPERIAL HEIGHT: 2'00"
IMPERIAL WEIGHT: 33.5 lbs.
METRIC HEIGHT: 0.6 m
METRIC WEIGHT: 15.2 kg
GENDER: ♂ ♀
ABILITIES: Static, Lightning Rod
WEAKNESSES: Ground

ELECTRIKE   MANECTRIC   MEGA MANECTRIC

ELECTRODE
Ball Pokémon

#0101

TYPE: ELECTRIC

The more energy it charges up, the faster it gets. But this also makes it more likely to explode.

It explodes in response to even minor stimuli. It is feared, with the nickname of the Bomb Ball.

HOW TO SAY IT: ee-LECK-trode
IMPERIAL HEIGHT: 3'11"
IMPERIAL WEIGHT: 146.8 lbs.
METRIC HEIGHT: 1.2 m
METRIC WEIGHT: 66.6 kg
GENDER: Unknown
ABILITIES: Soundproof, Static
WEAKNESSES: Ground

VOLTORB → **ELECTRODE**

HISUIAN ELECTRODE
Sphere Pokémon

#0101

TYPE: ELECTRIC-GRASS

The tissue on the surface of its body is curiously similar in composition to an Apricorn. When irritated, this Pokémon lets loose an electric current equal to 20 lightning bolts.

HOW TO SAY IT: ee-LECK-trode
IMPERIAL HEIGHT: 3'11"
IMPERIAL WEIGHT: 156.5 lbs.
METRIC HEIGHT: 1.2 m
METRIC WEIGHT: 71.0 kg
GENDER: Unknown
ABILITIES: N/A
WEAKNESSES: Fire, Ice, Poison, Bug

HISUIAN VOLTORB → **HISUIAN ELECTRODE**

ELEKID

Electric Pokémon

#0239

TYPE: ELECTRIC

When a storm approaches, this Pokémon gets restless. Once Elekid hears the sound of thunder, it gets full-on rowdy.

It's not good at storing electricity yet. This Pokémon sneaks into people's homes, looking for electrical outlets to eat electricity from.

HOW TO SAY IT: EL-eh-kid
IMPERIAL HEIGHT: 2'00"
IMPERIAL WEIGHT: 51.8 lbs.
METRIC HEIGHT: 0.6 m
METRIC WEIGHT: 23.5 kg
GENDER: ♂ ♀
ABILITIES: Static
WEAKNESSES: Ground

ELEKID **ELECTABUZZ** **ELECTIVIRE**

ELGYEM

Cerebral Pokémon

#0605

TYPE: PSYCHIC

If this Pokémon stands near a TV, strange scenery will appear on the screen. That scenery is said to be from its home.

This Pokémon was discovered about 50 years ago. Its highly developed brain enables it to exert its psychic powers.

HOW TO SAY IT: ELL-jee-ehm
IMPERIAL HEIGHT: 1'08"
IMPERIAL WEIGHT: 19.8 lbs.
METRIC HEIGHT: 0.5 m
METRIC WEIGHT: 9.0 kg
GENDER: ♂ ♀
ABILITIES: Telepathy, Synchronize
WEAKNESSES: Ghost, Dark, Bug

ELGYEM **BEHEEYEM**

EMBOAR #0500

Mega Fire Pig Pokémon

TYPE: FIRE-FIGHTING

It can throw a fire punch by setting its fists on fire with its fiery chin. It cares deeply about its friends.

It has mastered fast and powerful fighting moves. It grows a beard of fire.

HOW TO SAY IT: EHM-bohr
IMPERIAL HEIGHT: 5'03"
IMPERIAL WEIGHT: 330.7 lbs.
METRIC HEIGHT: 1.6 m
METRIC WEIGHT: 150.0 kg
GENDER: ♂ ♀
ABILITIES: Blaze
WEAKNESSES: Water, Psychic, Flying, Ground

TEPIG   PIGNITE   EMBOAR

#0587 EMOLGA
Sky Squirrel Pokémon

TYPE: ELECTRIC-FLYING

As Emolga flutters through the air, it crackles with electricity. This Pokémon is cute, but it can cause a lot of trouble.

This Pokémon absolutely loves sweet berries. Sometimes it stuffs its cheeks full of so much food that it can't fly properly.

HOW TO SAY IT: ee-MAHL-guh
IMPERIAL HEIGHT: 1'04"
IMPERIAL WEIGHT: 11.0 lbs.
METRIC HEIGHT: 0.4 m
METRIC WEIGHT: 5.0 kg
GENDER: ♂ ♀
ABILITIES: Static
WEAKNESSES: Ice, Rock

DOES NOT EVOLVE

#0395 EMPOLEON
Emperor Pokémon

TYPE: WATER-STEEL

It swims as fast as a jet boat. The edges of its wings are sharp and can slice apart drifting ice.

The three horns that extend from its beak attest to its power. The leader has the biggest horns.

HOW TO SAY IT: em-POH-lee-on
IMPERIAL HEIGHT: 5'07"
IMPERIAL WEIGHT: 186.3 lbs.
METRIC HEIGHT: 1.7 m
METRIC WEIGHT: 84.5 kg
GENDER: ♂ ♀
ABILITIES: Torrent
WEAKNESSES: Electric, Fighting, Ground

PIPLUP   PRINPLUP   EMPOLEON

ENAMORUS

Love-Hate Pokémon

#0905

TYPE: FAIRY-FLYING

INCARNATE FORME: When it flies to this land from across the sea, the bitter winter comes to an end. According to legend, this Pokémon's love gives rise to the budding of fresh life across Hisui.

THERIAN FORME: A different guise from its feminine humanoid form. From the clouds, it descends upon those who treat any form of life with disrespect and metes out wrathful, ruthless punishment.

HOW TO SAY IT: eh-NAM-or-us
IMPERIAL HEIGHT: 5'03"
IMPERIAL WEIGHT: 105.8 lbs.
METRIC HEIGHT: 1.6 m
METRIC WEIGHT: 48.0 kg
GENDER: ♀
ABILITIES: N/A
WEAKNESSES: Steel, Poison, Electric, Ice, Rock

INCARNATE FORME

THERIAN FORME

172

DOES NOT EVOLVE

ENTEI
Volcano Pokémon

#0244

TYPE: FIRE

Entei embodies the passion of magma. This Pokémon is thought to have been born in the eruption of a volcano. It sends up massive bursts of fire that utterly consume all that they touch.

HOW TO SAY IT: EN-tay
IMPERIAL HEIGHT: 6'11"
IMPERIAL WEIGHT: 436.5 lbs.
METRIC HEIGHT: 2.1 m
METRIC WEIGHT: 198.0 kg
GENDER: Unknown
ABILITIES: Pressure
WEAKNESSES: Water, Ground, Rock

DOES NOT EVOLVE

ESCAVALIER
Cavalry Pokémon

#0589

TYPE: BUG-STEEL

They use shells they've stolen from Shelmet to arm and protect themselves. They're very popular Pokémon in the Galar region.

It charges its enemies, lances at the ready. An image of one of its duels is captured in a famous painting of Escavalier clashing with Sirfetch'd.

HOW TO SAY IT: ess-KA-vuh-LEER
IMPERIAL HEIGHT: 3'03"
IMPERIAL WEIGHT: 72.8 lbs.
METRIC HEIGHT: 1.0 m
METRIC WEIGHT: 33.0 kg
GENDER: ♂ ♀
ABILITIES: Swarm, Shell Armor
WEAKNESSES: Fire

KARRABLAST **ESCAVALIER**

ESPATHRA

Ostrich Pokémon

#0956

TYPE: PSYCHIC

It immobilizes opponents by bathing them in psychic power from its large eyes. Despite its appearance, it has a vicious temperament.

It emits psychic power from the gaps between its multicolored frills and sprints at speeds greater than 120 mph.

HOW TO SAY IT: ess-PATH-ruh
IMPERIAL HEIGHT: 6'03"
IMPERIAL WEIGHT: 198.4 lbs.
METRIC HEIGHT: 1.9 m
METRIC WEIGHT: 90.0 kg
GENDER: ♂♀
ABILITIES: Opportunist, Frisk
WEAKNESSES: Ghost, Dark, Bug

FLITTLE → ESPATHRA

ESPEON

Sun Pokémon

#0196

TYPE: PSYCHIC

The tip of its forked tail quivers when it is predicting its opponent's next move.

It uses the fine hair that covers its body to sense air currents and predict its enemy's actions.

HOW TO SAY IT: ESS-pee-on
IMPERIAL HEIGHT: 2'11"
IMPERIAL WEIGHT: 58.4 lbs.
METRIC HEIGHT: 0.9 m
METRIC WEIGHT: 26.5 kg
GENDER: ♂♀
ABILITIES: Synchronize
WEAKNESSES: Ghost, Dark, Bug

EEVEE → ESPEON

ESPURR
Restraint Pokémon

TYPE: PSYCHIC

Though Espurr's expression never changes, behind that blank stare is an intense struggle to contain its devastating psychic power.

There's enough psychic power in Espurr to send a wrestler flying, but because this power can't be controlled, Espurr finds it troublesome.

ESPURR ➡ **MEOWSTIC**

HOW TO SAY IT: ESS-purr
IMPERIAL HEIGHT: 1'00"
IMPERIAL WEIGHT: 7.7 lbs.
METRIC HEIGHT: 0.3 m
METRIC WEIGHT: 3.5 kg
GENDER: ♂ ♀
ABILITIES: Keen Eye, Infiltrator
WEAKNESSES: Ghost, Dark, Bug

ETERNATUS
Gigantic Pokémon

#0890

LEGENDARY POKÉMON

TYPE: POISON-DRAGON

The core on its chest absorbs energy emanating from the lands of the Galar region. This energy is what allows Eternatus to stay active.

It was inside a meteorite that fell 20,000 years ago. There seems to be a connection between this Pokémon and the Dynamax phenomenon.

HOW TO SAY IT: ee-TURR-nuh-tuss
IMPERIAL HEIGHT: 65'07"
IMPERIAL WEIGHT: 2,094.4 lbs.
METRIC HEIGHT: 20.0 m
METRIC WEIGHT: 950.0 kg
GENDER: Unknown
ABILITIES: Pressure
WEAKNESSES: Psychic, Ground, Ice, Dragon

DOES NOT EVOLVE

EXCADRILL

Subterrene Pokémon

#0530

TYPE: GROUND-STEEL

It's not uncommon for tunnels that appear to have formed naturally to actually be a result of Excadrill's rampant digging.

Known as the Drill King, this Pokémon can tunnel through the terrain at speeds of over 90 mph.

HOW TO SAY IT: EKS-kuh-dril
IMPERIAL HEIGHT: 2'04"
IMPERIAL WEIGHT: 89.1 lbs.
METRIC HEIGHT: 0.7 m
METRIC WEIGHT: 40.4 kg
GENDER: ♂ ♀
ABILITIES: Sand Rush, Sand Force
WEAKNESSES: Fire, Water, Fighting, Ground

DRILBUR **EXCADRILL**

EXEGGCUTE

Egg Pokémon

#0102

TYPE: GRASS-PSYCHIC

Though it may look like it's just a bunch of eggs, it's a proper Pokémon. Exeggcute communicates with others of its kind via telepathy, apparently.

These Pokémon get nervous when they're not in a group of six. The minute even one member of the group goes missing, Exeggcute become cowardly.

HOW TO SAY IT: ECKS-egg-cute
IMPERIAL HEIGHT: 1'04"
IMPERIAL WEIGHT: 5.5 lbs.
METRIC HEIGHT: 0.4 m
METRIC WEIGHT: 2.5 kg
GENDER: ♂ ♀
ABILITIES: Chlorophyll
WEAKNESSES: Ghost, Fire, Flying, Ice, Dark, Poison, Bug

EXEGGUTOR

EXEGGCUTE

ALOLAN EXEGGUTOR

EXEGGUTOR
Coconut Pokémon

TYPE: GRASS-PSYCHIC

Each of Exeggutor's three heads is thinking different thoughts. The three don't seem to be very interested in one another.

When they work together, Exeggutor's three heads can put out powerful psychic energy. Cloudy days make this Pokémon sluggish.

HOW TO SAY IT: ecks-EGG-u-tore
IMPERIAL HEIGHT: 6'07"
IMPERIAL WEIGHT: 264.6 lbs.
METRIC HEIGHT: 2.0 m
METRIC WEIGHT: 120.0 kg
GENDER: ♂ ♀
ABILITIES: Chlorophyll
WEAKNESSES: Ghost, Fire, Flying, Ice, Dark, Poison, Bug

EXEGGCUTE → EXEGGUTOR

ALOLAN EXEGGUTOR
Coconut Pokémon

#0103

TYPE: GRASS-DRAGON

Blazing sunlight has brought out the true form and powers of this Pokémon.

This Pokémon's psychic powers aren't as strong as they once were. The head on this Exeggutor's tail scans surrounding areas with weak telepathy.

HOW TO SAY IT: ecks-EGG-u-tore
IMPERIAL HEIGHT: 35'09"
IMPERIAL WEIGHT: 916.2 lbs.
METRIC HEIGHT: 10.9 m
METRIC WEIGHT: 415.6 kg
GENDER: ♂ ♀
ABILITIES: Frisk
WEAKNESSES: Flying, Ice, Dragon, Poison, Fairy, Bug

  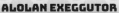

EXEGGCUTE → ALOLAN EXEGGUTOR

177

TYPE: NORMAL

In the past, people would use the loud voices of these Pokémon as a means of communication between distant cities.

This Pokémon can do more than just shout. To communicate with others of its kind, it'll emit all sorts of sounds from the holes in its body.

HOW TO SAY IT: ecks-PLOWD
IMPERIAL HEIGHT: 4'11"
IMPERIAL WEIGHT: 185.2 lbs.
METRIC HEIGHT: 1.5 m
METRIC WEIGHT: 84.0 kg
GENDER: ♂ ♀
ABILITIES: Soundproof
WEAKNESSES: Fighting

#0295

EXPLOUD
Loud Noise Pokémon

WHISMUR ➡ LOUDRED ➡ EXPLOUD

FALINKS
Formation Pokémon

#0870

TYPE: FIGHTING

The brass, which is the one that stands at the front and issues orders, is the strongest and smartest of the six.

The leader, known as the brass, uses its extendible horn to issue orders to the others when it's time to change formation.

HOW TO SAY IT: FAY-links
IMPERIAL HEIGHT: 9'10"
IMPERIAL WEIGHT: 136.7 lbs.
METRIC HEIGHT: 3.0 m
METRIC WEIGHT: 62.0 kg
GENDER: Unknown
ABILITIES: Battle Armor
WEAKNESSES: Psychic, Flying, Fairy

DOES NOT EVOLVE

FARFETCH'D
Wild Duck Pokémon

#0083

TYPE: NORMAL-FLYING

It can't live without the stalk it holds. That's why it defends the stalk from attackers with its life.

HOW TO SAY IT: FAR-fetched
IMPERIAL HEIGHT: 2'07"
IMPERIAL WEIGHT: 33.1 lbs.
METRIC HEIGHT: 0.8 m
METRIC WEIGHT: 15.0 kg
GENDER: ♂ ♀
ABILITIES: Keen Eye, Inner Focus
WEAKNESSES: Electric, Ice, Rock

DOES NOT EVOLVE

GALARIAN FARFETCH'D
Wild Duck Pokémon

#0083

TYPE: FIGHTING

The Farfetch'd of the Galar region are brave warriors, and they wield thick, tough leeks in battle.

The stalks of leeks are thicker and longer in the Galar region. Farfetch'd that adapted to these stalks took on a unique form.

HOW TO SAY IT: FAR-fetched
IMPERIAL HEIGHT: 2'07"
IMPERIAL WEIGHT: 92.6 lbs.
METRIC HEIGHT: 0.8 m
METRIC WEIGHT: 42.0 kg
GENDER: ♂ ♀
ABILITIES: Steadfast
WEAKNESSES: Psychic, Flying, Fairy

GALARIAN FARFETCH'D → SIRFETCH'D

FARIGIRAF

Long Neck Pokémon

#0981

TYPE: NORMAL-PSYCHIC

Now that the brain waves from the head and tail are synced up, the psychic power of this Pokémon is 10 times stronger than Girafarig's.

The hardened head from the tail protects the head of the main body as Farigiraf whips its long neck around to headbutt enemies.

HOW TO SAY IT: fuh-RIG-uh-ra
IMPERIAL HEIGHT: 10'06"
IMPERIAL WEIGHT: 352.7 lbs.
METRIC HEIGHT: 3.2 m
METRIC WEIGHT: 160.0 kg
GENDER: ♂ ♀
ABILITIES: Cud Chew, Armor Tail
WEAKNESSES: Dark, Bug

GIRAFARIG

FARIGIRAF

FEAROW
Beak Pokémon

TYPE: NORMAL-FLYING

A Pokémon that dates back many years. If it senses danger, it flies high and away, instantly.

HOW TO SAY IT: FEER-oh
IMPERIAL HEIGHT: 3'11"
IMPERIAL WEIGHT: 83.8 lbs.
METRIC HEIGHT: 1.2 m
METRIC WEIGHT: 38.0 kg
GENDER: ♂ ♀
ABILITIES: Keen Eye
WEAKNESSES: Electric, Ice, Rock

SPEAROW → FEAROW

FEEBAS
Fish Pokémon

#0349

TYPE: WATER

Although unattractive and unpopular, this Pokémon's marvelous vitality has made it a subject of research.

It is a shabby and ugly Pokémon. However, it is very hardy and can survive on little water.

HOW TO SAY IT: FEE-bass
IMPERIAL HEIGHT: 2'00"
IMPERIAL WEIGHT: 16.3 lbs.
METRIC HEIGHT: 0.6 m
METRIC WEIGHT: 7.4 kg
GENDER: ♂ ♀
ABILITIES: Swift Swim, Oblivious
WEAKNESSES: Grass, Electric

 FEEBAS → MILOTIC

FENNEKIN

Fox Pokémon

#0653

TYPE: FIRE

Eating a twig fills it with energy, and its roomy ears give vent to air hotter than 390 degrees Fahrenheit.

As it walks, it munches on a twig in place of a snack. It intimidates opponents by puffing hot air out of its ears.

HOW TO SAY IT: FEN-ik-in
IMPERIAL HEIGHT: 1'04"
IMPERIAL WEIGHT: 20.7 lbs.
METRIC HEIGHT: 0.4 m
METRIC WEIGHT: 9.4 kg
GENDER: ♂ ♀
ABILITIES: Blaze
WEAKNESSES: Water, Ground, Rock

FENNEKIN   BRAIXEN   DELPHOX

FERALIGATR

Big Jaw Pokémon

#0160

TYPE: WATER

Feraligatr intimidates its foes by opening its huge mouth. In battle, it will kick the ground hard with its thick and powerful hind legs to charge at the foe at an incredible speed.

HOW TO SAY IT: fer-AL-ee-gay-tur
IMPERIAL HEIGHT: 7'07"
IMPERIAL WEIGHT: 195.8 lbs.
METRIC HEIGHT: 2.3 m
METRIC WEIGHT: 88.8 kg
GENDER: ♂ ♀
ABILITIES: Torrent
WEAKNESSES: Grass, Electric

TOTODILE   CROCONAW   FERALIGATR

#0597 FERROSEED
Thorn Seed Pokémon

TYPE: GRASS-STEEL

It defends itself by launching spikes, but its aim isn't very good at first. Only after a lot of practice will it improve.

Mossy caves are their preferred dwellings. Enzymes contained in mosses help Ferroseed's spikes grow big and strong.

HOW TO SAY IT: fer-AH-seed
IMPERIAL HEIGHT: 2'00"
IMPERIAL WEIGHT: 41.4 lbs.
METRIC HEIGHT: 0.6 m
METRIC WEIGHT: 18.8 kg
GENDER: ♂ ♀
ABILITIES: Iron Barbs
WEAKNESSES: Fire, Fighting

FERROSEED → FERROTHORN

TYPE: GRASS-STEEL

This Pokémon scrapes its spikes across rocks, and then uses the tips of its feelers to absorb the nutrients it finds within the stone.

Its spikes are harder than steel. This Pokémon crawls across rock walls by stabbing the spikes on its feelers into the stone.

HOW TO SAY IT: fer-AH-thorn
IMPERIAL HEIGHT: 3'03"
IMPERIAL WEIGHT: 242.5 lbs.
METRIC HEIGHT: 1.0 m
METRIC WEIGHT: 110.0 kg
GENDER: ♂ ♀
ABILITIES: Iron Barbs
WEAKNESSES: Fire, Fighting

#0598 FERROTHORN
Thorn Pod Pokémon

FERROSEED → FERROTHORN

FIDOUGH
Puppy Pokémon
#0926

TYPE: FAIRY

This Pokémon is smooth and moist to the touch. Yeast in Fidough's breath induces fermentation in the Pokémon's vicinity.

The yeast in Fidough's breath is useful for cooking, so this Pokémon has been protected by people since long ago.

HOW TO SAY IT: FEYE-doh
IMPERIAL HEIGHT: 1'00"
IMPERIAL WEIGHT: 24.0 lbs.
METRIC HEIGHT: 0.3 m
METRIC WEIGHT: 10.9 kg
GENDER: ♂ ♀
ABILITIES: Own Tempo
WEAKNESSES: Steel, Poison

FIDOUGH　　**DACHSBUN**

FINIZEN
Dolphin Pokémon
#0963

TYPE: WATER

It likes playing with others of its kind using the water ring on its tail. It uses ultrasonic waves to sense the emotions of other living creatures.

Its water ring is made from seawater mixed with a sticky fluid that Finizen secretes from its blowhole.

HOW TO SAY IT: FIN-uh-zin
IMPERIAL HEIGHT: 4'03"
IMPERIAL WEIGHT: 132.7 lbs.
METRIC HEIGHT: 1.3 m
METRIC WEIGHT: 60.2 kg
GENDER: ♂ ♀
ABILITIES: Water Veil
WEAKNESSES: Grass, Electric

FINIZEN　　**PALAFIN**

#0456 FINNEON
Wing Fish Pokémon

TYPE: WATER

The line running down its side can store sunlight. It shines vividly at night.

It absorbs sunlight with the pink areas of its skin, which then shine. This appears to be a form of camouflage.

HOW TO SAY IT: FINN-ee-on
IMPERIAL HEIGHT: 1'04"   **METRIC HEIGHT:** 0.4 m
IMPERIAL WEIGHT: 15.4 lbs.   **METRIC WEIGHT:** 7.0 kg
GENDER: ♂ ♀
ABILITIES: Swift Swim, Storm Drain
WEAKNESSES: Grass, Electric

FINNEON ➡ **LUMINEON**

#0180 FLAAFFY
Wool Pokémon

TYPE: ELECTRIC

As a result of storing too much electricity, it developed patches where even downy wool won't grow.

Because of its rubbery, electricity-resistant skin, it can store lots of electricity in its fur.

HOW TO SAY IT: FLAH-fee
IMPERIAL HEIGHT: 2'07"
IMPERIAL WEIGHT: 29.3 lbs.
METRIC HEIGHT: 0.8 m
METRIC WEIGHT: 13.3 kg
GENDER: ♂ ♀
ABILITIES: Static
WEAKNESSES: Ground

MAREEP ➡ **FLAAFFY** ➡ **AMPHAROS** ➡ **MEGA AMPHAROS**

FLABÉBÉ

#0669

Single Bloom Pokémon

TYPE: FAIRY

This Pokémon can draw forth the power hidden within blooming wildflowers. It is particularly fond of red flowers.

This Flabébé rides a red flower. Immediately after birth, this Pokémon begins flying around in search of a flower it likes.

HOW TO SAY IT: flah-BAY-BAY
IMPERIAL HEIGHT: 0'04"
IMPERIAL WEIGHT: 0.2 lbs.
METRIC HEIGHT: 0.1 m
METRIC WEIGHT: 0.1 kg
GENDER: ♀
ABILITIES: Flower Veil
WEAKNESSES: Steel, Poison

FLABÉBÉ   FLOETTE   FLORGES

FLAMIGO

#0973

Synchronize Pokémon

TYPE: FLYING-FIGHTING

This Pokémon apparently ties the base of its neck into a knot so that energy stored in its belly does not escape from its beak.

Thanks to a behavior of theirs known as "synchronizing," an entire flock of these Pokémon can attack simultaneously in perfect harmony.

HOW TO SAY IT: fluh-MEE-goh
IMPERIAL HEIGHT: 5'03"
IMPERIAL WEIGHT: 81.6 lbs.
METRIC HEIGHT: 1.6 m
METRIC WEIGHT: 37.0 kg
GENDER: ♂ ♀
ABILITIES: Scrappy, Tangled Feet
WEAKNESSES: Psychic, Flying, Fairy, Electric, Ice

DOES NOT EVOLVE

FLAPPLE

Apple Wing Pokémon

TYPE: GRASS-DRAGON

It flutters around while seeking an opening in the opponent's guard, then attacks by spitting acidic liquid strong enough to melt metal.

It uses its own body fluid to repair its apple. Strong Flapple that have won many battles have apples that are clay colored all over.

HOW TO SAY IT: FLAP-puhl
IMPERIAL WEIGHT: 2.2 lbs.
IMPERIAL HEIGHT: 1'00"
METRIC HEIGHT: 0.3 m
METRIC WEIGHT: 1.0 kg
GENDER: ♂ ♀
ABILITIES: Ripen, Gluttony
WEAKNESSES: Flying, Ice, Dragon, Poison, Fairy, Bug

APPLIN → FLAPPLE

GIGANTAMAX FLAPPLE

Under the influence of Gigantamax energy, it produces much more sweet nectar, and its shape has changed to resemble a giant apple.

If it stretches its neck, the strong aroma of its nectar pours out. The scent is so sickeningly sweet that one whiff makes other Pokémon faint.

IMPERIAL HEIGHT: 78'09"+
IMPERIAL WEIGHT: ????.? lbs.
METRIC HEIGHT: 24.0+ m
METRIC WEIGHT: ???.? kg

FLAREON
Flame Pokémon
#0136

TYPE: FIRE

Inhaled air is carried to its flame sac, heated, and exhaled as fire that reaches over 3,000 degrees Fahrenheit.

It fluffs out its fur collar to cool down its body temperature, which can reach 1,650 degrees Fahrenheit.

HOW TO SAY IT: FLAIR-ee-on
IMPERIAL HEIGHT: 2'11"
IMPERIAL WEIGHT: 55.1 lbs.
METRIC HEIGHT: 0.9 m
METRIC WEIGHT: 25.0 kg
GENDER: ♂♀
ABILITIES: Flash Fire
WEAKNESSES: Water, Ground, Rock

EEVEE ➡ FLAREON

#0662
FLETCHINDER
Ember Pokémon

TYPE: FIRE-FLYING

Fletchinder scatters embers in tall grass where bug Pokémon might be hiding and then catches them as they come leaping out.

Its territory has a radius of just over a mile. If any bird Pokémon should enter, it will show them no mercy.

HOW TO SAY IT: FLETCH-in-der
IMPERIAL HEIGHT: 2'04"
IMPERIAL WEIGHT: 35.3 lbs.
METRIC HEIGHT: 0.7 m
METRIC WEIGHT: 16.0 kg
GENDER: ♂♀
ABILITIES: Flame Body
WEAKNESSES: Water, Electric, Rock

FLETCHLING   FLETCHINDER   TALONFLAME

FLETCHLING

Tiny Robin Pokémon

TYPE: NORMAL-FLYING

This Pokémon is normally calm, but once it enters battle, its hormonal balance changes and it becomes aggressive.

Fletchling can be found in both rural and urban areas. They once had a huge territorial dispute with Squawkabilly. Fights broke out all over town.

HOW TO SAY IT: FLETCH-ling
IMPERIAL HEIGHT: 1'00" **METRIC HEIGHT:** 0.3 m
IMPERIAL WEIGHT: 3.7 lbs. **METRIC WEIGHT:** 1.7 kg
GENDER: ♂ ♀
ABILITIES: Big Pecks
WEAKNESSES: Electric, Ice, Rock

FLETCHLING   **FLETCHINDER**   **TALONFLAME**

FLITTLE

Frill Pokémon

TYPE: PSYCHIC

Flittle's toes levitate about half an inch above the ground because of the psychic power emitted from the frills on the Pokémon's belly.

It spends its time running around wastelands. If anyone steals its beloved berries, it will chase them down and exact its revenge.

HOW TO SAY IT: FLIT-ull
IMPERIAL HEIGHT: 0'08"
IMPERIAL WEIGHT: 3.3 lbs.
METRIC HEIGHT: 0.2 m
METRIC WEIGHT: 1.5 kg
GENDER: ♂ ♀
ABILITIES: Anticipation, Frisk
WEAKNESSES: Ghost, Dark, Bug

FLITTLE   **ESPATHRA**

FLOATZEL

Sea Weasel Pokémon

#0419

TYPE: WATER

With its flotation sac inflated, it can carry people on its back. It deflates the sac before it dives.

It is a common sight around fishing ports. It is known to rescue people and help fishers carry what they caught.

HOW TO SAY IT: FLOAT-zul
IMPERIAL HEIGHT: 3'07"
IMPERIAL WEIGHT: 73.9 lbs.
METRIC HEIGHT: 1.1 m
METRIC WEIGHT: 33.5 kg
GENDER: ♂ ♀
ABILITIES: Swift Swim
WEAKNESSES: Grass, Electric

BUIZEL   **FLOATZEL**

#0670

FLOETTE

Single Bloom Pokémon

TYPE: FAIRY

This Pokémon draws forth what power is left in withered flowers to make them healthy again. It holds a red flower.

This Pokémon uses red wavelengths of light to pour its own energy into flowers and draw forth their latent potential.

HOW TO SAY IT: floh-ET
IMPERIAL HEIGHT: 0'08"
IMPERIAL WEIGHT: 2.0 lbs.
METRIC HEIGHT: 0.2 m
METRIC WEIGHT: 0.9 kg
GENDER: ♀
ABILITIES: Flower Veil
WEAKNESSES: Steel, Poison

FLABÉBÉ   **FLOETTE**   **FLORGES**

#0907

FLORAGATO
Grass Cat Pokémon

TYPE: GRASS

Floragato deftly wields the vine hidden beneath its long fur, slamming the hard flower bud against its opponents.

The hardness of Floragato's fur depends on the Pokémon's mood. When Floragato is prepared to battle, its fur becomes pointed and needle sharp.

HOW TO SAY IT: FLOR-uh-GAH-toh
IMPERIAL HEIGHT: 2'11"
IMPERIAL WEIGHT: 26.9 lbs.
METRIC HEIGHT: 0.9 m
METRIC WEIGHT: 12.2 kg
GENDER: ♂ ♀
ABILITIES: Overgrow
WEAKNESSES: Fire, Flying, Ice, Poison, Bug

SPRIGATITO FLORAGATO MEOWSCARADA

#0671

FLORGES
Garden Pokémon

TYPE: FAIRY

This Pokémon creates an impressive flower garden in its territory. It draws forth the power of the red flowers around its neck.

They say that flower gardens created by Florges are constantly showered with a power that can heal both body and spirit.

HOW TO SAY IT: FLORE-jess
IMPERIAL HEIGHT: 3'07"
IMPERIAL WEIGHT: 22.0 lbs.
METRIC HEIGHT: 1.1 m
METRIC WEIGHT: 10.0 kg
GENDER: ♀
ABILITIES: Flower Veil
WEAKNESSES: Steel, Poison

FLABÉBÉ   FLOETTE   FLORGES

FLUTTER MANE

Paradox Pokémon

#0987

TYPE: GHOST-FAIRY

This Pokémon has characteristics similar to those of Flutter Mane, a creature mentioned in a certain book.

It has similar features to a ghostly pterosaur that was covered in a paranormal magazine, but the two have little else in common.

HOW TO SAY IT: FLUH-ter mane
IMPERIAL HEIGHT: 4'07"
IMPERIAL WEIGHT: 8.8 lbs.
METRIC HEIGHT: 1.4 m
METRIC WEIGHT: 4.0 kg
GENDER: Unknown
ABILITIES: Protosynthesis
WEAKNESSES: Ghost, Steel

DOES NOT EVOLVE

FLYGON

Mystic Pokémon

#0330

TYPE: GROUND-DRAGON

This Pokémon hides in the heart of sandstorms it creates and seldom appears where people can see it.

It is nicknamed the Desert Spirit because the flapping of its wings sounds like a woman singing.

HOW TO SAY IT: FLY-gon
IMPERIAL HEIGHT: 6'07"
IMPERIAL WEIGHT: 180.8 lbs.
METRIC HEIGHT: 2.0 m
METRIC WEIGHT: 82.0 kg
GENDER: ♂ ♀
ABILITIES: Levitate
WEAKNESSES: Fairy, Ice, Dragon

 TRAPINCH VIBRAVA FLYGON

FOMANTIS

Sickle Grass Pokémon

#0753

TYPE: GRASS

Fomantis hates having its naps interrupted. It fires off beams using energy it gathers by bathing in the sun.

Many Trainers give their Fomantis their own flowerpots so they can sunbathe in peace and quiet.

HOW TO SAY IT: fo-MAN-tis
IMPERIAL HEIGHT: 1'00"
IMPERIAL WEIGHT: 3.3 lbs.
METRIC HEIGHT: 0.3 m
METRIC WEIGHT: 1.5 kg
GENDER: ♂ ♀
ABILITIES: Leaf Guard
WEAKNESSES: Fire, Flying, Ice, Poison, Bug

FOMANTIS   LURANTIS

#0590

FOONGUS

Mushroom Pokémon

TYPE: GRASS-POISON

There is a theory that the developer of the modern-day Poké Ball really liked Foongus, but this has not been confirmed.

This Pokémon prefers damp places. It spurts out poison spores to repel approaching enemies.

HOW TO SAY IT: FOON-gus
IMPERIAL HEIGHT: 0'08"
IMPERIAL WEIGHT: 2.2 lbs.
METRIC HEIGHT: 0.2 m
METRIC WEIGHT: 1.0 kg
GENDER: ♂ ♀
ABILITIES: Effect Spore
WEAKNESSES: Fire, Psychic, Flying, Ice

FOONGUS   AMOONGUSS

FORRETRESS

#0205

Bagworm Pokémon

TYPE: BUG-STEEL

It's usually found hanging on to a fat tree trunk. It shoots out bits of its shell when it sees action.

Its entire body is shielded by a steel-hard shell. What lurks inside this shell is a total mystery.

HOW TO SAY IT: FOR-it-tress
IMPERIAL HEIGHT: 3'11"
IMPERIAL WEIGHT: 277.3 lbs.
METRIC HEIGHT: 1.2 m
METRIC WEIGHT: 125.8 kg
GENDER: ♂ ♀
ABILITIES: Sturdy
WEAKNESSES: Fire

PINECO   FORRETRESS

FRAXURE

#0611

Axe Jaw Pokémon

TYPE: DRAGON

Because its tusks don't grow back once they break, this Pokémon apparently won't use them unless truly necessary.

Fraxure uses its thick tusks to neatly cut prey into two portions—one to eat now and one to save for later.

HOW TO SAY IT: FRAK-shur
IMPERIAL HEIGHT: 3'03"
IMPERIAL WEIGHT: 79.4 lbs.
METRIC HEIGHT: 1.0 m
METRIC WEIGHT: 36.0 kg
GENDER: ♂ ♀
ABILITIES: Rivalry, Mold Breaker
WEAKNESSES: Fairy, Ice, Dragon

AXEW

FRAXURE

HAXORUS

#0996 FRIGIBAX
Ice Fin Pokémon

TYPE: DRAGON-ICE

Frigibax absorbs heat through its dorsal fin and converts the heat into ice energy. The higher the temperature, the more energy Frigibax stores.

This Pokémon lives in forests and craggy areas. Using the power of its dorsal fin, it cools the inside of its nest like a refrigerator.

HOW TO SAY IT: FRI-juh-baks
IMPERIAL HEIGHT: 1'08"
IMPERIAL WEIGHT: 37.5 lbs.
METRIC HEIGHT: 0.5 m
METRIC WEIGHT: 17.0 kg
GENDER: ♂ ♀
ABILITIES: Thermal Exchange
WEAKNESSES: Steel, Fairy, Rock, Fighting, Dragon

FRIGIBAX **ARCTIBAX** **BAXCALIBUR**

FRILLISH #0592
Floating Pokémon

TYPE: WATER-GHOST

It envelops its prey in its veil-like arms and draws it down to the deeps, five miles below the ocean's surface.

Legend has it that the residents of a sunken ancient city changed into these Pokémon.

HOW TO SAY IT: FRIL-lish
IMPERIAL HEIGHT: 3'11"
IMPERIAL WEIGHT: 72.8 lbs.
METRIC HEIGHT: 1.2 m
METRIC WEIGHT: 33.0 kg
GENDER: ♂ ♀
ABILITIES: Water Absorb, Cursed Body
WEAKNESSES: Ghost, Dark, Grass, Electric

MALE FORM

FEMALE FORM

FRILLISH **JELLICENT**

195

FROAKIE

Bubble Frog Pokémon

#0656

TYPE: WATER

It secretes flexible bubbles from its chest and back. The bubbles reduce the damage it would otherwise take when attacked.

It protects its skin by covering its body in delicate bubbles. Beneath its happy-go-lucky air, it keeps a watchful eye on its surroundings.

HOW TO SAY IT: FRO-kee
IMPERIAL HEIGHT: 1'00"
IMPERIAL WEIGHT: 15.4 lbs.
METRIC HEIGHT: 0.3 m
METRIC WEIGHT: 7.0 kg
GENDER: ♂ ♀
ABILITIES: Torrent
WEAKNESSES: Grass, Electric

FROAKIE   FROGADIER   GRENINJA

FROGADIER

Bubble Frog Pokémon

#0657

TYPE: WATER

It can throw bubble-covered pebbles with precise control, hitting empty cans up to 100 feet away.

Its swiftness is unparalleled. It can scale a tower of more than 2,000 feet in a minute's time.

HOW TO SAY IT: FROG-uh-deer
IMPERIAL HEIGHT: 2'00"
IMPERIAL WEIGHT: 24.0 lbs.
METRIC HEIGHT: 0.6 m
METRIC WEIGHT: 10.9 kg
GENDER: ♂ ♀
ABILITIES: Torrent
WEAKNESSES: Grass, Electric

FROAKIE   FROGADIER   GRENINJA

FROSLASS

#0478

Snow Land Pokémon

TYPE: ICE-GHOST

When it finds humans or Pokémon it likes, it freezes them and takes them to its chilly den, where they become decorations.

It freezes prey by blowing its −58 degree Fahrenheit breath. It is said to then secretly display its prey.

HOW TO SAY IT: FROS-lass
IMPERIAL HEIGHT: 4'03"
IMPERIAL WEIGHT: 58.6 lbs.
METRIC HEIGHT: 1.3 m
METRIC WEIGHT: 26.6 kg
GENDER: ♀
ABILITIES: Snow Cloak
WEAKNESSES: Steel, Ghost, Fire, Dark, Rock

SNORUNT   FROSLASS

FROSMOTH

#0873

Frost Moth Pokémon

TYPE: ICE-BUG

Frosmoth senses air currents with its antennae. It sends its scales drifting on frigid air, making them fall like snow.

It causes blizzards as it flies around with its huge, chill-emanating wings. Clean meltwater is its favorite thing to drink.

HOW TO SAY IT: FRAHS-mahth
IMPERIAL HEIGHT: 4'03"
IMPERIAL WEIGHT: 92.6 lbs.
METRIC HEIGHT: 1.3 m
METRIC WEIGHT: 42.0 kg
GENDER: ♂ ♀
ABILITIES: Shield Dust
WEAKNESSES: Fire, Steel, Flying, Rock

SNOM   FROSMOTH

FUECOCO #0909

Fire Croc Pokémon

TYPE: FIRE

It lies on warm rocks and uses the heat absorbed by its square-shaped scales to create fire energy.

Its flame sac is small, so energy is always leaking out. This energy is released from the dent atop Fuecoco's head and flickers to and fro.

HOW TO SAY IT: fwey-KO-ko
IMPERIAL HEIGHT: 1'04"
IMPERIAL WEIGHT: 21.6 lbs.
METRIC HEIGHT: 0.4 m
METRIC WEIGHT: 9.8 kg
GENDER: ♂ ♀
ABILITIES: Blaze
WEAKNESSES: Water, Ground, Rock

FUECOCO **CROCALOR** **SKELEDIRGE**

FURFROU #0676

Poodle Pokémon

NATURAL FORM

TYPE: NORMAL

There was an era when aristocrats would compete to see who could trim their Furfrou's fur into the most exquisite style.

Left alone, its fur will grow longer and longer, but it will only allow someone it trusts to cut it.

HOW TO SAY IT: FUR-froo
IMPERIAL HEIGHT: 3'11"
IMPERIAL WEIGHT: 61.7 lbs.
METRIC HEIGHT: 1.2 m
METRIC WEIGHT: 28.0 kg
GENDER: ♂ ♀
ABILITIES: Fur Coat
WEAKNESSES: Fighting

HEART TRIM

STAR TRIM

DIAMOND TRIM

DOES NOT EVOLVE

#0162 FURRET
Long Body Pokémon

TYPE: NORMAL

Furret has a very slim build. When under attack, it can slickly squirm through narrow spaces and get away. In spite of its short limbs, this Pokémon is very nimble and fleet.

HOW TO SAY IT: FUR-ret
IMPERIAL HEIGHT: 5'11"
IMPERIAL WEIGHT: 71.7 lbs.
METRIC HEIGHT: 1.8 m
METRIC WEIGHT: 32.5 kg
GENDER: ♂ ♀
ABILITIES: Run Away, Keen Eye
WEAKNESSES: Fighting

SENTRET ➡ **FURRET**

#0444 GABITE
Cave Pokémon

TYPE: DRAGON-GROUND

In rare cases, it molts and sheds its scales. Medicine containing its scales as an ingredient will make a weary body feel invigorated.

It loves sparkly things. It seeks treasures in caves and hoards the loot in its nest.

HOW TO SAY IT: gab-BITE
IMPERIAL HEIGHT: 4'07"
IMPERIAL WEIGHT: 123.5 lbs.
METRIC HEIGHT: 1.4 m
METRIC WEIGHT: 56.0 kg
GENDER: ♂ ♀
ABILITIES: Sand Veil
WEAKNESSES: Fairy, Ice, Dragon

GIBLE   **GABITE**   **GARCHOMP**   **MEGA GARCHOMP**

GALLADE
Blade Pokémon

TYPE: PSYCHIC-FIGHTING

When trying to protect someone, it extends its elbows as if they were swords and fights savagely.

Because it can sense what its foe is thinking, its attacks burst out first, fast, and fierce.

HOW TO SAY IT: guh-LADE
IMPERIAL HEIGHT: 5'03"
IMPERIAL WEIGHT: 114.6 lbs.
METRIC HEIGHT: 1.6 m
METRIC WEIGHT: 52.0 kg
GENDER: ♂
ABILITIES: Steadfast, Sharpness
WEAKNESSES: Ghost, Fairy, Flying

MEGA GALLADE

TYPE: PSYCHIC-FIGHTING

Because it can sense what its foe is thinking, its attacks burst out first, fast, and fierce.

A master of courtesy and swordsmanship, it fights using extending swords on its elbows.

IMPERIAL HEIGHT: 5'03"
IMPERIAL WEIGHT: 124.3 lbs.
METRIC HEIGHT: 1.6 m
METRIC WEIGHT: 56.4 kg

RALTS   KIRLIA   GALLADE   MEGA GALLADE

GALVANTULA

EleSpider Pokémon

TYPE: BUG-ELECTRIC

It launches electrified fur from its abdomen as its means of attack. Opponents hit by the fur could be in for three full days and nights of paralysis.

It lays traps of electrified threads near the nests of bird Pokémon, aiming to snare chicks that are not yet good at flying.

HOW TO SAY IT: gal-VAN-choo-luh
IMPERIAL HEIGHT: 2'07"
IMPERIAL WEIGHT: 31.5 lbs.
METRIC HEIGHT: 0.8 m
METRIC WEIGHT: 14.3 kg
GENDER: ♂ ♀
ABILITIES: Compound Eyes, Unnerve
WEAKNESSES: Fire, Rock

JOLTIK

GALVANTULA

GARBODOR

Trash Heap Pokémon

#0569

TYPE: POISON

This Pokémon eats trash, which turns into poison inside its body. The main component of the poison depends on what sort of trash was eaten.

The toxic liquid it launches from its right arm is so virulent that it can kill a weakened creature instantly.

HOW TO SAY IT: gar-BOH-dur
IMPERIAL HEIGHT: 6'03"
IMPERIAL WEIGHT: 236.6 lbs.
METRIC HEIGHT: 1.9 m
METRIC WEIGHT: 107.3 kg
GENDER: ♂ ♀
ABILITIES: Stench, Weak Armor
WEAKNESSES: Psychic, Ground

TRUBBISH   GARBODOR

GIGANTAMAX GARBODOR

Due to Gigantamax energy, this Pokémon's toxic gas has become much thicker, congealing into masses shaped like discarded toys.

It sprays toxic gas from its mouth and fingers. If the gas engulfs you, the toxins will seep in all the way down to your bones.

IMPERIAL HEIGHT: 68'11"+
IMPERIAL WEIGHT: ????.? lbs.
METRIC HEIGHT: 21.0+ m
METRIC WEIGHT: ???.? kg

GARCHOMP

Mach Pokémon

TYPE: DRAGON-GROUND

It is said that when one runs at high speed, its wings create blades of wind that can fell nearby trees.

The protuberances on its head serve as sensors. It can even detect distant prey.

HOW TO SAY IT: GAR-chomp
IMPERIAL HEIGHT: 6'03"
IMPERIAL WEIGHT: 209.4 lbs.
METRIC HEIGHT: 1.9 m
METRIC WEIGHT: 95.0 kg
GENDER: ♂ ♀
ABILITIES: Sand Veil
WEAKNESSES: Fairy, Ice, Dragon

MEGA GARCHOMP

TYPE: DRAGON-GROUND

Its arms and wings melted into something like scythes. Mad with rage, it rampages on and on.

Its disposition is more vicious than before its Mega Evolution. Garchomp carves its opponents up with the scythes on both arms.

IMPERIAL HEIGHT: 6'03"
IMPERIAL WEIGHT: 209.4 lbs.
METRIC HEIGHT: 1.9 m
METRIC WEIGHT: 95.0 kg

GIBLE   GABITE   GARCHOMP   MEGA GARCHOMP

TYPE: PSYCHIC-FAIRY

To protect its Trainer, it will expend all its psychic power to create a small black hole.

It unleashes psychokinetic energy at full power when protecting a Trainer it has bonded closely with.

HOW TO SAY IT: GAR-dee-VWAR
IMPERIAL HEIGHT: 5'03"
IMPERIAL WEIGHT: 106.7 lbs.
METRIC HEIGHT: 1.6 m
METRIC WEIGHT: 48.4 kg
GENDER: ♂ ♀
ABILITIES: Synchronize, Trace
WEAKNESSES: Ghost, Steel, Poison

#0282 GARDEVOIR
Embrace Pokémon

MEGA GARDEVOIR

TYPE: PSYCHIC-FAIRY

Gardevoir has the ability to read the future. If it senses impending danger to its Trainer, this Pokémon is said to unleash its psychokinetic energy at full power.

Gardevoir has the psychokinetic power to distort the dimensions and create a small black hole. This Pokémon will try to protect its Trainer even at the risk of its own life.

IMPERIAL HEIGHT: 5'03"
IMPERIAL WEIGHT: 106.7 lbs.
METRIC HEIGHT: 1.6 m
METRIC WEIGHT: 48.4 kg

RALTS KIRLIA GARDEVOIR MEGA GARDEVOIR

GARGANACL
Rock Salt Pokémon

TYPE: ROCK

Garganacl will rub its fingertips together and sprinkle injured Pokémon with salt. Even severe wounds will promptly heal afterward.

Many Pokémon gather around Garganacl, hoping to lick at its mineral-rich salt.

HOW TO SAY IT: GAHR-gah-NAK-ull
IMPERIAL HEIGHT: 7'07"
IMPERIAL WEIGHT: 529.1 lbs.
METRIC HEIGHT: 2.3 m
METRIC WEIGHT: 240.0 kg
GENDER: ♂ ♀
ABILITIES: Purifying Salt, Sturdy
WEAKNESSES: Water, Steel, Grass, Fighting, Ground

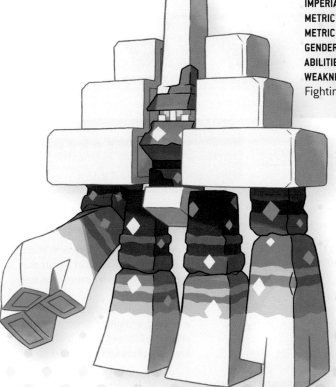

NACLI

NACLSTACK

GARGANACL

GASTLY
Gas Pokémon
#0092

TYPE: GHOST-POISON

It wraps its opponent in its gas-like body, slowly weakening its prey by poisoning it through the skin.

Its body is made of gas. Despite lacking substance, it can envelop an opponent of any size and cause suffocation.

HOW TO SAY IT: GAST-lee
IMPERIAL HEIGHT: 4'03"
IMPERIAL WEIGHT: 0.2 lbs.
METRIC HEIGHT: 1.3 m
METRIC WEIGHT: 0.1 kg
GENDER: ♂ ♀
ABILITIES: Levitate
WEAKNESSES: Ghost, Dark, Psychic, Ground

| GASTLY | HAUNTER | GENGAR | MEGA GENGAR |

#0423
GASTRODON
Sea Slug Pokémon

WEST SEA

EAST SEA

TYPE: WATER-GROUND

Its whole body is sticky with mucus. In the past, this form of Gastrodon was by far the more numerous one.

It appears on beaches where the waters are shallow. Once it catches prey, it will slowly melt them with its mucus before slurping them up.

HOW TO SAY IT: GAS-stroh-don
IMPERIAL HEIGHT: 2'11"
IMPERIAL WEIGHT: 65.9 lbs.
METRIC HEIGHT: 0.9 m
METRIC WEIGHT: 29.9 kg
GENDER: ♂ ♀
ABILITIES: Sticky Hold, Storm Drain
WEAKNESSES: Grass

SHELLOS   GASTRODON

GENESECT
Paleozoic Pokémon

TYPE: BUG-STEEL

This ancient bug Pokémon was altered by Team Plasma. They upgraded the cannon on its back.

This Pokémon existed 300 million years ago. Team Plasma altered it and attached a cannon to its back.

HOW TO SAY IT: JEN-uh-sekt
IMPERIAL HEIGHT: 4'11"
IMPERIAL WEIGHT: 181.9 lbs.
METRIC HEIGHT: 1.5 m
METRIC WEIGHT: 82.5 kg
GENDER: Unknown
ABILITIES: Download
WEAKNESSES: Fire

DOES NOT EVOLVE

GENGAR

Shadow Pokémon

#0094

TYPE: GHOST-POISON

To steal the life of its target, it slips into the prey's shadow and silently waits for an opportunity.

Hiding in people's shadows at night, it absorbs their heat. The chill it causes makes the victims shake.

HOW TO SAY IT: GHEN-gar
IMPERIAL HEIGHT: 4'11"
IMPERIAL WEIGHT: 89.3 lbs.
METRIC HEIGHT: 1.5 m
METRIC WEIGHT: 40.5 kg
GENDER: ♂ ♀
ABILITIES: Cursed Body
WEAKNESSES: Ghost, Dark, Psychic, Ground

MEGA GENGAR

TYPE: GHOST-POISON

It can pass through other dimensions and appear anywhere. It caused a stir one time when it stuck just one leg out of a wall.

IMPERIAL HEIGHT: 4'07"
IMPERIAL WEIGHT: 89.3 lbs.
METRIC HEIGHT: 1.4 m
METRIC WEIGHT: 40.5 kg

GASTLY

HAUNTER

GENGAR

MEGA GENGAR

GIGANTAMAX GENGAR

Rumor has it that its gigantic mouth leads not into its body, filled with cursed energy, but instead directly to the afterlife.

It lays traps, hoping to steal the lives of those it catches. If you stand in front of its mouth, you'll hear your loved ones' voices calling out to you.

IMPERIAL HEIGHT: 65'07"+
IMPERIAL WEIGHT: ????.? lbs.
METRIC HEIGHT: 20.0 m+
METRIC WEIGHT: ???.? kg

GEODUDE
Rock Pokémon

#0074

TYPE: ROCK-GROUND

Commonly found near mountain trails and the like. If you step on one by accident, it gets angry.

HOW TO SAY IT: JEE-oh-dude
IMPERIAL HEIGHT: 1'04"
IMPERIAL WEIGHT: 44.1 lbs.
METRIC HEIGHT: 0.4 m
METRIC WEIGHT: 20.0 kg
GENDER: ♂ ♀
ABILITIES: Rock Head, Sturdy
WEAKNESSES: Steel, Fighting, Water, Ice, Grass, Ground

GEODUDE   GRAVELER   GOLEM

ALOLAN GEODUDE
Rock Pokémon

#0074

TYPE: ROCK-ELECTRIC

Its stone head is imbued with electricity and magnetism. If you carelessly step on one, you'll be in for a painful shock.

HOW TO SAY IT: JEE-oh-dude
IMPERIAL HEIGHT: 1'04"
IMPERIAL WEIGHT: 44.8 lbs.
METRIC HEIGHT: 0.4 m
METRIC WEIGHT: 20.3 kg
GENDER: ♂ ♀
ABILITIES: Magnet Pull, Sturdy
WEAKNESSES: Water, Grass, Fighting, Ground

ALOLAN GEODUDE   ALOLAN GRAVELER   ALOLAN GOLEM

GHOLDENGO
Coin Entity Pokémon

TYPE: STEEL-GHOST

Its body seems to be made up of 1,000 coins. This Pokémon gets along well with others and is quick to make friends with anybody.

It has a sturdy body made up of stacked coins. Gholdengo overwhelms its enemies by firing coin after coin at them in quick succession.

HOW TO SAY IT: GOHL-den-goh
IMPERIAL HEIGHT: 3'11"
IMPERIAL WEIGHT: 66.1 lbs.
METRIC HEIGHT: 1.2 m
METRIC WEIGHT: 30.0 kg
GENDER: Unknown
ABILITIES: Good as Gold
WEAKNESSES: Fire, Ghost, Dark, Ground

GIMMIGHOUL   GHOLDENGO

TYPE: DRAGON-GROUND

GIBLE
Land Shark Pokémon

#0443

It skulks in caves, and when prey or an enemy passes by, it leaps out and chomps them. The force of its attack sometimes chips its teeth.

It nests in horizontal holes warmed by geothermal heat. Foes who get too close can expect to be pounced on and bitten.

HOW TO SAY IT: GIB-bull
IMPERIAL HEIGHT: 2'04"
IMPERIAL WEIGHT: 45.2 lbs.
METRIC HEIGHT: 0.7 m
METRIC WEIGHT: 20.5 kg
GENDER: ♂ ♀
ABILITIES: Sand Veil
WEAKNESSES: Fairy, Ice, Dragon

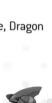   

GIBLE   **GABITE**   **GARCHOMP**   **MEGA GARCHOMP**

TYPE: ROCK

GIGALITH
Compressed Pokémon

#0526

This hardy Pokémon can often be found on construction sites and in mines, working alongside people and Copperajah.

Although its energy blasts can blow away a dump truck, they have a limitation—they can only be fired when the sun is out.

HOW TO SAY IT: GIH-gah-lith
IMPERIAL HEIGHT: 5'07"
IMPERIAL WEIGHT: 573.2 lbs.
METRIC HEIGHT: 1.7 m
METRIC WEIGHT: 260.0 kg
GENDER: ♂ ♀
ABILITIES: Sturdy, Sand Stream
WEAKNESSES: Water, Steel, Grass, Fighting, Ground

ROGGENROLA   **BOLDORE**   **GIGALITH**

GIMMIGHOUL

#0999

Coin Chest Pokémon

TYPE: GHOST

This Pokémon was born inside a treasure chest about 1,500 years ago. It sucks the life force out of scoundrels who try to steal the treasure.

It lives inside an old treasure chest. Sometimes it gets left in shop corners since no one realizes it's actually a Pokémon.

HOW TO SAY IT: GIH-mee-ghoul
IMPERIAL HEIGHT: 1'00"
IMPERIAL WEIGHT: 11.0 lbs.
METRIC HEIGHT: 0.3 m
METRIC WEIGHT: 5.0 kg
GENDER: Unknown
ABILITIES: Rattled
WEAKNESSES: Ghost, Dark

GIMMIGHOUL → **GHOLDENGO**

GIRAFARIG

#0203

Long Neck Pokémon

TYPE: NORMAL-PSYCHIC

Though very small, the brain in its tail is still considered an important organ because it emits powerful psychic energy.

Girafarig's tail has a small head. It instinctively bites at any foe that approaches the Pokémon from behind.

HOW TO SAY IT: jir-RAF-uh-rig
IMPERIAL HEIGHT: 4'11"
IMPERIAL WEIGHT: 91.5 lbs.
METRIC HEIGHT: 1.5 m
METRIC WEIGHT: 41.5 kg
GENDER: ♂ ♀
ABILITIES: Inner Focus, Early Bird
WEAKNESSES: Dark, Bug

GIRAFARIG → **FARIGIRAF**

LEGENDARY POKÉMON

GIRATINA
Renegade Pokémon

TYPE: GHOST-DRAGON

This Pokémon is said to live in a world on the reverse side of ours, where common knowledge is distorted and strange.

It was banished for its violence. It silently gazed upon the old world from the Distortion World.

HOW TO SAY IT: geer-ah-TEE-na
IMPERIAL HEIGHT: 14'09"
IMPERIAL WEIGHT: 1,653.5 lbs.
METRIC HEIGHT: 4.5 m
METRIC WEIGHT: 750.0 kg
GENDER: Unknown
ABILITIES: Pressure
WEAKNESSES: Ghost, Dark, Fairy, Ice, Dragon

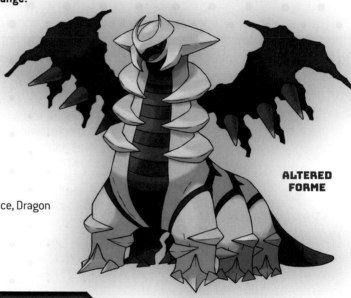

ALTERED FORME

GIRATINA ORIGIN FORME

IMPERIAL HEIGHT: 22'08"
IMPERIAL WEIGHT: 1,433.0 lbs.
METRIC HEIGHT: 6.9 m
METRIC WEIGHT: 650.0 kg

DOES NOT EVOLVE

TYPE: ICE

It can control its body temperature at will. This enables it to freeze the moisture in the atmosphere, creating flurries of diamond dust.

It lowers its body heat to freeze its fur. The hairs then become like needles it can fire.

HOW TO SAY IT: GLASE-ee-on
IMPERIAL HEIGHT: 2'07"
IMPERIAL WEIGHT: 57.1 lbs.
METRIC HEIGHT: 0.8 m
METRIC WEIGHT: 25.9 kg
GENDER: ♂ ♀
ABILITIES: Snow Cloak
WEAKNESSES: Fire, Steel, Fighting, Rock

EEVEE

GLACEON

#0362

GLALIE
Face Pokémon

TYPE: ICE

Its prey is instantaneously frozen stiff by the cold air it exhales from its huge mouth. While they're in that frozen state, it gobbles them up.

It prevents prey from escaping by instantaneously freezing moisture in the air.

HOW TO SAY IT: GLAY-lee
IMPERIAL HEIGHT: 4'11"
IMPERIAL WEIGHT: 565.5 lbs.
METRIC HEIGHT: 1.5 m
METRIC WEIGHT: 256.5 kg
GENDER: ♂ ♀
ABILITIES: Inner Focus, Ice Body
WEAKNESSES: Fire, Steel, Fighting, Rock

MEGA GLALIE

TYPE: ICE

When it spews stupendously cold air from its broken mouth, the entire area around it gets whited out.

The power of Mega Evolution was so strong that it smashed Glalie's jaw. Its inability to eat very well leaves Glalie irritated.

IMPERIAL HEIGHT: 6'11"
IMPERIAL WEIGHT: 772.1 lbs.
METRIC HEIGHT: 2.1 m
METRIC WEIGHT: 350.2 kg

SNORUNT

GLALIE

MEGA GLALIE

GLAMEOW
Catty Pokémon

#0431

TYPE: NORMAL

It claws if displeased and purrs when affectionate. Its fickleness is very popular among some.

When it's happy, Glameow demonstrates beautiful movements of its tail, like a dancing ribbon.

HOW TO SAY IT: GLAM-meow
IMPERIAL HEIGHT: 1'08"
IMPERIAL WEIGHT: 8.6 lbs.
METRIC HEIGHT: 0.5 m
METRIC WEIGHT: 3.9 kg
GENDER: ♂ ♀
ABILITIES: Limber, Own Tempo
WEAKNESSES: FIGHTING

GLAMEOW ➡ PURUGLY

LEGENDARY POKÉMON

#0896

GLASTRIER
Wild Horse Pokémon

TYPE: ICE

Glastrier emits intense cold from its hooves. It's also a belligerent Pokémon—anything it wants, it takes by force.

Glastrier has tremendous physical strength, and the mask of ice covering its face is 100 times harder than diamond.

HOW TO SAY IT: GLASS-treer
IMPERIAL HEIGHT: 7'03"
IMPERIAL WEIGHT: 1,763.7 lbs.
METRIC HEIGHT: 2.2 m
METRIC WEIGHT: 800.0 kg
GENDER: Unknown
ABILITIES: Chilling Neigh
WEAKNESSES: Fire, Steel, Fighting, Rock

DOES NOT EVOLVE

GLIGAR #0207
Fly Scorpion Pokémon

TYPE: GROUND-FLYING

Gligar glides through the air without a sound as if it were sliding. This Pokémon hangs on to the face of its foe using its clawed hind legs and the large pincers on its forelegs, then injects the prey with its poison barb.

HOW TO SAY IT: GLY-gar
IMPERIAL HEIGHT: 3'07"
IMPERIAL WEIGHT: 142.9 lbs.
METRIC HEIGHT: 1.1 m
METRIC WEIGHT: 64.8 kg
GENDER: ♂ ♀
ABILITIES: Hyper Cutter, Sand Veil
WEAKNESSES: Water, Ice

GLIGAR   GLISCOR

GLIMMET #0969
Ore Pokémon

TYPE: ROCK-POISON

It absorbs nutrients from cave walls. The petals it wears are made of crystallized poison.

Glimmet's toxic mineral crystals look just like flower petals. This Pokémon scatters poisonous powder like pollen to protect itself.

HOW TO SAY IT: GLIHM-miht
IMPERIAL HEIGHT: 2'04"
IMPERIAL WEIGHT: 17.6 lbs.
METRIC HEIGHT: 0.7 m
METRIC WEIGHT: 8.0 kg
GENDER: ♂ ♀
ABILITIES: Toxic Debris
WEAKNESSES: Steel, Water, Psychic, Ground

GLIMMET   GLIMMORA

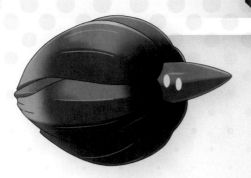

#0970 GLIMMORA
Ore Pokémon

TYPE: ROCK-POISON

When this Pokémon detects danger, it will open up its crystalline petals and fire beams from its conical body.

Glimmora's petals are made of crystallized poison energy. It has recently become evident that these petals resemble Tera Jewels.

HOW TO SAY IT: glihm-MOR-uh
IMPERIAL HEIGHT: 4'11"
IMPERIAL WEIGHT: 99.2 lbs.
METRIC HEIGHT: 1.5 m
METRIC WEIGHT: 45.0 kg
GENDER: ♂ ♀
ABILITIES: Toxic Debris
WEAKNESSES: Steel, Water, Psychic, Ground

GLIMMET → GLIMMORA

#0472 GLISCOR
Fang Scorpion Pokémon

TYPE: GROUND-FLYING

It observes prey while hanging inverted from branches. When the chance presents itself, it swoops!

Its flight is soundless. It uses its lengthy tail to carry off its prey . . . Then its elongated fangs do the rest.

HOW TO SAY IT: GLY-score
IMPERIAL HEIGHT: 6'07"
IMPERIAL WEIGHT: 93.7 lbs.
METRIC HEIGHT: 2.0 m
METRIC WEIGHT: 42.5 kg
GENDER: ♂ ♀
ABILITIES: Hyper Cutter, Sand Veil
WEAKNESSES: Water, Ice

GLIGAR → GLISCOR

TYPE: GRASS-POISON

Its pistils exude an incredibly foul odor. The horrid stench can cause fainting at a distance of 1.25 miles.

What appears to be drool is actually sweet honey. It is very sticky and clings stubbornly if touched.

HOW TO SAY IT: GLOOM
IMPERIAL HEIGHT: 2'07"
IMPERIAL WEIGHT: 19.0 lbs.
METRIC HEIGHT: 0.8 m
METRIC WEIGHT: 8.6 kg
GENDER: ♂ ♀
ABILITIES: Chlorophyll
WEAKNESSES: Fire, Psychic, Flying, Ice

GLOOM
Weed Pokémon

#0044

VILEPLUME

ODDISH → GLOOM

BELLOSSOM

GOGOAT
Mount Pokémon

#0673

TYPE: GRASS

It can sense the feelings of others by touching them with its horns. This species has assisted people with their work since 5,000 years ago.

These Pokémon live in herds in mountainous places. The victor in their contests of clashing horns will become the leader of the herd.

HOW TO SAY IT: GO-goat
IMPERIAL HEIGHT: 5'07"
IMPERIAL WEIGHT: 200.6 lbs.
METRIC HEIGHT: 1.7 m
METRIC WEIGHT: 91.0 kg
GENDER: ♂ ♀
ABILITIES: Sap Sipper
WEAKNESSES: Fire, Flying, Ice, Poison, Bug

SKIDDO   GOGOAT

GOLBAT
Bat Pokémon

#0042

TYPE: POISON-FLYING

It loves to drink other creatures' blood. It's said that if it finds others of its kind going hungry, it sometimes shares the blood it's gathered.

Its feet are tiny, but this Pokémon walks skillfully. It sneaks up on sleeping prey before sinking in its fangs and slurping up blood.

HOW TO SAY IT: GOHL-bat
IMPERIAL HEIGHT: 5'03"
IMPERIAL WEIGHT: 121.3 lbs.
METRIC HEIGHT: 1.6 m
METRIC WEIGHT: 55.0 kg
GENDER: ♂ ♀
ABILITIES: Inner Focus
WEAKNESSES: Psychic, Electric, Ice, Rock

ZUBAT → GOLBAT → CROBAT

TYPE: WATER

Its dorsal, pectoral, and tail fins wave elegantly in water. That is why it is known as the Water Dancer.

Its dorsal and pectoral fins are strongly developed like muscles. It can swim at a speed of five knots.

HOW TO SAY IT: GOL-deen
IMPERIAL HEIGHT: 2'00"
IMPERIAL WEIGHT: 33.1 lbs.
METRIC HEIGHT: 0.6 m
METRIC WEIGHT: 15.0 kg
GENDER: ♂ ♀
ABILITIES: Swift Swim, Water Veil
WEAKNESSES: Grass, Electric

GOLDEEN
Goldfish Pokémon

#0118

GOLDEEN → SEAKING

GOLDUCK

Duck Pokémon

#0555

TYPE: WATER

When it swims at full speed using its long, webbed limbs, its forehead somehow begins to glow.

It swims gracefully along on the quiet, slow-moving rivers and lakes of which it is so fond.

HOW TO SAY IT: GOL-duck
IMPERIAL HEIGHT: 5'07"
IMPERIAL WEIGHT: 168.9 lbs.
METRIC HEIGHT: 1.7 m
METRIC WEIGHT: 76.6 kg
GENDER: ♂ ♀
ABILITIES: Damp, Cloud Nine
WEAKNESSES: Grass, Electric

PSYDUCK

GOLDUCK

GOLEM

Megaton Pokémon

#0076

TYPE: ROCK-GROUND

Once it sheds its skin, its body turns tender and whitish. Its hide hardens when it's exposed to air.

HOW TO SAY IT: GO-lum
IMPERIAL HEIGHT: 4'07"
IMPERIAL WEIGHT: 661.4 lbs.
METRIC HEIGHT: 1.4 m
METRIC WEIGHT: 300.0 kg
GENDER: ♂ ♀
ABILITIES: Rock Head, Sturdy
WEAKNESSES: Steel, Fighting, Water, Ice, Grass, Ground

GEODUDE   GRAVELER   GOLEM

ALOLAN GOLEM

Megaton Pokémon

#0076

TYPE: ROCK-ELECTRIC

It uses magnetism to accelerate and fire off rocks tinged with electricity. Even if it doesn't score a direct hit, the jolt of electricity will do the job.

HOW TO SAY IT: GO-lum
IMPERIAL HEIGHT: 5'07"
IMPERIAL WEIGHT: 696.7 lbs.
METRIC HEIGHT: 1.7 m
METRIC WEIGHT: 316.0 kg
GENDER: ♂ ♀
ABILITIES: Magnet Pull, Sturdy
WEAKNESSES: Water, Grass, Fighting, Ground

ALOLAN
GEODUDE   ALOLAN
GRAVELER   ALOLAN
GOLEM

#0622 GOLETT
Automaton Pokémon

TYPE: GROUND-GHOST

They were sculpted from clay in ancient times. No one knows why, but some of them are driven to continually line up boulders.

This Pokémon was created from clay. It received orders from its master many thousands of years ago, and it still follows those orders to this day.

HOW TO SAY IT: GO-let
IMPERIAL HEIGHT: 3'03"
IMPERIAL WEIGHT: 202.8 lbs.
METRIC HEIGHT: 1.0 m
METRIC WEIGHT: 92.0 kg
GENDER: Unknown
ABILITIES: Iron Fist, Klutz
WEAKNESSES: Water, Ghost, Grass, Dark, Ice

GOLETT → GOLURK

#0768 GOLISOPOD
Hard Scale Pokémon

TYPE: BUG-WATER

It will do anything to win, taking advantage of every opening and finishing opponents off with the small claws on its front legs.

They live in sunken ships or in holes in the seabed. When Golisopod and Grapploct battle, the loser becomes the winner's meal.

HOW TO SAY IT: go-LIE-suh-pod
IMPERIAL HEIGHT: 6'07"
IMPERIAL WEIGHT: 238.1 lbs.
METRIC HEIGHT: 2.0 m
METRIC WEIGHT: 108.0 kg
GENDER: ♂ ♀
ABILITIES: Emergency Exit
WEAKNESSES: Flying, Electric, Rock

WIMPOD   GOLISOPOD

TYPE: GROUND-GHOST

#0623

GOLURK
Automaton Pokémon

Artillery platforms built into the walls of ancient castles served as perches from which Golurk could fire energy beams.

There's a theory that inside Golurk is a perpetual motion machine that produces limitless energy, but this belief hasn't been proven.

HOW TO SAY IT: GO-lurk
IMPERIAL HEIGHT: 9'02"
IMPERIAL WEIGHT: 727.5 lbs.
METRIC HEIGHT: 2.8 m
METRIC WEIGHT: 330.0 kg
GENDER: Unknown
ABILITIES: Iron Fist, Klutz
WEAKNESSES: Water, Ghost, Grass, Dark, Ice

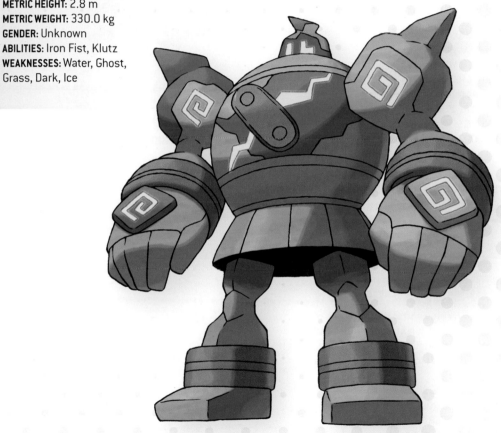

GOLETT **GOLURK**

GOODRA

Dragon Pokémon

#0706

TYPE: DRAGON

It loves the rain. This mellow Pokémon can be seen walking around on the plains and in the mountains on rainy days.

This Pokémon is uncontrollable when enraged. It rampages on and on, lashing its tail with enough power to send a dump truck flying.

HOW TO SAY IT: GOO-druh
IMPERIAL HEIGHT: 6'07"
IMPERIAL WEIGHT: 331.8 lbs.
METRIC HEIGHT: 2.0 m
METRIC WEIGHT: 150.5 kg
GENDER: ♂ ♀
ABILITIES: Sap Sipper, Hydration
WEAKNESSES: Fairy, Ice, Dragon

GOOMY → **SLIGGOO** → **GOODRA**

HISUIAN GOODRA

Shell Bunker Pokémon

#0706

TYPE: STEEL-DRAGON

Able to freely control the hardness of its metallic shell. It loathes solitude and is extremely clingy—it will fume and run riot if those dearest to it ever leave its side.

HOW TO SAY IT: GOO-druh
IMPERIAL HEIGHT: 5'07"
IMPERIAL WEIGHT: 736.6 lbs.
METRIC HEIGHT: 1.7 m
METRIC WEIGHT: 334.1 kg
GENDER: ♂ ♀
ABILITIES: N/A
WEAKNESSES: Fighting, Ground

GOOMY → **HISUIAN SLIGGOO** → **HISUIAN GOODRA**

#0704

GOOMY
Soft Tissue Pokémon

GOOMY

SLIGGOO   GOODRA

HISUIAN   HISUIAN
SLIGGOO   GOODRA

TYPE: DRAGON

Most of a Goomy's body is water. A membrane covers the whole Pokémon to prevent it from shriveling up in dry weather.

Goomy's horns are excellent sensory organs that cover all five of Goomy's senses. Goomy picks up on danger from the movement of the air.

HOW TO SAY IT: GOO-mee
IMPERIAL HEIGHT: 1'00"
IMPERIAL WEIGHT: 6.2 lbs.
METRIC HEIGHT: 0.3 m
METRIC WEIGHT: 2.8 kg
GENDER: ♂ ♀
ABILITIES: Sap Sipper, Hydration
WEAKNESSES: Fairy, Ice, Dragon

#0368

GOREBYSS
South Sea Pokémon

TYPE: WATER

The color of its body changes with the water temperature. The coloration of Gorebyss in Alola is almost blindingly vivid.

It sucks bodily fluids out of its prey. The leftover meat sinks to the seafloor, where it becomes food for other Pokémon.

HOW TO SAY IT: GORE-a-biss
IMPERIAL HEIGHT: 5'11"
IMPERIAL WEIGHT: 49.8 lbs.
METRIC HEIGHT: 1.8 m
METRIC WEIGHT: 22.6 kg
GENDER: ♂ ♀
ABILITIES: Swift Swim
WEAKNESSES: Grass, Electric

CLAMPERL

GOREBYSS

GOSSIFLEUR
Flowering Pokémon

#0829

TYPE: GRASS

It anchors itself in the ground with its single leg, then basks in the sun. After absorbing enough sunlight, its petals spread as it blooms brilliantly.

It whirls around in the wind while singing a joyous song. This delightful display has charmed many into raising this Pokémon.

HOW TO SAY IT: GAH-sih-fluhr
IMPERIAL HEIGHT: 1'04"
IMPERIAL WEIGHT: 4.9 lbs.
METRIC HEIGHT: 0.4 m
METRIC WEIGHT: 2.2 kg
GENDER: ♂ ♀
ABILITIES: Cotton Down, Regenerator
WEAKNESSES: Fire, Flying, Ice, Poison, Bug

GOSSIFLEUR   ELDEGOSS

#0574

GOTHITA
Fixation Pokémon

TYPE: PSYCHIC

This Pokémon is normally very innocent. When it is staring at something invisible, it is unblinking and utterly silent.

Beware of touching the ribbon-shaped feelers that control its psychic power. Gothita will begin bawling if you do.

HOW TO SAY IT: GAH-THEE-tah
IMPERIAL HEIGHT: 1'04"
IMPERIAL WEIGHT: 12.8 lbs.
METRIC HEIGHT: 0.4 m
METRIC WEIGHT: 5.8 kg
GENDER: ♂ ♀
ABILITIES: Frisk, Competitive
WEAKNESSES: Ghost, Dark, Bug

GOTHITA   GOTHORITA   GOTHITELLE

GOTHITELLE
Astral Body Pokémon

#0576

TYPE: PSYCHIC

Gothitelle unleashes psychic energy and shows opponents dreams of the universe's end. These dreams are apparently ethereal and beautiful.

It gazes at the stars to predict the future. It acts somewhat detached because it has seen the end of all existence.

HOW TO SAY IT: GAH-thih-tell
IMPERIAL HEIGHT: 4'11"
IMPERIAL WEIGHT: 97.0 lbs.
METRIC HEIGHT: 1.5 m
METRIC WEIGHT: 44.0 kg
GENDER: ♂ ♀
ABILITIES: Frisk, Competitive
WEAKNESSES: Ghost, Dark, Bug

GOTHITA   GOTHORITA   GOTHITELLE

GOTHORITA
Manipulate Pokémon

#0575

TYPE: PSYCHIC

This Pokémon will hypnotize children to put them to sleep before carrying them away. Be wary of nights when the starlight is bright.

Using its psychic power, it arranges pebbles to form the shapes of constellations. Some people believe this Pokémon came from outer space.

HOW TO SAY IT: GAH-thoh-REE-tah
IMPERIAL HEIGHT: 2'04"
IMPERIAL WEIGHT: 39.7 lbs.
METRIC HEIGHT: 0.7 m
METRIC WEIGHT: 18.0 kg
GENDER: ♂ ♀
ABILITIES: Frisk, Competitive
WEAKNESSES: Ghost, Dark, Bug

GOTHITA   GOTHORITA   GOTHITELLE

GOURGEIST

Pumpkin Pokémon

#0711

TYPE: GHOST-GRASS

Eerie cries emanate from its body in the dead of night. The sounds are said to be the wails of spirits who are suffering in the afterlife.

In the darkness of a new-moon night, Gourgeist will come knocking. Whoever answers the door will be swept off to the afterlife.

HOW TO SAY IT: GORE-guyst
IMPERIAL HEIGHT: 2'11"
IMPERIAL WEIGHT: 27.6 lbs.
METRIC HEIGHT: 0.9 m
METRIC WEIGHT: 12.5 kg
GENDER: ♂ ♀
ABILITIES: Pickup, Frisk
WEAKNESSES: Ghost, Fire, Flying, Dark, Ice

PUMPKABOO ➡ GOURGEIST

GRAFAIAI

Toxic Monkey Pokémon

#0945

TYPE: POISON-NORMAL

The color of the poisonous saliva depends on what the Pokémon eats. Grafaiai covers its fingers in its saliva and draws patterns on trees in forests.

Each Grafaiai paints its own individual pattern, and it will paint that same pattern over and over again throughout its life.

HOW TO SAY IT: gruh-FEYE-eye
IMPERIAL HEIGHT: 2'04"
IMPERIAL WEIGHT: 60.0 lbs.
METRIC HEIGHT: 0.7 m
METRIC WEIGHT: 27.2 kg
GENDER: ♂ ♀
ABILITIES: Unburden, Poison Touch
WEAKNESSES: Psychic, Ground

SHROODLE ➡ GRAFAIAI

#0210

GRANBULL
Fairy Pokémon

TYPE: FAIRY

While it has powerful jaws, it doesn't care for disputes, so it rarely has a chance to display their might.

Although it's popular with young people, Granbull is timid and sensitive, so it's totally incompetent as a watchdog.

HOW TO SAY IT: GRAN-bull
IMPERIAL HEIGHT: 4'07"
IMPERIAL WEIGHT: 107.4 lbs.
METRIC HEIGHT: 1.4 m
METRIC WEIGHT: 48.7 kg
GENDER: ♂ ♀
ABILITIES: Intimidate, Quick Feet
WEAKNESSES: Steel, Poison

SNUBBULL GRANBULL

#0853

GRAPPLOCT
Jujitsu Pokémon

TYPE: FIGHTING

A body made up of nothing but muscle makes the grappling moves this Pokémon performs with its tentacles tremendously powerful.

Searching for an opponent to test its skills against, it emerges onto land. Once the battle is over, it returns to the sea.

HOW TO SAY IT: GRAP-lahct
IMPERIAL HEIGHT: 5'03"
IMPERIAL WEIGHT: 86.0 lbs.
METRIC HEIGHT: 1.6 m
METRIC WEIGHT: 39.0 kg
GENDER: ♂ ♀
ABILITIES: Limber
WEAKNESSES: Psychic, Flying, Fairy

CLOBBOPUS GRAPPLOCT

GRAVELER #0075

Rock Pokémon

TYPE: ROCK-GROUND

Often seen rolling down mountain trails. Obstacles are just things to roll straight over, not avoid.

HOW TO SAY IT: GRAV-el-ler
IMPERIAL HEIGHT: 3'03"
IMPERIAL WEIGHT: 231.5 lbs.
METRIC HEIGHT: 1.0 m
METRIC WEIGHT: 105.0 kg
GENDER: ♂ ♀
ABILITIES: Rock Head, Sturdy
WEAKNESSES: Steel, Fighting, Water, Ice, Grass, Ground

GEODUDE　　GRAVELER　　GOLEM

ALOLAN GRAVELER #0075

Rock Pokémon

TYPE: ROCK-ELECTRIC

When it comes rolling down a mountain path, anything in its way gets zapped by electricity and sent flying.

HOW TO SAY IT: GRAV-el-ler
IMPERIAL HEIGHT: 3'03"
IMPERIAL WEIGHT: 242.5 lbs.
METRIC HEIGHT: 1.0 m
METRIC WEIGHT: 110.0 kg
GENDER: ♂ ♀
ABILITIES: Magnet Pull, Sturdy
WEAKNESSES: Water, Grass, Fighting, Ground

ALOLAN GEODUDE　　ALOLAN GRAVELER　　ALOLAN GOLEM

#0984

GREAT TUSK
Paradox Pokémon

TYPE: GROUND-FIGHTING

Sightings of this Pokémon have occurred in recent years. The name Great Tusk was taken from a creature listed in a certain book.

This creature resembles a mysterious Pokémon that, according to a paranormal magazine, has lived since ancient times.

HOW TO SAY IT: GREAT TUSK
IMPERIAL HEIGHT: 7'03"
IMPERIAL WEIGHT: 705.5 lbs.
METRIC HEIGHT: 2.2 m
METRIC WEIGHT: 320.0 kg
GENDER: Unknown
ABILITIES: Protosynthesis
WEAKNESSES: Psychic, Flying, Ice, Water, Fairy, Grass

DOES NOT EVOLVE

#0971

GREAVARD
Ghost Dog Pokémon

TYPE: GHOST

It is said that a dog Pokémon that died in the wild without ever interacting with a human was reborn as this Pokémon.

This friendly Pokémon doesn't like being alone. Pay it even the slightest bit of attention, and it will follow you forever.

HOW TO SAY IT: GREE-verd
IMPERIAL HEIGHT: 2'00"
IMPERIAL WEIGHT: 77.2 lbs.
METRIC HEIGHT: 0.6 m
METRIC WEIGHT: 35.0 kg
GENDER: ♂ ♀
ABILITIES: Pickup
WEAKNESSES: Ghost, Dark

GREAVARD **HOUNDSTONE**

GREEDENT

Greedy Pokémon

#0820

TYPE: NORMAL

If it spots a berry tree, it will immediately go to gather berries without a sideways glance— even if it's in the middle of a battle.

This Pokémon makes off with heaps of fallen berries by wrapping them in its tail, which is roughly twice the length of its body.

HOW TO SAY IT: GREE-dent
IMPERIAL HEIGHT: 2'00"
IMPERIAL WEIGHT: 13.2 lbs.
METRIC HEIGHT: 0.6 m
METRIC WEIGHT: 6.0 kg
GENDER: ♂ ♀
ABILITIES: Cheek Pouch
WEAKNESSES: Fighting

SKWOVET → **GREEDENT**

TYPE: WATER-DARK

#0658

GRENINJA

Ninja Pokémon

It creates throwing stars out of compressed water. When it spins them and throws them at high speed, these stars can split metal in two.

It appears and vanishes with a ninja's grace. It toys with its enemies using swift movements, while slicing them with throwing stars of sharpest water.

HOW TO SAY IT: greh-NIN-jah
IMPERIAL HEIGHT: 4'11"
IMPERIAL WEIGHT: 88.2 lbs.
METRIC HEIGHT: 1.5 m
METRIC WEIGHT: 40.0 kg
GENDER: ♂ ♀
ABILITIES: Torrent
WEAKNESSES: Fairy, Grass, Electric, Fighting, Bug

FROAKIE → **FROGADIER** → **GRENINJA**

GRIMER
Sludge Pokémon

#0088

TYPE: POISON

Born from sludge, these Pokémon now gather in polluted places and increase the bacteria in their bodies.

When two of these Pokémon's bodies are combined together, new poisons are created.

HOW TO SAY IT: GRY-mur
IMPERIAL HEIGHT: 2'11"
IMPERIAL WEIGHT: 66.1 lbs.
METRIC HEIGHT: 0.9 m
METRIC WEIGHT: 30.0 kg
GENDER: ♂ ♀
ABILITIES: Stench, Sticky Hold
WEAKNESSES: Psychic, Ground

GRIMER ➡ MUK

ALOLAN GRIMER
Sludge Pokémon

#0088

TYPE: POISON-DARK

It has a passion for trash above all else, speedily digesting it and creating brilliant crystals of sparkling poison.

HOW TO SAY IT: GRY-mur
IMPERIAL HEIGHT: 2'04"
IMPERIAL WEIGHT: 92.6 lbs.
METRIC HEIGHT: 0.7 m
METRIC WEIGHT: 42.0 kg
GENDER: ♂ ♀
ABILITIES: Poison Touch, Gluttony
WEAKNESSES: Ground

ALOLAN GRIMER   ALOLAN MUK

GRIMMSNARL

Bulk Up Pokémon

#0861

TYPE: DARK-FAIRY

This Pokémon has complete control over its hair. Grimmsnarl normally keeps its hair wrapped around its body to support its muscles.

It lives deep within the forest. Even after evolving into this splendid form, it hasn't given up on its petty misdeeds and pranks.

HOW TO SAY IT: GRIM-snarl
IMPERIAL HEIGHT: 4'11"
IMPERIAL WEIGHT: 134.5 lbs.
METRIC HEIGHT: 1.5 m
METRIC WEIGHT: 61.0 kg
GENDER: ♂
ABILITIES: Prankster, Frisk
WEAKNESSES: Steel, Fairy, Poison

IMPIDIMP ➡ **MORGREM** ➡ **GRIMMSNARL**

GIGANTAMAX GRIMMSNARL

By transforming its leg hair, this Pokémon delivers power-packed drill kicks that can bore huge holes in Galar's terrain.

Gigantamax energy has caused more hair to sprout all over its body. With the added strength, it can jump over the world's tallest building.

IMPERIAL HEIGHT: 105'00"+
IMPERIAL WEIGHT: ????.? lbs.
METRIC HEIGHT: 32.0+ m
METRIC WEIGHT: ???.? kg

GROOKEY

Chimp Pokémon

#0810

TYPE: GRASS

When it uses its special stick to strike up a beat, the sound waves produced carry revitalizing energy to the plants and flowers in the area.

It attacks with rapid beats of its stick. As it strikes with amazing speed, it gets more and more pumped.

HOW TO SAY IT: GROO-kee
IMPERIAL HEIGHT: 1'00"
IMPERIAL WEIGHT: 11.0 lbs.
METRIC HEIGHT: 0.3 m
METRIC WEIGHT: 5.0 kg
GENDER: ♂ ♀
ABILITIES: Overgrow
WEAKNESSES: Fire, Flying, Ice, Poison, Bug

GROOKEY   THWACKEY   RILLABOOM

GROTLE

Grove Pokémon

#0388

TYPE: GRASS

It lives along water in forests. In the daytime, it leaves the forest to sunbathe its treed shell.

It knows where pure water wells up. It carries fellow Pokémon there on its back.

HOW TO SAY IT: GRAH-tul
IMPERIAL HEIGHT: 3'07"
IMPERIAL WEIGHT: 213.8 lbs.
METRIC HEIGHT: 1.1 m
METRIC WEIGHT: 97.0 kg
GENDER: ♂ ♀
ABILITIES: Overgrow
WEAKNESSES: Fire, Flying, Ice, Poison, Bug

TURTWIG   GROTLE   TORTERRA

GROUDON
Continent Pokémon

TYPE: GROUND

Groudon is said to be the personification of the land itself. Legends tell of its many clashes against Kyogre, as each sought to gain the power of nature.

Through Primal Reversion and with nature's full power, it will take back its true form. It can cause magma to erupt and expand the landmass of the world.

HOW TO SAY IT: GRAU-DON
IMPERIAL HEIGHT: 11'06"
IMPERIAL WEIGHT: 2,094.4 lbs.
METRIC HEIGHT: 3.5 m
METRIC WEIGHT: 950.0 kg
GENDER: Unknown
ABILITIES: Drought
WEAKNESSES: Water, Grass, Ice

PRIMAL GROUDON

TYPE: GROUND-FIRE

IMPERIAL HEIGHT: 16'05"
IMPERIAL WEIGHT: 2,204.0 lbs.
METRIC HEIGHT: 5.0 m
METRIC WEIGHT: 999.7 kg
ABILITIES: Desolate Land
WEAKNESSES: Water, Ground

GROUDON   PRIMAL GROUDON

GROVYLE
Wood Gecko Pokémon

TYPE: GRASS

The leaves growing out of Grovyle's body are convenient for camouflaging it from enemies in the forest. This Pokémon is a master at climbing trees in jungles.

This Pokémon adeptly flies from branch to branch in trees. In a forest, no Pokémon can ever hope to catch a fleeing Grovyle however fast they may be.

HOW TO SAY IT: GROW-vile
IMPERIAL HEIGHT: 2'11" **METRIC HEIGHT:** 0.9 m
IMPERIAL WEIGHT: 47.6 lbs. **METRIC WEIGHT:** 21.6 kg
GENDER: ♂ ♀
ABILITIES: Overgrow
WEAKNESSES: Fire, Flying, Ice, Poison, Bug

 TREECKO **GROVYLE**   **SCEPTILE**  **MEGA SCEPTILE** 239

GROWLITHE

Puppy Pokémon

#0058

TYPE: FIRE

It has a brave and trustworthy nature. It fearlessly stands up to bigger and stronger foes.

It's very friendly and faithful to people. It will try to repel enemies by barking and biting.

HOW TO SAY IT: GROWL-lith
IMPERIAL HEIGHT: 2'04"
IMPERIAL WEIGHT: 41.9 lbs.
METRIC HEIGHT: 0.7 m
METRIC WEIGHT: 19.0 kg
GENDER: ♂ ♀
ABILITIES: Intimidate, Flash Fire
WEAKNESSES: Water, Ground, Rock

GROWLITHE   ARCANINE

HISUIAN GROWLITHE

Scout Pokémon

#0058

TYPE: FIRE-ROCK

They patrol their territory in pairs. I believe the igneous rock components in the fur of this species are the result of volcanic activity in its habitat.

HOW TO SAY IT: GROWL-lith
IMPERIAL HEIGHT: 2'07"
IMPERIAL WEIGHT: 50.0 lbs.
METRIC HEIGHT: 0.8 m
METRIC WEIGHT: 22.7 kg
GENDER: ♂ ♀
ABILITIES: N/A
WEAKNESSES: Water, Ground, Fighting, Rock

HISUIAN GROWLITHE   HISUIAN ARCANINE

TYPE: BUG

Its natural enemies, like Rookidee, may flee rather than risk getting caught in its large mandibles that can snap thick tree branches.

It uses its big jaws to dig nests into the forest floor, and it loves to feed on sweet tree sap.

HOW TO SAY IT: GRUB-bin
IMPERIAL HEIGHT: 1'04"
IMPERIAL WEIGHT: 9.7 lbs.
METRIC HEIGHT: 0.4 m
METRIC WEIGHT: 4.4 kg
GENDER: ♂ ♀
ABILITIES: Swarm
WEAKNESSES: Fire, Flying, Rock

GRUBBIN
Larva Pokémon
#0736

GRUBBIN   **CHARJABUG**   **VIKAVOLT**

#0326

GRUMPIG
Manipulate Pokémon

TYPE: PSYCHIC

It can perform odd dance steps to influence foes. Its style of dancing became hugely popular overseas.

It uses black pearls to amplify its psychic power. It does a strange dance to control foes' minds.

HOW TO SAY IT: GRUM-pig
IMPERIAL HEIGHT: 2'11"
IMPERIAL WEIGHT: 157.6 lbs.
METRIC HEIGHT: 0.9 m
METRIC WEIGHT: 71.5 kg
GENDER: ♂ ♀
ABILITIES: Thick Fat, Own Tempo
WEAKNESSES: Ghost, Dark, Bug

SPOINK   **GRUMPIG**

GULPIN

Stomach Pokémon

#0316

TYPE: POISON

There is nothing its stomach can't digest. While it is digesting, vile, overpowering gases are expelled.

It has a small heart and brain. Its stomach comprises most of its body, with enzymes to dissolve anything.

HOW TO SAY IT: GULL-pin
IMPERIAL HEIGHT: 1'04"
IMPERIAL WEIGHT: 22.7 lbs.
METRIC HEIGHT: 0.4 m
METRIC WEIGHT: 10.3 kg
GENDER: ♂ ♀
ABILITIES: Liquid Ooze, Sticky Hold
WEAKNESSES: Psychic, Ground

GULPIN **SWALOT**

GUMSHOOS

Stakeout Pokémon

#0735

TYPE: NORMAL

Once it finds signs of prey, it will patiently stake out the location, waiting until the sun goes down.

Gumshoos specializes in relentlessly tracking down prey. The simple-minded Skwovet doesn't seem to provide Gumshoos enough challenge.

HOW TO SAY IT: GUM-shooss
IMPERIAL HEIGHT: 2'04"
IMPERIAL WEIGHT: 31.3 lbs.
METRIC HEIGHT: 0.7 m
METRIC WEIGHT: 14.2 kg
GENDER: ♂ ♀
ABILITIES: Stakeout, Strong Jaw
WEAKNESSES: Fighting

YUNGOOS **GUMSHOOS**

TYPE: FIGHTING

GURDURR
Muscular Pokémon

It shows off its muscles to Machoke and other Gurdurr. If it fails to measure up to the other Pokémon, it lies low for a little while.

Gurdurr excels at demolition—construction is not its forte. In any case, there's skill in the way this Pokémon wields its metal beam.

HOW TO SAY IT: GUR-dur
IMPERIAL HEIGHT: 3'11"
IMPERIAL WEIGHT: 88.2 lbs.
METRIC HEIGHT: 1.2 m
METRIC WEIGHT: 40.0 kg
GENDER: ♂ ♀
ABILITIES: Guts, Sheer Force
WEAKNESSES: Psychic, Flying, Fairy

TIMBURR ➡ **GURDURR** ➡ **CONKELDURR**

ULTRA BEAST

#0799

GUZZLORD
Junkivore Pokémon

TYPE: DARK-DRAGON

Although it's alien to this world and a danger here, it's apparently a common organism in the world where it normally lives.

An unknown life-form called a UB. It may be constantly hungry—it is certainly always devouring something.

HOW TO SAY IT: GUZZ-lord
IMPERIAL HEIGHT: 18'01"
IMPERIAL WEIGHT: 1,957.7 lbs.
METRIC HEIGHT: 5.5 m
METRIC WEIGHT: 888.0 kg
GENDER: Unknown
ABILITIES: Beast Boost
WEAKNESSES: Fairy, Fighting, Bug, Ice, Dragon

DOES NOT EVOLVE

GYARADOS

Atrocious Pokémon

#0130

TYPE: WATER-FLYING

Once it appears, it goes on a rampage. It remains enraged until it demolishes everything around it.

It appears whenever there is world conflict, burning down any place it travels through.

HOW TO SAY IT: GARE-uh-dos
IMPERIAL HEIGHT: 21'04"
IMPERIAL WEIGHT: 518.1 lbs.
METRIC HEIGHT: 6.5 m
METRIC WEIGHT: 235.0 kg
GENDER: ♂ ♀
ABILITIES: Intimidate
WEAKNESSES: Electric, Rock

MEGA GYARADOS

TYPE: WATER-DARK

Although it obeys its instinctive drive to destroy everything within its reach, it will respond to orders from a Trainer it truly trusts.

IMPERIAL HEIGHT: 21'04"
IMPERIAL WEIGHT: 672.4 lbs.
METRIC HEIGHT: 6.5 m
METRIC WEIGHT: 305.0 kg

MAGIKARP

GYARADOS

MEGA GYARADOS

HAKAMO-O

Scaly Pokémon

#0783

TYPE: DRAGON-FIGHTING

The scaleless, scarred parts of its body are signs of its strength. It shows them off to defeated opponents.

Before attacking its enemies, it clashes its scales together and roars. Its sharp claws shred the opposition.

HOW TO SAY IT: HAH-kah-MOH-oh
IMPERIAL HEIGHT: 3'11"
IMPERIAL WEIGHT: 103.6 lbs.
METRIC HEIGHT: 1.2 m
METRIC WEIGHT: 47.0 kg
GENDER: ♂ ♀
ABILITIES: Bulletproof, Soundproof
WEAKNESSES: Fairy, Flying, Psychic, Ice, Dragon

JANGMO-O   **HAKAMO-O**   **KOMMO-O**

HAPPINY

Playhouse Pokémon

#0440

TYPE: NORMAL

It carries a round, white rock in its belly pouch. If it gets along well with someone, it will sometimes give that person the rock.

It carefully carries a round, white rock that it thinks is an egg. It's bothered by how curly its hair looks.

HOW TO SAY IT: hap-PEE-nee
IMPERIAL HEIGHT: 2'00"
IMPERIAL WEIGHT: 53.8 lbs.
METRIC HEIGHT: 0.6 m
METRIC WEIGHT: 24.4 kg
GENDER: ♀
ABILITIES: Natural Cure, Serene Grace
WEAKNESSES: Fighting

HAPPINY   **CHANSEY**   **BLISSEY**

HARIYAMA

Arm Thrust Pokémon

#0297

TYPE: FIGHTING

It loves challenging others to tests of strength. It has the power to stop a train with a slap.

It stomps on the ground to build power. It can send a 10-ton truck flying with a straight-arm punch.

HOW TO SAY IT: HAR-ee-YAH-mah
IMPERIAL HEIGHT: 7'07"
IMPERIAL WEIGHT: 559.5 lbs.
METRIC HEIGHT: 2.3 m
METRIC WEIGHT: 253.8 kg
GENDER: ♂ ♀
ABILITIES: Thick Fat, Guts
WEAKNESSES: Psychic, Flying, Fairy

MAKUHITA **HARIYAMA**

HATENNA

Calm Pokémon

#0856

TYPE: PSYCHIC

Because the emotions of others constantly flow into its head, this Pokémon prefers environments where no other creatures live.

It senses the feelings of other living creatures. Be careful not to expose it to strong emotions for too long, or it will end up exhausted.

HOW TO SAY IT: hat-EN-nuh
IMPERIAL HEIGHT: 1'04"
IMPERIAL WEIGHT: 7.5 lbs.
METRIC HEIGHT: 0.4 m
METRIC WEIGHT: 3.4 kg
GENDER: ♀
ABILITIES: Healer, Anticipation
WEAKNESSES: Ghost, Dark, Bug

HATENNA **HATTREM** **HATTERENE**

#0858 HATTERENE
Silent Pokémon

TYPE: PSYCHIC-FAIRY

Hatterene knocks out those that intrude in its home forest by blasting them with a beam, then slashing with claws enhanced by psychic power.

Beware of forests that show no signs of living creatures within. You may have wandered into Hatterene's territory.

HOW TO SAY IT: HAT-eh-reen
IMPERIAL HEIGHT: 6'11"
IMPERIAL WEIGHT: 11.2 lbs.
METRIC HEIGHT: 2.1 m
METRIC WEIGHT: 5.1 kg
GENDER: ♀
ABILITIES: Healer, Anticipation
WEAKNESSES: Ghost, Steel, Poison

HATENNA → HATTREM → HATTERENE

GIGANTAMAX HATTERENE

This Pokémon can read the emotions of creatures over 30 miles away. The minute it senses hostility, it goes on the attack.

Beams like lightning shoot down from its tentacles. It's known to some as the Raging Goddess.

IMPERIAL HEIGHT: 85'04"+
IMPERIAL WEIGHT: ????.? lbs.
METRIC HEIGHT: 26.0+ m
METRIC WEIGHT: ???.? kg

HATTREM #0857

Serene Pokémon

TYPE: PSYCHIC

To this Pokémon, strong emotions apparently feel like incredibly loud noises— even if the emotions are happy ones.

The moment this Pokémon finds someone who's emitting strong emotions, it will pummel them senseless with its braids to silence them.

HOW TO SAY IT: HAT-trum
IMPERIAL HEIGHT: 2'00"
IMPERIAL WEIGHT: 10.6 lbs.
METRIC HEIGHT: 0.6 m
METRIC WEIGHT: 4.8 kg
GENDER: ♀
ABILITIES: Healer, Anticipation
WEAKNESSES: Ghost, Dark, Bug

HATENNA   HATTREM   HATTERENE

HAUNTER #0093

Gas Pokémon

TYPE: GHOST-POISON

It likes to lurk in the dark and tap shoulders with a gaseous hand. Its touch causes endless shuddering.

In total darkness, where nothing is visible, Haunter lurks, silently stalking its next victim.

HOW TO SAY IT: HAUNT-ur
IMPERIAL HEIGHT: 5'03"
IMPERIAL WEIGHT: 0.2 lbs.
METRIC HEIGHT: 1.6 m
METRIC WEIGHT: 0.1 kg
GENDER: ♂ ♀
ABILITIES: Levitate
WEAKNESSES: Ghost, Dark, Psychic, Ground

GASTLY   HAUNTER   GENGAR   MEGA GENGAR

TYPE: FIGHTING-FLYING

HAWLUCHA
Wrestling Pokémon

Its elegant finishing moves—performed by nimbly leaping around using its wings—are polished in the forest where it was born and raised.

Hawlucha live quietly without flocking together. They fight constantly with their natural enemies: noisy groups of Primeape.

HOW TO SAY IT: haw-LOO-cha
IMPERIAL HEIGHT: 2'07"
IMPERIAL WEIGHT: 47.4 lbs.
METRIC HEIGHT: 0.8 m
METRIC WEIGHT: 21.5 kg
GENDER: ♂ ♀
ABILITIES: Limber, Unburden
WEAKNESSES: Electric, Psychic, Flying, Ice, Fairy

DOES NOT EVOLVE

#0612

HAXORUS
Axe Jaw Pokémon

TYPE: DRAGON

This Pokémon nests in caves and abandoned mines. It is docile, but it will become incredibly angry if its tusks are touched, so beware.

It overwhelms enemies with its prized tusks, which are sharp enough to cut through a metal transmission tower in one strike.

HOW TO SAY IT: HAK-soar-us
IMPERIAL HEIGHT: 5'11"
IMPERIAL WEIGHT: 232.6 lbs.
METRIC HEIGHT: 1.8 m
METRIC WEIGHT: 105.5 kg
GENDER: ♂ ♀
ABILITIES: Rivalry, Mold Breaker
WEAKNESSES: Ice, Dragon, Fairy

AXEW → **FRAXURE** → **HAXORUS**

HEATMOR

Anteater Pokémon

#0631

TYPE: FIRE

There's a hole in its tail that allows it to draw in the air it needs to keep its fire burning. If the hole gets blocked, this Pokémon will fall ill.

A flame serves as its tongue, melting through the hard shell of Durant so that Heatmor can devour their insides.

HOW TO SAY IT: HEET-mohr
IMPERIAL HEIGHT: 4'07"
IMPERIAL WEIGHT: 127.9 lbs.
METRIC HEIGHT: 1.4 m
METRIC WEIGHT: 58.0 kg
GENDER: ♂ ♀
ABILITIES: Gluttony, Flash Fire
WEAKNESSES: Water, Ground, Rock

DOES NOT EVOLVE

HEATRAN

Lava Dome Pokémon

#0485

LEGENDARY POKÉMON

TYPE: FIRE-STEEL

It dwells in volcanic caves. It digs in with its cross-shaped feet to crawl on ceilings and walls.

Boiling blood, like magma, circulates through its body. It makes its dwelling place in volcanic caves.

HOW TO SAY IT: HEET-tran
IMPERIAL HEIGHT: 5'07"
IMPERIAL WEIGHT: 948.0 lbs.
METRIC HEIGHT: 1.7 m
METRIC WEIGHT: 430.0 kg
GENDER: ♂ ♀
ABILITIES: Flash Fire
WEAKNESSES: Water, Fighting, Ground

DOES NOT EVOLVE

TYPE: ELECTRIC-NORMAL

A now-vanished desert culture treasured these Pokémon. Appropriately, when Heliolisk came to the Galar region, treasure came with them.

One Heliolisk basking in the sun with its frill outspread is all it would take to produce enough electricity to power a city.

HOW TO SAY IT: HEE-lee-oh-lisk
IMPERIAL HEIGHT: 3'03"
IMPERIAL WEIGHT: 46.3 lbs.
METRIC HEIGHT: 1.0 m
METRIC WEIGHT: 21.0 kg
GENDER: ♂ ♀
ABILITIES: Dry Skin, Sand Veil
WEAKNESSES: Fighting, Ground

HELIOLISK
Generator Pokémon

#0695

HELIOPTILE ➡ HELIOLISK

HELIOPTILE
Generator Pokémon

#0694

TYPE: ELECTRIC-NORMAL

When spread, the frills on its head act like solar panels, generating the power behind this Pokémon's electric moves.

The sun powers this Pokémon's electricity generation. Interruption of that process stresses Helioptile to the point of weakness.

HOW TO SAY IT: hee-lee-AHP-tile
IMPERIAL HEIGHT: 1'08"
IMPERIAL WEIGHT: 13.2 lbs.
METRIC HEIGHT: 0.5 m
METRIC WEIGHT: 6.0 kg
GENDER: ♂ ♀
ABILITIES: Dry Skin, Sand Veil
WEAKNESSES: Fighting, Ground

HELIOPTILE   HELIOLISK

HERACROSS
Single Horn Pokémon

#0214

TYPE: BUG-FIGHTING

It loves sweet nectar. To keep all the nectar to itself, it hurls rivals away with its prized horn.

With its herculean powers, it can easily throw around an object that is 100 times its own weight.

HOW TO SAY IT: HAIR-uh-cross
IMPERIAL HEIGHT: 4'11"
IMPERIAL WEIGHT: 119.0 lbs.
METRIC HEIGHT: 1.5 m
METRIC WEIGHT: 54.0 kg
GENDER: ♂ ♀
ABILITIES: Swarm, Guts
WEAKNESSES: Fire, Psychic, Flying, Fairy

MEGA HERACROSS

TYPE: BUG-FIGHTING

It can grip things with its two horns and lift 500 times its own body weight.

A tremendous influx of energy builds it up, but when Mega Evolution ends, Heracross is bothered by terrible soreness in its muscles.

IMPERIAL HEIGHT: 5'07"
IMPERIAL WEIGHT: 137.8 lbs.
METRIC HEIGHT: 1.7 m
METRIC WEIGHT: 62.5 kg

HERACROSS ➡ MEGA HERACROSS

TYPE: NORMAL

Herdier is a very smart and friendly Pokémon. So much so that there's a theory that Herdier was the first Pokémon to partner with people.

The black fur that covers this Pokémon's body is dense and springy. Even sharp fangs bounce right off.

HOW TO SAY IT: HERD-ee-er
IMPERIAL HEIGHT: 2'11"
IMPERIAL WEIGHT: 32.4 lbs.
METRIC HEIGHT: 0.9 m
METRIC WEIGHT: 14.7 kg
GENDER: ♂ ♀
ABILITIES: Intimidate, Sand Rush
WEAKNESSES: Fighting

#0507

HERDIER
Loyal Dog Pokémon

LILLIPUP → **HERDIER** → **STOUTLAND**

#0449

HIPPOPOTAS
Hippo Pokémon

TYPE: GROUND

It shuts its nostrils tight, then travels through sand as if walking. They form colonies of around 10.

It shrouds itself in sand to ward off germs. It travels easily through the sands of the desert.

HOW TO SAY IT: HIP-poh-puh-TOSS
IMPERIAL HEIGHT: 2'07"
IMPERIAL WEIGHT: 109.1 lbs.
METRIC HEIGHT: 0.8 m
METRIC WEIGHT: 49.5 kg
GENDER: ♂ ♀
ABILITIES: Sand Stream
WEAKNESSES: Water, Grass, Ice

HIPPOPOTAS → **HIPPOWDON**

HIPPOWDON

Heavyweight Pokémon

#0450

TYPE: GROUND

It is surprisingly quick to anger. It holds its mouth agape as a display of its strength.

It brandishes its gaping mouth in a display of fearsome strength. It raises vast quantities of sand while attacking.

HOW TO SAY IT: hip-POW-don
IMPERIAL HEIGHT: 6'07"
IMPERIAL WEIGHT: 661.4 lbs.
METRIC HEIGHT: 2.0 m
METRIC WEIGHT: 300.0 kg
GENDER: ♂ ♀
ABILITIES: Sand Stream
WEAKNESSES: Water, Grass, Ice

HIPPOPOTAS　　　**HIPPOWDON**

HITMONCHAN

Punching Pokémon

#0107

TYPE: FIGHTING

Its punches slice the air. They are launched at such high speed, even a slight graze could cause a burn.

Its punches slice the air. However, it seems to need a short break after fighting for three minutes.

HOW TO SAY IT: HIT-mon-CHAN
IMPERIAL HEIGHT: 4'07"
IMPERIAL WEIGHT: 110.7 lbs.
METRIC HEIGHT: 1.4 m
METRIC WEIGHT: 50.2 kg
GENDER: ♂
ABILITIES: Keen Eye, Iron Fist
WEAKNESSES: Psychic, Flying, Fairy

TYROGUE　　**HITMONCHAN**

TYPE: FIGHTING

This amazing Pokémon has an awesome sense of balance. It can kick in succession from any position.

The legs freely contract and stretch. The stretchy legs allow it to hit a distant foe with a rising kick.

HOW TO SAY IT: HIT-mon-LEE
IMPERIAL HEIGHT: 4'11"
IMPERIAL WEIGHT: 109.8 lbs.
METRIC HEIGHT: 1.5m
METRIC WEIGHT: 49.8 kg
GENDER: ♂
ABILITIES: Limber, Reckless
WEAKNESSES: Psychic, Flying, Fairy

#0106 HITMONLEE
Kicking Pokémon

TYROGUE ➡ **HITMONLEE**

#0237 HITMONTOP
Handstand Pokémon

TYPE: FIGHTING

It launches kicks while spinning. If it spins at high speed, it may bore its way into the ground.

After doing a handstand to throw off the opponent's timing, it presents its fancy kick moves.

HOW TO SAY IT: HIT-mon-TOP
IMPERIAL HEIGHT: 4'07"
IMPERIAL WEIGHT: 105.8 lbs.
METRIC HEIGHT: 1.4 m
METRIC WEIGHT: 48.0 kg
GENDER: ♂
ABILITIES: Intimidate, Technician
WEAKNESSES: Psychic, Flying, Fairy

TYROGUE ➡ **HITMONTOP**

HO-OH

Rainbow Pokémon

#0250

LEGENDARY POKÉMON

TYPE: FIRE-FLYING

Ho-Oh's feathers glow in seven colors depending on the angle at which they are struck by light. These feathers are said to bring happiness to the bearers. This Pokémon is said to live at the foot of a rainbow.

HOW TO SAY IT: HOE-OH
IMPERIAL HEIGHT: 12'06"
IMPERIAL WEIGHT: 438.7 lbs.
METRIC HEIGHT: 3.8 m
METRIC WEIGHT: 199.0 kg
GENDER: Unknown
ABILITIES: Pressure
WEAKNESSES: Water, Electric, Rock

DOES NOT EVOLVE

TYPE: DARK-FLYING

It is merciless by nature. It is said that it never forgives the mistakes of its Murkrow followers.

A single cry from this nocturnal Pokémon, and more than 100 of its Murkrow cronies will assemble.

HOW TO SAY IT: HONCH-krow
IMPERIAL HEIGHT: 2'11"
IMPERIAL WEIGHT: 60.2 lbs.
METRIC HEIGHT: 0.9 m
METRIC WEIGHT: 27.3 kg
GENDER: ♂ ♀
ABILITIES: Insomnia, Super Luck
WEAKNESSES: Electric, Ice, Rock, Fairy

#0430

HONCHKROW
Big Boss Pokémon

MURKROW → HONCHKROW

#0679

HONEDGE
Sword Pokémon

TYPE: STEEL-GHOST

Honedge's soul once belonged to a person who was killed a long time ago by the sword that makes up Honedge's body.

The blue eye on the sword's handguard is the true body of Honedge. With its old cloth, it drains people's lives away.

HOW TO SAY IT: HONE-ej
IMPERIAL HEIGHT: 2'07"
IMPERIAL WEIGHT: 4.4 lbs.
METRIC HEIGHT: 0.8 m
METRIC WEIGHT: 2.0 kg
GENDER: ♂ ♀
ABILITIES: No Guard
WEAKNESSES: Fire, Ghost, Dark, Ground

HONEDGE   DOUBLADE   AEGISLASH

HOOPA CONFINED

Mischief Pokémon

#0720

TYPE: PSYCHIC-GHOST

In its true form, it possesses a huge amount of power. Legends of its avarice tell how it once carried off an entire castle to gain the treasure hidden within.

It is said to be able to seize anything it desires with its six rings and six huge arms. With its power sealed, it is transformed into a much smaller form.

HOW TO SAY IT: HOO-pah
IMPERIAL HEIGHT: 1'08"
IMPERIAL WEIGHT: 19.8 lbs.
METRIC HEIGHT: 0.5 m
METRIC WEIGHT: 9.0 kg
GENDER: Unknown
ABILITIES: Magician
WEAKNESSES: Ghost, Dark

HOOPA UNBOUND

Djinn Pokémon

TYPE: PSYCHIC-DARK

IMPERIAL HEIGHT: 21'04"
IMPERIAL WEIGHT: 1,080.3 lbs.
METRIC HEIGHT: 6.5 m
METRIC WEIGHT: 490.0 kg
ABILITIES: Magician
WEAKNESSES: Fairy, Bug

DOES NOT EVOLVE

TYPE: NORMAL-FLYING

HOOTHOOT

#0163

Owl Pokémon

It always stands on one foot. It changes feet so fast, the movement can rarely be seen.

It begins to hoot at the same time every day. Some Trainers use them in place of clocks.

HOW TO SAY IT: HOOT-HOOT
IMPERIAL HEIGHT: 2'04"
IMPERIAL WEIGHT: 46.7 lbs.
METRIC HEIGHT: 0.7 m
METRIC WEIGHT: 21.2 kg
GENDER: ♂ ♀
ABILITIES: Insomnia, Keen Eye
WEAKNESSES: Electric, Ice, Rock

HOOTHOOT → **NOCTOWL**

HOPPIP

Cottonweed Pokémon

#0187

TYPE: GRASS-FLYING

This Pokémon is blown across vast distances by the wind. It is unclear where the Hoppip of Paldea originally came from.

Outside of cold regions, Hoppip can be found practically everywhere. This is because the wind carries this species all over the world.

HOW TO SAY IT: HOP-pip
IMPERIAL HEIGHT: 1'04"
IMPERIAL WEIGHT: 1.1 lbs.
METRIC HEIGHT: 0.4 m
METRIC WEIGHT: 0.5 kg
GENDER: ♂ ♀
ABILITIES: Chlorophyll, Leaf Guard
WEAKNESSES: Fire, Flying, Ice, Poison, Rock

HOPPIP   SKIPLOOM   JUMPLUFF

#0116

HORSEA
Dragon Pokémon

TYPE: WATER

Horsea makes its home in oceans with gentle currents. If this Pokémon is under attack, it spits out pitch-black ink and escapes.

They swim with dance-like motions and cause whirlpools to form. Horsea compete to see which of them can generate the biggest whirlpool.

HOW TO SAY IT: HOR-see
IMPERIAL HEIGHT: 1'04"
IMPERIAL WEIGHT: 17.6 lbs.
METRIC HEIGHT: 0.4 m
METRIC WEIGHT: 8.0 kg
GENDER: ♂ ♀
ABILITIES: Swift Swim, Sniper
WEAKNESSES: Grass, Electric

HORSEA   SEADRA   KINGDRA

HOUNDOOM
Dark Pokémon

TYPE: DARK-FIRE

If you are burned by the flames it shoots from its mouth, the pain will never go away.

Upon hearing its eerie howls, other Pokémon get the shivers and head straight back to their nests.

HOW TO SAY IT: HOWN-doom
IMPERIAL HEIGHT: 4'07"
IMPERIAL WEIGHT: 77.2 lbs.
METRIC HEIGHT: 1.4 m
METRIC WEIGHT: 35.0 kg
GENDER: ♂ ♀
ABILITIES: Early Bird, Flash Fire
WEAKNESSES: Water, Ground, Fighting, Rock

MEGA HOUNDOOM

TYPE: DARK-FIRE

Its red claws and the tips of its tail are melting from high internal temperatures that are painful to Houndoom itself.

Houndoom's entire body generates heat when it Mega Evolves. Its fearsome fiery breath turns its opponents to ash.

IMPERIAL HEIGHT: 6'03"
IMPERIAL WEIGHT: 109.1 lbs.
METRIC HEIGHT: 1.9 m
METRIC WEIGHT: 49.5 kg

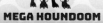
HOUNDOUR   **HOUNDOOM**   **MEGA HOUNDOOM**

HOUNDOUR

Dark Pokémon

#0228

TYPE: DARK-FIRE

It is smart enough to hunt in packs. It uses a variety of cries for communicating with others.

It uses different kinds of cries for communicating with others of its kind and for pursuing its prey.

HOW TO SAY IT: HOWN-dowr
IMPERIAL HEIGHT: 2'00"
IMPERIAL WEIGHT: 23.8 lbs.
METRIC HEIGHT: 0.6 m
METRIC WEIGHT: 10.8 kg
GENDER: ♂ ♀
ABILITIES: Early Bird, Flash Fire
WEAKNESSES: Water, Ground, Fighting, Rock

| HOUNDOUR | HOUNDOOM | MEGA HOUNDOOM |

HOUNDSTONE

Ghost Dog Pokémon

#0972

TYPE: GHOST

Houndstone spends most of its time sleeping in graveyards. Among all the dog Pokémon, this one is most loyal to its master.

A lovingly mourned Pokémon was reborn as Houndstone. It doesn't like anyone touching the protuberance atop its head.

HOW TO SAY IT: HOUND-stone
IMPERIAL HEIGHT: 6'07"
IMPERIAL WEIGHT: 33.1 lbs.
METRIC HEIGHT: 2.0 m
METRIC WEIGHT: 15.0 kg
GENDER: ♂ ♀
ABILITIES: Sand Rush
WEAKNESSES: Ghost, Dark

| GREAVARD | HOUNDSTONE |

#0367 HUNTAIL
Deep Sea Pokémon

TYPE: WATER

It's not the strongest swimmer. It wags its tail to lure in its prey and then gulps them down as soon as they get close.

Deep seas are their habitat. According to tradition, when Huntail wash up onshore, something unfortunate will happen.

HOW TO SAY IT: HUN-tail
IMPERIAL HEIGHT: 5'07"
IMPERIAL WEIGHT: 59.5 lbs.
METRIC HEIGHT: 1.7 m
METRIC WEIGHT: 27.0 kg
GENDER: ♂ ♀
ABILITIES: Swift Swim
WEAKNESSES: Grass, Electric

CLAMPERL → HUNTAIL

HYDREIGON #0635
Brutal Pokémon

TYPE: DARK-DRAGON

Only the central head has a brain. It is very intelligent, but it thinks only of destruction.

It's said that Hydreigon grew ferocious because people in times long past loathed it, considering it to be evil incarnate and attacking it relentlessly.

HOW TO SAY IT: hy-DRY-guhn
IMPERIAL HEIGHT: 5'11"
IMPERIAL WEIGHT: 352.7 lbs.
METRIC HEIGHT: 1.8 m
METRIC WEIGHT: 160.0 kg
GENDER: ♂ ♀
ABILITIES: Levitate
WEAKNESSES: Ice, Fighting, Bug, Dragon, Fairy

DEINO → ZWEILOUS → HYDREIGON

HYPNO
Hypnosis Pokémon

#0097

TYPE: PSYCHIC

When it locks eyes with an enemy, it will use a mix of psi moves, such as Hypnosis and Confusion.

Always holding a pendulum that it swings at a steady rhythm, it causes drowsiness in anyone nearby.

HOW TO SAY IT: HIP-no
IMPERIAL HEIGHT: 5'03"
IMPERIAL WEIGHT: 166.7 lbs.
METRIC HEIGHT: 1.6 m
METRIC WEIGHT: 75.6 kg
GENDER: ♂ ♀
ABILITIES: Insomnia, Forewarn
WEAKNESSES: Ghost, Dark, Bug

DROWZEE → **HYPNO**

IGGLYBUFF
Balloon Pokémon

#0174

TYPE: NORMAL-FAIRY

Its body has a faintly sweet scent and is bouncy and soft. If it bounces even once, it cannot stop.

It likes to sing but is not yet good at it. With praise and encouragement, it will get better little by little.

HOW TO SAY IT: IG-lee-buff
IMPERIAL HEIGHT: 1'00"
IMPERIAL WEIGHT: 2.2 lbs.
METRIC HEIGHT: 0.3 m
METRIC WEIGHT: 1.0 kg
GENDER: ♂ ♀
ABILITIES: Cute Charm, Competitive
WEAKNESSES: Steel, Poison

IGGLYBUFF **JIGGLYPUFF** **WIGGLYTUFF**

ILLUMISE

Firefly Pokémon

#0314

TYPE: BUG

Illumise attracts a swarm of Volbeat using a sweet fragrance. Once the Volbeat have gathered, this Pokémon leads the lit-up swarm in drawing geometric designs on the canvas of the night sky.

Illumise leads a flight of illuminated Volbeat to draw signs in the night sky. This Pokémon is said to earn greater respect from its peers by composing more complex designs in the sky.

HOW TO SAY IT: EE-loom-MEE-zay
IMPERIAL HEIGHT: 2'00"
IMPERIAL WEIGHT: 39.0 lbs.
METRIC HEIGHT: 0.6 m
METRIC WEIGHT: 17.7 kg
GENDER: ♀
ABILITIES: Oblivious, Tinted Lens
WEAKNESSES: Fire, Flying, Rock

DOES NOT EVOLVE

IMPIDIMP

Wily Pokémon

#0859

TYPE: DARK-FAIRY

The reason this Pokémon causes trouble for those it feels close to is because Impidimp itself gets irritable if it can't absorb negative emotions.

They live in groups, pestering and playing pranks on each other to polish their troublemaking skills.

HOW TO SAY IT: IMP-ih-dimp
IMPERIAL HEIGHT: 1'04"
IMPERIAL WEIGHT: 12.1 lbs.
METRIC HEIGHT: 0.4 m
METRIC WEIGHT: 5.5 kg
GENDER: ♂
ABILITIES: Prankster, Frisk
WEAKNESSES: Steel, Fairy, Poison

IMPIDIMP **MORGREM** **GRIMMSNARL**

265

INCINEROAR

Heel Pokémon

#0727

TYPE: FIRE-DARK

Although it's rough mannered and egotistical, it finds beating down unworthy opponents boring. It gets motivated for stronger opponents.

When its fighting spirit is set alight, the flames around its waist become especially intense.

HOW TO SAY IT: in-SIN-uh-roar
IMPERIAL HEIGHT: 5'11"
IMPERIAL WEIGHT: 183.0 lbs.
METRIC HEIGHT: 1.8 m
METRIC WEIGHT: 83.0 kg
GENDER: ♂ ♀
ABILITIES: Blaze
WEAKNESSES: Water, Ground, Fighting, Rock

LITTEN → **TORRACAT** → **INCINEROAR**

TYPE: PSYCHIC-NORMAL

INDEEDEE

#0876

Emotion Pokémon

This Pokémon picks up on the positive emotions of other creatures via its horns and uses those emotions to fuel itself.

This Pokémon never leaves its Trainer's side. It predicts their actions with its psychic power and takes care of their day-to-day needs.

HOW TO SAY IT: in-DEE-dee
IMPERIAL HEIGHT: 2'11"
IMPERIAL WEIGHT: 61.7 lbs.
METRIC HEIGHT: 0.9 m
METRIC WEIGHT: 28.0 kg
GENDER: ♂ ♀
ABILITIES: Inner Focus, Synchronize
WEAKNESSES: Dark, Bug

MALE FORM

FEMALE FORM

DOES NOT EVOLVE

INFERNAPE

Flame Pokémon

#0392

TYPE: FIRE-FIGHTING

Its crown of fire is indicative of its fiery nature. It is beaten by none in terms of quickness.

It tosses its enemies around with agility. It uses all its limbs to fight in its own unique style.

HOW TO SAY IT: in-FUR-nape
IMPERIAL HEIGHT: 3'11"
IMPERIAL WEIGHT: 121.3 lbs.
METRIC HEIGHT: 1.2 m
METRIC WEIGHT: 55.0 kg
GENDER: ♂ ♀
ABILITIES: Blaze
WEAKNESSES: Water, Psychic, Flying, Ground

CHIMCHAR **MONFERNO** **INFERNAPE**

INKAY

Revolving Pokémon

#0686

TYPE: DARK-PSYCHIC

It spins while making its luminescent spots flash. These spots allow it to communicate with others by using different patterns of light.

By exposing foes to the blinking of its luminescent spots, Inkay demoralizes them, and then it seizes the chance to flee.

HOW TO SAY IT: IN-kay
IMPERIAL HEIGHT: 1'04"
IMPERIAL WEIGHT: 7.7 lbs.
METRIC HEIGHT: 0.4 m
METRIC WEIGHT: 3.5 kg
GENDER: ♂ ♀
ABILITIES: Contrary, Suction Cups
WEAKNESSES: Fairy, Bug

INKAY **MALAMAR**

INTELEON
Secret Agent Pokémon

#0818

TYPE: WATER

It has many hidden capabilities, such as fingertips that can shoot water and a membrane on its back that it can use to glide through the air.

Its nictitating membranes let it pick out foes' weak points so it can precisely blast them with water that shoots from its fingertips at Mach 3.

HOW TO SAY IT: in-TELL-ee-un
IMPERIAL HEIGHT: 6'03"
IMPERIAL WEIGHT: 99.6 lbs.
METRIC HEIGHT: 1.9 m
METRIC WEIGHT: 45.2 kg
GENDER: ♂ ♀
ABILITIES: Torrent
WEAKNESSES: Grass, Electric

SOBBLE → DRIZZILE → INTELEON

GIGANTAMAX INTELEON

Gigantamax Inteleon's Water Gun move fires at Mach 7. As the Pokémon takes aim, it uses the crest on its head to gauge wind and temperature.

It has excellent sniping skills. Shooting a berry rolling along over nine miles away is a piece of cake for this Pokémon.

IMPERIAL HEIGHT: 131'03"+
IMPERIAL WEIGHT: ????.? lbs.
METRIC HEIGHT: 40.0+ m
METRIC WEIGHT: ???.? kg

#0991

IRON BUNDLE
Paradox Pokémon

DOES NOT EVOLVE

TYPE: ICE-WATER

Its shape is similar to a robot featured in a paranormal magazine article. The robot was said to have been created by an ancient civilization.

It resembles a mysterious object mentioned in an old book. There are only two reported sightings of this Pokémon.

HOW TO SAY IT: EYE-ern BUN-del
IMPERIAL HEIGHT: 2'00"
IMPERIAL WEIGHT: 24.3 lbs.
METRIC HEIGHT: 0.6 m
METRIC WEIGHT: 11.0 kg
GENDER: Unknown
ABILITIES: Quark Drive
WEAKNESSES: Grass, Electric, Fighting, Rock

#0992

IRON HANDS
Paradox Pokémon

DOES NOT EVOLVE

TYPE: FIGHTING-ELECTRIC

It is very similar to a cyborg covered exclusively by a paranormal magazine. The cyborg was said to be the modified form of a certain athlete.

This Pokémon shares many similarities with Iron Hands, an object mentioned in a certain expedition journal.

HOW TO SAY IT: EYE-ern HANDS
IMPERIAL HEIGHT: 5'11"
IMPERIAL WEIGHT: 839.3 lbs.
METRIC HEIGHT: 1.8 m
METRIC WEIGHT: 380.7 kg
GENDER: Unknown
ABILITIES: Quark Drive
WEAKNESSES: Psychic, Fairy, Ground

IRON JUGULIS
Paradox Pokémon

TYPE: DARK-FLYING

It resembles a certain Pokémon introduced in a paranormal magazine, described as the offspring of a Hydreigon that fell in love with a robot.

It's possible that Iron Jugulis, an object described in an old book, may actually be this Pokémon.

HOW TO SAY IT: EYE-ern JUH-gyoo-lihs
IMPERIAL HEIGHT: 4'03"
IMPERIAL WEIGHT: 244.7 lbs.
METRIC HEIGHT: 1.3 m
METRIC WEIGHT: 111.0 kg
GENDER: Unknown
ABILITIES: Quark Drive
WEAKNESSES: Fairy, Electric, Ice, Rock

DOES NOT EVOLVE

IRON MOTH
Paradox Pokémon

TYPE: FIRE-POISON

This Pokémon resembles an Unknown object described in a paranormal magazine as a UFO sent to observe humanity.

No records exist of this species being caught. Data is lacking, but the Pokémon's traits match up with an object described in an old book.

HOW TO SAY IT: EYE-ern MAHTH
IMPERIAL HEIGHT: 3'11"
IMPERIAL WEIGHT: 79.4 lbs.
METRIC HEIGHT: 1.2 m
METRIC WEIGHT: 36.0 kg
GENDER: Unknown
ABILITIES: Quark Drive
WEAKNESSES: Water, Psychic, Ground, Rock

DOES NOT EVOLVE

#0995

IRON THORNS
Paradox Pokémon

TYPE: ROCK-ELECTRIC

It has some similarities to a Pokémon introduced in a dubious magazine as a Tyranitar from one billion years into the future.

Some of its notable features match those of an object named within a certain expedition journal as Iron Thorns.

HOW TO SAY IT: EYE-ern THORNS
IMPERIAL HEIGHT: 5'03"
IMPERIAL WEIGHT: 668.0 lbs.
METRIC HEIGHT: 1.6 m
METRIC WEIGHT: 303.0 kg
GENDER: Unknown
ABILITIES: Quark Drive
WEAKNESSES: Water, Grass, Fighting, Ground

DOES NOT EVOLVE

PARADOX POKÉMON

#0990

IRON TREADS
Paradox Pokémon

TYPE: GROUND-STEEL

This Pokémon closely resembles a scientific weapon that a paranormal magazine claimed was sent to this planet by aliens.

Sightings of this Pokémon have occurred in recent years. It resembles a mysterious object described in an old expedition journal.

HOW TO SAY IT: EYE-ern TREDS
IMPERIAL HEIGHT: 2'11"
IMPERIAL WEIGHT: 529.1 lbs.
METRIC HEIGHT: 0.9 m
METRIC WEIGHT: 240.0 kg
GENDER: Unknown
ABILITIES: Quark Drive
WEAKNESSES: Fire, Water, Fighting, Ground

DOES NOT EVOLVE

IRON VALIANT
Paradox Pokémon

#1006

PARADOX POKÉMON

TYPE: FAIRY-FIGHTING

It has some similarities to a mad scientist's invention covered in a paranormal magazine.

It's possible that this is the object listed as Iron Valiant in a certain expedition journal.

HOW TO SAY IT: EYE-ern VAL-ee-ent
IMPERIAL HEIGHT: 4'07"
IMPERIAL WEIGHT: 77.2 lbs.
METRIC HEIGHT: 1.4 m
METRIC WEIGHT: 35.0 kg
GENDER: Unknown
ABILITIES: Quark Drive
WEAKNESSES: Steel, Psychic, Flying, Fairy, Poison

IVYSAUR
Seed Pokémon

#0002

TYPE: GRASS-POISON

When the bulb on its back grows large, it appears to lose the ability to stand on its hind legs.

Exposure to sunlight adds to its strength. Sunlight also makes the bud on its back grow larger.

HOW TO SAY IT: EYE-vee-sore
IMPERIAL HEIGHT: 3'03"
IMPERIAL WEIGHT: 28.7 lbs.
METRIC HEIGHT: 1.0 m
METRIC WEIGHT: 13.0 kg
GENDER: ♂ ♀
ABILITIES: Overgrow
WEAKNESSES: Fire, Psychic, Flying, Ice

BULBASAUR

IVYSAUR

VENUSAUR

MEGA VENUSAUR

JANGMO-O
Scaly Pokémon

#0782

TYPE: DRAGON

They learn to fight by smashing their head scales together. The dueling strengthens both their skills and their spirits.

Jangmo-o strikes its scales to communicate with others of its kind. Its scales are actually fur that's become as hard as metal.

HOW TO SAY IT: JANG-MOH-oh
IMPERIAL HEIGHT: 2'00"
IMPERIAL WEIGHT: 65.5 lbs.
METRIC HEIGHT: 0.6 m
METRIC WEIGHT: 29.7 kg
GENDER: ♂ ♀
ABILITIES: Bulletproof, Soundproof
WEAKNESSES: Fairy, Ice, Dragon

JANGMO-O **HAKAMO-O** **KOMMO-O**

#0593

JELLICENT
Floating Pokémon

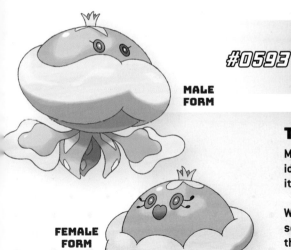

MALE FORM

FEMALE FORM

TYPE: WATER-GHOST

Most of this Pokémon's body composition is identical to sea water. It makes sunken ships its lair.

Whenever a full moon hangs in the night sky, schools of Jellicent gather near the surface of the sea, waiting for their prey to appear.

HOW TO SAY IT: JEL-ih-sent
IMPERIAL HEIGHT: 7'03"
IMPERIAL WEIGHT: 297.6 lbs.
METRIC HEIGHT: 2.2 m
METRIC WEIGHT: 135.0 kg
GENDER: ♂ ♀
ABILITIES: Water Absorb, Cursed Body
WEAKNESSES: Ghost, Dark, Grass, Electric

FRILLISH **JELLICENT**

#0039 JIGGLYPUFF
Balloon Pokémon

TYPE: NORMAL-FAIRY

When its huge eyes waver, it sings a mysteriously soothing melody that lulls its enemies to sleep.

If it inflates to sing a lullaby, it can perform longer and cause sure drowsiness in its audience.

HOW TO SAY IT: JIG-lee-puff
IMPERIAL HEIGHT: 1'08"
IMPERIAL WEIGHT: 12.1 lbs.
METRIC HEIGHT: 0.5 m
METRIC WEIGHT: 5.5 kg
GENDER: ♂ ♀
ABILITIES: Cute Charm, Competitive
WEAKNESSES: Steel, Poison

IGGLYBUFF ➡ **JIGGLYPUFF** ➡ **WIGGLYTUFF**

JIRACHI #0385
Wish Pokémon

MYTHICAL POKÉMON

TYPE: STEEL-PSYCHIC

A legend states that Jirachi will make true any wish that is written on notes attached to its head when it awakens. If this Pokémon senses danger, it will fight without awakening.

Jirachi will awaken from its sleep of a thousand years if you sing to it in a voice of purity. It is said to make true any wish that people desire.

HOW TO SAY IT: jir-AH-chi
IMPERIAL HEIGHT: 1'00"
IMPERIAL WEIGHT: 2.4 lbs.
METRIC HEIGHT: 0.3 m
METRIC WEIGHT: 1.1 kg
GENDER: Unknown
ABILITIES: Serene Grace
WEAKNESSES: Ghost, Fire, Dark, Ground

DOES NOT EVOLVE

#0135

JOLTEON
Lightning Pokémon

TYPE: ELECTRIC

It concentrates the weak electric charges emitted by its cells and launches wicked lightning bolts.

If agitated, it uses electricity to straighten out its fur and launch it in small bunches.

HOW TO SAY IT: JOL-tee-on
IMPERIAL HEIGHT: 2'07"
IMPERIAL WEIGHT: 54.0 lbs.
METRIC HEIGHT: 0.8 m
METRIC WEIGHT: 24.5 kg
GENDER: ♂ ♀
ABILITIES: Volt Absorb
WEAKNESSES: Ground

EEVEE → JOLTEON

#0595

JOLTIK
Attaching Pokémon

TYPE: BUG-ELECTRIC

Joltik can be found clinging to other Pokémon. It's soaking up static electricity because it can't produce a charge on its own.

Joltik latch on to other Pokémon and suck out static electricity. They're often found sticking to Yamper's hindquarters.

HOW TO SAY IT: JOHL-tik
IMPERIAL HEIGHT: 0'04"
IMPERIAL WEIGHT: 1.3 lbs.
METRIC HEIGHT: 0.1 m
METRIC WEIGHT: 0.6 kg
GENDER: ♂ ♀
ABILITIES: Compound Eyes, Unnerve
WEAKNESSES: Fire, Rock

JOLTIK   GALVANTULA

JUMPLUFF

Cottonweed Pokémon

#0189

TYPE: GRASS-FLYING

Jumpluff travels on seasonal winds. Once its cotton spores run out, its journey ends, as does its life.

Beware its cotton spores. If you accidentally breathe them in, you'll be racked with coughs and itchiness.

HOW TO SAY IT: JUM-pluff
IMPERIAL HEIGHT: 2'07"
IMPERIAL WEIGHT: 6.6 lbs.
METRIC HEIGHT: 0.8 m
METRIC WEIGHT: 3.0 kg
GENDER: ♂♀
ABILITIES: Chlorophyll, Leaf Guard
WEAKNESSES: Fire, Flying, Ice, Poison, Rock

| HOPPIP | SKIPLOOM | JUMPLUFF |

JYNX

Human Shape Pokémon

#0124

TYPE: ICE-PSYCHIC

In certain parts of Galar, Jynx was once feared and worshiped as the Queen of Ice.

The Jynx of Galar often have beautiful and delicate voices. Some of these Pokémon have even gathered a fan base.

HOW TO SAY IT: JINX
IMPERIAL HEIGHT: 4'07"
IMPERIAL WEIGHT: 89.5 lbs.
METRIC HEIGHT: 1.4 m
METRIC WEIGHT: 40.6 kg
GENDER: ♀
ABILITIES: Oblivious, Forewarn
WEAKNESSES: Steel, Ghost, Fire, Dark, Rock, Bug

| SMOOCHUM | JYNX |

#0140

KABUTO

Shellfish Pokémon

TYPE: ROCK-WATER

This species is almost entirely extinct. Kabuto molt every three days, making their shells harder and harder.

While some say this species has gone extinct, Kabuto sightings are apparently fairly common in some places.

KABUTO → KABUTOPS

HOW TO SAY IT: ka-BOO-toe
IMPERIAL HEIGHT: 1'08"
IMPERIAL WEIGHT: 25.4 lbs.
METRIC HEIGHT: 0.5 m
METRIC WEIGHT: 11.5 kg
GENDER: ♂ ♀
ABILITIES: Swift Swim, Battle Armor
WEAKNESSES: Grass, Electric, Fighting, Ground

#0141

KABUTOPS

Shellfish Pokémon

TYPE: ROCK-WATER

Kabutops slices its prey apart and sucks out the fluids. The discarded body parts become food for other Pokémon.

The cause behind the extinction of this species is unknown. Kabutops were aggressive Pokémon that inhabited warm seas.

HOW TO SAY IT: KA-boo-tops
IMPERIAL HEIGHT: 4'03"
IMPERIAL WEIGHT: 89.3 lbs.
METRIC HEIGHT: 1.3 m
METRIC WEIGHT: 40.5 kg
GENDER: ♂ ♀
ABILITIES: Swift Swim, Battle Armor
WEAKNESSES: Grass, Electric, Fighting, Ground

KABUTO → KABUTOPS

KADABRA

Psi Pokémon

#0064

TYPE: PSYCHIC

Using its psychic power, Kadabra levitates as it sleeps. It uses its springy tail as a pillow.

This Pokémon's telekinesis is immensely powerful. To prepare for evolution, Kadabra stores up psychic energy in the star on its forehead.

HOW TO SAY IT: kuh-DAB-ra
IMPERIAL HEIGHT: 4'03"
IMPERIAL WEIGHT: 124.6 lbs.
METRIC HEIGHT: 1.3 m
METRIC WEIGHT: 56.5 kg
GENDER: ♂ ♀
ABILITIES: Synchronize, Inner Focus
WEAKNESSES: Ghost, Dark, Bug

ABRA   KADABRA   ALAKAZAM   MEGA ALAKAZAM

KAKUNA

Cocoon Pokémon

#0014

TYPE: BUG-POISON

Able to move only slightly. When endangered, it may stick out its stinger and poison its enemy.

HOW TO SAY IT: kah-KOO-na
IMPERIAL HEIGHT: 2'00"
IMPERIAL WEIGHT: 22.0 lbs.
METRIC HEIGHT: 0.6 m
METRIC WEIGHT: 10.0 kg
GENDER: ♂ ♀
ABILITIES: Shed Skin
WEAKNESSES: Fire, Psychic, Flying, Rock

WEEDLE   KAKUNA   BEEDRILL   MEGA BEEDRILL

KANGASKHAN

#0115

Parent Pokémon

TYPE: NORMAL

Although it's carrying its baby in a pouch on its belly, Kangaskhan is swift on its feet. It intimidates its opponents with quick jabs.

There are records of a lost human child being raised by a childless Kangaskhan.

HOW TO SAY IT: KANG-gas-con
IMPERIAL HEIGHT: 7'03"
IMPERIAL WEIGHT: 176.4 lbs.
METRIC HEIGHT: 2.2 m
METRIC WEIGHT: 80.0 kg
GENDER: ♀
ABILITIES: Early Bird, Scrappy
WEAKNESSES: Fighting

MEGA KANGASKHAN

TYPE: NORMAL

Its child has grown rapidly, thanks to the energy of Mega Evolution. Mother and child show off their harmonious teamwork in battle.

IMPERIAL HEIGHT: 7'03"
IMPERIAL WEIGHT: 220.5 lbs.
METRIC HEIGHT: 2.2 m
METRIC WEIGHT: 100.0 kg

KANGASKHAN

MEGA KANGASKHAN

KARRABLAST

Clamping Pokémon

#0588

TYPE: BUG

Its strange physiology reacts to electrical energy in interesting ways. The presence of a Shelmet will cause this Pokémon to evolve.

It spits a liquid from its mouth to melt through Shelmet's shell. Karrablast doesn't eat the shell—it eats only the contents.

HOW TO SAY IT: KAIR-ruh-blast
IMPERIAL HEIGHT: 1'08"
IMPERIAL WEIGHT: 13.0 lbs.
METRIC HEIGHT: 0.5 m
METRIC WEIGHT: 5.9 kg
GENDER: ♂ ♀
ABILITIES: Swarm, Shed Skin
WEAKNESSES: Fire, Flying, Rock

KARRABLAST   ESCAVALIER

KARTANA

Drawn Sword Pokémon

#0798

ULTRA BEAST

TYPE: GRASS-STEEL

This Ultra Beast's body, which is as thin as paper, is like a sharpened sword.

Although it's alien to this world and a danger here, it's apparently a common organism in the world where it normally lives.

HOW TO SAY IT: kar-TAH-nuh
IMPERIAL HEIGHT: 1'00"
IMPERIAL WEIGHT: 0.2 lbs.
METRIC HEIGHT: 0.3 m
METRIC WEIGHT: 0.1 kg
GENDER: Unknown
ABILITIES: Beast Boost
WEAKNESSES: Fire, Fighting

DOES NOT EVOLVE

#0352 **KECLEON**
Color Swap Pokémon

TYPE: NORMAL

It changes its hue to blend into its surroundings. If no one takes notice of it for too long, it will pout and never reveal itself.

Its color changes for concealment and also when its mood or health changes. The darker the color, the healthier it is.

HOW TO SAY IT: KEH-clee-on
IMPERIAL HEIGHT: 3'03"
IMPERIAL WEIGHT: 48.5 lbs.
METRIC HEIGHT: 1.0 m
METRIC WEIGHT: 22.0 kg
GENDER: ♂ ♀
ABILITIES: Color Change
WEAKNESSES: Fighting

DOES NOT EVOLVE

MYTHICAL POKÉMON

#0647 **KELDEO**
Colt Pokémon

TYPE: WATER-FIGHTING

It crosses the world, running over the surfaces of oceans and rivers. It appears at scenic waterfronts.

When it is resolute, its body fills with power and it becomes swifter. Its jumps are then too fast to follow.

HOW TO SAY IT: KELL-dee-oh
IMPERIAL HEIGHT: 4'07"
IMPERIAL WEIGHT: 106.9 lbs.
METRIC HEIGHT: 1.4 m
METRIC WEIGHT: 48.5 kg
GENDER: Unknown
ABILITIES: Justified
WEAKNESSES: Fairy, Grass, Flying, Psychic, Electric

ORDINARY FORM

RESOLUTE FORM

DOES NOT EVOLVE

KILOWATTREL

Frigatebird Pokémon

#0941

TYPE: ELECTRIC-FLYING

Kilowattrel inflates its throat sac to amplify its electricity. By riding the wind, this Pokémon can fly over 430 miles in a day.

It uses its throat sac to store electricity generated by its wings. There's hardly any oil in its feathers, so it is a poor swimmer.

HOW TO SAY IT: KIH-loh-WAHT-rel
IMPERIAL HEIGHT: 4'07"
IMPERIAL WEIGHT: 85.1 lbs.
METRIC HEIGHT: 1.4 m
METRIC WEIGHT: 38.6 kg
GENDER: ♂ ♀
ABILITIES: Wind Power, Volt Absorb
WEAKNESSES: Ice, Rock

WATTREL

KILOWATTREL

KINGAMBIT

#0983

Big Blade Pokémon

TYPE: DARK-STEEL

Only a Bisharp that stands above all others in its vast army can evolve into Kingambit.

Though it commands a massive army in battle, it's not skilled at devising complex strategies. It just uses brute strength to keep pushing.

HOW TO SAY IT: kihn-GAM-bet
IMPERIAL HEIGHT: 6'07"
IMPERIAL WEIGHT: 264.6 lbs.
METRIC WEIGHT: 120.0 kg
METRIC HEIGHT: 2.0 m
GENDER: ♂ ♀
ABILITIES: Defiant, Supreme Overlord
WEAKNESSES: Fire, Fighting, Ground

PAWNIARD **BISHARP** **KINGAMBIT**

KINGDRA

#0230

Dragon Pokémon

TYPE: WATER-DRAGON

With the arrival of a storm at sea, this Pokémon will show itself on the surface. When a Kingdra and a Dragonite meet, a fierce battle ensues.

Scales shed by this Pokémon have such a splendorous gleam to them that they've been given to royalty as gifts.

HOW TO SAY IT: KING-dra
IMPERIAL HEIGHT: 5'11"
IMPERIAL WEIGHT: 335.1 lbs.
METRIC HEIGHT: 1.8 m
METRIC WEIGHT: 152.0 kg
GENDER: ♂ ♀
ABILITIES: Swift Swim, Sniper
WEAKNESSES: Fairy, Dragon

HORSEA

SEADRA

KINGDRA

TYPE: WATER

#0099

KINGLER

Pincer Pokémon

The larger pincer has 10,000-horsepower strength. However, it is so heavy, it is difficult to aim.

HOW TO SAY IT: KING-lur
IMPERIAL HEIGHT: 4'03"
IMPERIAL WEIGHT: 132.3 lbs.
METRIC HEIGHT: 1.3 m
METRIC WEIGHT: 60.0 kg
GENDER: ♂ ♀
ABILITIES: Hyper Cutter, Shell Armor
WEAKNESSES: Grass, Electric

KRABBY → KINGLER

GIGANTAMAX KINGLER

The flow of Gigantamax energy has spurred this Pokémon's left pincer to grow to an enormous size. That claw can pulverize anything.

The bubbles it spews out are strongly alkaline. Any opponents hit by them will have their bodies quickly melted away.

IMPERIAL HEIGHT: 62'04"+
IMPERIAL WEIGHT: ????.? lbs.
METRIC HEIGHT: 19.0+ m
METRIC WEIGHT: ???.? kg

KIRLIA
Emotion Pokémon

#0281

TYPE: PSYCHIC-FAIRY

It has a psychic power that enables it to distort the space around it and see into the future.

The cheerful spirit of its Trainer gives it energy for its psychokinetic power. It spins and dances when happy.

HOW TO SAY IT: KERL-lee-ah
IMPERIAL HEIGHT: 2'07"　　**METRIC HEIGHT:** 0.8 m
IMPERIAL WEIGHT: 44.5 lbs.　**METRIC WEIGHT:** 20.2 kg
GENDER: ♂ ♀
ABILITIES: Synchronize, Trace
WEAKNESSES: Ghost, Steel, Poison

GARDEVOIR　　MEGA GARDEVOIR

RALTS　　KIRLIA

GALLADE　　MEGA GALLADE

KLANG
Gear Pokémon

#0600

TYPE: STEEL

When Klang goes all out, the minigear links up perfectly with the outer part of the big gear, and this Pokémon's rotation speed increases sharply.

Many companies in the Galar region choose Klang as their logo. This Pokémon is considered the symbol of industrial technology.

HOW TO SAY IT: KLANG
IMPERIAL HEIGHT: 2'00"　　**METRIC HEIGHT:** 0.6 m
IMPERIAL WEIGHT: 112.4 lbs.　**METRIC WEIGHT:** 51.0 kg
GENDER: Unknown
ABILITIES: Plus, Minus
WEAKNESSES: Fire, Fighting, Ground

KLINK　　　KLANG　　　KLINKLANG

KLAWF

Ambush Pokémon

#0950

TYPE: ROCK

Klawf hangs upside down from cliffs, waiting for prey. But Klawf can't remain in this position for long because its blood rushes to its head.

This Pokémon lives on sheer cliffs. It sidesteps opponents' attacks, then lunges for their weak spots with its claws.

HOW TO SAY IT: KLAWF
IMPERIAL HEIGHT: 4'03"
IMPERIAL WEIGHT: 174.2 lbs.
METRIC HEIGHT: 1.3 m
METRIC WEIGHT: 79.0 kg
GENDER: ♂ ♀
ABILITIES: Anger Shell, Shell Armor
WEAKNESSES: Water, Steel, Grass, Fighting, Ground

DOES NOT EVOLVE

KLEAVOR

Axe Pokémon

#0900

TYPE: BUG-ROCK

A violent creature that fells towering trees with its crude axes and shields itself with hard stone. If one should chance upon this Pokémon in the wilds, one's only recourse is to flee.

HOW TO SAY IT: KLEE-vor
IMPERIAL HEIGHT: 5'11"
IMPERIAL WEIGHT: 196.2 lbs.
METRIC HEIGHT: 1.8 m
METRIC WEIGHT: 89.0 kg
GENDER: ♂ ♀
ABILITIES: N/A
WEAKNESSES: Steel, Water, Rock

SCYTHER   ➡   KLEAVOR

TYPE: STEEL-FAIRY

KLEFKI

#0707

Key Ring Pokémon

Once it absorbs a key's metal ions, it discards the key without a second thought. However, it will hang on to keys it favors for decades.

In the past, noble families entrusted their vault keys to a Klefki. They passed the Klefki down through the generations, taking good care of it.

HOW TO SAY IT: KLEF-key
IMPERIAL HEIGHT: 0'08"
IMPERIAL WEIGHT: 6.6 lbs.
METRIC HEIGHT: 0.2 m
METRIC WEIGHT: 3.0 kg
GENDER: ♂ ♀
ABILITIES: Prankster
WEAKNESSES: Fire, Ground

DOES NOT EVOLVE

TYPE: STEEL

KLINK

#0599

Gear Pokémon

The two minigears that compose this Pokémon are closer than twins. They mesh well only with each other.

It's suspected that Klink were the inspiration behind ancient people's invention of the first gears.

HOW TO SAY IT: KLEENK
IMPERIAL HEIGHT: 1'00"
IMPERIAL WEIGHT: 46.3 lbs.
METRIC HEIGHT: 0.3 m
METRIC WEIGHT: 21.0 kg
GENDER: Unknown
ABILITIES: Plus, Minus
WEAKNESSES: Fire, Fighting, Ground

KLINK **KLANG** **KLINKLANG**

KLINKLANG

Gear Pokémon

#0601

TYPE: STEEL

From its spikes, it launches powerful blasts of electricity. Its red core contains an enormous amount of energy.

The three gears that compose this Pokémon spin at high speed. Its new spiked gear isn't a living creature.

HOW TO SAY IT: KLEENK-klang
IMPERIAL HEIGHT: 2'00"
IMPERIAL WEIGHT: 178.6 lbs.
METRIC HEIGHT: 0.6 m
METRIC WEIGHT: 81.0 kg
GENDER: Unknown
ABILITIES: Plus, Minus
WEAKNESSES: Fire, Fighting, Ground

| KLINK | KLANG | KLINKLANG |

KOFFING

Poison Gas Pokémon

#0109

TYPE: POISON

Its body is full of poisonous gas. It floats into garbage dumps, seeking out the fumes of raw, rotting trash.

It adores polluted air. Some claim that Koffing used to be more plentiful in the Galar region than they are now.

HOW TO SAY IT: KOFF-ing
IMPERIAL HEIGHT: 2'00"
IMPERIAL WEIGHT: 2.2 lbs.
METRIC HEIGHT: 0.6 m
METRIC WEIGHT: 1.0 kg
GENDER: ♂ ♀
ABILITIES: Levitate, Neutralizing Gas
WEAKNESSES: Psychic, Ground

WEEZING

KOFFING

GALARIAN WEEZING

#0775

KOMALA
Drowsing Pokémon

TYPE: NORMAL

Komala spends its entire life sleeping. It feeds on leaves that contain a potent poison only Komala can break down.

A potent anesthetic can be made by diluting Komala's drool. This anesthetic was used for surgeries in the past.

HOW TO SAY IT: koh-MAH-luh
IMPERIAL HEIGHT: 1'04"
IMPERIAL WEIGHT: 43.9 lbs.
METRIC HEIGHT: 0.4 m
METRIC WEIGHT: 19.9 kg
GENDER: ♂ ♀
ABILITIES: Comatose
WEAKNESSES: Fighting

DOES NOT EVOLVE

#0784

KOMMO-O
Scaly Pokémon

TYPE: DRAGON-FIGHTING

It clatters its tail scales to unnerve opponents. This Pokémon will battle only those who stand steadfast in the face of this display.

Certain ruins have paintings of ancient warriors wearing armor made of Kommo-o scales.

HOW TO SAY IT: koh-MOH-oh
IMPERIAL HEIGHT: 5'03"   **METRIC HEIGHT:** 1.6 m
IMPERIAL WEIGHT: 172.4 lbs.   **METRIC WEIGHT:** 78.2 kg
GENDER: ♂ ♀
ABILITIES: Bulletproof, Soundproof
WEAKNESSES: Fairy, Flying, Psychic, Ice, Dragon

 JANGMO-O ➡ **HAKAMO-O** ➡ **KOMMO-O**

KORAIDON

Paradox Pokémon

#1007

LEGENDARY POKÉMON

TYPE: FIGHTING-DRAGON

This seems to be the Winged King mentioned in an old expedition journal. It was said to have split the land with its bare fists.

This Pokémon resembles Cyclizar, but it is far burlier and more ferocious. Nothing is known about its ecology or other features.

HOW TO SAY IT: koh-RAI-dahn
IMPERIAL HEIGHT: 8'02"
IMPERIAL WEIGHT: 668.0 lbs.
METRIC HEIGHT: 2.5 m
METRIC WEIGHT: 303.0 kg
GENDER: Unknown
ABILITIES: Orichalcum Pulse
WEAKNESSES: Psychic, Flying, Fairy, Ice, Dragon

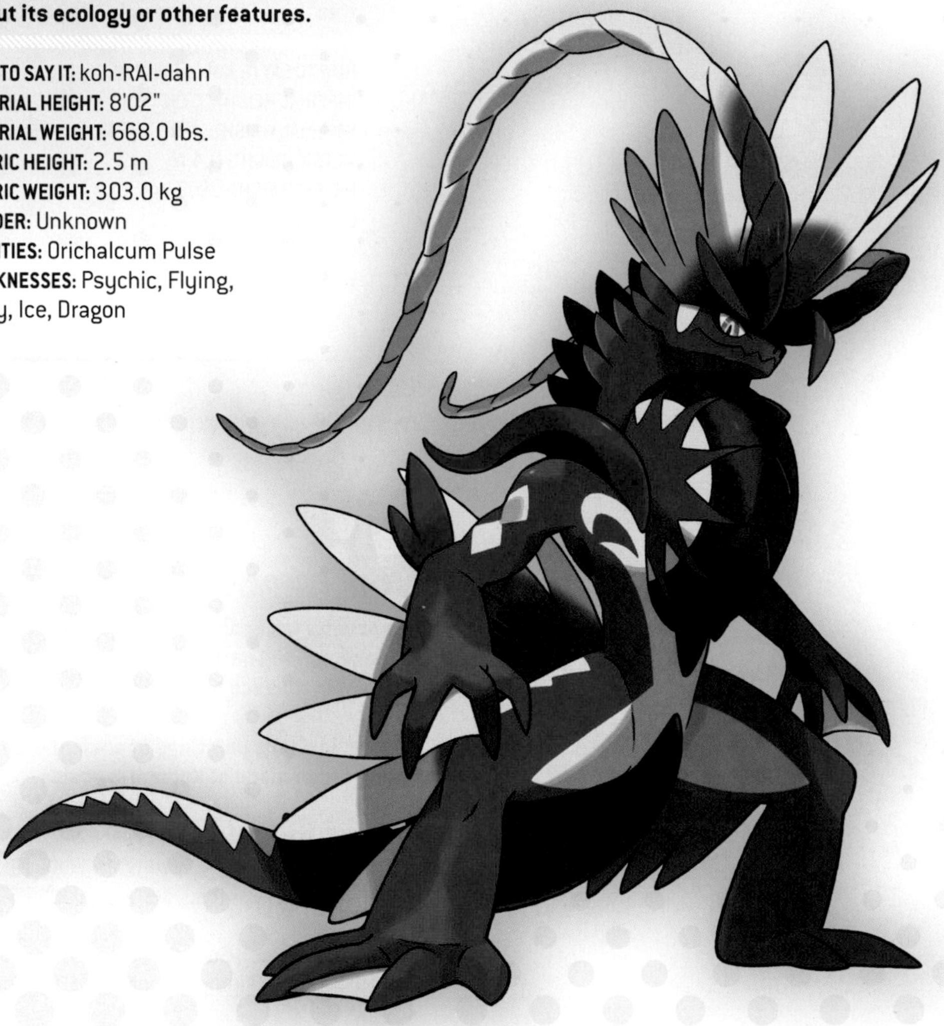

DOES NOT EVOLVE

KRABBY
River Crab Pokémon

#0098

TYPE: WATER

It can be found near the sea. The large pincers grow back if they are torn out of their sockets.

If it senses danger approaching, it cloaks itself with bubbles from its mouth so it will look bigger.

HOW TO SAY IT: KRAB-ee
IMPERIAL HEIGHT: 1'04"
IMPERIAL WEIGHT: 14.3 lbs.
METRIC HEIGHT: 0.4 m
METRIC WEIGHT: 6.5 kg
GENDER: ♂ ♀
ABILITIES: Hyper Cutter, Shell Armor
WEAKNESSES: Grass, Electric

KRABBY **KINGLER**

KRICKETOT
Cricket Pokémon

#0401

TYPE: BUG

Its legs are short. Whenever it stumbles, its stiff antennae clack with a xylophone-like sound.

When its antennae hit each other, it sounds like the music of a xylophone.

HOW TO SAY IT: KRICK-eh-tot
IMPERIAL HEIGHT: 1'00"
IMPERIAL WEIGHT: 4.9 lbs.
METRIC HEIGHT: 0.3 m
METRIC WEIGHT: 2.2 kg
GENDER: ♂ ♀
ABILITIES: Shed Skin
WEAKNESSES: Fire, Flying, Rock

KRICKETOT **KRICKETUNE**

TYPE: BUG

By allowing its cry to resonate in the hollow of its belly, it produces a captivating sound.

There is a village that hosts a contest based on the amazingly variable cries of this Pokémon.

HOW TO SAY IT: KRICK-eh-toon
IMPERIAL HEIGHT: 3'03"
IMPERIAL WEIGHT: 56.2 lbs.
METRIC HEIGHT: 1.0 m
METRIC WEIGHT: 25.5 kg
GENDER: ♂ ♀
ABILITIES: Swarm
WEAKNESSES: Fire, Flying, Rock

#0402

KRICKETUNE
Cricket Pokémon

KRICKETOT ▶ **KRICKETUNE**

#0552

KROKOROK
Desert Croc Pokémon

TYPE: GROUND-DARK

Protected by thin membranes, their eyes can see even in the dead of night. They live in groups of a few individuals.

Thanks to the special membrane covering its eyes, it can see its surroundings clearly, even in the middle of the night.

HOW TO SAY IT: KRAHK-oh-rahk
IMPERIAL HEIGHT: 3'03"
IMPERIAL WEIGHT: 73.6 lbs.
METRIC HEIGHT: 1.0 m
METRIC WEIGHT: 33.4 kg
GENDER: ♂ ♀
ABILITIES: Intimidate, Moxie
WEAKNESSES: Ice, Water, Fighting, Fairy, Grass, Bug

SANDILE   **KROKOROK**   **KROOKODILE**

KROOKODILE
Intimidation Pokémon

#0553

TYPE: GROUND-DARK

After clamping down with its powerful jaws, it twists its body around to rip its prey in half.

Its unique faculty of sight can detect small prey more than 30 miles away, even in the midst of a sandstorm.

HOW TO SAY IT: KROOK-oh-dyle
IMPERIAL HEIGHT: 4'11"
IMPERIAL WEIGHT: 212.3 lbs.
METRIC HEIGHT: 1.5 m
METRIC WEIGHT: 96.3 kg
GENDER: ♂ ♀
ABILITIES: Intimidate, Moxie
WEAKNESSES: Ice, Water, Fighting, Fairy, Grass, Bug

SANDILE → **KROKOROK** → **KROOKODILE**

LEGENDARY POKÉMON

#0891

KUBFU
Wushu Pokémon

TYPE: FIGHTING

Kubfu trains hard to perfect its moves. The moves it masters will determine which form it takes when it evolves.

If Kubfu pulls the long white hair on its head, its fighting spirit heightens and power wells up from the depths of its belly.

HOW TO SAY IT: kub-foo
IMPERIAL HEIGHT: 2'00"
IMPERIAL WEIGHT: 26.5 lbs.
METRIC HEIGHT: 0.6 m
METRIC WEIGHT: 12.0 kg
GENDER: ♂ ♀
ABILITIES: Inner Focus
WEAKNESSES: Psychic, Flying, Fairy

KUBFU **URSHIFU**

LEGENDARY POKÉMON

KYOGRE
Sea Basin Pokémon

TYPE: WATER

Through Primal Reversion and with nature's full power, it will take back its true form. It can summon storms that cause the sea levels to rise.

Kyogre is said to be the personification of the sea itself. Legends tell of its many clashes against Groudon, as each sought to gain the power of nature.

HOW TO SAY IT: kai-OH-gurr
IMPERIAL HEIGHT: 14'09"
IMPERIAL WEIGHT: 776.0 lbs.
METRIC HEIGHT: 4.5 m
METRIC WEIGHT: 352.0 kg
GENDER: Unknown
ABILITIES: Drizzle
WEAKNESSES: Grass, Electric

PRIMAL KYOGRE

TYPE: WATER

IMPERIAL HEIGHT: 32'02"
IMPERIAL WEIGHT: 948.0 lbs.
METRIC HEIGHT: 9.8 m
METRIC WEIGHT: 430.0 kg
ABILITIES: Primodial Sea
WEAKNESSES: Grass, Electric

KYOGRE PRIMAL KYOGRE

KYUREM

Boundary Pokémon

#0646

LEGENDARY POKÉMON

TYPE: DRAGON-ICE

This legendary ice Pokémon waits for a hero to fill in the missing parts of its body with truth or ideals.

It generates a powerful, freezing energy inside itself, but its body became frozen when the energy leaked out.

HOW TO SAY IT: KYOO-rem
IMPERIAL HEIGHT: 9'10"
    Black Kyurem: 10'10"
    White Kyurem: 11'10"
IMPERIAL WEIGHT: 716.5 lbs.
METRIC HEIGHT: 3.0 m
BLACK KYUREM: 3.3m
WHITE KYUREM: 3.6m
METRIC WEIGHT: 325.0 kg
GENDER: Unknown
ABILITIES: Pressure
    Black Kyurem: Teravolt
    White Kyurem: Turboblaze
WEAKNESSES: Steel, Fairy, Rock, Fighting, Dragon

BLACK KYUREM

WHITE KYUREM

DOES NOT EVOLVE

TYPE: STEEL-ROCK

Lairon live in mountains brimming with spring water and iron ore, so these Pokémon often came into conflict with humans in the past.

During territorial disputes, Lairon fight by slamming into each other. Close inspection of their steel armor reveals scratches and dents.

HOW TO SAY IT: LAIR-ron
IMPERIAL HEIGHT: 2'11" **METRIC HEIGHT:** 0.9 m
IMPERIAL WEIGHT: 264.6 lbs. **METRIC WEIGHT:** 120.0 kg
GENDER: ♂ ♀
ABILITIES: Sturdy, Rock Head
WEAKNESSES: Water, Fighting, Ground

#0305

LAIRON
Iron Armor Pokémon

ARON **LAIRON** **AGGRON** **MEGA AGGRON**

#0608

LAMPENT
Lamp Pokémon

TYPE: GHOST-FIRE

This Pokémon appears just before someone passes away, so it's feared as an emissary of death.

It lurks in cities, pretending to be a lamp. Once it finds someone whose death is near, it will trail quietly after them.

HOW TO SAY IT: LAM-pent
IMPERIAL HEIGHT: 2'00" **METRIC HEIGHT:** 0.6 m
IMPERIAL WEIGHT: 28.7 lbs. **METRIC WEIGHT:** 13.0 kg
GENDER: ♂ ♀
ABILITIES: Flash Fire, Flame Body
WEAKNESSES: Ghost, Dark, Ground, Water, Rock

LITWICK **LAMPENT** **CHANDELURE**

LANDORUS

Abundance Pokémon

#0645

TYPE: GROUND-FLYING

Lands visited by Landorus grant such bountiful crops that it has been hailed as "The Guardian of the Fields."

From the forces of lightning and wind, it creates energy to give nutrients to the soil and make the land abundant.

HOW TO SAY IT: LAN-duh-rus
IMPERIAL HEIGHT: Incarnate Forme: 4'11"
                             Therian Forme: 4'03"
IMPERIAL WEIGHT: 149.9 lbs.
METRIC HEIGHT: Incarnate Forme: 1.5 m
                           Therian Forme: 1.3 m
METRIC WEIGHT: 68.0 kg
GENDER: ♂
ABILITIES: Incarnate Forme: Sand Force
                    Therian Forme: Intimidate
WEAKNESSES: Water, Ice

INCARNATE FORME

THERIAN FORME

DOES NOT EVOLVE

TYPE: WATER-ELECTRIC

The light it emits is so bright that it can illuminate the sea's surface from a depth of over three miles.

This Pokémon flashes a bright light that blinds its prey. This creates an opening for it to deliver an electrical attack.

HOW TO SAY IT: LAN-turn
IMPERIAL HEIGHT: 3'11"
IMPERIAL WEIGHT: 49.6 lbs.
METRIC HEIGHT: 1.2 m
METRIC WEIGHT: 22.5 kg
GENDER: ♂ ♀
ABILITIES: Volt Absorb, Illuminate
WEAKNESSES: Grass, Ground

#0171

LANTURN
Light Pokémon

CHINCHOU

LANTURN

LAPRAS
Transport Pokémon

TYPE: WATER-ICE

It loves crossing the sea with people and Pokémon on its back. It understands human speech.

HOW TO SAY IT: LAP-rus
IMPERIAL HEIGHT: 8'02"
IMPERIAL WEIGHT: 485.0 lbs.
METRIC HEIGHT: 2.5 m
METRIC WEIGHT: 220.0 kg
GENDER: ♂ ♀
ABILITIES: Water Absorb, Shell Armor
WEAKNESSES: Grass, Electric, Fighting, Rock

DOES NOT EVOLVE

GIGANTAMAX LAPRAS

Over 5,000 people can ride on its shell at once. And it's a very comfortable ride, without the slightest shaking or swaying.

It surrounds itself with a huge ring of gathered ice particles. It uses the ring to smash any icebergs that might impede its graceful swimming.

IMPERIAL HEIGHT: 78'09"+
IMPERIAL WEIGHT: ????.? lbs.
METRIC HEIGHT: 24.0+ m
METRIC WEIGHT: ???.? kg

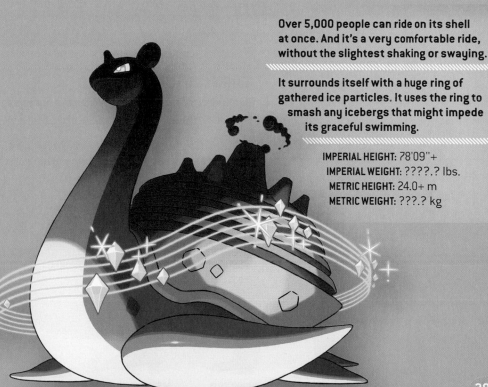

#0636 LARVESTA
Torch Pokémon

TYPE: BUG-FIRE

This Pokémon was called the Larva That Stole the Sun. The fire Larvesta spouts from its horns can cut right through a sheet of iron.

In ancient times, Larvesta was worshiped as the emissary of the sun. However, it was also viewed as a burden since it often caused forest fires.

HOW TO SAY IT: lar-VESS-tah
IMPERIAL HEIGHT: 3'07" **METRIC HEIGHT:** 1.1 m
IMPERIAL WEIGHT: 63.5 lbs. **METRIC WEIGHT:** 28.8 kg
GENDER: ♂ ♀
ABILITIES: Flame Body
WEAKNESSES: Water, Flying, Rock

LARVESTA → VOLCARONA

#0246 LARVITAR
Rock Skin Pokémon

TYPE: ROCK-GROUND

Born deep underground, this Pokémon becomes a pupa after eating enough dirt to make a mountain.

It is born deep underground. It can't emerge until it has entirely consumed the soil around it.

HOW TO SAY IT: LAR-vuh-tar
IMPERIAL HEIGHT: 2'00" **METRIC HEIGHT:** 0.6 m
IMPERIAL WEIGHT: 158.7 lbs. **METRIC WEIGHT:** 72.0 kg
GENDER: ♂ ♀
ABILITIES: Guts
WEAKNESSES: Grass, Water, Fighting, Ground, Ice, Steel

 LARVITAR PUPITAR TYRANITAR  MEGA TYRANITAR

TYPE: DRAGON-PSYCHIC

Latias is highly sensitive to the emotions of people. If it senses any hostility, this Pokémon ruffles the feathers all over its body and cries shrilly to intimidate the foe.

Latias is highly intelligent and capable of understanding human speech. It is covered with a glass-like down. The Pokémon enfolds its body with its down and refracts light to alter its appearance.

HOW TO SAY IT: LAT-ee-ahs
IMPERIAL HEIGHT: 4'07"
IMPERIAL WEIGHT: 88.2 lbs.
METRIC HEIGHT: 1.4 m
METRIC WEIGHT: 40.0 kg
GENDER: ♀
ABILITIES: Levitate
WEAKNESSES: Ghost, Ice, Dragon, Dark, Fairy, Bug

MEGA LATIAS

TYPE: DRAGON-PSYCHIC

IMPERIAL HEIGHT: 5'11"
IMPERIAL WEIGHT: 114.6 lbs.
METRIC HEIGHT: 1.8 m
METRIC WEIGHT: 52.0 kg

LATIAS

MEGA LATIAS

LATIOS
Eon Pokémon

#0381

TYPE: DRAGON-PSYCHIC

Latios has the ability to make others see an image of what it has seen or imagines in its head. This Pokémon is intelligent and understands human speech.

Latios will only open its heart to a Trainer with a compassionate spirit. This Pokémon can fly faster than a jet plane by folding its forelegs to minimize air resistance.

HOW TO SAY IT: LAT-ee-ose
IMPERIAL HEIGHT: 6'07"
IMPERIAL WEIGHT: 132.3 lbs.
METRIC HEIGHT: 2.0 m
METRIC WEIGHT: 60.0 kg
GENDER: ♂
ABILITIES: Levitate
WEAKNESSES: Ghost, Ice, Dragon, Dark, Fairy, Bug

MEGA LATIOS

TYPE: DRAGON-PSYCHIC

IMPERIAL HEIGHT: 7'07"
IMPERIAL WEIGHT: 154.3 lbs.
METRIC HEIGHT: 2.3 m
METRIC WEIGHT: 70.0 kg

LATIOS

MEGA LATIOS

LEAFEON

Verdant Pokémon

#0470

TYPE: GRASS

When you see Leafeon asleep in a patch of sunshine, you'll know it is using photosynthesis to produce clean air.

The younger they are, the more they smell like fresh grass. With age, their fragrance takes on the odor of fallen leaves.

HOW TO SAY IT: LEAF-ee-on
IMPERIAL HEIGHT: 3'03"
IMPERIAL WEIGHT: 56.2 lbs.
METRIC HEIGHT: 1.0 m
METRIC WEIGHT: 25.5 kg
GENDER: ♂ ♀
ABILITIES: Leaf Guard
WEAKNESSES: Bug, Fire, Flying, Ice, Poison

EEVEE　　　**LEAFEON**

LEAVANNY

Nurturing Pokémon

#0542

TYPE: BUG-GRASS

Upon finding a small Pokémon, it weaves clothing for it from leaves by using the sticky silk secreted from its mouth.

It keeps its eggs warm with heat from fermenting leaves. It also uses leaves to make warm wrappings for Sewaddle.

HOW TO SAY IT: lee-VAN-nee
IMPERIAL HEIGHT: 3'11"　　**METRIC HEIGHT:** 1.2 m
IMPERIAL WEIGHT: 45.2 lbs.　　**METRIC WEIGHT:** 20.5 kg
GENDER: ♂ ♀
ABILITIES: Swarm, Chlorophyll
WEAKNESSES: Fire, Flying, Ice, Poison, Rock, Bug

SEWADDLE　　**SWADLOON**　　**LEAVANNY**

LECHONK
Hog Pokémon

#0915

TYPE: NORMAL

It searches for food all day. It possesses a keen sense of smell but doesn't use it for anything other than foraging.

This Pokémon spurns all but the finest of foods. Its body gives off an herblike scent that bug Pokémon detest.

HOW TO SAY IT: leh-CHAHNK
IMPERIAL HEIGHT: 1'08"
IMPERIAL WEIGHT: 22.5 lbs.
METRIC HEIGHT: 0.5 m
METRIC WEIGHT: 10.2 kg
GENDER: ♂ ♀
ABILITIES: Aroma Veil, Gluttony
WEAKNESSES: Fighting

LECHONK

OINKOLOGNE

LEDIAN
Five Star Pokémon

TYPE: BUG-FLYING

It's said that the patterns on its back are related to the stars in the night sky, but the details of that relationship remain unclear.

It flies through the night sky, sprinkling sparkly dust. According to some, if that dust sticks to you, good things will happen to you.

HOW TO SAY IT: LEH-dee-an
IMPERIAL HEIGHT: 4'07"
IMPERIAL WEIGHT: 78.5 lbs.
METRIC HEIGHT: 1.4 m
METRIC WEIGHT: 35.6 kg
GENDER: ♂ ♀
ABILITIES: Swarm, Early Bird
WEAKNESSES: Fire, Flying, Electric, Ice, Rock

LEDYBA → **LEDIAN**

LEDYBA
Five Star Pokémon

TYPE: BUG-FLYING

This Pokémon is very sensitive to cold. In the warmth of Alola, it appears quite lively.

These very cowardly Pokémon join together and use Reflect to protect their nest.

HOW TO SAY IT: LEH-dee-bah
IMPERIAL HEIGHT: 3'03"
IMPERIAL WEIGHT: 23.8 lbs.
METRIC HEIGHT: 1.0 m
METRIC WEIGHT: 10.8 kg
GENDER: ♂ ♀
ABILITIES: Swarm, Early Bird
WEAKNESSES: Fire, Flying, Electric, Ice, Rock

LEDYBA **LEDIAN**

LICKILICKY

Licking Pokémon

#0463

TYPE: NORMAL

Lickilicky's strange tongue can stretch to many times the length of its body. No one has figured out how Lickilicky's tongue can stretch so far.

Lickilicky can do just about anything with its tongue, which is as dexterous as the human hand. In contrast, Lickilicky's use of its fingers is clumsy.

HOW TO SAY IT: LICK-ee-LICK-ee
IMPERIAL HEIGHT: 5'07"
IMPERIAL WEIGHT: 308.6 lbs.
METRIC HEIGHT: 1.7 m
METRIC WEIGHT: 140.0 kg
GENDER: ♂ ♀
ABILITIES: Own Tempo, Oblivious
WEAKNESSES: Fighting

LICKITUNG　　LICKILICKY

LICKITUNG

Licking Pokémon

#0108

TYPE: NORMAL

If this Pokémon's sticky saliva gets on you and you don't clean it off, an intense itch will set in. The itch won't go away, either.

Bug Pokémon are Lickitung's main food source. This Pokémon paralyzes its prey with a lick from its long tongue, then swallows the prey whole.

HOW TO SAY IT: LICK-it-tung
IMPERIAL HEIGHT: 3'11"
IMPERIAL WEIGHT: 144.4 lbs.
METRIC HEIGHT: 1.2 m
METRIC WEIGHT: 65.5 kg
GENDER: ♂ ♀
ABILITIES: Own Tempo, Oblivious
WEAKNESSES: Fighting

LICKITUNG　　LICKILICKY

#0510 LIEPARD
Cruel Pokémon

TYPE: DARK

Don't be fooled by its gorgeous fur and elegant figure. This is a moody and vicious Pokémon.

This stealthy Pokémon sneaks up behind prey without making any sound at all. It competes with Thievul for territory.

HOW TO SAY IT: LY-purd
IMPERIAL HEIGHT: 3'07"
IMPERIAL WEIGHT: 82.7 lbs.
METRIC HEIGHT: 1.1 m
METRIC WEIGHT: 37.5 kg
GENDER: ♂ ♀
ABILITIES: Limber, Unburden
WEAKNESSES: Fairy, Bug, Fighting

PURRLOIN ➡ LIEPARD

#0345 LILEEP
Sea Lily Pokémon

TYPE: ROCK-GRASS

This Pokémon was restored from a fossil. Lileep once lived in warm seas that existed approximately 100,000,000 years ago.

Lileep clings to rocks on the seabed. When prey comes close, this Pokémon entangles it with petallike tentacles.

HOW TO SAY IT: lil-LEEP
IMPERIAL HEIGHT: 3'03"
IMPERIAL WEIGHT: 52.5 lbs.
METRIC HEIGHT: 1.0 m
METRIC WEIGHT: 23.8 kg
GENDER: ♂ ♀
ABILITIES: Suction Cups
WEAKNESSES: Steel, Ice, Fighting, Bug

LILEEP CRADILY

LILLIGANT

Flowering Pokémon

#0549

TYPE: GRASS

The fragrance of the garland on its head has a relaxing effect, but taking care of it is very difficult.

No matter how much time and money is spent raising it, its flowers are the most beautiful when they bloom in the wild.

HOW TO SAY IT: LIL-lih-gunt
IMPERIAL HEIGHT: 3'07"
IMPERIAL WEIGHT: 35.9 lbs.
METRIC HEIGHT: 1.1 m
METRIC WEIGHT: 16.3 kg
GENDER: ♀
ABILITIES: Chlorophyll, Own Tempo
WEAKNESSES: Fire, Flying, Ice, Poison, Bug

PETILIL   LILLIGANT

HISUIAN LILLIGANT

Spinning Pokémon

#0549

TYPE: GRASS-FIGHTING

I suspect that its well-developed legs are the result of a life spent on mountains covered in deep snow. The scent it exudes from its flower crown heartens those in proximity.

HOW TO SAY IT: LIL-uh-gunt
IMPERIAL HEIGHT: 3'11"
IMPERIAL WEIGHT: 42.3 lbs.
METRIC HEIGHT: 1.2 m
METRIC WEIGHT: 19.2 kg
GENDER: ♀
ABILITIES: N/A
WEAKNESSES: Fire, Psychic, Flying, Ice, Poison, Fairy

PETILIL   HISUIAN
LILLIGANT

TYPE: NORMAL

This Pokémon is courageous but also cautious. It uses the soft fur covering its face to collect information about its surroundings.

This Pokémon is far brighter than the average child, and Lillipup won't forget the love it receives or any abuse it suffers.

HOW TO SAY IT: LIL-ee-pup
IMPERIAL HEIGHT: 1'04"
IMPERIAL WEIGHT: 9.0 lbs.
METRIC HEIGHT: 0.4 m
METRIC WEIGHT: 4.1 kg
GENDER: ♂ ♀
ABILITIES: Vital Spirit, Pickup
WEAKNESSES: Fighting

#0506

LILLIPUP
Puppy Pokémon

 LILLIPUP → **HERDIER** →  **STOUTLAND**

LINOONE
Rushing Pokémon

#0264

TYPE: NORMAL

It charges prey at speeds over 60 mph. However, because it can only run straight, it often fails.

HOW TO SAY IT: line-NOON
IMPERIAL HEIGHT: 1'08"
IMPERIAL WEIGHT: 71.7 lbs.
METRIC HEIGHT: 0.5 m
METRIC WEIGHT: 32.5 kg
GENDER: ♂ ♀
ABILITIES: Pickup, Gluttony
WEAKNESSES: Fighting

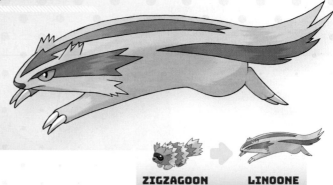

ZIGZAGOON → LINOONE

#0264

GALARIAN LINOONE
Rushing Pokémon

TYPE: DARK-NORMAL

It uses its long tongue to taunt opponents. Once the opposition is enraged, this Pokémon hurls itself at the opponent, tackling them forcefully.

This very aggressive Pokémon will recklessly challenge opponents stronger than itself.

HOW TO SAY IT: line-NOON
IMPERIAL HEIGHT: 1'08"
IMPERIAL WEIGHT: 71.7 lbs.
METRIC HEIGHT: 0.5 m
METRIC WEIGHT: 32.5 kg
GENDER: ♂ ♀
ABILITIES: Pickup, Gluttony
WEAKNESSES: Fairy, Bug, Fighting

GALARIAN ZIGZAGOON → GALARIAN LINOONE → OBSTAGOON

LITLEO

Lion Cub Pokémon

#0667

TYPE: FIRE-NORMAL

When Litleo are young, female Pyroar will teach them how to hunt. Once the Litleo mature, they will leave the pride and set out on their own.

The more a Litleo trains its body and spirit by battling mighty enemies, the hotter its mane will grow.

HOW TO SAY IT: LIT-lee-oh
IMPERIAL HEIGHT: 2'00"
IMPERIAL WEIGHT: 29.8 lbs.
METRIC HEIGHT: 0.6 m
METRIC WEIGHT: 13.5 kg
GENDER: ♂ ♀
ABILITIES: Rivalry, Unnerve
WEAKNESSES: Water, Ground, Fighting, Rock

LITLEO **PYROAR**

LITTEN

Fire Cat Pokémon

#0725

TYPE: FIRE

If you try too hard to get close to it, it won't open up to you. Even if you do grow close, giving it too much affection is still a no-no.

Its coat regrows twice a year. When the time comes, Litten sets its own body on fire and burns away the old fur.

HOW TO SAY IT: LIT-n
IMPERIAL HEIGHT: 1'04"
IMPERIAL WEIGHT: 9.5 lbs.
METRIC HEIGHT: 0.4 m
METRIC WEIGHT: 4.3 kg
GENDER: ♂ ♀
ABILITIES: Blaze
WEAKNESSES: Water, Ground, Rock

LITTEN **TORRACAT** **INCINEROAR**

LITWICK

Candle Pokémon

#0607

TYPE: GHOST-FIRE

The flame on its head keeps its body slightly warm. This Pokémon takes lost children by the hand to guide them to the spirit world.

The younger the life this Pokémon absorbs, the brighter and eerier the flame on its head burns.

HOW TO SAY IT: LIT-wik
IMPERIAL HEIGHT: 1'00"
IMPERIAL WEIGHT: 6.8 lbs.
METRIC HEIGHT: 0.3 m
METRIC WEIGHT: 3.1 kg
GENDER: ♂ ♀
ABILITIES: Flash Fire, Flame Body
WEAKNESSES: Ghost, Dark, Ground, Water, Rock

LITWICK   LAMPENT   CHANDELURE

LOKIX

Grasshopper Pokémon

#0920

TYPE: BUG-DARK

When it decides to fight all out, it stands on its previously folded legs to enter Showdown Mode. It neutralizes its enemies in short order.

It uses its normally folded third set of legs when in Showdown Mode. This places a huge burden on its body, so it can't stay in this mode for long.

HOW TO SAY IT: low-kicks
IMPERIAL HEIGHT: 3'03"
IMPERIAL WEIGHT: 38.6 lbs.
METRIC HEIGHT: 1.0 m
METRIC WEIGHT: 17.5 kg
GENDER: ♂ ♀
ABILITIES: Swarm
WEAKNESSES: Fire, Fairy, Flying, Bug, Rock

NYMBLE   LOKIX

LOMBRE
Jolly Pokémon

TYPE: WATER-GRASS

It is nocturnal and becomes active at nightfall. It feeds on aquatic mosses that grow in the riverbed.

It lives at the water's edge where it is sunny. It sleeps on a bed of water grass by day and becomes active at night.

HOW TO SAY IT: LOM-brey
IMPERIAL HEIGHT: 3'11"
IMPERIAL WEIGHT: 71.7 lbs.
METRIC HEIGHT: 1.2 m
METRIC WEIGHT: 32.5 kg
GENDER: ♂ ♀
ABILITIES: Swift Swim, Rain Dish
WEAKNESSES: Flying, Bug, Poison

LOTAD   LOMBRE   LUDICOLO

LOPUNNY

Rabbit Pokémon

#0428

TYPE: NORMAL

Lopunny is constantly monitoring its surroundings. If danger approaches, this Pokémon responds with superdestructive kicks.

Once hot seasons are over, Lopunny's coat will be replaced with fur that holds a lot of insulating air in preparation for colder weather.

HOW TO SAY IT: LAH-pun-nee
IMPERIAL HEIGHT: 3'11"
IMPERIAL WEIGHT: 73.4 lbs.
METRIC HEIGHT: 1.2 m
METRIC WEIGHT: 33.3 kg
GENDER: ♂ ♀
ABILITIES: Cute Charm, Klutz
WEAKNESSES: Fighting

MEGA LOPUNNY

TYPE: NORMAL-FIGHTING

It swings its ears like whips and strikes its enemies with them. It has an intensely combative disposition.

Mega Evolution awakens its combative instincts. It has shed any fur that got in the way of its attacks.

IMPERIAL HEIGHT: 4'03"
IMPERIAL WEIGHT: 62.4 lbs.
METRIC HEIGHT: 1.3 m
METRIC WEIGHT: 28.3 kg

BUNEARY   LOPUNNY   MEGA LOPUNNY

LOTAD
Water Weed Pokémon

TYPE: WATER-GRASS

It searches about for clean water. If it does not drink water for too long, the leaf on its head wilts.

Its leaf grew too large for it to live on land. That is how it began to live floating in the water.

HOW TO SAY IT: LOW-tad
IMPERIAL HEIGHT: 1'08"
IMPERIAL WEIGHT: 5.7 lbs.
METRIC HEIGHT: 0.5 m
METRIC WEIGHT: 2.6 kg
GENDER: ♂ ♀
ABILITIES: Swift Swim, Rain Dish
WEAKNESSES: Flying, Bug, Poison

LOTAD → **LOMBRE** → **LUDICOLO**

#0294

LOUDRED
Big Voice Pokémon

TYPE: NORMAL

Loudred's ears serve as speakers, and they can put out sound waves powerful enough to blow away a house.

The force of this Pokémon's loud voice isn't just the sound—it's also the wave of air pressure that blows opponents away and damages them.

HOW TO SAY IT: LOUD-red
IMPERIAL HEIGHT: 3'03"
IMPERIAL WEIGHT: 89.3 lbs.
METRIC HEIGHT: 1.0 m
METRIC WEIGHT: 40.5 kg
GENDER: ♂ ♀
ABILITIES: Soundproof
WEAKNESSES: Fighting

WHISMUR **LOUDRED** **EXPLOUD**

LUCARIO

Aura Pokémon

#0448

TYPE: FIGHTING-STEEL

It's said that no foe can remain invisible to Lucario, since it can detect auras—even those of foes it could not otherwise see.

A well-trained one can use its aura to identify and take in the feelings of creatures over half a mile away.

HOW TO SAY IT: loo-CAR-ee-oh
IMPERIAL HEIGHT: 3'11"
IMPERIAL WEIGHT: 119.0 lbs.
METRIC HEIGHT: 1.2 m
METRIC WEIGHT: 54.0 kg
GENDER: ♂ ♀
ABILITIES: Steadfast, Inner Focus
WEAKNESSES: Fighting, Fire, Ground

MEGA LUCARIO

TYPE: FIGHTING-STEEL

Its aura has expanded due to Mega Evolution. Governed only by its combative instincts, it strikes enemies without mercy.

Bathed in explosive energy, its combative instincts have awakened. For its enemies, it has no mercy whatsoever.

IMPERIAL HEIGHT: 4'03"
IMPERIAL WEIGHT: 126.8 lbs.
METRIC HEIGHT: 1.3 m
METRIC WEIGHT: 57.5 kg

RIOLU

LUCARIO

MEGA LUCARIO

#0272

LUDICOLO
Carefree Pokémon

TYPE: WATER-GRASS

The rhythm of bright, festive music activates Ludicolo's cells, making it more powerful.

If it hears festive music, it begins moving in rhythm in order to amplify its power.

HOW TO SAY IT: LOO-dee-KO-low
IMPERIAL HEIGHT: 4'11"
IMPERIAL WEIGHT: 121.3 lbs.
METRIC HEIGHT: 1.5 m
METRIC WEIGHT: 55.0 kg
GENDER: ♂ ♀
ABILITIES: Swift Swim, Rain Dish
WEAKNESSES: Flying, Bug, Poison

LOTAD → **LOMBRE** → **LUDICOLO**

LEGENDARY POKÉMON

#0249

LUGIA
Diving Pokémon

TYPE: PSYCHIC-FLYING

Lugia's wings pack devastating power—a light fluttering of its wings can blow apart regular houses. As a result, this Pokémon chooses to live out of sight deep under the sea.

HOW TO SAY IT: LOO-gee-uh
IMPERIAL HEIGHT: 17'01"
IMPERIAL WEIGHT: 476.2 lbs.
METRIC HEIGHT: 5.2 m
METRIC WEIGHT: 216.0 kg
GENDER: Unknown
ABILITIES: Pressure
WEAKNESSES: Ghost, Dark, Electric, Ice, Rock

DOES NOT EVOLVE

LUMINEON
Neon Pokémon

#0457

TYPE: WATER

With its shining light, it lures its prey close. However, the light also happens to attract ferocious fish Pokémon—its natural predators.

Lumineon swimming in the darkness of the deep sea look like stars shining in the night sky.

HOW TO SAY IT: loo-MIN-ee-on
IMPERIAL HEIGHT: 3'11"
IMPERIAL WEIGHT: 52.9 lbs.
METRIC HEIGHT: 1.2 m
METRIC WEIGHT: 24.0 kg
GENDER: ♂ ♀
ABILITIES: Swift Swim, Storm Drain
WEAKNESSES: Grass, Electric

FINNEON   LUMINEON

LUNALA
Moone Pokémon

#0792

LEGENDARY POKÉMON

TYPE: PSYCHIC-GHOST

Records of it exist in writings from long, long ago, where it was known by the name "the beast that calls the moon."

It sometimes summons unknown powers and life-forms here to this world from holes that lead to other worlds.

HOW TO SAY IT: loo-NAH-luh
IMPERIAL HEIGHT: 13'01"
IMPERIAL WEIGHT: 264.6 lbs.
METRIC HEIGHT: 4.0 m
METRIC WEIGHT: 120.0 kg
GENDER: Unknown
ABILITIES: Shadow Shield
WEAKNESSES: Ghost, Dark

COSMOG   COSMOEM   LUNALA

#0337 LUNATONE
Meteorite Pokémon

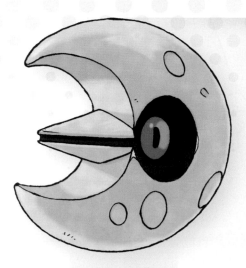

DOES NOT EVOLVE

TYPE: ROCK-PSYCHIC

The phase of the moon apparently has some effect on its power. It's active on the night of a full moon.

It was discovered at the site of a meteor strike 40 years ago. Its stare can lull its foes to sleep.

HOW TO SAY IT: LOO-nuh-tone
IMPERIAL HEIGHT: 3'03"
IMPERIAL WEIGHT: 370.4 lbs.
METRIC HEIGHT: 1.0 m
METRIC WEIGHT: 168.0 kg
GENDER: Unknown
ABILITIES: Levitate
WEAKNESSES: Steel, Ghost, Water, Dark, Grass, Bug, Ground

#0754 LURANTIS
Bloom Sickle Pokémon

TYPE: GRASS

By masquerading as a bug Pokémon, it lowers the guard of actual bug Pokémon lured in by a scent of sweet flowers. Its sickles bring them down.

A lot of time and effort is required to maintain the vivid colors of its petals. This Pokémon puts its Trainer's attentiveness to the test.

HOW TO SAY IT: loor-RAN-tis
IMPERIAL HEIGHT: 2'11"
IMPERIAL WEIGHT: 40.8 lbs.
METRIC HEIGHT: 0.9 m
METRIC WEIGHT: 18.5 kg
GENDER: ♂ ♀
ABILITIES: Leaf Guard
WEAKNESSES: Fire, Flying, Ice, Poison, Bug

FOMANTIS   LURANTIS

LUVDISC

Rendezvous Pokémon

#0370

TYPE: WATER

Its heart-shaped body makes it popular. In some places, you would give a Luvdisc to someone you love.

During the spawning season, countless Luvdisc congregate at coral reefs, turning the waters pink.

HOW TO SAY IT: LOVE-disk
IMPERIAL HEIGHT: 2'00"
IMPERIAL WEIGHT: 19.2 lbs.
METRIC HEIGHT: 0.6 m
METRIC WEIGHT: 8.7 kg
GENDER: ♂ ♀
ABILITIES: Swift Swim
WEAKNESSES: Grass, Electric

DOES NOT EVOLVE

LUXIO

Spark Pokémon

#0404

TYPE: ELECTRIC

Strong electricity courses through the tips of its sharp claws. A light scratch causes fainting in foes.

By gathering their tails together, they collectively generate powerful electricity from their claws.

HOW TO SAY IT: LUCKS-ee-oh
IMPERIAL HEIGHT: 2'11"
IMPERIAL WEIGHT: 67.2 lbs.
METRIC HEIGHT: 0.9 m
METRIC WEIGHT: 30.5 kg
GENDER: ♂ ♀
ABILITIES: Rivalry, Intimidate
WEAKNESSES: Ground

SHINX

LUXIO

LUXRAY

LUXRAY
Gleam Eyes Pokémon

TYPE: ELECTRIC

It can see clearly through walls to track down its prey and seek its lost young.

Luxray's ability to see through objects comes in handy when it's scouting for danger.

HOW TO SAY IT: LUCKS-ray
IMPERIAL HEIGHT: 4'07"
IMPERIAL WEIGHT: 92.6 lbs.
METRIC HEIGHT: 1.4 m
METRIC WEIGHT: 42.0 kg
GENDER: ♂ ♀
ABILITIES: Rivalry, Intimidate
WEAKNESSES: Ground

SHINX

LUXIO

LUXRAY

LYCANROC DUSK FORM

#0745

Wolf Pokémon

TYPE: ROCK

Normally this Pokémon doesn't even bark, but once it enters battle, it will relentlessly drive the opponent into a corner.

These Pokémon have both calm and ferocious qualities. It's said that this form of Lycanroc is the most troublesome to raise.

HOW TO SAY IT: LIE-can-rock
IMPERIAL HEIGHT: 2'07"
IMPERIAL WEIGHT: 55.1 lbs.
METRIC HEIGHT: 0.8 m
METRIC WEIGHT: 25.0 kg
GENDER: ♂ ♀
ABILITIES: Tough Claws
WEAKNESSES: Water, Steel, Grass, Fighting, Ground

ROCKRUFF   **LYCANROC**
(DUSK FORM)

#0745 LYCANROC MIDDAY FORM

Wolf Pokémon

TYPE: ROCK

Lycanroc attacks its prey with its sharp claws and fangs. It loyally obeys the instructions of a Trainer it trusts.

It has a calm and collected demeanor. It swiftly closes in on its prey, then slices them with the rocks in its mane.

HOW TO SAY IT: LIE-can-rock
IMPERIAL HEIGHT: 2'07"
IMPERIAL WEIGHT: 55.1 lbs.
METRIC HEIGHT: 0.8 m
METRIC WEIGHT: 25.0 kg
GENDER: ♂ ♀
ABILITIES: Keen Eye, Sand Rush
WEAKNESSES: Water, Steel, Grass, Fighting, Ground

ROCKRUFF   **LYCANROC**
(MIDDAY FORM)

LYCANROC MIDNIGHT FORM

Wolf Pokémon

#0745

TYPE: ROCK

This Pokémon uses its rocky mane to slash any who approach. It will even disobey its Trainer if it dislikes the orders it was given.

This Lycanroc has an extremely vicious temperament. It will happily sustain injuries for the sake of taking down its opponent.

HOW TO SAY IT: LIE-can-rock
IMPERIAL HEIGHT: 3'07"
IMPERIAL WEIGHT: 55.1 lbs.
METRIC HEIGHT: 1.1 m
METRIC WEIGHT: 25.0 kg
GENDER: ♂ ♀
ABILITIES: Keen Eye, Vital Spirit
WEAKNESSES: Water, Steel, Grass, Fighting, Ground

ROCKRUFF → LYCANROC (MIDNIGHT FORM)

#0943

MABOSSTIFF

Boss Pokémon

TYPE: DARK

This Pokémon can store energy in its large dewlap. Mabosstiff unleashes this energy all at once to blow away enemies.

Mabosstiff loves playing with children. Though usually gentle, it takes on an intimidating look when protecting its family.

HOW TO SAY IT: mah-BAWS-tif
IMPERIAL HEIGHT: 3'07"
IMPERIAL WEIGHT: 134.5 lbs.
METRIC HEIGHT: 1.1 m
METRIC WEIGHT: 61.0 kg
GENDER: ♂ ♀
ABILITIES: Intimidate, Guard Dog
WEAKNESSES: Fairy, Bug, Fighting

MASCHIFF → MABOSSTIFF

MACHAMP
Superpower Pokémon

#0068

TYPE: FIGHTING

It punches with its four arms at blinding speed. It can launch 1,000 punches in two seconds.

It can knock a train flying with a punch. However, it is terrible at delicate work using its fingers.

HOW TO SAY IT: muh-CHAMP
IMPERIAL HEIGHT: 5'03"
IMPERIAL WEIGHT: 286.6 lbs.
METRIC HEIGHT: 1.6 m
METRIC WEIGHT: 130.0 kg
GENDER: ♂ ♀
ABILITIES: Guts, No Guard
WEAKNESSES: Psychic, Flying, Fairy

MACHOP → MACHOKE → MACHAMP

GIGANTAMAX MACHAMP

The Gigantamax energy coursing through its arms makes its punches hit as hard as bomb blasts.

One of these Pokémon once used its immeasurable strength to lift a large ship that was in trouble. It then carried the ship to port.

IMPERIAL HEIGHT: 82'00"+
IMPERIAL WEIGHT: ????.? lbs.
METRIC HEIGHT: 25.0+ m
METRIC WEIGHT: ???.? kg

MACHOKE
Superpower Pokémon

#0067

TYPE: FIGHTING

Its muscular body is so powerful, it must wear a power-save belt to be able to regulate its motions.

Its formidable body never gets tired. It helps people by doing work such as the moving of heavy goods.

HOW TO SAY IT: muh-CHOKE
IMPERIAL HEIGHT: 4'11"
IMPERIAL WEIGHT: 155.4 lbs.
METRIC HEIGHT: 1.5 m
METRIC WEIGHT: 70.5 kg
GENDER: ♂ ♀
ABILITIES: Guts, No Guard
WEAKNESSES: Psychic, Flying, Fairy

MACHOP **MACHOKE** **MACHAMP**

#0066

MACHOP
Superpower Pokémon

TYPE: FIGHTING

Its whole body is composed of muscles. Even though it's the size of a human child, it can hurl 100 grown-ups.

Always brimming with power, it passes time by lifting boulders. Doing so makes it even stronger.

HOW TO SAY IT: muh-CHOP
IMPERIAL HEIGHT: 2'07"
IMPERIAL WEIGHT: 43.0 lbs.
METRIC HEIGHT: 0.8 m
METRIC WEIGHT: 19.5 kg
GENDER: ♂ ♀
ABILITIES: Guts, No Guard
WEAKNESSES: Psychic, Flying, Fairy

MACHOP **MACHOKE** **MACHAMP**

#0240 MAGBY
Live Coal Pokémon

TYPE: FIRE

This Pokémon is still small and timid. Whenever Magby gets excited or surprised, flames leak from its mouth and its nose.

This Pokémon makes its home near volcanoes. At the end of the day, Magby soaks in magma, resting and recovering from the day's fatigue.

HOW TO SAY IT: MAG-bee
IMPERIAL HEIGHT: 2'04"   **METRIC HEIGHT:** 0.7 m
IMPERIAL WEIGHT: 47.2 lbs.   **METRIC WEIGHT:** 21.4 kg
GENDER: ♂ ♀
ABILITIES: Flame Body
WEAKNESSES: Water, Ground, Rock

MAGBY   MAGMAR   MAGMORTAR

MAGCARGO #0219
Lava Pokémon

TYPE: FIRE-ROCK

Magcargo's shell is actually its skin that hardened as a result of cooling. Its shell is very brittle and fragile—just touching it causes it to crumble apart. This Pokémon returns to its original size by dipping itself in magma.

Magcargo's body temperature is approximately 18,000 degrees Fahrenheit. Water is vaporized on contact. If this Pokémon is caught in the rain, the raindrops instantly turn into steam, cloaking the area in a thick fog.

HOW TO SAY IT: mag-CAR-go
IMPERIAL HEIGHT: 2'07"   **METRIC HEIGHT:** 0.8 m
IMPERIAL WEIGHT: 121.3 lbs.   **METRIC WEIGHT:** 55.0 kg
GENDER: ♂ ♀
ABILITIES: Magma Armor, Flame Body
WEAKNESSES: Water, Ground, Fighting, Rock

SLUGMA   MAGCARGO

MAGEARNA

Artificial Pokémon

MYTHICAL POKÉMON

TYPE: STEEL-FAIRY

It synchronizes its consciousness with others to understand their feelings. This faculty makes it useful for taking care of people.

Built roughly 500 years ago by a scientist, the part called the Soul-Heart is the actual life-form.

HOW TO SAY IT: muh-GEER-nuh
IMPERIAL HEIGHT: 3'03"
IMPERIAL WEIGHT: 177.5 lbs.
METRIC HEIGHT: 1.0 m
METRIC WEIGHT: 80.5 kg
GENDER: Unknown
ABILITIES: Soul-Heart
WEAKNESSES: Fire, Ground

DOES NOT EVOLVE

MAGIKARP

Fish Pokémon

TYPE: WATER

An underpowered, pathetic Pokémon. It may jump high on rare occasions but never more than seven feet.

In the distant past, it was somewhat stronger than the horribly weak descendants that exist today.

HOW TO SAY IT: MADGE-eh-karp
IMPERIAL HEIGHT: 2'11"
IMPERIAL WEIGHT: 22.0 lbs.
METRIC HEIGHT: 0.9 m
METRIC WEIGHT: 10.0 kg
GENDER: ♂ ♀
ABILITIES: Swift Swim
WEAKNESSES: Electric, Grass

MAGIKARP   **GYARADOS**   **MEGA GYARADOS**

TYPE: FIRE

Magmar dispatches its prey with fire. But it regrets this habit once it realizes that it has burned its intended prey to a charred crisp.

These Pokémon's bodies are constantly burning. Magmar are feared as one of the causes behind fires.

HOW TO SAY IT: MAG-marr
IMPERIAL HEIGHT: 4'03"
IMPERIAL WEIGHT: 98.1 lbs.
METRIC HEIGHT: 1.3 m
METRIC WEIGHT: 44.5 kg
GENDER: ♂ ♀
ABILITIES: Flame Body
WEAKNESSES: Water, Ground, Rock

#0126

MAGMAR
Spitfire Pokémon

MAGBY **MAGMAR** **MAGMORTAR**

MAGMORTAR
Blast Pokémon

#0467

TYPE: FIRE

When Magmortar inhales deeply, the fire burning in its belly intensifies, rising in temperature to over 3,600 degrees Fahrenheit.

Living in the crater of a volcano has caused this Pokémon's body to resemble its environment—it has an organ similar to a magma chamber.

HOW TO SAY IT: mag-MORT-ur
IMPERIAL HEIGHT: 5'03"
IMPERIAL WEIGHT: 149.9 lbs.
METRIC HEIGHT: 1.6 m
METRIC WEIGHT: 68.0 kg
GENDER: ♂ ♀
ABILITIES: Flame Body
WEAKNESSES: Water, Ground, Rock

MAGBY **MAGMAR** **MAGMORTAR**

MAGNEMITE
Magnet Pokémon

#0081

TYPE: ELECTRIC-STEEL

The electromagnetic waves emitted by the units at the sides of its head expel antigravity, which allows it to float.

It moves while constantly hovering. It discharges electromagnetic waves and so on from the units at its sides.

HOW TO SAY IT: MAG-ne-mite
IMPERIAL HEIGHT: 1'00"
IMPERIAL WEIGHT: 13.2 lbs.
METRIC HEIGHT: 0.3 m
METRIC WEIGHT: 6.0 kg
GENDER: Unknown
ABILITIES: Magnet Pull, Sturdy
WEAKNESSES: Fire, Fighting, Ground

MAGNEMITE   MAGNETON   MAGNEZONE

TYPE: ELECTRIC-STEEL

MAGNETON
Magnet Pokémon

#0082

Three Magnemite are linked by a strong magnetic force. Earaches will occur if you get too close.

They're formed by several Magnemite linked together. They frequently appear when sunspots flare up.

HOW TO SAY IT: MAG-ne-ton
IMPERIAL HEIGHT: 3'03"
IMPERIAL WEIGHT: 132.3 lbs.
METRIC HEIGHT: 1.0 m
METRIC WEIGHT: 60.0 kg
GENDER: Unknown
ABILITIES: Magnet Pull, Sturdy
WEAKNESSES: Fire, Fighting, Ground

MAGNEMITE   MAGNETON   MAGNEZONE

MAGNEZONE

Magnet Area Pokémon

#0462

TYPE: ELECTRIC-STEEL

As it zooms through the sky, this Pokémon seems to be receiving signals of unknown origin while transmitting signals of unknown purpose.

Exposure to a special magnetic field changed Magneton's molecular structure, turning it into Magnezone.

HOW TO SAY IT: MAG-nuh-zone
IMPERIAL HEIGHT: 3'11"
IMPERIAL WEIGHT: 396.8 lbs.
METRIC HEIGHT: 1.2 m
METRIC WEIGHT: 180.0 kg
GENDER: Unknown
ABILITIES: Magnet Pull, Sturdy
WEAKNESSES: Fire, Fighting, Ground

MAGNEMITE   MAGNETON   MAGNEZONE

MAKUHITA

Guts Pokémon

#0296

TYPE: FIGHTING

It grows stronger by enduring harsh training. It is a gutsy Pokémon that can withstand any attack.

It toughens up by slamming into thick trees over and over. It gains a sturdy body and dauntless spirit.

HOW TO SAY IT: MAK-oo-HEE-ta
IMPERIAL HEIGHT: 3'03"
IMPERIAL WEIGHT: 190.5 lbs.
METRIC HEIGHT: 1.0 m
METRIC WEIGHT: 86.4 kg
GENDER: ♂ ♀
ABILITIES: Thick Fat, Guts
WEAKNESSES: Psychic, Flying, Fairy

MAKUHITA   HARIYAMA

MALAMAR

Overturning Pokémon

#0687

TYPE: DARK-PSYCHIC

Gazing at its luminescent spots will quickly induce a hypnotic state, putting the observer under Malamar's control.

It's said that Malamar's hypnotic powers played a role in certain history-changing events.

HOW TO SAY IT: MAL-uh-MAR
IMPERIAL HEIGHT: 4'11"
IMPERIAL WEIGHT: 103.6 lbs.
METRIC HEIGHT: 1.5 m
METRIC WEIGHT: 47.0 kg
GENDER: ♂ ♀
ABILITIES: Contrary, Suction Cups
WEAKNESSES: Fairy, Bug

INKAY   **MALAMAR**

MAMOSWINE

Twin Tusk Pokémon

#0473

TYPE: ICE-GROUND

This Pokémon can be spotted in wall paintings from as far back as 10,000 years ago. For a while, it was thought to have gone extinct.

It looks strong, and that's exactly what it is. As the weather grows colder, its ice tusks grow longer, thicker, and more impressive.

HOW TO SAY IT: MAM-oh-swine
IMPERIAL HEIGHT: 8'02"
IMPERIAL WEIGHT: 641.5 lbs.
METRIC HEIGHT: 2.5 m
METRIC WEIGHT: 291.0 kg
GENDER: ♂ ♀
ABILITIES: Oblivious, Snow Cloak
WEAKNESSES: Steel, Fire, Grass, Water, Fighting

SWINUB   **PILOSWINE**   **MAMOSWINE**

MYTHICAL POKÉMON

#0490

MANAPHY
Seafaring Pokémon

TYPE: WATER

It is born with a wondrous power that lets it bond with any kind of Pokémon.

It starts its life with a wondrous power that permits it to bond with any kind of Pokémon.

HOW TO SAY IT: MAN-ah-fee
IMPERIAL HEIGHT: 1'00"
IMPERIAL WEIGHT: 3.1 lbs.
METRIC HEIGHT: 0.3 m
METRIC WEIGHT: 1.4 kg
GENDER: Unknown
ABILITIES: Hydration
WEAKNESSES: Grass, Electric

DOES NOT EVOLVE

#0630

MANDIBUZZ
Bone Vulture Pokémon

TYPE: DARK-FLYING

Although it's a bit of a ruffian, this Pokémon will take lost Vullaby under its wing and care for them till they're ready to leave the nest.

They adorn themselves with bones. There seem to be fashion trends among them, as different bones come into and fall out of popularity.

HOW TO SAY IT: MAN-dih-buz
IMPERIAL HEIGHT: 3'11"
IMPERIAL WEIGHT: 87.1 lbs.
METRIC HEIGHT: 1.2 m
METRIC WEIGHT: 39.5 kg
GENDER: ♀
ABILITIES: Big Pecks, Overcoat
WEAKNESSES: Fairy, Electric, Ice, Rock

VULLABY   MANDIBUZZ

MANECTRIC

Discharge Pokémon

#0310

TYPE: ELECTRIC

It stimulates its own muscles with electricity, so it can move quickly. It eases its soreness with electricity, too, so it can recover quickly as well.

It rarely appears before people. It is said to nest where lightning has fallen.

HOW TO SAY IT: mane-EK-trick
IMPERIAL HEIGHT: 4'11"
IMPERIAL WEIGHT: 88.6 lbs.
METRIC HEIGHT: 1.5 m
METRIC WEIGHT: 40.2 kg
GENDER: ♂ ♀
ABILITIES: Static, Lightning Rod
WEAKNESSES: Ground

MEGA MANECTRIC

TYPE: ELECTRIC

Mega Evolution fills its body with a tremendous amount of electricity, but it's too much for Manectric to fully control.

Too much electricity has built up in its body, irritating Manectric. Its explosive speed is equal to that of a lightning bolt.

IMPERIAL HEIGHT: 5'11"
IMPERIAL WEIGHT: 97.0 lbs.
METRIC HEIGHT: 1.8 m
METRIC WEIGHT: 44.0 kg

ELECTRIKE   MANECTRIC   MEGA MANECTRIC

MANKEY

Pig Monkey Pokémon

#0056

TYPE: FIGHTING

It lives in groups in the treetops. If it loses sight of its group, it becomes infuriated by its loneliness.

It is extremely quick to anger. It could be docile one moment, then thrashing away the next instant.

HOW TO SAY IT: MANG-key
IMPERIAL HEIGHT: 1'08"
IMPERIAL WEIGHT: 61.7 lbs.
METRIC HEIGHT: 0.5 m
METRIC WEIGHT: 28.0 kg
GENDER: ♂ ♀
ABILITIES: Vital Spirit, Anger Point
WEAKNESSES: Psychic, Flying, Fairy

MANKEY → PRIMEAPE → ANNIHILAPE

MANTINE

Kite Pokémon

#0226

TYPE: WATER-FLYING

If it builds up enough speed swimming, it can jump out above the waves and glide for over 300 feet.

As it majestically swims, it doesn't care if Remoraid attach to it to scavenge for its leftovers.

HOW TO SAY IT: MAN-teen
IMPERIAL HEIGHT: 6'11"
IMPERIAL WEIGHT: 485.0 lbs.
METRIC HEIGHT: 2.1 m
METRIC WEIGHT: 220.0 kg
GENDER: ♂ ♀
ABILITIES: Swift Swim, Water Absorb
WEAKNESSES: Electric, Rock

MANTYKE   MANTINE

MANTYKE

Kite Pokémon

#0458

TYPE: WATER-FLYING

Mantyke living in Galar seem to be somewhat sluggish. The colder waters of the seas in this region may be the cause.

It swims along with a school of Remoraid, and they'll all fight together to repel attackers.

HOW TO SAY IT: MAN-tike
IMPERIAL HEIGHT: 3'03"
IMPERIAL WEIGHT: 143.3 lbs.
METRIC HEIGHT: 1.0 m
METRIC WEIGHT: 65.0 kg
GENDER: ♂ ♀
ABILITIES: Swift Swim, Water Absorb
WEAKNESSES: Electric, Rock

MANTYKE   MANTINE

MARACTUS

Cactus Pokémon

#0556

TYPE: GRASS

With noises that could be mistaken for the rattles of maracas, it creates an upbeat rhythm, startling bird Pokémon and making them fly off in a hurry.

Once each year, this Pokémon scatters its seeds. They're jam-packed with nutrients, making them a precious food source out in the desert.

HOW TO SAY IT: mah-RAK-tus
IMPERIAL HEIGHT: 3'03"
IMPERIAL WEIGHT: 61.7 lbs.
METRIC HEIGHT: 1.0 m
METRIC WEIGHT: 28.0 kg
GENDER: ♂ ♀
ABILITIES: Water Absorb, Chlorophyll
WEAKNESSES: Fire, Flying, Ice, Poison, Bug

DOES NOT EVOLVE

MAREANIE

Brutal Star Pokémon

#0747

TYPE: POISON-WATER

This Pokémon wanders the seaside looking for food. It often gets electric shocks from broken Pincurchin spines that it tries to eat.

It has excellent regenerative capabilities. Legs that a Mareanie has lost have a very bitter, astringent flavor—they're not suitable as food.

HOW TO SAY IT: muh-REE-nee
IMPERIAL HEIGHT: 1'04"
IMPERIAL WEIGHT: 17.6 lbs.
METRIC HEIGHT: 0.4 m
METRIC WEIGHT: 8.0 kg
GENDER: ♂ ♀
ABILITIES: Merciless, Limber
WEAKNESSES: Psychic, Electric, Ground

MAREANIE **TOXAPEX**

MAREEP

Wool Pokémon

#0179

TYPE: ELECTRIC

If static electricity builds in its body, its fleece doubles in volume. Touching it will shock you.

Its fleece grows continually. In the summer, the fleece is fully shed, but it grows back in a week.

HOW TO SAY IT: mah-REEP
IMPERIAL HEIGHT: 2'00"
IMPERIAL WEIGHT: 17.2 lbs.
METRIC HEIGHT: 0.6 m
METRIC WEIGHT: 7.8 kg
GENDER: ♂ ♀
ABILITIES: Static
WEAKNESSES: Ground

MAREEP   **FLAAFFY**   **AMPHAROS**   **MEGA AMPHAROS**

MARILL

Aqua Mouse Pokémon

#0183

TYPE: WATER-FAIRY

The fur on its body naturally repels water. It can stay dry even when it plays in the water.

The oil-filled tail functions as a buoy, so it's fine even in rivers with strong currents.

HOW TO SAY IT: MARE-rull
IMPERIAL HEIGHT: 1'04"
IMPERIAL WEIGHT: 18.7 lbs.
METRIC HEIGHT: 0.4 m
METRIC WEIGHT: 8.5 kg
GENDER: ♂ ♀
ABILITIES: Thick Fat, Huge Power
WEAKNESSES: Grass, Electric, Poison

AZURILL   **MARILL**   **AZUMARILL**

MAROWAK

Bone Keeper Pokémon

#0105

TYPE: GROUND

This Pokémon overcame its sorrow to evolve a sturdy new body. Marowak faces its opponents bravely, using a bone as a weapon.

When this Pokémon evolved, the skull of its mother fused to it. Marowak's temperament also turned vicious at the same time.

HOW TO SAY IT: MARE-oh-wack
IMPERIAL HEIGHT: 3'03"   **METRIC HEIGHT:** 1.0 m
IMPERIAL WEIGHT: 99.2 lbs.   **METRIC WEIGHT:** 45.0 kg
GENDER: ♂ ♀
ABILITIES: Rock Head, Lightning Rod
WEAKNESSES: Water, Grass, Ice

CUBONE → MAROWAK

ALOLAN MAROWAK

#0105

Bone Keeper Pokémon

TYPE: FIRE-GHOST

This Pokémon sets the bone it holds on fire and dances through the night as a way to mourn its fallen allies.

The cursed flames that light up the bone carried by this Pokémon are said to cause both mental and physical pain that will never fade.

HOW TO SAY IT: MARE-oh-wack
IMPERIAL HEIGHT: 3'03"
IMPERIAL WEIGHT: 75.0 lbs.
METRIC HEIGHT: 1.0 m
METRIC WEIGHT: 34.0 kg
GENDER: ♂ ♀
ABILITIES: Cursed Body, Lightning Rod
WEAKNESSES: Water, Ghost, Ground, Dark, Rock

CUBONE → ALOLAN MAROWAK

TYPE: FIGHTING-GHOST

It slips into the shadows of others and mimics their powers and movements. As it improves, it becomes stronger than those it's imitating.

It sinks into the shadows of people and Pokémon, where it can understand their feelings and copy their capabilities.

HOW TO SAY IT: mar-SHAD-oh
IMPERIAL HEIGHT: 2'04'
IMPERIAL WEIGHT: 48.9 lbs.
METRIC HEIGHT: 0.7m
METRIC WEIGHT: 22.2 kg
GENDER: Unknown
ABILITIES: Technician
WEAKNESSES: Ghost, Psychic, Flying, Fairy

ZENITH MARSHADOW

MARSHTOMP
Mud Fish Pokémon
#0259

TYPE: WATER-GROUND

The surface of Marshtomp's body is enveloped by a thin, sticky film that enables it to live on land. This Pokémon plays in mud on beaches when the ocean tide is low.

Marshtomp is much faster at traveling through mud than it is at swimming. This Pokémon's hindquarters exhibit obvious development, giving it the ability to walk on just its hind legs.

HOW TO SAY IT: MARSH-stomp
IMPERIAL HEIGHT: 2'04"
IMPERIAL WEIGHT: 61.7 lbs.
GENDER: ♂ ♀
ABILITIES: Torrent
WEAKNESSES: Grass

METRIC HEIGHT: 0.7 m
METRIC WEIGHT: 28.0 kg

MUDKIP → **MARSHTOMP** → **SWAMPERT** → **MEGA SWAMPERT**

MASCHIFF
Rascal Pokémon
#0942

TYPE: DARK

It always scowls in an attempt to make opponents take it seriously, but even crying children will burst into laughter when they see Maschiff's face.

Its well-developed jaw and fangs are strong enough to crunch through boulders, and its thick fat makes for an excellent defense.

HOW TO SAY IT: MAS-chif
IMPERIAL HEIGHT: 1'08"
IMPERIAL WEIGHT: 35.3 lbs.
GENDER: ♂ ♀
ABILITIES: Intimidate, Run Away
WEAKNESSES: Fairy, Bug, Fighting

METRIC HEIGHT: 0.5 m
METRIC WEIGHT: 16.0 kg

MASCHIFF → **MABOSSTIFF**

#0284

MASQUERAIN
Eyeball Pokémon

TYPE: BUG-FLYING

It flaps its four wings to hover and fly freely in any direction—to and fro and sideways.

The antennae have distinctive patterns that look like eyes. When it rains, they grow heavy, making flight impossible.

HOW TO SAY IT: mas-ker-RAIN
IMPERIAL HEIGHT: 2'07"
IMPERIAL WEIGHT: 7.9 lbs.
METRIC HEIGHT: 0.8 m
METRIC WEIGHT: 3.6 kg
GENDER: ♂ ♀
ABILITIES: Intimidate
WEAKNESSES: Fire, Flying, Electric, Ice, Rock

SURSKIT **MASQUERAIN**

#0925

MAUSHOLD
Family Pokémon

TYPE: NORMAL

The two little ones just appeared one day. The group might be a family of related Pokémon, but nobody knows for sure.

The larger pair protects the little ones during battles. When facing strong opponents, the whole group will join the fight.

HOW TO SAY IT: MOUSE-hold
IMPERIAL HEIGHT: 1'00"
IMPERIAL WEIGHT: 6.2 lbs.
METRIC HEIGHT: 0.3 m
METRIC WEIGHT: 2.8 kg
GENDER: Unknown
ABILITIES: Friend Guard, Cheek Pouch
WEAKNESSES: Fighting

TANDEMAUS **MAUSHOLD**

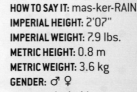

MAWILE

Deceiver Pokémon

#0303

TYPE: STEEL-FAIRY

It uses its docile-looking face to lull foes into complacency, then bites with its huge, relentless jaws.

It chomps with its gaping mouth. Its huge jaws are actually steel horns that have been transformed.

HOW TO SAY IT: MAW-while
IMPERIAL HEIGHT: 2'00"
IMPERIAL WEIGHT: 25.4 lbs.
METRIC HEIGHT: 0.6 m
METRIC WEIGHT: 11.5 kg
GENDER: ♂ ♀
ABILITIES: Hyper Cutter, Intimidate
WEAKNESSES: Fire, Ground

MEGA MAWILE

TYPE: STEEL-FAIRY

It has an extremely vicious disposition. It grips prey in its two sets of jaws and tears them apart with raw power.

Its two sets of jaws thrash about violently as if they each had a will of their own. One gnash from them can turn a boulder to dust.

IMPERIAL HEIGHT: 3'03"
IMPERIAL WEIGHT: 51.8 lbs.
METRIC HEIGHT: 1.0 m
METRIC WEIGHT: 23.5 kg

MAWILE

MEGA MAWILE

MEDICHAM

#0308

Meditate Pokémon

TYPE: FIGHTING-PSYCHIC

Through yoga training, it gained the psychic power to predict its foe's next move.

It elegantly avoids attacks with dance-like steps, then launches a devastating blow in the same motion.

HOW TO SAY IT: MED-uh-cham
IMPERIAL HEIGHT: 4'03"
IMPERIAL WEIGHT: 69.4 lbs.
METRIC HEIGHT: 1.3 m
METRIC WEIGHT: 31.5 kg
GENDER: ♂ ♀
ABILITIES: Pure Power
WEAKNESSES: Ghost, Fairy, Flying

MEGA MEDICHAM

TYPE: FIGHTING-PSYCHIC

It is said that through meditation, Medicham heightens energy inside its body and sharpens its sixth sense. This Pokémon hides its presence by merging itself with fields and mountains.

Through the power of meditation, Medicham developed its sixth sense. It gained the ability to use psychokinetic powers. This Pokémon is known to meditate for a whole month without eating.

IMPERIAL HEIGHT: 4'03"
IMPERIAL WEIGHT: 69.4 lbs.
METRIC HEIGHT: 1.3 m
METRIC WEIGHT: 31.5 kg

MEDITITE

MEDICHAM

MEGA MEDICHAM

MEDITITE

Meditate Pokémon

#0307

TYPE: FIGHTING-PSYCHIC

It never skips its daily yoga training. It heightens its inner strength through meditation.

It meditates to heighten its inner energy and to float in the air. It eats one berry a day.

HOW TO SAY IT: MED-uh-tite
IMPERIAL HEIGHT: 2'00"
IMPERIAL WEIGHT: 24.7 lbs.
METRIC HEIGHT: 0.6 m
METRIC WEIGHT: 11.2 kg
GENDER: ♂ ♀
ABILITIES: Pure Power
WEAKNESSES: Ghost, Fairy, Flying

MEDITITE   **MEDICHAM**   **MEGA MEDICHAM**

MEGANIUM

Herb Pokémon

#0154

TYPE: GRASS

The fragrance of Meganium's flower soothes and calms emotions. In battle, this Pokémon gives off more of its becalming scent to blunt the foe's fighting spirit.

HOW TO SAY IT: meg-GAY-nee-um
IMPERIAL HEIGHT: 5'11"
IMPERIAL WEIGHT: 221.6 lbs.
METRIC HEIGHT: 1.8 m
METRIC WEIGHT: 100.5 kg
GENDER: ♂ ♀
ABILITIES: Overgrow
WEAKNESSES: Fire, Flying, Ice, Poison, Bug

CHIKORITA   **BAYLEEF**   **MEGANIUM**

#0809

MELMETAL
Hex Nut Pokémon

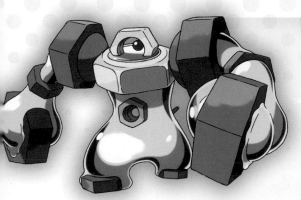

TYPE: STEEL

At the end of its life span, Melmetal will rust and fall apart. The small shards left behind will eventually be reborn as Meltan.

Centrifugal force is behind the punches of Melmetal's heavy hex-nut arms. Melmetal is said to deliver the strongest punches of all Pokémon.

HOW TO SAY IT: MEL-metal
IMPERIAL HEIGHT: 8'02"
IMPERIAL WEIGHT: 1,763.7 lbs.
METRIC HEIGHT: 2.5 m
METRIC WEIGHT: 800.0 kg
GENDER: Unknown
ABILITIES: Iron Fist
WEAKNESSES: Fire, Fighting, Ground

MELTAN   MELMETAL

GIGANTAMAX MELMETAL

In a distant land, there are legends about a cyclopean giant. In fact, the giant was a Melmetal that was flooded with Gigantamax energy.

It can send electric beams streaking out from the hole in its belly. The beams' tremendous energy can vaporize an opponent in one shot.

IMPERIAL HEIGHT: 82'00"+
IMPERIAL WEIGHT: ????.? lbs.
METRIC HEIGHT: 25.0+ m
METRIC WEIGHT: ???.? kg

MELOETTA

Melody Pokémon

#0648

PIROUETTE FORME

ARIA FORME TYPE: NORMAL-PSYCHIC PIROUETTE FORME TYPE: NORMAL-FIGHTING

The melodies sung by Meloetta have the power to make Pokémon that hear them happy or sad.

Its melodies are sung with a special vocalization method that can control the feelings of those who hear it.

HOW TO SAY IT: mell-oh-ET-tuh
IMPERIAL HEIGHT: 2'00"
IMPERIAL WEIGHT: 14.3 lbs.
METRIC HEIGHT: 0.6 m
METRIC WEIGHT: 6.5 kg
GENDER: Unknown
ABILITIES: Serene Grace
WEAKNESSES: Aria Forme: Dark, Bug/
Pirouette Forme: Fighting,
Flying, Psychic, Fairy

DOES NOT EVOLVE

ARIA FORME

MELTAN

Hex Nut Pokémon

#0808

MYTHICAL POKÉMON

TYPE: STEEL

It melts particles of iron and other metals found in the subsoil, so it can absorb them into its body of molten steel.

HOW TO SAY IT: MEL-tan
IMPERIAL HEIGHT: 0'08"
IMPERIAL WEIGHT: 17.6 lbs.
METRIC HEIGHT: 0.2 m
METRIC WEIGHT: 8.0 kg
GENDER: Unknown
ABILITIES: Magnet Pull
WEAKNESSES: Fire, Fighting, Ground

MELTAN

MELMETAL

#0908

MEOWSCARADA
Magician Pokémon

TYPE: GRASS-DARK

This Pokémon uses the reflective fur lining its cape to camouflage the stem of its flower, creating the illusion that the flower is floating.

With skillful misdirection, it rigs foes with pollen-packed flower bombs. Meowscarada sets off the bombs before its foes realize what's going on.

HOW TO SAY IT: MEOW-skah-RAH-da
IMPERIAL HEIGHT: 4'11"
IMPERIAL WEIGHT: 68.8 lbs.
METRIC HEIGHT: 1.5 m
METRIC WEIGHT: 31.2 kg
GENDER: ♂ ♀
ABILITIES: Overgrow
WEAKNESSES: Ice, Fire, Flying, Poison, Fighting, Fairy, Bug

SPRIGATITO ➡ **FLORAGATO** ➡ **MEOWSCARADA**

TYPE: PSYCHIC

Revealing the eyelike patterns on the insides of its ears will unleash its psychic powers. It normally keeps the patterns hidden, however.

The defensive instinct of the males is strong. It's when they're protecting themselves or their partners that they unleash their full power.

HOW TO SAY IT: MYOW-stik
IMPERIAL HEIGHT: 2'00"
IMPERIAL WEIGHT: 18.7 lbs.
METRIC HEIGHT: 0.6 m
METRIC WEIGHT: 8.5 kg
GENDER: ♂ ♀
ABILITIES: Keen Eye, Infiltrator
WEAKNESSES: Ghost, Dark, Bug

#0678

MEOWSTIC
Constraint Pokémon

MALE FORM

FEMALE FORM

ESPURR **MEOWSTIC**

MEOWTH
Scratch Cat Pokémon

#0052

TYPE: NORMAL

All it does is sleep during the daytime. At night, it patrols its territory with its eyes aglow.

It loves things that sparkle. When it sees a shiny object, the gold coin on its head shines, too.

HOW TO SAY IT: mee-OWTH
IMPERIAL HEIGHT: 1'04"
METRIC HEIGHT: 0.4 m
IMPERIAL WEIGHT: 9.3 lbs.
METRIC WEIGHT: 4.2 kg
GENDER: ♂ ♀
ABILITIES: Pickup, Technician
WEAKNESSES: Fighting

MEOWTH   PERSIAN

GIGANTAMAX MEOWTH

The pattern that has appeared on its giant coin is thought to be the key to unlocking the secrets of the Dynamax phenomenon.

Its body has grown incredibly long and the coin on its forehead has grown incredibly large—all thanks to Gigantamax power.

IMPERIAL HEIGHT: 108'03"+
IMPERIAL WEIGHT: ????.? lbs.
METRIC HEIGHT: 33.0+ m
METRIC WEIGHT: ???.? kg

ALOLAN MEOWTH

Scratch Cat Pokémon

TYPE: DARK

It's accustomed to luxury because it used to live with Alolan royalty. As a result, it's very picky about food.

Deeply proud and keenly smart, this Pokémon moves with cunning during battle and relentlessly attacks enemies' weak points.

HOW TO SAY IT: mee-OWTH
IMPERIAL HEIGHT: 1'04"
IMPERIAL WEIGHT: 9.3 lbs.
METRIC HEIGHT: 0.4 m
METRIC WEIGHT: 4.2 kg
GENDER: ♂ ♀
ABILITIES: Pickup, Technician
WEAKNESESS: Fairy, Bug, Fighting

ALOLAN MEOWTH   **ALOLAN PERSIAN**

GALARIAN MEOWTH

Scratch Cat Pokémon

TYPE: STEEL

Living with a savage, seafaring people has toughened this Pokémon's body so much that parts of it have turned to iron.

These daring Pokémon have coins on their foreheads. Darker coins are harder, and harder coins garner more respect among Meowth.

HOW TO SAY IT: mee-OWTH
IMPERIAL HEIGHT: 1'04"
IMPERIAL WEIGHT: 16.5 lbs.
METRIC HEIGHT: 0.4 m
METRIC WEIGHT: 7.5 kg
GENDER: ♂ ♀
ABILITIES: Pickup, Tough Claws
WEAKNESSES: Fire, Fighting, Ground

GALARIAN MEOWTH   **PERRSERKER**

TYPE: PSYCHIC

Known as "The Being of Emotion." It taught humans the nobility of sorrow, pain, and joy.

It sleeps at the bottom of a lake. Its spirit is said to leave its body to fly on the lake's surface.

HOW TO SAY IT: MESS-sprit
IMPERIAL HEIGHT: 1'00"
IMPERIAL WEIGHT: 0.7 lbs.
METRIC HEIGHT: 0.3 m
METRIC WEIGHT: 0.3 kg
GENDER: Unknown
ABILITIES: Levitate
WEAKNESSES: Ghost, Dark, Bug

DOES NOT EVOLVE

METAGROSS

Iron Leg Pokémon

TYPE: STEEL-PSYCHIC

Because the magnetic powers of these Pokémon get stronger in freezing temperatures, Metagross living on snowy mountains are full of energy.

Metagross is the result of the fusion of two Metang. This Pokémon defeats its opponents through use of its supercomputer-level brain.

HOW TO SAY IT: MET-uh-gross
IMPERIAL HEIGHT: 5'03"
IMPERIAL WEIGHT: 1,212.5 lbs.
METRIC HEIGHT: 1.6 m
METRIC WEIGHT: 550.0 kg
GENDER: Unknown
ABILITIES: Clear Body
WEAKNESSES: Ghost, Fire, Dark, Ground

MEGA METAGROSS

TYPE: STEEL-PSYCHIC

Its intellect surpasses its previous level, resulting in battles so cruel, they'll make you want to cover your eyes.

When it knows it can't win, it digs the claws on its legs into its opponent and starts the countdown to a big explosion.

IMPERIAL HEIGHT: 8'02"
IMPERIAL WEIGHT: 2,078.7 lbs.
METRIC HEIGHT: 2.5 m
METRIC WEIGHT: 942.9 kg

BELDUM

METANG

METAGROSS

MEGA METAGROSS

METANG

Iron Claw Pokémon

#0375

TYPE: STEEL-PSYCHIC

Two Beldum have become stuck together via their own magnetic forces. With two brains, the resulting Metang has doubled psychic powers.

Using magnetic forces to stay aloft, this Pokémon flies at high speeds, weaving through harsh mountain terrain in pursuit of prey.

HOW TO SAY IT: met-TANG
IMPERIAL HEIGHT: 3'11"
IMPERIAL WEIGHT: 446.4 lbs.
METRIC HEIGHT: 1.2 m
METRIC WEIGHT: 202.5 kg
GENDER: Unknown
ABILITIES: Clear Body
WEAKNESSES: Ghost, Fire, Dark, Ground

BELDUM   **METANG**   **METAGROSS**   **MEGA METAGROSS**

METAPOD

Cocoon Pokémon

#0011

TYPE: BUG

It is waiting for the moment to evolve. At this stage, it can only harden, so it remains motionless to avoid attack.

Even though it is encased in a sturdy shell, the body inside is tender. It can't withstand a harsh attack.

HOW TO SAY IT: MET-uh-pod
IMPERIAL HEIGHT: 2'04"
IMPERIAL WEIGHT: 21.8 lbs.
METRIC HEIGHT: 0.7 m
METRIC WEIGHT: 9.9 kg
GENDER: ♂ ♀
ABILITIES: Shed Skin
WEAKNESSES: Fire, Flying, Rock

CATERPIE   **METAPOD**   **BUTTERFREE**

#0151

MEW
New Species Pokémon

TYPE: PSYCHIC

When viewed through a microscope, this Pokémon's short, fine, delicate hair can be seen.

HOW TO SAY IT: MUE
IMPERIAL HEIGHT: 1'04"
IMPERIAL WEIGHT: 8.8 lbs.
METRIC HEIGHT: 0.4 m
METRIC WEIGHT: 4.0 kg
GENDER: Unknown
ABILITIES: Synchronize
WEAKNESSES: Ghost, Dark, Bug

DOES NOT EVOLVE

#0150

MEWTWO
Genetic Pokémon

TYPE: PSYCHIC

Its DNA is almost the same as Mew's. However, its size and disposition are vastly different.

HOW TO SAY IT: MUE-TOO
IMPERIAL HEIGHT: 6'07"
METRIC HEIGHT: 2.0 m
IMPERIAL WEIGHT: 269.0 lbs.
METRIC WEIGHT: 122.0 kg
GENDER: Unknown
ABILITIES: Pressure
WEAKNESSES: Ghost, Dark, Bug

MEGA MEWTWO X

TYPE: PSYCHIC-FIGHTING

Psychic power has augmented its muscles. It has a grip strength of one ton and can sprint a hundred meters in two seconds flat!

IMPERIAL HEIGHT: 7'07"
IMPERIAL WEIGHT: 280.0 lbs.
METRIC HEIGHT: 2.3 m
METRIC WEIGHT: 127.0 kg

MEGA MEWTWO Y

TYPE: PSYCHIC

Despite its diminished size, its mental power has grown phenomenally. With a mere thought, it can smash a skyscraper to smithereens.

IMPERIAL HEIGHT: 4'11"
IMPERIAL WEIGHT: 72.8 lbs.
METRIC HEIGHT: 1.5 m
METRIC WEIGHT: 33.0 kg

MEGA
MEWTWO X

MEWTWO

MEGA
MEWTWO Y

MIENFOO

#0619

Martial Arts Pokémon

TYPE: FIGHTING

In one minute, a well-trained Mienfoo can chop with its arms more than 100 times.

Though small, Mienfoo's temperament is fierce. Any creature that approaches Mienfoo carelessly will be greeted with a flurry of graceful attacks.

HOW TO SAY IT: MEEN-FOO
IMPERIAL HEIGHT: 2'11"
IMPERIAL WEIGHT: 44.1 lbs.
METRIC HEIGHT: 0.9 m
METRIC WEIGHT: 20.0 kg
GENDER: ♂ ♀
ABILITIES: Inner Focus, Regenerator
WEAKNESSES: Psychic, Flying, Fairy

MIENFOO   MIENSHAO

MIENSHAO

#0620

Martial Arts Pokémon

TYPE: FIGHTING

When Mienshao comes across a truly challenging opponent, it will lighten itself by biting off the fur on its arms.

Delivered at blinding speeds, kicks from this Pokémon can shatter massive boulders into tiny pieces.

HOW TO SAY IT: MEEN-SHAU
IMPERIAL HEIGHT: 4'07"
IMPERIAL WEIGHT: 78.3 lbs.
METRIC HEIGHT: 1.4 m
METRIC WEIGHT: 35.5 kg
GENDER: ♂ ♀
ABILITIES: Inner Focus, Regenerator
WEAKNESSES: Psychic, Flying, Fairy

MIENFOO   MIENSHAO

MIGHTYENA

Bite Pokémon

#0262

TYPE: DARK

Mightyena gives obvious signals when it is preparing to attack. It starts to growl deeply and then flattens its body. This Pokémon will bite savagely with its sharply pointed fangs.

Mightyena travel and act as a pack in the wild. The memory of its life in the wild compels the Pokémon to obey only those Trainers that it recognizes to possess superior skill.

HOW TO SAY IT: MY-tee-EH-nah
IMPERIAL HEIGHT: 3'03"
IMPERIAL WEIGHT: 81.6 lbs.
METRIC HEIGHT: 1.0 m
METRIC WEIGHT: 37.0 kg
GENDER: ♂ ♀
ABILITIES: Intimidate, Quick Feet
WEAKNESSES: Fairy, Bug, Fighting

POOCHYENA   MIGHTYENA

MILCERY

Cream Pokémon

#0868

TYPE: FAIRY

This Pokémon was born from sweet-smelling particles in the air. Its body is made of cream.

They say that any patisserie visited by Milcery is guaranteed success and good fortune.

HOW TO SAY IT: MIHL-suh-ree
IMPERIAL HEIGHT: 0'08"
IMPERIAL WEIGHT: 0.7 lbs.
METRIC HEIGHT: 0.2 m
METRIC WEIGHT: 0.3 kg
GENDER: ♀
ABILITIES: Sweet Veil
WEAKNESSES: Steel, Poison

MILCERY   ALCREMIE

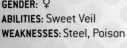

TYPE: WATER

Milotic has provided inspiration to many artists. It has even been referred to as the most beautiful Pokémon of all.

It's said that a glimpse of a Milotic and its beauty will calm any hostile emotions you're feeling.

HOW TO SAY IT: MY-low-tic
IMPERIAL HEIGHT: 20'04"
IMPERIAL WEIGHT: 357.1 lbs.
METRIC HEIGHT: 6.2 m
METRIC WEIGHT: 162.0 kg
GENDER: ♂ ♀
ABILITIES: Marvel Scale, Competitive
WEAKNESSES: Grass, Electric

#0350

MILOTIC
Tender Pokémon

FEEBAS   MILOTIC

MILTANK

Milk Cow Pokémon

#0241

TYPE: NORMAL

Miltank produces highly nutritious milk, so it's been supporting the lives of people and other Pokémon since ancient times.

This Pokémon needs to be milked every day, or else it will fall ill. The flavor of Miltank milk changes with the seasons.

HOW TO SAY IT: MILL-tank
IMPERIAL HEIGHT: 3'11"
IMPERIAL WEIGHT: 166.4 lbs.
METRIC HEIGHT: 1.2 m
METRIC WEIGHT: 75.5 kg
GENDER: ♀
ABILITIES: Thick Fat, Scrappy
WEAKNESSES: Fighting

DOES NOT EVOLVE

MIME JR.

Mime Pokémon

#0439

TYPE: PSYCHIC-FAIRY

It mimics everyone it sees, but it puts extra effort into copying the graceful dance steps of Mr. Rime as practice.

It looks for a Mr. Rime that's a good dancer and carefully copies the Mr. Rime's steps like an apprentice.

HOW TO SAY IT: mime JOO-nyur
IMPERIAL HEIGHT: 2'00"
IMPERIAL WEIGHT: 28.7 lbs.
METRIC HEIGHT: 0.6 m
METRIC WEIGHT: 13.0 kg
GENDER: ♂ ♀
ABILITIES: Soundproof, Filter
WEAKNESSES: Ghost, Steel, Poison

MIME JR.

MR. MIME

GALARIAN
MR. MIME

MR. RIME

TYPE: GHOST-FAIRY

This Pokémon lives in dark places untouched by sunlight. When it appears before humans, it hides itself under a cloth that resembles a Pikachu.

Mimikyu was only recently identified as a Pokémon. Previously, people thought it was just a ghost wearing a cloth.

HOW TO SAY IT: MEE-mee-kyoo
IMPERIAL HEIGHT: 0'08"
IMPERIAL WEIGHT: 1.5 lbs.
METRIC HEIGHT: 0.2 m
METRIC WEIGHT: 0.7 kg
GENDER: ♂ ♀
ABILITIES: Disguise
WEAKNESSES: Ghost, Steel

#0778

MIMIKYU
Disguise Pokémon

DOES NOT EVOLVE

#0572

MINCCINO
Chinchilla Pokémon

TYPE: NORMAL

The way it brushes away grime with its tail can be helpful when cleaning. But its focus on spotlessness can make cleaning more of a hassle.

They pet each other with their tails as a form of greeting. Of the two, the one whose tail is fluffier is a bit more boastful.

HOW TO SAY IT: min-CHEE-noh
IMPERIAL HEIGHT: 1'04"
IMPERIAL WEIGHT: 12.8 lbs.
METRIC HEIGHT: 0.4 m
METRIC WEIGHT: 5.8 kg
GENDER: ♂ ♀
ABILITIES: Cute Charm, Technician
WEAKNESSES: Fighting

MINCCINO

CINCCINO

MINIOR

Meteor Pokémon

#0774

TYPE: ROCK-FLYING

It lives in the ozone layer, where it becomes food for stronger Pokémon. When it tries to run away, it falls to the ground.

Although its outer shell is uncommonly durable, the shock of falling to the ground smashes the shell to smithereens.

HOW TO SAY IT: MIN-ee-or
IMPERIAL HEIGHT: 1'00"
IMPERIAL WEIGHT: Meteor Form: 88.2 lbs. /
　　　　　　　　Red Core Form: 0.7 lbs.
METRIC HEIGHT: 0.3 m
METRIC WEIGHT: Meteor Form: 40.0 kg /
　　　　　　　　Red Core Form: 0.3 kg
GENDER: Unknown
ABILITIES: Shields Down
WEAKNESSES: Steel, Water, Electric, Ice, Rock

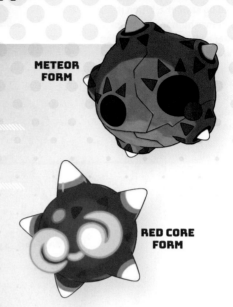

METEOR FORM

RED CORE FORM

DOES NOT EVOLVE

MINUN

Cheering Pokémon

#0312

TYPE: ELECTRIC

Minun is more concerned about cheering on its partners than its own safety. It shorts out the electricity in its body to create brilliant showers of sparks to cheer on its teammates.

Minun loves to cheer on its partner in battle. It gives off sparks from its body while it is doing so. If its partner is in trouble, this Pokémon gives off increasing amounts of sparks.

HOW TO SAY IT: MY-nun
IMPERIAL HEIGHT: 1'04"
IMPERIAL WEIGHT: 9.3 lbs.
METRIC HEIGHT: 0.4 m
METRIC WEIGHT: 4.2 kg
GENDER: ♂ ♀
ABILITIES: Minus
WEAKNESSES: Ground

DOES NOT EVOLVE

MIRAIDON
Paradox Pokémon

TYPE: ELECTRIC-DRAGON

Much remains Unknown about this creature. It resembles Cyclizar, but it is far more ruthless and powerful.

This seems to be the Iron Serpent mentioned in an old book. The Iron Serpent is said to have turned the land to ash with its lightning.

HOW TO SAY IT: meer-RAI-dahn
IMPERIAL HEIGHT: 11'06"
IMPERIAL WEIGHT: 529.1 lbs.
METRIC HEIGHT: 3.5 m
METRIC WEIGHT: 240.0 kg
GENDER: Unknown
ABILITIES: Hadron Engine
WEAKNESSES: Fairy, Ground, Ice, Dragon

DOES NOT EVOLVE

MISDREAVUS
Screech Pokémon

#0200

TYPE: GHOST

This Pokémon startles people in the middle of the night. It gathers fear as its energy.

It loves to bite and yank people's hair from behind without warning, just to see their shocked reactions.

HOW TO SAY IT: mis-DREE-vuss
IMPERIAL HEIGHT: 2'04"
IMPERIAL WEIGHT: 2.2 lbs.
METRIC HEIGHT: 0.7 m
METRIC WEIGHT: 1.0 kg
GENDER: ♂ ♀
ABILITIES: Levitate
WEAKNESSES: Ghost, Dark

MISDREAVUS   MISMAGIUS

#0429

MISMAGIUS
Magical Pokémon

TYPE: GHOST

Its cry sounds like an incantation. It is said the cry may rarely be imbued with happiness-giving power.

Its cries sound like incantations to torment the foe. It appears where you least expect it.

HOW TO SAY IT: miss-MAG-ee-us
IMPERIAL HEIGHT: 2'11"
IMPERIAL WEIGHT: 9.7 lbs.
METRIC HEIGHT: 0.9 m
METRIC WEIGHT: 4.4 kg
GENDER: ♂ ♀
ABILITIES: Levitate
WEAKNESSES: Ghost, Dark

MISDREAVUS   MISMAGIUS

LEGENDARY POKÉMON

#0146

MOLTRES
Flame Pokémon

TYPE: FIRE-FLYING

It is one of the legendary bird Pokémon. Its appearance is said to indicate the coming of spring.

HOW TO SAY IT: MOHL-trace
IMPERIAL HEIGHT: 6'07"
IMPERIAL WEIGHT: 132.3 lbs.
METRIC HEIGHT: 2.0 m
METRIC WEIGHT: 60.0 kg
GENDER: Unknown
ABILITIES: Pressure
WEAKNESSES: Water, Electric, Rock

DOES NOT EVOLVE

LEGENDARY POKÉMON

#0146

GALARIAN MOLTRES
Malevolent Pokémon

TYPE: DARK-FLYING

This Pokémon's sinister, flame-like aura will consume the spirit of any creature it hits. Victims become burned-out shadows of themselves.

The sinister aura that blazes like molten fire around this Pokémon is what inspired the name "Moltres."

HOW TO SAY IT: MOHL-trace
IMPERIAL HEIGHT: 6'07"
IMPERIAL WEIGHT: 145.5 lbs.
METRIC HEIGHT: 2.0 m
METRIC WEIGHT: 66.0 kg
GENDER: Unknown
ABILITIES: Berserk
WEAKNESSES: Fairy, Electric, Ice, Rock

DOES NOT EVOLVE

TYPE: FIRE-FIGHTING

It skillfully controls the intensity of the fire on its tail to keep its foes at an ideal distance.

It uses ceilings and walls to launch aerial attacks. Its fiery tail is but one weapon.

#0391

MONFERNO
Playful Pokémon

HOW TO SAY IT: mon-FUR-no
IMPERIAL HEIGHT: 2'11"
IMPERIAL WEIGHT: 48.5 lbs.
METRIC HEIGHT: 0.9 m
METRIC WEIGHT: 22.0 kg
GENDER: ♂ ♀
ABILITIES: Blaze
WEAKNESSES: Water, Psychic, Flying, Ground

CHIMCHAR

MONFERNO

INFERNAPE

MORELULL #0755
Illuminating Pokémon

MORELULL → **SHIINOTIC**

TYPE: GRASS-FAIRY

Pokémon living in the forest eat the delicious caps on Morelull's head. The caps regrow overnight.

Morelull live in forests that stay dark even during the day. They scatter flickering spores that put enemies to sleep.

HOW TO SAY IT: MORE-eh-lull
IMPERIAL HEIGHT: 0'08"
IMPERIAL WEIGHT: 3.3 lbs.
METRIC HEIGHT: 0.2 m
METRIC WEIGHT: 1.5 kg
GENDER: ♂ ♀
ABILITIES: Illuminate, Effect Spore
WEAKNESSES: Steel, Fire, Flying, Ice, Poison

MORGREM #0860
Devious Pokémon

TYPE: DARK-FAIRY

Morgrem prefers dirty tactics, like ambushing, because it doesn't have confidence in its brawn.

This Pokémon absorbs negative emotions and turns them into energy. It's popular with people who tend to think gloomy thoughts.

HOW TO SAY IT: MOHR-grehm
IMPERIAL HEIGHT: 2'07"
IMPERIAL WEIGHT: 27.6 lbs.
METRIC HEIGHT: 0.8 m
METRIC WEIGHT: 12.5 kg
GENDER: ♂
ABILITIES: Prankster, Frisk
WEAKNESSES: Steel, Fairy, Poison

IMPIDIMP

MORGREM

GRIMMSNARL

MORPEKO

Two-Sided Pokémon

#0877

FULL BELLY MODE

HANGRY MODE

TYPE: ELECTRIC-DARK

As it eats the seeds stored up in its pocket-like pouches, this Pokémon is not just satisfying its constant hunger. It's also generating electricity.

It carries electrically roasted seeds with it as if they're precious treasures. No matter how much it eats, it always gets hungry again in short order.

HOW TO SAY IT: mohr-PEH-koh
IMPERIAL HEIGHT: 1'00"
IMPERIAL WEIGHT: 6.6 lbs.
METRIC HEIGHT: 0.3 m
METRIC WEIGHT: 3.0 kg
GENDER: ♂ ♀
ABILITIES: Hunger Switch
WEAKNESSES: Fairy, Bug, Fighting, Ground

DOES NOT EVOLVE

TYPE: BUG-FLYING

It loves the honey of flowers and steals honey collected by Combee.

It flutters around at night and steals honey from the Combee hive.

HOW TO SAY IT: MOTH-im
IMPERIAL HEIGHT: 2'11"
IMPERIAL WEIGHT: 51.4 lbs.
METRIC HEIGHT: 0.9 m
METRIC WEIGHT: 23.3 kg
GENDER: ♂
ABILITIES: Swarm
WEAKNESSES: Fire, Flying, Electric, Ice, Rock

#0414

MOTHIM

Moth Pokémon

BURMY   MOTHIM

MR. MIME

Barrier Pokémon

#0122

TYPE: PSYCHIC-FAIRY

It is a pantomime expert that can create invisible but solid walls using miming gestures.

Emanations from its fingertips solidify the air into invisible walls that repel even harsh attacks.

HOW TO SAY IT: MIS-ter MIME
IMPERIAL HEIGHT: 4'03"
IMPERIAL WEIGHT: 120.2 lbs.
METRIC HEIGHT: 1.3 m
METRIC WEIGHT: 54.5 kg
GENDER: ♂ ♀
ABILITIES: Soundproof, Filter
WEAKNESSES: Ghost, Steel, Poison

MIME JR.　　MR. MIME

GALARIAN MR. MIME

Dancing Pokémon

#0122

TYPE: ICE-PSYCHIC

Its talent is tap-dancing. It can also manipulate temperatures to create a floor of ice, which this Pokémon can kick up to use as a barrier.

It can radiate chilliness from the bottoms of its feet. It'll spend the whole day tap-dancing on a frozen floor.

HOW TO SAY IT: MIS-ter MIME
IMPERIAL HEIGHT: 4'07"
IMPERIAL WEIGHT: 125.2 lbs.
METRIC HEIGHT: 1.4 m
METRIC WEIGHT: 56.8 kg
GENDER: ♂ ♀
ABILITIES: Vital Spirit, Screen Cleaner
WEAKNESSES: Steel, Ghost, Fire, Dark, Rock, Bug

MIME JR.　　GALARIAN MR. MIME　　MR. RIME

TYPE: ICE-PSYCHIC

It's highly skilled at tap-dancing. It waves its cane of ice in time with its graceful movements.

Its amusing movements make it very popular. It releases its psychic power from the pattern on its belly.

HOW TO SAY IT: MIS-ter RYME
IMPERIAL HEIGHT: 4'11"
IMPERIAL WEIGHT: 128.3 lbs.
METRIC HEIGHT: 1.5 m
METRIC WEIGHT: 58.2 kg
GENDER: ♂ ♀
ABILITIES: Tangled Feet, Screen Cleaner
WEAKNESSES: Steel, Ghost, Fire, Dark, Rock, Bug

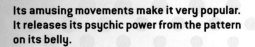

MR. RIME
Comedian Pokémon
#0866

| MIME JR. | GALARIAN MR. MIME | MR. RIME |

#0749

MUDBRAY
Donkey Pokémon

TYPE: GROUND

This Pokémon covers itself in mud that it has regurgitated. The mud won't dry out even if it's exposed to the sun for a long time.

Though a slow walker, Mudbray is plenty strong. Its pace doesn't change even when it's loaded with 50 times its own body weight.

HOW TO SAY IT: MUD-bray
IMPERIAL HEIGHT: 3'03"
IMPERIAL WEIGHT: 242.5 lbs.
METRIC HEIGHT: 1.0 m
METRIC WEIGHT: 110.0 kg
GENDER: ♂ ♀
ABILITIES: Own Tempo, Stamina
WEAKNESSES: Water, Grass, Ice

MUDBRAY   MUDSDALE

MUDKIP

Mud Fish Pokémon

TYPE: WATER

The fin on Mudkip's head acts as a highly sensitive radar. Using this fin to sense movements of water and air, this Pokémon can determine what is taking place around it without using its eyes.

In water, Mudkip breathes using the gills on its cheeks. If it is faced with a tight situation in battle, this Pokémon will unleash its amazing power—it can crush rocks bigger than itself.

HOW TO SAY IT: MUD-kip
IMPERIAL HEIGHT: 1'04"　　**METRIC HEIGHT:** 0.4 m
IMPERIAL WEIGHT: 16.8 lbs.　**METRIC WEIGHT:** 7.6 kg
GENDER: ♂ ♀
ABILITIES: Torrent
WEAKNESSES: Grass, Electric

 ➡ ➡ ➡

| MUDKIP | MARSHTOMP | SWAMPERT | MEGA SWAMPERT |

MUDSDALE

Draft Horse Pokémon

TYPE: GROUND

This Pokémon has been treasured not just for its physical labor, but also because it produces high-quality mud used for making pottery.

Its legs are fortified with mud and harder than stone, and they can reduce a large truck to scrap with one kick.

HOW TO SAY IT: MUDZ-dale
IMPERIAL HEIGHT: 8'02"　　　**METRIC HEIGHT:** 2.5 m
IMPERIAL WEIGHT: 2,028.3 lbs.　**METRIC WEIGHT:** 920.0 kg
GENDER: ♂ ♀
ABILITIES: Own Tempo, Stamina
WEAKNESSES: Water, Grass, Ice

| MUDBRAY | MUDSDALE |

MUK

Sludge Pokémon

#0089

TYPE: POISON

It's thickly covered with a filthy, vile sludge. It is so toxic, even its footprints contain poison.

It's so stinky! Muk's body contains toxic elements, and any plant will wilt when it passes by.

HOW TO SAY IT: MUCK
IMPERIAL HEIGHT: 3'11"
IMPERIAL WEIGHT: 66.1 lbs.
METRIC HEIGHT: 1.2 m
METRIC WEIGHT: 30.0 kg
GENDER: ♂ ♀
ABILITIES: Stench, Sticky Hold
WEAKNESSES: Psychic, Ground

GRIMER   MUK

ALOLAN MUK

Sludge Pokémon

#0089

TYPE: POISON-DARK

Muk's coloration becomes increasingly vivid the more it feasts on its favorite dish—trash.

HOW TO SAY IT: MUCK
IMPERIAL HEIGHT: 3'03"
IMPERIAL WEIGHT: 114.6 lbs.
METRIC HEIGHT: 1.0 m
METRIC WEIGHT: 52.0 kg
GENDER: ♂ ♀
ABILITIES: Poison Touch, Gluttony
WEAKNESSES: Ground

ALOLAN GRIMER   ALOLAN MUK

MUNCHLAX #0446

Big Eater Pokémon

TYPE: NORMAL

Stuffing itself with vast amounts of food is its only concern. Whether the food is rotten or fresh, yummy or tasteless—it does not care.

It stores food beneath its fur. It might share just one bite, but only if it really trusts you.

HOW TO SAY IT: MUNCH-lax
IMPERIAL HEIGHT: 2'00"
IMPERIAL WEIGHT: 231.5 lbs.
METRIC HEIGHT: 0.6 m
METRIC WEIGHT: 105.0 kg
GENDER: ♂ ♀
ABILITIES: Pickup, Thick Fat
WEAKNESSES: Fighting

MUNCHLAX   SNORLAX

MUNNA #0517

Dream Eater Pokémon

TYPE: PSYCHIC

Late at night, it appears beside people's pillows. As it feeds on dreams, the patterns on its body give off a faint glow.

It eats dreams and releases mist. The mist is pink when it's eating a good dream, and black when it's eating a nightmare.

HOW TO SAY IT: MOON-nuh
IMPERIAL HEIGHT: 2'00"
IMPERIAL WEIGHT: 51.4 lbs.
METRIC HEIGHT: 0.6 m
METRIC WEIGHT: 23.3 kg
GENDER: ♂ ♀
ABILITIES: Forewarn, Synchronize
WEAKNESSES: Ghost, Dark, Bug

MUNNA

MUSHARNA

TYPE: DARK-FLYING

Feared and loathed by many, it is believed to bring misfortune to all those who see it at night.

If spotted, it will lure an unwary person into chasing it, then lose the pursuer on mountain trails.

HOW TO SAY IT: MUR-crow
IMPERIAL HEIGHT: 1'08"
IMPERIAL WEIGHT: 4.6 lbs.
METRIC HEIGHT: 0.5 m
METRIC WEIGHT: 2.1 kg
GENDER: ♂ ♀
ABILITIES: Insomnia, Super Luck
WEAKNESSES: Fairy, Electric, Ice, Rock

MURKROW

Darkness Pokémon

#0198

MURKROW ➡ HONCHKROW

TYPE: PSYCHIC

When dark mists emanate from its body, don't get too near. If you do, your nightmares will become reality.

It drowses and dreams all the time. It's best to leave it be if it's just woken up, as it's a terrible grump when freshly roused from sleep.

HOW TO SAY IT: moo-SHAHR-nuh
IMPERIAL HEIGHT: 3'07"
IMPERIAL WEIGHT: 133.4 lbs.
METRIC HEIGHT: 1.1 m
METRIC WEIGHT: 60.5 kg
GENDER: ♂ ♀
ABILITIES: Forewarn, Synchronize
WEAKNESSES: Ghost, Dark, Bug

MUSHARNA

Drowsing Pokémon

#0518

MUNNA ➡ MUSHARNA

NACLI
Rock Salt Pokémon

TYPE: ROCK

It was born in a layer of rock salt deep under the earth. This species was particularly treasured in the old days, as they would share precious salt.

The ground scrapes its body as it travels, causing it to leave salt behind. Salt is constantly being created and replenished inside Nacli's body.

HOW TO SAY IT: NAK-lee
IMPERIAL HEIGHT: 1'04"
IMPERIAL WEIGHT: 35.3 lbs.
METRIC HEIGHT: 0.4 m
METRIC WEIGHT: 16.0 kg
GENDER: ♂ ♀
ABILITIES: Purifying Salt, Sturdy
WEAKNESSES: Water, Steel, Grass, Fighting, Ground

NACLI   NACLSTACK   GARGANACL

NACLSTACK
Rock Salt Pokémon

TYPE: ROCK

This Pokémon dry cures its prey by spraying salt over them. The curing process steals away the water in the prey's body.

It compresses rock salt inside its body and shoots out hardened salt pellets with enough force to perforate an iron sheet.

HOW TO SAY IT: NAK-ull-stak
IMPERIAL HEIGHT: 2'00"
IMPERIAL WEIGHT: 231.5 lbs.
METRIC HEIGHT: 0.6 m
METRIC WEIGHT: 105.0 kg
GENDER: ♂ ♀
ABILITIES: Purifying Salt, Sturdy
WEAKNESSES: Water, Steel, Grass, Fighting, Ground

NACLI   NACLSTACK   GARGANACL

NAGANADEL
Poison Pin Pokémon

#0804

TYPE: POISON-DRAGON

It stores hundreds of liters of poisonous liquid inside its body. It is one of the organisms known as UBs.

One kind of Ultra Beast, it fires a glowing, venomous liquid from its needles. This liquid is also immensely adhesive.

HOW TO SAY IT: NAW-guh-NAW-duhl
IMPERIAL HEIGHT: 11'10"
IMPERIAL WEIGHT: 330.7 lbs.
METRIC HEIGHT: 3.6 m
METRIC WEIGHT: 150.0 kg
GENDER: Unknown
ABILITIES: Beast Boost
WEAKNESSES: Psychic, Ground, Ice, Dragon

POIPOLE → NAGANADEL

NATU
Tiny Bird Pokémon

#0877

TYPE: PSYCHIC-FLYING

It is extremely good at climbing tree trunks and likes to eat the new sprouts on the trees.

Because its wings aren't yet fully grown, it has to hop to get around. It is always staring at something.

HOW TO SAY IT: NAH-too
IMPERIAL HEIGHT: 0'08"
IMPERIAL WEIGHT: 4.4 lbs.
METRIC HEIGHT: 0.2 m
METRIC WEIGHT: 2.0 kg
GENDER: ♂ ♀
ABILITIES: Synchronize, Early Bird
WEAKNESSES: Ghost, Dark, Electric, Ice, Rock

NATU → XATU

NECROZMA

Prism Pokémon

TYPE: PSYCHIC

It looks somehow pained as it rages around in search of light, which serves as its energy. It's apparently from another world.

Light is the source of its energy. If it isn't devouring light, impurities build up in it and on it, and Necrozma darkens and stops moving.

HOW TO SAY IT: neh-KROHZ-muh
IMPERIAL HEIGHT: 7'10"
IMPERIAL WEIGHT: 507.1 lbs.
METRIC HEIGHT: 2.4 m
METRIC WEIGHT: 230.0 kg
GENDER: Unknown
ABILITIES: Prism Armor
WEAKNESSES: Ghost, Dark, Bug

DUSK MANE NECROZMA

ULTRA NECROZMA

DAWN WINGS NECROZMA

DOES NOT EVOLVE

NICKIT
Fox Pokémon

#0827

TYPE: DARK

Aided by the soft pads on its feet, it silently raids the food stores of other Pokémon. It survives off its ill-gotten gains.

Cunning and cautious, this Pokémon survives by stealing food from others. It erases its tracks with swipes of its tail as it makes off with its plunder.

HOW TO SAY IT: NICK-it
IMPERIAL HEIGHT: 2'00"
IMPERIAL WEIGHT: 19.6 lbs.
METRIC WEIGHT: 8.9 kg
METRIC HEIGHT: 0.6 m
GENDER: ♂ ♀
ABILITIES: Run Away, Unburden
WEAKNESSES: Fairy, Bug, Fighting

NICKIT   THIEVUL

NIDOKING
Drill Pokémon

TYPE: POISON-GROUND

When it goes on a rampage, it's impossible to control. But in the presence of a Nidoqueen it's lived with for a long time, Nidoking calms down.

Nidoking prides itself on its strength. It's forceful and spirited in battle, making use of its thick tail and diamond-crushing horn.

HOW TO SAY IT: NEE-do-king
IMPERIAL HEIGHT: 4'07"
IMPERIAL WEIGHT: 136.7 lbs.
METRIC HEIGHT: 1.4 m
METRIC WEIGHT: 62.0 kg
GENDER: ♂
ABILITIES: Poison Point, Rivalry
WEAKNESSES: Water, Psychic, Ice, Ground

NIDORAN♂   **NIDORINO**   **NIDOKING**

TYPE: POISON-GROUND

#0031

NIDOQUEEN
Drill Pokémon

Nidoqueen is better at defense than offense. With scales like armor, this Pokémon will shield its children from any kind of attack.

It pacifies offspring by placing them in the gaps between the spines on its back. The spines will never secrete poison while young are present.

HOW TO SAY IT: NEE-do-kween
IMPERIAL HEIGHT: 4'03"
IMPERIAL WEIGHT: 132.3 lbs.
METRIC HEIGHT: 1.3 m
METRIC WEIGHT: 60.0 kg
GENDER: ♀
ABILITIES: Poison Point, Rivalry
WEAKNESSES: Water, Psychic, Ice, Ground

NIDORAN ♀   **NIDORINA**   **NIDOQUEEN**

NIDORAN♀

Poison Pin Pokémon

#0029

TYPE: POISON

Females are more sensitive to smells than males. While foraging, they'll use their whiskers to check wind direction and stay downwind of predators.

It uses its hard incisor teeth to crush and eat berries. The tip of a female Nidoran's horn is a bit more rounded than the tip of a male's horn.

HOW TO SAY IT: NEE-do-ran
IMPERIAL HEIGHT: 1'04"
IMPERIAL WEIGHT: 15.4 lbs.
METRIC HEIGHT: 0.4 m
METRIC WEIGHT: 7.0 kg
GENDER: ♀
ABILITIES: Poison Point, Rivalry
WEAKNESSES: Psychic, Ground

NIDORAN♀   **NIDORINA**   **NIDOQUEEN**

NIDORAN♂

Poison Pin Pokémon

#0032

TYPE: POISON

The horn on a male Nidoran's forehead contains a powerful poison. This is a very cautious Pokémon, always straining its large ears.

Small but brave, this Pokémon will hold its ground and even risk its life in battle to protect the female it's friendly with.

HOW TO SAY IT: NEE-do-ran
IMPERIAL HEIGHT: 1'08"
IMPERIAL WEIGHT: 19.8 lbs.
METRIC HEIGHT: 0.5 m
METRIC WEIGHT: 9.0 kg
GENDER: ♂
ABILITIES: Poison Point, Rivalry
WEAKNESSES: Psychic, Ground

NIDORAN♂   **NIDORINO**   **NIDOKING**

#0030

NIDORINA
Poison Pin Pokémon

TYPE: POISON

The horn on its head has atrophied. It's thought that this happens so Nidorina's children won't get poked while their mother is feeding them.

If the group is threatened, these Pokémon will band together to assault enemies with a chorus of ultrasonic waves.

HOW TO SAY IT: NEE-do-REE-na
IMPERIAL HEIGHT: 2'07"
IMPERIAL WEIGHT: 44.1 lbs.
METRIC HEIGHT: 0.8 m
METRIC WEIGHT: 20.0 kg
GENDER: ♀
ABILITIES: Poison Point, Rivalry
WEAKNESSES: Psychic, Ground

NIDORAN ♀   **NIDORINA**   **NIDOQUEEN**

#0033

NIDORINO
Poison Pin Pokémon

TYPE: POISON

With a horn that's harder than diamond, this Pokémon goes around shattering boulders as it searches for a moon stone.

It's nervous and quick to act aggressively. The potency of its poison increases along with the level of adrenaline present in its body.

HOW TO SAY IT: NEE-do-REE-no
IMPERIAL HEIGHT: 2'11"
IMPERIAL WEIGHT: 43.0 lbs.
METRIC HEIGHT: 0.9 m
METRIC WEIGHT: 19.5 kg
GENDER: ♂
ABILITIES: Poison Point, Rivalry
WEAKNESSES: Psychic, Ground

NIDORAN ♂   **NIDORINO**   **NIDOKING**

NIHILEGO

Parasite Pokémon

#0793

TYPE: ROCK-POISON

A life-form from another world, it was dubbed a UB and is thought to produce a strong neurotoxin.

It appeared in this world from an Ultra Wormhole. Nihilego appears to be a parasite that lives by feeding on people and Pokémon.

HOW TO SAY IT: NIE-uh-LEE-go
IMPERIAL HEIGHT: 3'11"
IMPERIAL WEIGHT: 122.4 lbs.
METRIC HEIGHT: 1.2 m
METRIC WEIGHT: 55.5 kg
GENDER: Unknown
ABILITIES: Beast Boost
WEAKNESSES: Steel, Water, Psychic, Ground

DOES NOT EVOLVE

NINCADA

Trainee Pokémon

#0290

TYPE: BUG-GROUND

Because it lived almost entirely underground, it is nearly blind. It uses its antennae instead.

It can sometimes live underground for more than 10 years. It absorbs nutrients from the roots of trees.

HOW TO SAY IT: nin-KAH-da
IMPERIAL HEIGHT: 1'08"
IMPERIAL WEIGHT: 12.1 lbs.
METRIC HEIGHT: 0.5 m
METRIC WEIGHT: 5.5 kg
GENDER: ♂ ♀
ABILITIES: Compund Eyes
WEAKNESSES: Fire, Water, Flying, Ice

NINJASK

NINCADA

SHEDINJA

TYPE: FIRE

It is said to live 1,000 years, and each of its tails is loaded with supernatural powers.

Very smart and very vengeful. Grabbing one of its many tails could result in a 1,000-year curse.

HOW TO SAY IT: NINE-tails
IMPERIAL HEIGHT: 3'07"
IMPERIAL WEIGHT: 43.9 lbs.
METRIC HEIGHT: 1.1 m
METRIC WEIGHT: 19.9 kg
GENDER: ♂ ♀
ABILITIES: Flash Fire
WEAKNESSES: Water, Ground, Rock

#0038

NINETALES
Fox Pokémon

VULPIX ➡ **NINETALES**

#0038

ALOLAN NINETALES
Fox Pokémon

TYPE: ICE-FAIRY

A deity resides in the snowy mountains where this Pokémon lives. In ancient times, it was worshiped as that deity's incarnation.

While it will guide travelers who get lost on a snowy mountain down to the mountain's base, it won't forgive anyone who harms nature.

HOW TO SAY IT: NINE-tails
IMPERIAL HEIGHT: 3'07"
IMPERIAL WEIGHT: 43.9 lbs.
METRIC HEIGHT: 1.1 m
METRIC WEIGHT: 19.9 kg
GENDER: ♂ ♀
ABILITIES: Snow Cloak
WEAKNESSES: Fire, Steel, Poison, Rock

ALOLAN VULPIX   **ALOLAN NINETALES**

NINJASK
Ninja Pokémon
#0291

TYPE: BUG-FLYING

Its cry leaves a lasting headache if heard for too long. It moves so quickly that it is almost invisible.

This Pokémon is so quick, it is said to be able to avoid any attack. It loves to feed on tree sap.

HOW TO SAY IT: NIN-jask
IMPERIAL HEIGHT: 2'07"
IMPERIAL WEIGHT: 26.5 lbs.
METRIC HEIGHT: 0.8 m
METRIC WEIGHT: 12.0 kg
GENDER: ♂ ♀
ABILITIES: Speed Boost
WEAKNESSES: Fire, Flying, Electric, Ice, Rock

NINCADA   NINJASK

NOCTOWL
Owl Pokémon
#0164

TYPE: NORMAL-FLYING

Its eyes are specially developed to enable it to see clearly even in murky darkness and minimal light.

When it needs to think, it rotates its head 180 degrees to sharpen its intellectual power.

HOW TO SAY IT: NAHK-towl
IMPERIAL HEIGHT: 5'03"
IMPERIAL WEIGHT: 89.9 lbs.
METRIC HEIGHT: 1.6 m
METRIC WEIGHT: 40.8 kg
GENDER: ♂ ♀
ABILITIES: Insomnia, Keen Eye
WEAKNESSES: Electric, Ice, Rock

HOOTHOOT   NOCTOWL

NOIBAT
Sound Wave Pokémon

TYPE: FLYING-DRAGON

This Pokémon emits ultrasonic waves from its large ears to search for fruit to eat. It mistakes Applin for its food.

Noibat can change the frequency of its sound waves at will, and it generates ultrasonic waves of up to 200,000 hertz.

HOW TO SAY IT: NOY-bat
IMPERIAL HEIGHT: 1'08"
IMPERIAL WEIGHT: 17.6 lbs.
METRIC HEIGHT: 0.5 m
METRIC WEIGHT: 8.0 kg
GENDER: ♂ ♀
ABILITIES: Frisk, Infiltrator
WEAKNESSES: Fairy, Rock, Ice, Dragon

NOIBAT **NOIVERN**

NOIVERN
Sound Wave Pokémon

TYPE: FLYING-DRAGON

Ultrasonic waves emitted by a Noivern can pulverize a large boulder. This Pokémon has a cruel disposition.

In the dark, even Hydreigon are terrified of this Pokémon. But in the light, Noivern is the one that avoids battle.

HOW TO SAY IT: NOY-vurn
IMPERIAL HEIGHT: 4'11"
IMPERIAL WEIGHT: 187.4 lbs.
METRIC HEIGHT: 1.5 m
METRIC WEIGHT: 85.0 kg
GENDER: ♂ ♀
ABILITIES: Frisk, Infiltrator
WEAKNESSES: Fairy, Rock, Ice, Dragon

NOIBAT **NOIVERN**

NOSEPASS #0299

Compass Pokémon

TYPE: ROCK

It moves less than an inch a year, but when it's in a jam, it will spin and drill down into the ground in a split second.

It hunts without twitching a muscle by pulling in its prey with powerful magnetism. But sometimes it pulls natural enemies in close.

HOW TO SAY IT: NOSE-pass
IMPERIAL HEIGHT: 3'03"
IMPERIAL WEIGHT: 213.8 lbs.
METRIC HEIGHT: 1.0 m
METRIC WEIGHT: 97.0 kg
GENDER: ♂ ♀
ABILITIES: Sturdy, Magnet Pull
WEAKNESSES: Water, Steel, Grass, Fighting, Ground

NOSEPASS   PROBOPASS

NUMEL #0322

Numb Pokémon

TYPE: FIRE-GROUND

Magma of almost 2,200 degrees Fahrenheit courses through its body. When it grows cold, the magma hardens and slows it.

The flaming magma it stores in the hump on its back is the source of its tremendous power.

HOW TO SAY IT: NUM-mull
IMPERIAL HEIGHT: 2'04"
IMPERIAL WEIGHT: 52.9 lbs.
METRIC HEIGHT: 0.7 m
METRIC WEIGHT: 24.0 kg
GENDER: ♂ ♀
ABILITIES: Oblivious, Simple
WEAKNESSES: Water, Ground

NUMEL   CAMERUPT   MEGA CAMERUPT

#0274 NUZLEAF
Wily Pokémon

TYPE: GRASS-DARK

It lives deep in forests. With the leaf on its head, it makes a flute whose song makes listeners uneasy.

They live in holes bored in large trees. The sound of Nuzleaf's grass flute fills listeners with dread.

HOW TO SAY IT: NUHZ-leef
IMPERIAL HEIGHT: 3'03"
IMPERIAL WEIGHT: 61.7 lbs.
METRIC HEIGHT: 1.0 m
METRIC WEIGHT: 28.0 kg
GENDER: ♂ ♀
ABILITIES: Chlorophyll, Early Bird
WEAKNESSES: Ice, Fire, Flying, Poison, Fighting, Fairy, Bug

SEEDOT ➡ **NUZLEAF** ➡ **SHIFTRY**

#0919 NYMBLE
Grasshopper Pokémon

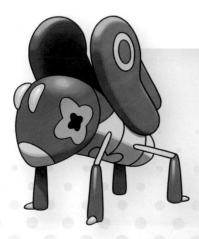

TYPE: BUG

It has its third set of legs folded up. When it's in a tough spot, this Pokémon jumps over 30 feet using the strength of its legs.

It's highly skilled at a fighting style in which it uses its jumping capabilities to dodge incoming attacks while also dealing damage to opponents.

HOW TO SAY IT: NIHM-bul
IMPERIAL HEIGHT: 0'08"
IMPERIAL WEIGHT: 2.2 lbs.
METRIC HEIGHT: 0.2 m
METRIC WEIGHT: 1.0 kg
GENDER: ♂ ♀
ABILITIES: Swarm
WEAKNESSES: Fire, Flying, Rock

NYMBLE ➡ **LOKIX**

OBSTAGOON
Blocking Pokémon

#0862

TYPE: DARK-NORMAL

Its voice is staggering in volume. Obstagoon has a tendency to take on a threatening posture and shout—this move is known as Obstruct.

It evolved after experiencing numerous fights. While crossing its arms, it lets out a shout that would make any opponent flinch.

HOW TO SAY IT: AHB-stuh-goon
IMPERIAL HEIGHT: 5'03"
IMPERIAL WEIGHT: 101.4 lbs.
METRIC HEIGHT: 1.6 m
METRIC WEIGHT: 46.0 kg
GENDER: ♂ ♀
ABILITIES: Reckless, Guts
WEAKNESSES: Fairy, Bug, Fighting

GALARIAN ZIGZAGOON → **GALARIAN LINOONE** → **OBSTAGOON**

OCTILLERY
Jet Pokémon

#0224

TYPE: WATER

It has a tendency to want to be in holes. It prefers rock crags or pots and sprays ink from them before attacking.

It traps enemies with its suction-cupped tentacles, then smashes them with its rock-hard head.

HOW TO SAY IT: ock-TILL-er-ree
IMPERIAL HEIGHT: 2'11"
IMPERIAL WEIGHT: 62.8 lbs.
GENDER: ♂ ♀
ABILITIES: Suction Cups, Sniper
WEAKNESSES: Grass, Electric

METRIC HEIGHT: 0.9 m
METRIC WEIGHT: 28.5 kg

REMORAID **OCTILLERY**

ODDISH
Weed Pokémon

#0043

TYPE: GRASS-POISON

If exposed to moonlight, it starts to move. It roams far and wide at night to scatter its seeds.

During the day, it stays in the cold underground to avoid the sun. It grows by bathing in moonlight.

HOW TO SAY IT: ODD-ish
IMPERIAL HEIGHT: 1'08"
IMPERIAL WEIGHT: 11.9 lbs.
METRIC HEIGHT: 0.5 m
METRIC WEIGHT: 5.4 kg
GENDER: ♂ ♀
ABILITIES: Chlorophyll
WEAKNESSES: Fire, Psychic, Flying, Ice

VILEPLUME

ODDISH

GLOOM

BELLOSSOM

#0916

OINKOLOGNE
Hog Pokémon

MALE

TYPE: NORMAL

Oinkologne is proud of its fine, glossy skin. It emits a concentrated scent from the tip of its tail.

It entrances female Pokémon with the sweet, alluring scent that wafts from all over its body.

HOW TO SAY IT: OIN-koh-lohn
IMPERIAL HEIGHT: 3'03"
IMPERIAL WEIGHT: 264.4 lbs.
METRIC HEIGHT: 1.0 m
METRIC WEIGHT: 120.0 kg
GENDER: ♂ ♀
ABILITIES: Gluttony, Lingering Aroma
WEAKNESSES: Fighting

FEMALE

LECHONK

OINKOLOGNE

#0138

OMANYTE
Spiral Pokémon

TYPE: ROCK-WATER

Because some Omanyte manage to escape after being restored or are released into the wild by people, this species is becoming a problem.

This Pokémon is a member of an ancient, extinct species. Omanyte paddles through water with its 10 tentacles, looking like it's just drifting along.

HOW TO SAY IT: AH-man-ite
IMPERIAL HEIGHT: 1'04"
IMPERIAL WEIGHT: 16.5 lbs.
METRIC HEIGHT: 0.4 m
METRIC WEIGHT: 7.5 kg
GENDER: ♂ ♀
ABILITIES: Swift Swim, Shell Armor
WEAKNESSES: Grass, Electric, Fighting, Ground

OMANYTE → OMASTAR

#0139

OMASTAR
Spiral Pokémon

TYPE: ROCK-WATER

Weighed down by a large and heavy shell, Omastar couldn't move very fast. Some say it went extinct because it was unable to catch food.

Omastar's sharp fangs could crush rock, but the Pokémon can attack only the prey that come within reach of its tentacles.

HOW TO SAY IT: AH-mah-star
IMPERIAL HEIGHT: 3'03"
IMPERIAL WEIGHT: 77.2 lbs.
METRIC HEIGHT: 1.0 m
METRIC WEIGHT: 35.0 kg
GENDER: ♂ ♀
ABILITIES: Swift Swim, Shell Armor
WEAKNESSES: Grass, Electric, Fighting, Ground

OMANYTE → OMASTAR

#0095

ONIX
Rock Snake Pokémon

TYPE: ROCK-GROUND

As it digs through the ground, it absorbs many hard objects. This is what makes its body so solid.

It rapidly bores through the ground at 50 mph by squirming and twisting its massive, rugged body.

HOW TO SAY IT: ON-icks
IMPERIAL HEIGHT: 28'10"
IMPERIAL WEIGHT: 463.0 lbs.
METRIC HEIGHT: 8.8 m
METRIC WEIGHT: 210.0 kg
GENDER: ♂ ♀
ABILITIES: Rock Head, Sturdy
WEAKNESSES: Steel, Fighting, Water, Ice, Grass, Ground

ONIX   STEELIX

#0765

ORANGURU
Sage Pokémon

TYPE: NORMAL-PSYCHIC

People used to mistake Oranguru for a human when they saw it issue command after command to the other Pokémon of the forest.

This Pokémon lives quietly in the depths of the forest. The purple, cape-like fur gets longer and longer as Oranguru ages.

HOW TO SAY IT: or-RANG-goo-roo
IMPERIAL HEIGHT: 4'11"
IMPERIAL WEIGHT: 167.6 lbs.
METRIC HEIGHT: 1.5 m
METRIC WEIGHT: 76.0 kg
GENDER: ♂ ♀
ABILITIES: Inner Focus, Telepathy
WEAKNESSES: Dark, Bug

DOES NOT EVOLVE

ORBEETLE

Seven Spot Pokémon

#0826

TYPE: BUG-PSYCHIC

It's famous for its high level of intelligence, and the large size of its brain is proof that it also possesses immense psychic power.

It emits psychic energy to observe and study what's around it—and what's around it can include things over six miles away.

HOW TO SAY IT: OR-BEE-dul
IMPERIAL HEIGHT: 1'04"
METRIC HEIGHT: 0.4 m
IMPERIAL WEIGHT: 89.9 lbs.
METRIC WEIGHT: 40.8 kg
GENDER: ♂ ♀
ABILITIES: Swarm, Frisk
WEAKNESSES: Ghost, Fire, Flying, Dark, Rock, Bug

BLIPBUG **DOTTLER** **ORBEETLE**

GIGANTAMAX ORBEETLE

Its brain has grown to a gargantuan size, as has the rest of its body. This Pokémon's intellect and psychic abilities are overpowering.

If it were to utilize every last bit of its power, it could control the minds of every living being in its vicinity.

IMPERIAL HEIGHT: 45'11"+
IMPERIAL WEIGHT: ????.? lbs.
METRIC HEIGHT: 14.0 m+
METRIC WEIGHT: ???.? kg

ORICORIO BAILE STYLE

Dancing Pokémon

TYPE: FIRE-FLYING

This Pokémon is incredibly popular, possibly because its passionate dancing is a great match with the temperament of Paldean people.

This form of Oricorio has sipped red nectar. It whips up blazing flames as it moves to the steps of its passionate dance.

HOW TO SAY IT: or-ih-KOR-ee-oh
IMPERIAL HEIGHT: 2'00"
IMPERIAL WEIGHT: 7.5 lbs.
METRIC HEIGHT: 0.6 m
METRIC WEIGHT: 3.4 kg
GENDER: ♂ ♀
ABILITIES: Dancer
WEAKNESSES: Water, Electric, Rock

DOES NOT EVOLVE

ORICORIO PA'U STYLE

#0741

Dancing Pokémon

TYPE: PSYCHIC-FLYING

The airy dance of these Oricorio is popular as a means of maintaining good health, but the Oricorio themselves are hard to find in Paldea.

This form of Oricorio has sipped pink nectar. It elevates its mind with the gentle steps of its dance, then unleashes its psychic energy.

HOW TO SAY IT: or-ih-KOR-ee-oh
IMPERIAL HEIGHT: 2'00"
IMPERIAL WEIGHT: 7.5 lbs.
METRIC HEIGHT: 0.6 m
METRIC WEIGHT: 3.4 kg
GENDER: ♂ ♀
ABILITIES: Dancer
WEAKNESSES: Ghost, Dark, Electric, Ice, Rock

DOES NOT EVOLVE

ORICORIO POM-POM STYLE

Dancing Pokémon

TYPE: ELECTRIC-FLYING

This form of Oricorio has sipped yellow nectar. It uses nimble steps to approach opponents, then knocks them out with electric punches.

The energetic, cheerful dance of these Oricorio is popular with children, but the Oricorio themselves are hard to find in Paldea.

HOW TO SAY IT: or-ih-KOR-ee-oh
IMPERIAL HEIGHT: 2'00"
IMPERIAL WEIGHT: 7.5 lbs.
METRIC HEIGHT: 0.6 m
METRIC WEIGHT: 3.4 kg
GENDER: ♂ ♀
ABILITIES: Dancer
WEAKNESSES: Ice, Rock

DOES NOT EVOLVE

ORICORIO SENSU STYLE

Dancing Pokémon

TYPE: GHOST-FLYING

This form of Oricorio has sipped purple nectar. It uses ethereal dance steps to call forth the spirits of the dead.

The elegant, attractive dance of these Oricorio is popular with adults, but the Oricorio themselves are hard to find in Paldea.

HOW TO SAY IT: or-ih-KOR-ee-oh
IMPERIAL HEIGHT: 2'00"
IMPERIAL WEIGHT: 7.5 lbs.
METRIC HEIGHT: 0.6 m
METRIC WEIGHT: 3.4 kg
GENDER: ♂ ♀
ABILITIES: Dancer
WEAKNESSES: Ghost, Dark, Electric, Ice, Rock

DOES NOT EVOLVE

#0968 ORTHWORM
Earthworm Pokémon

TYPE: STEEL

When attacked, this Pokémon will wield the tendrils on its body like fists and pelt the opponent with a storm of punches.

This Pokémon lives in arid deserts. It maintains its metal body by consuming iron from the soil.

HOW TO SAY IT: ORTH-werm
IMPERIAL HEIGHT: 8'02"
IMPERIAL WEIGHT: 683.4 lbs.
METRIC HEIGHT: 2.5 m
METRIC WEIGHT: 310.0 kg
GENDER: ♂ ♀
ABILITIES: Earth Eater
WEAKNESSES: Fire, Fighting, Ground

DOES NOT EVOLVE

#0501 OSHAWOTT
Sea Otter Pokémon

TYPE: WATER

The scalchop on its stomach isn't just used for battle—it can be used to break open hard berries as well.

It fights using the scalchop on its stomach. In response to an attack, it retaliates immediately by slashing.

HOW TO SAY IT: AH-shuh-waht
IMPERIAL HEIGHT: 1'08"
IMPERIAL WEIGHT: 13.0 lbs.
METRIC HEIGHT: 0.5 m
METRIC WEIGHT: 5.9 kg
GENDER: ♂ ♀
ABILITIES: Torrent
WEAKNESSES: Grass, Electric

OSHAWOTT

DEWOTT　　**SAMUROTT**

HISUIAN SAMUROTT

OVERQWIL

Pin Cluster Pokémon

#0904

TYPE: DARK-POISON

Its lancelike spikes and savage temperament have earned it the nickname "sea fiend." It slurps up poison to nourish itself.

HOW TO SAY IT: OH-ver-kwill
IMPERIAL HEIGHT: 8'02"
IMPERIAL WEIGHT: 133.4 lbs.
METRIC HEIGHT: 2.5 m
METRIC WEIGHT: 60.5 kg
GENDER: ♂ ♀
ABILITIES: N/A
WEAKNESSES: Ground

HISUIAN QWILFISH → OVERQWIL

PACHIRISU

EleSquirrel Pokémon

#0417

TYPE: ELECTRIC

It's one of the kinds of Pokémon with electric cheek pouches. It shoots charges from its tail.

A pair may be seen rubbing their cheek pouches together in an effort to share stored electricity.

HOW TO SAY IT: patch-ee-ree-sue
IMPERIAL HEIGHT: 1'04"
IMPERIAL WEIGHT: 8.6 lbs.
METRIC HEIGHT: 0.4 m
METRIC WEIGHT: 3.9 kg
GENDER: ♂ ♀
ABILITIES: Run Away, Pickup
WEAKNESSES: Ground

DOES NOT EVOLVE

PALAFIN ZERO FORM

Dolphin Pokémon

TYPE: WATER

This Pokémon changes its appearance if it hears its allies calling for help. Palafin will never show anybody its moment of transformation.

Its physical capabilities are no different than a Finizen's, but when its allies are in danger, it transforms and powers itself up.

HOW TO SAY IT: PAL-uh-fin
IMPERIAL HEIGHT: 4'03"
IMPERIAL WEIGHT: 132.7 lbs.
METRIC HEIGHT: 1.3 m
METRIC WEIGHT: 60.2 kg
GENDER: ♂ ♀
ABILITIES: Zero to Hero
WEAKNESSES: Grass, Electric

PALAFIN HERO FORM

Hero Pokémon

TYPE: WATER

This Pokémon's ancient genes have awakened. It is now so extraordinarily strong that it can easily lift a cruise ship with one fin.

This hero of the ocean swims at a speed of 50 knots and saves drowning people and Pokémon.

IMPERIAL HEIGHT: 5'11"
IMPERIAL WEIGHT: 214.7 lbs.
METRIC HEIGHT: 1.8 m
METRIC WEIGHT: 97.4 kg

FINIZEN   PALAFIN

PALKIA

Spatial Pokémon

#0484

TYPE: WATER-DRAGON

It has the ability to distort space. It is described as a deity in Sinnoh-region mythology.

It is said to live in a gap in the spatial dimension parallel to ours. It appears in mythology.

HOW TO SAY IT: PALL-kee-ah
IMPERIAL HEIGHT: 13'09"
IMPERIAL WEIGHT: 740.8 lbs.
METRIC HEIGHT: 4.2 m
METRIC WEIGHT: 336.0 kg
GENDER: Unknown
ABILITIES: Pressure
WEAKNESSES: Fairy, Dragon

PALKIA ORIGIN FORME

It soars across the sky in a form that greatly resembles the creator of all things. Perhaps this imitation of appearance is Palkia's strategy for gaining Arceus's powers.

IMPERIAL HEIGHT: 20'08"
IMPERIAL WEIGHT: 1,455.1 lbs.
METRIC HEIGHT: 6.3 m
METRIC WEIGHT: 660.0 kg

DOES NOT EVOLVE

PALOSSAND
Sand Castle Pokémon

#0770

TYPE: GHOST-GROUND

The terrifying Palossand drags smaller Pokémon into its sandy body. Once its victims are trapped, it drains them of their vitality whenever it pleases.

From the hollows in its arms, it fires the bones of its victims, which are all dried up after being drained of their vitality.

HOW TO SAY IT: PAL-uh-sand
IMPERIAL HEIGHT: 4'03"
IMPERIAL WEIGHT: 551.2 lbs.
METRIC HEIGHT: 1.3 m
METRIC WEIGHT: 250.0 kg
GENDER: ♂ ♀
ABILITIES: Water Compaction
WEAKNESSES: Ghost, Dark, Grass, Water, Ice

SANDYGAST　　**PALOSSAND**

PALPITOAD
Vibration Pokémon

#0536

TYPE: WATER-GROUND

It weakens its prey with sound waves intense enough to cause headaches, then entangles them with its sticky tongue.

On occasion, their cries are sublimely pleasing to the ear. Palpitoad with larger lumps on their bodies can sing with a wider range of sounds.

HOW TO SAY IT: PAL-pih-tohd
IMPERIAL HEIGHT: 2'07"
IMPERIAL WEIGHT: 37.5 lbs.
METRIC HEIGHT: 0.8 m
METRIC WEIGHT: 17.0 kg
GENDER: ♂ ♀
ABILITIES: Swift Swim, Hydration
WEAKNESSES: Grass

TYMPOLE　　**PALPITOAD**　　**SEISMITOAD**

PANCHAM
Playful Pokémon

#0674

TYPE: FIGHTING

It chooses a Pangoro as its master and then imitates its master's actions. This is how it learns to battle and hunt for prey.

Wanting to make sure it's taken seriously, Pancham's always giving others a glare. But if it's not focusing, it ends up smiling.

HOW TO SAY IT: PAN-chum
IMPERIAL HEIGHT: 2'00"
IMPERIAL WEIGHT: 17.6 lbs.
METRIC HEIGHT: 0.6 m
METRIC WEIGHT: 8.0 kg
GENDER: ♂ ♀
ABILITIES: Iron Fist, Mold Breaker
WEAKNESSES: Psychic, Flying, Fairy

PANCHAM   PANGORO

TYPE: FIGHTING-DARK

#0675

PANGORO
Daunting Pokémon

This Pokémon is quick to anger, and it has no problem using its prodigious strength to get its way. It lives for duels against Obstagoon.

Using its leaf, Pangoro can predict the moves of its opponents. It strikes with punches that can turn a dump truck into scrap with just one hit.

HOW TO SAY IT: PAN-go-roh
IMPERIAL HEIGHT: 6'11"
IMPERIAL WEIGHT: 299.8 lbs.
METRIC HEIGHT: 2.1 m
METRIC WEIGHT: 136.0 kg
GENDER: ♂ ♀
ABILITIES: Iron Fist, Mold Breaker
WEAKNESSES: Fairy, Flying, Fighting

PANCHAM   PANGORO

#0515

PANPOUR
Spray Pokémon

TYPE: WATER

The water stored inside the tuft on its head is full of nutrients. It waters plants with it using its tail.

The water stored inside the tuft on its head is full of nutrients. Plants that receive its water grow large.

HOW TO SAY IT: PAN-por
IMPERIAL HEIGHT: 2'00"
IMPERIAL WEIGHT: 29.8 lbs.
METRIC HEIGHT: 0.6 m
METRIC WEIGHT: 13.5 kg
GENDER: ♂ ♀
ABILITIES: Gluttony
WEAKNESSES: Grass, Electric

PANPOUR → **SIMIPOUR**

PANSAGE
Grass Monkey Pokémon

#0511

TYPE: GRASS

It shares the leaf on its head with weary-looking Pokémon. These leaves are known to relieve stress.

It's good at finding berries and gathers them from all over. It's kind enough to share them with friends.

HOW TO SAY IT: PAN-sayj
IMPERIAL HEIGHT: 2'00"
IMPERIAL WEIGHT: 23.1 lbs.
METRIC HEIGHT: 0.6 m
METRIC WEIGHT: 10.5 kg
GENDER: ♂ ♀
ABILITIES: Gluttony
WEAKNESSES: Fire, Flying, Ice, Poison, Bug

PANSAGE → **SIMISAGE**

PANSEAR

High Temp Pokémon

#0513

TYPE: FIRE

Very intelligent, it roasts berries before eating them. It likes to help people.

This Pokémon lives in caves in volcanoes. The fire within the tuft on its head can reach 600 degrees Fahrenheit.

HOW TO SAY IT: PAN-seer
IMPERIAL HEIGHT: 2'00"
IMPERIAL WEIGHT: 24.3 lbs.
METRIC HEIGHT: 0.6 m
METRIC WEIGHT: 11.0 kg
GENDER: ♂ ♀
ABILITIES: Gluttony
WEAKNESSES: Water, Ground, Rock

PANSEAR   SIMISEAR

PARAS

Mushroom Pokémon

#0046

TYPE: BUG-GRASS

Burrows under the ground to gnaw on tree roots. The mushrooms on its back absorb most of the nutrition.

HOW TO SAY IT: PAIR-ihs
IMPERIAL HEIGHT: 1'00"
IMPERIAL WEIGHT: 11.9 lbs.
METRIC HEIGHT: 0.3 m
METRIC WEIGHT: 5.4 kg
GENDER: ♂ ♀
ABILITIES: Effect Spore, Dry Skin
WEAKNESSES: Fire, Flying, Ice, Poison, Rock, Bug

PARAS   PARASECT

PARASECT
Mushroom Pokémon

TYPE: BUG-GRASS

The bug host is drained of energy by the mushroom on its back. The mushroom appears to do all the thinking.

HOW TO SAY IT: PARA-sekt
IMPERIAL HEIGHT: 3'03"
IMPERIAL WEIGHT: 65.0 lbs.
METRIC HEIGHT: 1.0 m
METRIC WEIGHT: 29.5 kg
GENDER: ♂ ♀
ABILITIES: Effect Spore, Dry Skin
WEAKNESSES: Fire, Flying, Ice, Poison, Rock, Bug

PARAS

PARASECT

PASSIMIAN
Teamwork Pokémon

#0766

TYPE: FIGHTING

This Pokémon battles by throwing hard berries. It won't obey a Trainer who throws Poké Balls without skill.

The boss chooses 10 members of the group to go out hunting. The hunting party will evenly split the food they find with the rest of the group.

HOW TO SAY IT: pass-SIM-ee-uhn
IMPERIAL HEIGHT: 6'07"
IMPERIAL WEIGHT: 182.5 lbs.
METRIC HEIGHT: 2.0 m
METRIC WEIGHT: 82.8 kg
GENDER: ♂ ♀
ABILITIES: Receiver
WEAKNESSES: Psychic, Flying, Fairy

DOES NOT EVOLVE

#0504

PATRAT
Scout Pokémon

TYPE: NORMAL

Using food stored in cheek pouches, they can keep watch for days. They use their tails to communicate with others.

Extremely cautious, one of them will always be on the lookout, but it won't notice a foe coming from behind.

HOW TO SAY IT: pat-RAT
IMPERIAL HEIGHT: 1'08"
IMPERIAL WEIGHT: 25.6 lbs.
METRIC HEIGHT: 0.5 m
METRIC WEIGHT: 11.6 kg
GENDER: ♂ ♀
ABILITIES: Run Away, Keen Eye
WEAKNESSES: Fighting

PATRAT   **WATCHOG**

#0921

PAWMI
Mouse Pokémon

TYPE: ELECTRIC

It has underdeveloped electric sacs on its cheeks. These sacs can produce electricity only if Pawmi rubs them furiously with the pads on its forepaws.

The pads of its paws are electricity-discharging organs. Pawmi fires electricity from its forepaws while standing unsteadily on its hind legs.

HOW TO SAY IT: PAW-mi
IMPERIAL HEIGHT: 1'00"
IMPERIAL WEIGHT: 5.5 lbs.
METRIC HEIGHT: 0.3 m
METRIC WEIGHT: 2.5 kg
GENDER: ♂ ♀
ABILITIES: Static, Natural Cure
WEAKNESSES: Ground

PAWMI → PAWMO → PAWMOT

#0922

PAWMO
Mouse Pokémon

TYPE: ELECTRIC-FIGHTING

When its group is attacked, Pawmo is the first to leap into battle, defeating enemies with a fighting technique that utilizes electric shocks.

Pawmo uses a unique fighting technique in which it uses its forepaws to strike foes and zap them with electricity from its paw pads simultaneously.

HOW TO SAY IT: PAW-moh
IMPERIAL HEIGHT: 1'04"
IMPERIAL WEIGHT: 14.3 lbs.
METRIC HEIGHT: 0.4 m
METRIC WEIGHT: 6.5 kg
GENDER: ♂ ♀
ABILITIES: Volt Absorb, Natural Cure
WEAKNESSES: Psychic, Fairy, Ground

PAWMI PAWMO PAWMOT

PAWMOT

Hands-On Pokémon

#0923

TYPE: ELECTRIC-FIGHTING

This Pokémon normally is slow to react, but once it enters battle, it will strike down its enemies with lightning-fast movements.

Pawmot's fluffy fur acts as a battery. It can store the same amount of electricity as an electric car.

HOW TO SAY IT: PAW-met
IMPERIAL HEIGHT: 2'11"
IMPERIAL WEIGHT: 90.4 lbs.
METRIC HEIGHT: 0.9 m
METRIC WEIGHT: 41.0 kg
GENDER: ♂ ♀
ABILITIES: Volt Absorb, Natural Cure
WEAKNESSES: Psychic, Fairy, Ground

PAWMI → PAWMO → PAWMOT

PAWNIARD

Sharp Blade Pokémon

#0624

TYPE: DARK-STEEL

Pawniard will fearlessly challenge even powerful foes. In a pinch, it will cling to opponents and pierce them with the blades all over its body.

Any chips in its blades would prove fatal for it. After each battle, it diligently maintains its blades using its favorite sharpening stone.

HOW TO SAY IT: PAWN-yard
IMPERIAL HEIGHT: 1'08"
IMPERIAL WEIGHT: 22.5 lbs.
METRIC HEIGHT: 0.5 m
METRIC WEIGHT: 10.2 kg
GENDER: ♂ ♀
ABILITIES: Defiant, Inner Focus
WEAKNESSES: Fighting, Fire, Ground

PAWNIARD → BISHARP → KINGAMBIT

PELIPPER

Water Bird Pokémon

#0279

TYPE: WATER-FLYING

It is a flying transporter that carries small Pokémon in its beak. It bobs on the waves to rest its wings.

It protects its young in its beak. It bobs on waves, resting on them on days when the waters are calm.

HOW TO SAY IT: PEL-ip-purr
IMPERIAL HEIGHT: 3'11"
IMPERIAL WEIGHT: 61.7 lbs.
METRIC HEIGHT: 1.2 m
METRIC WEIGHT: 28.0 kg
GENDER: ♂ ♀
ABILITIES: Keen Eye, Drizzle
WEAKNESSES: Electric, Rock

WINGULL   PELIPPER

PERRSERKER

Viking Pokémon

#0863

TYPE: STEEL

What appears to be an iron helmet is actually hardened hair. This Pokémon lives for the thrill of battle.

After many battles, it evolved dangerous claws that come together to form daggers when extended.

HOW TO SAY IT: purr-ZURR-kurr
IMPERIAL HEIGHT: 2'07"
IMPERIAL WEIGHT: 61.7 lbs.
METRIC HEIGHT: 0.8 m
METRIC WEIGHT: 28.0 kg
GENDER: ♂ ♀
ABILITIES: Battle Armor, Tough Claws
WEAKNESSES: Fire, Fighting, Ground

GALARIAN MEOWTH   PERRSERKER

PERSIAN
Classy Cat Pokémon
#0053

TYPE: NORMAL

Although its fur has many admirers, it is tough to raise as a pet because of its fickle meanness.

It has a vicious temperament. Beware if it raises its tail straight up. This is a signal that it is about to pounce and bite.

HOW TO SAY IT: PER-zhun
IMPERIAL HEIGHT: 3'03"
IMPERIAL WEIGHT: 70.5 lbs.
METRIC HEIGHT: 1.0 m
METRIC WEIGHT: 32.0 kg
GENDER: ♂ ♀
ABILITIES: Limber, Technician
WEAKNESSES: Fighting

MEOWTH → PERSIAN

ALOLAN PERSIAN
Classy Cat Pokémon
#0053

TYPE: DARK

The round face of Alolan Persian is considered to be a symbol of prosperity in the Alola region, so these Pokémon are very well cared for.

This Pokémon is one tough opponent. Not only does it have formidable physical abilities, but it's also not above fighting dirty.

HOW TO SAY IT: PER-zhun
IMPERIAL HEIGHT: 3'07"
IMPERIAL WEIGHT: 72.8 lbs.
METRIC HEIGHT: 1.1 m
METRIC WEIGHT: 33.0 kg
GENDER: ♂ ♀
ABILITIES: Fur Coat, Technician
WEAKNESSES: Fairy, Bug, Fighting

ALOLAN MEOWTH → ALOLAN PERSIAN

PETILIL

Bulb Pokémon

#0548

TYPE: GRASS

The leaves on its head grow right back even if they fall out. These bitter leaves refresh those who eat them.

If the leaves on its head are pruned with regularity, this Pokémon can be grown into a fine plump shape.

HOW TO SAY IT: PEH-tuh-LIL
IMPERIAL HEIGHT: 1'08"
IMPERIAL WEIGHT: 14.6 lbs.
METRIC HEIGHT: 0.5 m
METRIC WEIGHT: 6.6 kg
GENDER: ♀
ABILITIES: Chlorophyll, Own Tempo
WEAKNESSES: Fire, Flying, Ice, Poison, Bug

PETILIL

LILLIGANT

HISUIAN
LILLIGANT

PHANPY

Long Nose Pokémon

#0231

TYPE: GROUND

This Pokémon lives and nests on a riverbank. After playing in the mud, it won't be able to settle down unless it washes its body.

It is far stronger than it appears. If a Phanpy is swinging its trunk around and your arm gets hit by it, your arm bone will shatter.

HOW TO SAY IT: FAN-pee
IMPERIAL HEIGHT: 1'08"
IMPERIAL WEIGHT: 73.9 lbs.
METRIC HEIGHT: 0.5 m
METRIC WEIGHT: 33.5 kg
GENDER: ♂ ♀
ABILITIES: Pickup
WEAKNESSES: Water, Grass, Ice

PHANPY

DONPHAN

PHANTUMP
Stump Pokémon

#0708

TYPE: GHOST-GRASS

After a lost child perished in the forest, their spirit possessed a tree stump, causing the spirit's rebirth as this Pokémon.

With a voice like a human child's, it cries out to lure adults deep into the forest, getting them lost among the trees.

HOW TO SAY IT: FAN-tump
IMPERIAL HEIGHT: 1'04"
IMPERIAL WEIGHT: 15.4 lbs.
METRIC HEIGHT: 0.4 m
METRIC WEIGHT: 7.0 kg
GENDER: ♂ ♀
ABILITIES: Natural Cure, Frisk
WEAKNESSES: Ghost, Fire, Flying, Dark, Ice

PHANTUMP   TREVENANT

ULTRA BEAST

#0795

PHEROMOSA
Lissome Pokémon

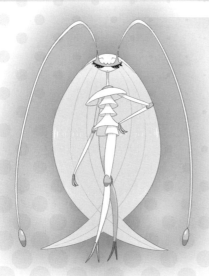

TYPE: BUG-FIGHTING

A life-form that lives in another world, its body is thin and supple, but it also possesses great power.

Although it's alien to this world and a danger here, it's apparently a common organism in the world where it normally lives.

HOW TO SAY IT: fair-uh-MO-suh
IMPERIAL HEIGHT: 5'11"
IMPERIAL WEIGHT: 55.1 lbs.
METRIC HEIGHT: 1.8 m
METRIC WEIGHT: 25.0 kg
GENDER: Unknown
ABILITIES: Beast Boost
WEAKNESSES: Fire, Psychic, Flying, Fairy

DOES NOT EVOLVE

PHIONE

Sea Drifter Pokémon

#0489

TYPE: WATER

When the water warms, they inflate the flotation sac on their heads and drift languidly on the sea in packs.

It drifts in warm seas. It always returns to where it was born, no matter how far it may have drifted.

HOW TO SAY IT: fee-OH-nay
IMPERIAL HEIGHT: 1'04"
IMPERIAL WEIGHT: 6.8 lbs.
METRIC HEIGHT: 0.4 m
METRIC WEIGHT: 3.1 kg
GENDER: Unknown
ABILITIES: Hydration
WEAKNESSES: Grass, Electric

DOES NOT EVOLVE

#0172

PICHU

Tiny Mouse Pokémon

TYPE: ELECTRIC

It is unskilled at storing electric power. Any kind of shock causes it to discharge energy spontaneously.

Despite this Pokémon's cute appearance, those who want to live with one should prepare to be on the receiving end of its electric jolts.

HOW TO SAY IT: PEE-choo
IMPERIAL HEIGHT: 1'00"
IMPERIAL WEIGHT: 4.4 lbs.
METRIC HEIGHT: 0.3 m
METRIC WEIGHT: 2.0 kg
GENDER: ♂ ♀
ABILITIES: Static
WEAKNESSES: Ground

RAICHU

PICHU **PIKACHU**

ALOLAN RAICHU

PIDGEOT

Bird Pokémon

#0018

TYPE: NORMAL-FLYING

This Pokémon flies at Mach 2 speed, seeking prey. Its large talons are feared as wicked weapons.

HOW TO SAY IT: PIDG-ee-ott
IMPERIAL HEIGHT: 4'11"
IMPERIAL WEIGHT: 87.1 lbs.
METRIC HEIGHT: 1.5 m
METRIC WEIGHT: 39.5 kg
GENDER: ♂ ♀
ABILITIES: Keen Eye, Tangled Feet
WEAKNESSES: Electric, Ice, Rock

MEGA PIDGEOT

TYPE: NORMAL-FLYING

With its muscular strength now greatly increased, it can fly continuously for two weeks without resting.

IMPERIAL HEIGHT: 7'03"
IMPERIAL WEIGHT: 111.3 lbs.
METRIC HEIGHT: 2.2 m
METRIC WEIGHT: 50.5 kg

PIDGEY

PIDGEOTTO

PIDGEOT

MEGA PIDGEOT

PIDGEOTTO
Bird Pokémon

#0017

TYPE: NORMAL-FLYING

This Pokémon is full of vitality. It constantly flies around its large territory in search of prey.

HOW TO SAY IT: PIDG-ee-OH-toe
IMPERIAL HEIGHT: 3'07"
IMPERIAL WEIGHT: 66.1 lbs.
METRIC HEIGHT: 1.1 m
METRIC WEIGHT: 30.0 kg
GENDER: ♂ ♀
ABILITIES: Keen Eye, Tangled Feet
WEAKNESSES: Electric, Ice, Rock

PIDGEY   PIDGEOTTO   PIDGEOT   MEGA PIDGEOT

PIDGEY
Tiny Bird Pokémon

#0016

TYPE: NORMAL-FLYING

Very docile. If attacked, it will often kick up sand to protect itself rather than fight back.

HOW TO SAY IT: PIDG-ee
IMPERIAL HEIGHT: 1'00"
IMPERIAL WEIGHT: 4.0 lbs.
METRIC HEIGHT: 0.3 m
METRIC WEIGHT: 1.8 kg
GENDER: ♂ ♀
ABILITIES: Keen Eye, Tangled Feet
WEAKNESSES: Electric, Ice, Rock

PIDGEY   PIDGEOTTO   PIDGEOT   MEGA PIDGEOT

PIDOVE

#0519

Tiny Pigeon Pokémon

TYPE: NORMAL-FLYING

Where people go, these Pokémon follow. If you're scattering food for them, be careful—several hundred of them can gather at once.

It's forgetful and not very bright, but many Trainers love it anyway for its friendliness and sincerity.

HOW TO SAY IT: pih-DUV
IMPERIAL HEIGHT: 1'00"
IMPERIAL WEIGHT: 4.6 lbs.
METRIC HEIGHT: 0.3 m
METRIC WEIGHT: 2.1 kg
GENDER: ♂ ♀
ABILITIES: Big Pecks., Super Luck
WEAKNESSES: Electric, Ice, Rock

PIDOVE   TRANQUILL   UNFEZANT

PIGNITE

#0499

Fire Pig Pokémon

TYPE: FIRE-FIGHTING

The more it eats, the more fuel it has to make the fire in its stomach stronger. This fills it with even more power.

When its internal fire flares up, its movements grow sharper and faster. When in trouble, it emits smoke.

HOW TO SAY IT: pig-NYTE
IMPERIAL HEIGHT: 3'03"
IMPERIAL WEIGHT: 122.4 lbs.
METRIC HEIGHT: 1.0 m
METRIC WEIGHT: 55.5 kg
GENDER: ♂ ♀
ABILITIES: Blaze
WEAKNESSE: Water, Psychic, Flying, Ground

TEPIG   PIGNITE   EMBOAR

#0025

PIKACHU
Mouse Pokémon

RAICHU

PICHU   PIKACHU

ALOLAN RAICHU

TYPE: ELECTRIC

When it is angered, it immediately discharges the energy stored in the pouches in its cheeks. cheek sacs that are extra soft and super stretchy.

When several of these Pokémon gather, their electricity can build and cause lightning storms.

HOW TO SAY IT: PEE-ka-choo
IMPERIAL HEIGHT: 1'04"
IMPERIAL WEIGHT: 13.2 lbs.
METRIC HEIGHT: 0.4 m
METRIC WEIGHT: 6.0 kg
GENDER: ♂ ♀
ABILITIES: Static
WEAKNESSES: Ground

PIKACHU LIBRE
SPECIAL MOVE:
Flying Press

PIKACHU BELLE
SPECIAL MOVE:
Icicle Crash

PIKACHU PHD
SPECIAL MOVE:
Electric Terrain

PIKACHU POP STAR
SPECIAL MOVE:
Draining Kiss

PIKACHU ROCK STAR
SPECIAL MOVE:
Meteor Mash

413

GIGANTAMAX
PIKACHU

Its Gigantamax power expanded, forming its supersized body and towering tail.

When it smashes its opponents with its bolt-shaped tail, it delivers a surge of electricity equivalent to a lightning strike.

IMPERIAL HEIGHT: 68'11"+
IMPERIAL WEIGHT: ?????.? lbs.
METRIC HEIGHT: 21.0+ m
METRIC WEIGHT: ???.? kg

PIKIPEK

Woodpecker Pokémon

#0731

TYPE: NORMAL-FLYING

It pecks at trees with its hard beak. You can get some idea of its mood or condition from the rhythm of its pecking.

It may look spindly, but its neck muscles are heavy-duty. It can peck at a tree 16 times per second!

HOW TO SAY IT: PICK-kee-peck
IMPERIAL HEIGHT: 1'00"
IMPERIAL WEIGHT: 2.6 lbs.
METRIC HEIGHT: 0.3 m
METRIC WEIGHT: 1.2 kg
GENDER: ♂ ♀
ABILITIES: Keen Eye, Skill Link
WEAKNESSES: Electric, Ice, Rock

PIKIPEK   TRUMBEAK   TOUCANNON

PILOSWINE

Swine Pokémon

#0221

TYPE: ICE-GROUND

If it charges at an enemy, the hairs on its back stand up straight. It is very sensitive to sound.

Although its legs are short, its rugged hooves prevent it from slipping, even on icy ground.

HOW TO SAY IT: PILE-oh-swine
IMPERIAL HEIGHT: 3'07"
IMPERIAL WEIGHT: 123.0 lbs.
METRIC HEIGHT: 1.1 m
METRIC WEIGHT: 55.8 kg
GENDER: ♂ ♀
ABILITIES: Oblivious, Snow Cloak
WEAKNESSES: Steel, Fire, Grass, Water, Fighting

SWINUB   PILOSWINE   MAMOSWINE

PINCURCHIN

Sea Urchin Pokémon

#0871

TYPE: ELECTRIC

This Pokémon generates electricity when it digests food. It uses its five hard teeth to scrape seaweed off surfaces and eat it.

This Pokémon is so timid that even brushing against seaweed will make it discharge electricity in surprise. Its lips do not conduct electricity.

HOW TO SAY IT: PIN-kur-chin
IMPERIAL HEIGHT: 1'00"
IMPERIAL WEIGHT: 2.2 lbs.
METRIC HEIGHT: 0.3 m
METRIC WEIGHT: 1.0 kg
GENDER: ♂ ♀
ABILITIES: Lightning Rod
WEAKNESSES: Ground

DOES NOT EVOLVE

#0204

PINECO

Bagworm Pokémon

TYPE: BUG

It likes to make its shell thicker by adding layers of tree bark. The additional weight doesn't bother it.

It spits out a fluid that it uses to glue tree bark to its body. The fluid hardens when it touches air.

HOW TO SAY IT: PINE-co
IMPERIAL HEIGHT: 2'00"
IMPERIAL WEIGHT: 15.9 lbs.
METRIC HEIGHT: 0.6 m
METRIC WEIGHT: 7.2 kg
GENDER: ♂ ♀
ABILITIES: Sturdy
WEAKNESSES: Fire, Flying, Rock

 PINECO → **FORRETRESS**

PINSIR

Stag Beetle Pokémon

TYPE: BUG

These Pokémon judge one another based on pincers. Thicker, more impressive pincers make for more popularity with the opposite gender.

This Pokémon clamps its pincers down on its prey and then either splits the prey in half or flings it away.

HOW TO SAY IT: PIN-sir
IMPERIAL HEIGHT: 4'11"
IMPERIAL WEIGHT: 121.3 lbs.
METRIC HEIGHT: 1.5 m
METRIC WEIGHT: 55.0 kg
GENDER: ♂ ♀
ABILITIES: Hyper Cutter, Mold Breaker
WEAKNESSES: Fire, Flying, Rock

MEGA PINSIR

TYPE: BUG-FLYING

With its vaunted horns, it can lift an opponent 10 times heavier than itself and fly about with ease.

IMPERIAL HEIGHT: 5'07"
IMPERIAL WEIGHT: 130.1 lbs.
METRIC HEIGHT: 1.7 m
METRIC WEIGHT: 59.0 kg

PINSIR   MEGA PINSIR

PIPLUP

Penguin Pokémon

#0393

TYPE: WATER

It doesn't like to be taken care of. It's difficult to bond with since it won't listen to its Trainer.

Because it is very proud, it hates accepting food from people. Its thick down guards it from cold.

HOW TO SAY IT: PIP-lup
IMPERIAL HEIGHT: 1'04"
IMPERIAL WEIGHT: 11.5 lbs.
METRIC HEIGHT: 0.4 m
METRIC WEIGHT: 5.2 kg
GENDER: ♂ ♀
ABILITIES: Torrent
WEAKNESSES: Grass, Electric

PIPLUP → PRINPLUP → EMPOLEON

PLUSLE

Cheering Pokémon

#0311

TYPE: ELECTRIC

Plusle always acts as a cheerleader for its partners. Whenever a teammate puts out a good effort in battle, this Pokémon shorts out its body to create the crackling noises of sparks to show its joy.

When Plusle is cheering on its partner, it flashes with electric sparks from all over its body. If its partner loses, this Pokémon cries loudly.

HOW TO SAY IT: PLUS-ull
IMPERIAL HEIGHT: 1'04"
IMPERIAL WEIGHT: 9.3 lbs.
METRIC HEIGHT: 0.4 m
METRIC WEIGHT: 4.2 kg
GENDER: ♂ ♀
ABILITIES: Plus
WEAKNESSES: Ground

DOES NOT EVOLVE

POIPOLE

Poison Pin Pokémon

#0803

TYPE: POISON

This Ultra Beast is well enough liked to be chosen as a first partner in its own world.

An Ultra Beast that lives in a different world, it cackles wildly as it sprays its opponents with poison from the needles on its head.

HOW TO SAY IT: POY-pull
IMPERIAL HEIGHT: 2'00"
IMPERIAL WEIGHT: 4.0 lbs.
METRIC HEIGHT: 0.6 m
METRIC WEIGHT: 1.8 kg
GENDER: Unknown
ABILITIES: Beast Boost
WEAKNESSES: Psychic, Ground

POIPOLE   NAGANADEL

#0186

POLITOED

Frog Pokémon

TYPE: WATER

At nightfall, these Pokémon appear on the shores of lakes. They announce their territorial claims by letting out cries that sound like shouting.

The cry of a male is louder than that of a female. Male Politoed with deep, menacing voices find more popularity with the opposite gender.

HOW TO SAY IT: PAUL-lee-TOED
IMPERIAL HEIGHT: 3'07"
IMPERIAL WEIGHT: 74.7 lbs.
METRIC HEIGHT: 1.1 m
METRIC WEIGHT: 33.9 kg
GENDER: ♂ ♀
ABILITIES: Water Absorb, Damp
WEAKNESSES: Grass, Electric

POLIWAG   POLIWHIRL   POLITOED

POLIWAG
Tadpole Pokémon

TYPE: WATER

For Poliwag, swimming is easier than walking. The swirl pattern on its belly is actually part of the Pokémon's innards showing through the skin.

In rivers with fast-flowing water, this Pokémon will cling to a rock by using its thick lips, which act like a suction cup.

POLIWRATH

POLITOED

POLIWAG POLIWHIRL

HOW TO SAY IT: PAUL-lee-wag
IMPERIAL HEIGHT: 2'00"
IMPERIAL WEIGHT: 27.3 lbs.
METRIC HEIGHT: 0.6 m
METRIC WEIGHT: 12.4 kg
GENDER: ♂ ♀
ABILITIES: Water Absorb, Damp
WEAKNESSES: Grass, Electric

POLIWHIRL
Tadpole Pokémon

#0061

TYPE: WATER

Staring at the swirl on its belly causes drowsiness. This trait of Poliwhirl's has been used in place of lullabies to get children to go to sleep.

This Pokémon's sweat is a slimy mucus. When captured, Poliwhirl can slither from its enemies' grasp and escape.

HOW TO SAY IT: PAUL-lee-wirl
IMPERIAL HEIGHT: 3'03"
IMPERIAL WEIGHT: 44.1 lbs.
METRIC HEIGHT: 1.0 m
METRIC WEIGHT: 20.0 kg
GENDER: ♂ ♀
ABILITIES: Water Absorb, Damp
WEAKNESSES: Grass, Electric

POLIWRATH

POLIWAG POLIWHIRL

POLITOED

POLIWRATH
Tadpole Pokémon

#0062

TYPE: WATER-FIGHTING

Its body is solid muscle. When swimming through cold seas, Poliwrath uses its impressive arms to smash through drift ice and plow forward.

Poliwrath is skilled at both swimming and martial arts. It uses its well-trained arms to dish out powerful punches.

HOW TO SAY IT: PAUL-lee-rath
IMPERIAL HEIGHT: 4'03"
IMPERIAL WEIGHT: 119.0 lbs.
METRIC HEIGHT: 1.3 m
METRIC WEIGHT: 54.0 kg
GENDER: ♂ ♀
ABILITIES: Water Absorb, Damp
WEAKNESSES: Fairy, Grass, Flying, Psychic, Electric

POLIWAG → POLIWHIRL → POLIWRATH

POLTEAGEIST
Black Tea Pokémon

#0855

TYPE: GHOST

The tea that composes Polteageist's body has a distinct and enjoyable flavor. Drinking too much, however, can be fatal.

These Pokémon multiply by creeping into teapots and pouring themselves into leftover tea.

HOW TO SAY IT: POHL-tee-guyst
IMPERIAL HEIGHT: 0'08"
IMPERIAL WEIGHT: 0.9 lbs.
METRIC HEIGHT: 0.2 m
METRIC WEIGHT: 0.4 kg
GENDER: Unknown
ABILITIES: Weak Armor
WEAKNESSES: Ghost, Dark

SINISTEA   POLTEAGEIST

PONYTA #0077

Fire Horse Pokémon

TYPE: FIRE

About an hour after birth, Ponyta's fiery mane and tail grow out, giving the Pokémon an impressive appearance.

Its legs grow strong while it chases after its parents. It runs all day in fields and on mountains.

HOW TO SAY IT: POH-nee-tah
IMPERIAL HEIGHT: 3'03"
IMPERIAL WEIGHT: 66.1 lbs.
METRIC HEIGHT: 1.0 m
METRIC WEIGHT: 30.0 kg
GENDER: ♂ ♀
ABILITIES: Run Away, Flash Fire
WEAKNESSES: Water, Ground, Rock

PONYTA → RAPIDASH

GALARIAN PONYTA #0077

Unique Horn Pokémon

TYPE: PSYCHIC

Its small horn hides a healing power. With a few rubs from this Pokémon's horn, any slight wound you have will be healed.

This Pokémon will look into your eyes and read the contents of your heart. If it finds evil there, it promptly hides away.

HOW TO SAY IT: POH-nee-tah
IMPERIAL HEIGHT: 2'07"
IMPERIAL WEIGHT: 52.9 lbs.
METRIC HEIGHT: 0.8 m
METRIC WEIGHT: 24.0 kg
GENDER: ♂ ♀
ABILITIES: Run Away, Pastel Veil
WEAKNESSES: Ghost, Dark, Bug

GALARIAN PONYTA → GALARIAN RAPIDASH

POOCHYENA
Bite Pokémon

POOCHYENA → **MIGHTYENA**

TYPE: DARK

At first sight, Poochyena takes a bite at anything that moves. This Pokémon chases after prey until the victim becomes exhausted. However, it may turn tail if the prey strikes back.

Poochyena is an omnivore—it will eat anything. A distinguishing feature is how large its fangs are compared to its body. This Pokémon tries to intimidate its foes by making the hair on its tail bristle out.

HOW TO SAY IT: POO-chee-EN-nah
IMPERIAL HEIGHT: 1'08"
IMPERIAL WEIGHT: 30.0 lbs.
METRIC HEIGHT: 0.5 m
METRIC WEIGHT: 13.6 kg
GENDER: ♂ ♀
ABILITIES: Run Away, Quick Feet
WEAKNESSES: Fairy, Bug, Fighting

POPPLIO
Sea Lion Pokémon

TYPE: WATER

The balloons it inflates with its nose grow larger and larger as it practices day by day.

Popplio gets on top of its bouncy water balloons to jump higher. It's quite the acrobatic fighter!

HOW TO SAY IT: POP-lee-oh
IMPERIAL HEIGHT: 1'04"
IMPERIAL WEIGHT: 16.5 lbs.
METRIC HEIGHT: 0.4 m
METRIC WEIGHT: 7.5 kg
GENDER: ♂ ♀
ABILITIES: Torrent
WEAKNESSES: Grass, Electric

POPPLIO   **BRIONNE**   **PRIMARINA**

PORYGON #0137

Virtual Pokémon

TYPE: NORMAL

State-of-the-art technology was used to create Porygon. It was the first artificial Pokémon to be created via computer programming.

In recent years, this species has been very helpful in cyberspace. These Pokémon will go around checking to make sure no suspicious data exists.

HOW TO SAY IT: PORE-ee-gon
IMPERIAL HEIGHT: 2'07"
IMPERIAL WEIGHT: 80.5 lbs.
METRIC HEIGHT: 0.8 m
METRIC WEIGHT: 36.5 kg
GENDER: Unknown
ABILITIES: Trace, Download
WEAKNESSES: Fighting

PORYGON   **PORYGON2**   **PORYGON-Z**

PORYGON2 #0233

Virtual Pokémon

TYPE: NORMAL

This is a Porygon that was updated with special data. Porygon2 develops itself by learning about many different subjects all on its own.

After artificial intelligence was implemented in Porygon2, the Pokémon began using a strange language that only other Porygon2 understand.

HOW TO SAY IT: PORE-ee-gon TWO
IMPERIAL HEIGHT: 2'00"
IMPERIAL WEIGHT: 71.6 lbs.
METRIC HEIGHT: 0.6 m
METRIC WEIGHT: 32.5 kg
GENDER: Unknown
ABILITIES: Trace, Download
WEAKNESSES: Fighting

PORYGON   **PORYGON2**   **PORYGON-Z**

#0474

PORYGON-Z
Virtual Pokémon

TYPE: NORMAL

Porygon-Z had a program installed to allow it to move between dimensions, but the program also caused instability in Porygon-Z's behavior.

Some say an additional program made this Pokémon evolve, but even academics can't agree on whether Porygon-Z is really an Evolution.

HOW TO SAY IT: PORE-ee-gon ZEE
IMPERIAL HEIGHT: 2'11"
IMPERIAL WEIGHT: 75.0 lbs.
METRIC HEIGHT: 0.9 m
METRIC WEIGHT: 34.0 kg
GENDER: Unknown
ABILITIES: Adaptability, Download
WEAKNESSES: Fighting

PORYGON **PORYGON2** **PORYGON-Z**

#0730

PRIMARINA
Soloist Pokémon

TYPE: WATER-FAIRY

To Primarina, every battle is a stage. It takes down its prey with beautiful singing and dancing.

Also known as a songstress, it has a fantastical look on moonlit nights when it leads its colony in song.

HOW TO SAY IT: PREE-muh-REE-nuh
IMPERIAL HEIGHT: 5'11"
IMPERIAL WEIGHT: 97.0 lbs.
METRIC HEIGHT: 1.8 m
METRIC WEIGHT: 44.0 kg
GENDER: ♂ ♀
ABILITIES: Torrent
WEAKNESSES: Grass, Electric, Poison

POPPLIO **BRIONNE** **PRIMARINA**

PRIMEAPE

Pig Monkey Pokémon

#0057

TYPE: FIGHTING

It becomes wildly furious if it even senses someone looking at it. It chases anyone that meets its glare.

Some researchers theorize that Primeape remains angry even when inside a Poké Ball.

HOW TO SAY IT: PRIME-ape
IMPERIAL HEIGHT: 3'03"
IMPERIAL WEIGHT: 70.5 lbs.
METRIC HEIGHT: 1.0 m
METRIC WEIGHT: 32.0 kg
GENDER: ♂ ♀
ABILITIES: Vital Spirit, Anger Point
WEAKNESSES: Psychic, Flying, Fairy

MANKEY   PRIMEAPE   ANNIHILAPE

PRINPLUP

Penguin Pokémon

#0394

TYPE: WATER

It lives alone, away from others. Apparently, every one of them believes it is the most important.

It lives a solitary life. Its wings deliver wicked blows that can snap even the thickest of trees.

HOW TO SAY IT: PRIN-plup
IMPERIAL HEIGHT: 2'07"
IMPERIAL WEIGHT: 50.7 lbs.
METRIC HEIGHT: 0.8 m
METRIC WEIGHT: 23.0 kg
GENDER: ♂ ♀
ABILITIES: Torrent
WEAKNESSES: Grass, Electric

PIPLUP   PRINPLUP   EMPOLEON

TYPE: ROCK-STEEL

Although it can control its units known as Mini-Noses, they sometimes get lost and don't come back.

It uses three small units to catch prey and battle enemies. The main body mostly just gives orders.

HOW TO SAY IT: PRO-bow-pass
IMPERIAL HEIGHT: 4'07"
IMPERIAL WEIGHT: 749.6 lbs.
METRIC HEIGHT: 1.4 m
METRIC WEIGHT: 340.0 kg
GENDER: ♂ ♀
ABILITIES: Sturdy, Magnet Pull
WEAKNESSES: Water, Fighting, Ground

#0476

PROBOPASS
Compass Pokémon

NOSEPASS → **PROBOPASS**

#0054

PSYDUCK
Duck Pokémon

TYPE: WATER

It is constantly wracked by a headache. When the headache turns intense, it begins using mysterious powers.

If its chronic headache peaks, it may exhibit odd powers. It seems unable to recall such an episode.

HOW TO SAY IT: SY-duck
IMPERIAL HEIGHT: 2'07"
IMPERIAL WEIGHT: 43.2 lbs.
METRIC HEIGHT: 0.8 m
METRIC WEIGHT: 19.6 kg
GENDER: ♂ ♀
ABILITIES: Damp, Cloud Nine
WEAKNESSES: Grass, Electric

PSYDUCK **GOLDUCK**

PUMPKABOO

Pumpkin Pokémon

#0710

TYPE: GHOST-GRASS

Spirits that wander this world are placed into Pumpkaboo's body. They're then moved on to the afterlife.

The light that streams out from the holes in the pumpkin can hypnotize and control the people and Pokémon that see it.

HOW TO SAY IT: PUMP-kuh-boo
IMPERIAL HEIGHT: 1'04"
IMPERIAL WEIGHT: 11.0 lbs.
METRIC HEIGHT: 0.4 m
METRIC WEIGHT: 5.0 kg
GENDER: ♂ ♀
ABILITIES: Pickup, Frisk
WEAKNESSES: Ghost, Fire, Flying, Dark, Ice

PUMPKABOO   **GOURGEIST**

PUPITAR

Hard Shell Pokémon

#0247

TYPE: ROCK-GROUND

This pupa flies around wildly by venting with great force the gas pressurized inside its body.

Its shell is as hard as bedrock, and it is also very strong. Its thrashing can topple a mountain.

HOW TO SAY IT: PUE-puh-tar
IMPERIAL HEIGHT: 3'11"
IMPERIAL WEIGHT: 335.1 lbs.
METRIC HEIGHT: 1.2 m
METRIC WEIGHT: 152.0 kg
GENDER: ♂ ♀
ABILITIES: Shed Skin
WEAKNESSES: Grass, Water, Fighting, Ground, Ice, Steel

LARVITAR   **PUPITAR**   **TYRANITAR**   **MEGA TYRANITAR**

#0509

PURRLOIN
Devious Pokémon

TYPE: DARK

It steals things from people just to amuse itself with their frustration. A rivalry exists between this Pokémon and Nickit.

Opponents that get drawn in by its adorable behavior come away with stinging scratches from its claws and stinging pride from its laughter.

HOW TO SAY IT: PUR-loyn
IMPERIAL HEIGHT: 1'04"
IMPERIAL WEIGHT: 22.3 lbs.
METRIC HEIGHT: 0.4 m
METRIC WEIGHT: 10.1 kg
GENDER: ♂ ♀
ABILITIES: Limber, Unburden
WEAKNESSES: Fairy, Bug, Fighting

PURRLOIN   LIEPARD

#0432

PURUGLY
Tiger Cat Pokémon

TYPE: NORMAL

It would claim another Pokémon's nest as its own if it finds a nest sufficiently comfortable.

To make itself appear intimidatingly beefy, it tightly cinches its waist with its twin tails.

HOW TO SAY IT: pur-UGG-lee
IMPERIAL HEIGHT: 3'03"
IMPERIAL WEIGHT: 96.6 lbs.
METRIC HEIGHT: 1.0 m
METRIC WEIGHT: 43.8 kg
GENDER: ♂ ♀
ABILITIES: Thick Fat, Own Tempo
WEAKNESSES: Fighting

GLAMEOW   PURUGLY

PYROAR

Royal Pokémon

#0668

MALE FORM

FEMALE FORM

TYPE: FIRE-NORMAL

The females of a pride work together to bring down prey. It's thanks to them that their pride doesn't starve.

The mane of a male Pyroar heats up to over 3,600 degrees Fahrenheit during battle. Merely approaching it will cause severe burns.

HOW TO SAY IT: PIE-roar
IMPERIAL HEIGHT: 4'11"
IMPERIAL WEIGHT: 179.7 lbs.
METRIC HEIGHT: 1.5 m
METRIC WEIGHT: 81.5 kg
GENDER: ♂ ♀
ABILITIES: Rivalry, Unnerve
WEAKNESSES: Water, Ground, Fighting, Rock

LITLEO　**PYROAR**

PYUKUMUKU

Sea Cucumber Pokémon

#0771

TYPE: WATER

It lives in warm, shallow waters. If it encounters a foe, it will spit out its internal organs as a means to punch them.

It's covered in a slime that keeps its skin moist, allowing it to stay on land for days without drying up.

HOW TO SAY IT: PYOO-koo-MOO-koo
IMPERIAL HEIGHT: 1'00"
IMPERIAL WEIGHT: 2.6 lbs.
METRIC HEIGHT: 0.3 m
METRIC WEIGHT: 1.2 kg
GENDER: ♂ ♀
ABILITIES: Innards Out
WEAKNESSES: Grass, Electric

DOES NOT EVOLVE

#0195

QUAGSIRE
Water Fish Pokémon

TYPE: WATER-GROUND

It has an easygoing nature. It doesn't care if it bumps its head on boats and boulders while swimming.

Its body is always slimy. It often bangs its head on the river bottom as it swims but seems not to care.

HOW TO SAY IT: KWAG-sire
IMPERIAL HEIGHT: 4'07"
IMPERIAL WEIGHT: 165.3 lbs.
METRIC HEIGHT: 1.4 m
METRIC WEIGHT: 75.0 kg
GENDER: ♂ ♀
ABILITIES: Damp, Water Absorb
WEAKNESSES: Grass

WOOPER **QUAGSIRE**

#0914

QUAQUAVAL
Dancer Pokémon

TYPE: WATER-FIGHTING

A single kick from a Quaquaval can send a truck rolling. This Pokémon uses its powerful legs to perform striking dances from far-off lands.

Dancing in ways that evoke far-away places, this Pokémon mesmerizes all that see it. Flourishes of its decorative water feathers slice into its foes.

HOW TO SAY IT: KWACK-wuh-vul
IMPERIAL HEIGHT: 5'11"
IMPERIAL WEIGHT: 136.5 lbs.
METRIC HEIGHT: 1.8 m
METRIC WEIGHT: 61.9 kg
GENDER: ♂ ♀
ABILITIES: Torrent
WEAKNESSES: Fairy, Grass, Flying, Psychic, Electric

QUAXLY **QUAXWELL** **QUAQUAVAL**

QUAXLY

Duckling Pokémon

#0912

TYPE: WATER

This Pokémon migrated to Paldea from distant lands long ago. The gel secreted by its feathers repels water and grime.

Its strong legs let it easily swim around in even fast-flowing rivers. It likes to keep things tidy and is prone to overthinking things.

HOW TO SAY IT: KWACKS-lee
IMPERIAL HEIGHT: 1'08"
IMPERIAL WEIGHT: 13.4 lbs.
METRIC HEIGHT: 0.5 m
METRIC WEIGHT: 6.1 kg
GENDER: ♂ ♀
ABILITIES: Torrent
WEAKNESSES: Grass, Electric

QUAXLY   QUAXWELL   QUAQUAVAL

QUAXWELL

Practicing Pokémon

#0913

TYPE: WATER

These Pokémon constantly run through shallow waters to train their legs, then compete with each other to see which of them kicks most gracefully.

The hardworking Quaxwell observes people and Pokémon from various regions and incorporates their movements into its own dance routines.

HOW TO SAY IT: KWACKS-well
IMPERIAL HEIGHT: 3'11"
IMPERIAL WEIGHT: 47.4 lbs.
METRIC HEIGHT: 1.2 m
METRIC WEIGHT: 21.5 kg
GENDER: ♂ ♀
ABILITIES: Torrent
WEAKNESSES: Grass, Electric

QUAXLY   QUAXWELL   QUAQUAVAL

TYPE: FIRE

Quilava keeps its foes at bay with the intensity of its flames and gusts of superheated air. This Pokémon applies its outstanding nimbleness to dodge attacks even while scorching the foe with flames.

QUILAVA
Volcano Pokémon

HOW TO SAY IT: kwi-LAH-va
IMPERIAL HEIGHT: 2'11"
IMPERIAL WEIGHT: 41.9 lbs.
METRIC HEIGHT: 0.9 m
METRIC WEIGHT: 19.0 kg
GENDER: ♂ ♀
ABILITIES: Blaze
WEAKNESSES: Water, Ground, Rock

TYPHLOSION

HISUIAN TYPHLOSION

CYNDAQUIL   **QUILAVA**

#0651

QUILLADIN
Spiny Armor Pokémon

TYPE: GRASS

It relies on its sturdy shell to deflect predators' attacks. It counterattacks with its sharp quills.

They strengthen their lower bodies by running into one another. They are very kind and won't start fights.

HOW TO SAY IT: QUILL-uh-din
IMPERIAL HEIGHT: 2'04"
IMPERIAL WEIGHT: 63.9 lbs.
METRIC HEIGHT: 0.7 m
METRIC WEIGHT: 29.0 kg
GENDER: ♂ ♀
ABILITIES: Overgrow
WEAKNESSES: Fire, Flying, Ice, Poison, Bug

CHESPIN   **QUILLADIN**   **CHESNAUGHT**

QWILFISH

Balloon Pokémon

#0211

TYPE: WATER-POISON

Be cautious if this Pokémon starts sucking in water—it will soon attack by scattering the toxic spikes that grow all over its body.

Experienced fishers say they try to catch Qwilfish in the brief moment that these Pokémon become defenseless just after launching poisonous spikes.

HOW TO SAY IT: KWILL-fish
IMPERIAL HEIGHT: 1'08"
IMPERIAL WEIGHT: 8.6 lbs.
METRIC HEIGHT: 0.5 m
METRIC WEIGHT: 3.9 kg
GENDER: ♂ ♀
ABILITIES: Poison Point, Swift Swim
WEAKNESSES: Psychic, Electric, Ground

DOES NOT EVOLVE

HISUIAN QWILFISH

Balloon Pokémon

#0211

TYPE: DARK-POISON

Fishers detest this troublesome Pokémon because it sprays poison from its spines, getting it everywhere. A different form of Qwilfish lives in other regions.

HOW TO SAY IT: KWILL-fish
IMPERIAL HEIGHT: 1'08"
IMPERIAL WEIGHT: 8.6 lbs.
METRIC HEIGHT: 0.5 m
METRIC WEIGHT: 3.9 kg
GENDER: ♂ ♀
ABILITIES: N/A
WEAKNESSES: Ground

HISUIAN QWILFISH

OVERQWIL

TYPE: FIRE

Its thick and fluffy fur protects it from the cold and enables it to use hotter fire moves.

It kicks berries right off the branches of trees and then juggles them with its feet, practicing its footwork.

HOW TO SAY IT: RAB-boot
IMPERIAL HEIGHT: 2'00"
IMPERIAL WEIGHT: 19.8 lbs.
METRIC HEIGHT: 0.6 m
METRIC WEIGHT: 9.0 kg
GENDER: ♂ ♀
ABILITIES: Blaze
WEAKNESSES: Water, Ground, Rock

#0814

RABOOT
Rabbit Pokémon

SCORBUNNY → **RABOOT** → **CINDERACE**

#0954

RABSCA
Rolling Pokémon

TYPE: BUG-PSYCHIC

The body that supports the ball barely moves. Therefore, it is thought that the true body of this Pokémon is actually inside the ball.

An infant sleeps inside the ball. Rabsca rolls the ball soothingly with its legs to ensure the infant sleeps comfortably.

HOW TO SAY IT: RABB-skuh
IMPERIAL HEIGHT: 1'00"
IMPERIAL WEIGHT: 7.7 lbs.
METRIC HEIGHT: 0.3 m
METRIC WEIGHT: 3.5 kg
GENDER: ♂ ♀
ABILITIES: Synchronize
WEAKNESSES: Ghost, Fire, Flying, Dark, Rock, Bug

RELLOR → **RABSCA**

RAICHU

Mouse Pokémon

#0026

TYPE: ELECTRIC

Its tail discharges electricity into the ground, protecting it from getting shocked.

If the electric pouches in its cheeks become fully charged, both ears will stand straight up.

HOW TO SAY IT: RYE-choo
IMPERIAL HEIGHT: 2'07"
IMPERIAL WEIGHT: 66.1 lbs.
METRIC HEIGHT: 0.8 m
METRIC WEIGHT: 30.0 kg
GENDER: ♂ ♀
ABILITIES: Static
WEAKNESSES: Ground

PICHU → PIKACHU → RAICHU

ALOLAN RAICHU

Mouse Pokémon

#0026

TYPE: ELECTRIC-PSYCHIC

It's believed that the weather, climate, and food of the Alola region all play a part in causing Pikachu to evolve into this form of Raichu.

This Pokémon rides on its tail while it uses its psychic powers to levitate. It attacks with star-shaped thunderbolts.

HOW TO SAY IT: RYE-choo
IMPERIAL HEIGHT: 2'04"
IMPERIAL WEIGHT: 46.3 lbs.
METRIC HEIGHT: 0.7 m
METRIC WEIGHT: 21.0 kg
GENDER: ♂ ♀
ABILITIES: Surge Surfer
WEAKNESSES: Ghost, Dark, Bug, Ground

PICHU PIKACHU ALOLAN RAICHU

TYPE: ELECTRIC

Raikou embodies the speed of lightning. The roars of this Pokémon send shock waves shuddering through the air and shake the ground as if lightning bolts had come crashing down.

HOW TO SAY IT: RYE-koh
IMPERIAL HEIGHT: 6'03"
IMPERIAL WEIGHT: 392.4 lbs.
METRIC HEIGHT: 1.9 m
METRIC WEIGHT: 178.0 kg
GENDER: Unknown
ABILITIES: Pressure
WEAKNESSES: Ground

DOES NOT EVOLVE

RALTS

Feeling Pokémon

#0280

TYPE: PSYCHIC-

The horns on its head provide a strong power that enables it to sense people's emotions.

It is highly attuned to the emotions of people and Pokémon. It hides if it senses hostility.

HOW TO SAY IT: RALTS
IMPERIAL HEIGHT: 1'04"
IMPERIAL WEIGHT: 14.6 lbs.
METRIC HEIGHT: 0.4 m
METRIC WEIGHT: 6.6 kg
GENDER: ♂ ♀
ABILITIES: Synchronize, Trace
WEAKNESSES: Ghost, Steel, Poison

RALTS **KIRLIA**

GARDEVOIR **MEGA GARDEVOIR**

GALLADE **MEGA GALLADE**

RAMPARDOS

Head Butt Pokémon

#0409

TYPE: ROCK

In ancient times, people would dig up fossils of this Pokémon and use its skull, which is harder than steel, to make helmets.

This ancient Pokémon used headbutts skillfully. Its brain was really small, so some theories suggest that its stupidity led to its extinction.

HOW TO SAY IT: ram-PAR-dose
IMPERIAL HEIGHT: 5'03"
IMPERIAL WEIGHT: 226.0 lbs.
METRIC HEIGHT: 1.6 m
METRIC WEIGHT: 102.5 kg
GENDER: ♂ ♀
ABILITIES: Mold Breaker
WEAKNESSES: Water, Steel, Grass, Fighting, Ground

CRANIDOS **RAMPARDOS**

RAPIDASH
Fire Horse Pokémon

TYPE: FIRE

It gallops at nearly 150 mph. With its mane blazing ferociously, it races as if it were an arrow.

It has astounding acceleration. From a standstill, it can reach top speed within 10 steps.

HOW TO SAY IT: RAP-id-dash
IMPERIAL HEIGHT: 5'07"
IMPERIAL WEIGHT: 209.4 lbs.
METRIC HEIGHT: 1.7 m
METRIC WEIGHT: 95.0 kg
GENDER: ♂ ♀
ABILITIES: Run Away, Flash Fire
WEAKNESSES: Water, Ground, Rock

PONYTA → RAPIDASH

GALARIAN RAPIDASH
Unique Horn Pokémon

TYPE: PSYCHIC-FAIRY

Little can stand up to its Psycho Cut. Unleashed from this Pokémon's horn, the move will punch a hole right through a thick metal sheet.

Brave and prideful, this Pokémon dashes airily through the forest, its steps aided by the psychic power stored in the fur on its fetlocks.

HOW TO SAY IT: RAP-id-dash
IMPERIAL HEIGHT: 5'07"
IMPERIAL WEIGHT: 176.4 lbs.
METRIC HEIGHT: 1.7 m
METRIC WEIGHT: 80.0 kg
GENDER: ♂ ♀
ABILITIES: Run Away, Pastel Veil
WEAKNESSES: Ghost, Steel, Poison

GALARIAN PONYTA

GALARIAN RAPIDASH

RATICATE

Mouse Pokémon

#0020

TYPE: NORMAL

Its hind feet are webbed. They act as flippers, so it can swim in rivers and hunt for prey.

HOW TO SAY IT: RAT-ih-kate
IMPERIAL HEIGHT: 2'04"
IMPERIAL WEIGHT: 40.8 lbs.
METRIC HEIGHT: 0.7 m
METRIC WEIGHT: 18.5 kg
GENDER: ♂ ♀
ABILITIES: Run Away, Guts
WEAKNESSES: Fighting

RATTATA   **RATICATE**

ALOLAN RATICATE

Mouse Pokémon

#0020

TYPE: DARK-NORMAL

It makes its Rattata underlings gather food for it, dining solely on the most nutritious and delicious fare.

HOW TO SAY IT: RAT-ih-kate
IMPERIAL HEIGHT: 2'04"
IMPERIAL WEIGHT: 56.2 lbs.
METRIC HEIGHT: 0.7 m
METRIC WEIGHT: 25.5 kg
GENDER: ♂ ♀
ABILITIES: Gluttony, Hustle
WEAKNESSES: Fairy, Bug, Fighting

 ALOLAN RATTATA   **ALOLAN RATICATE**

RATTATA

Mouse Pokémon

TYPE: NORMAL

Will chew on anything with its fangs. If you see one, you can be certain that 40 more live in the area.

HOW TO SAY IT: RA-TAT-ta
IMPERIAL HEIGHT: 1'00"
IMPERIAL WEIGHT: 7.7 lbs.
METRIC HEIGHT: 0.3 m
METRIC WEIGHT: 3.5 kg
GENDER: ♂ ♀
ABILITIES: Run Away, Guts
WEAKNESSES: Fighting

RATTATA ➡ RATICATE

#0019

ALOLAN RATTATA

Mouse Pokémon

TYPE: DARK-NORMAL

Its whiskers provide it with a keen sense of smell, enabling it to pick up the scent of hidden food and locate it instantly.

HOW TO SAY IT: RA-TAT-ta
IMPERIAL HEIGHT: 1'00"
IMPERIAL WEIGHT: 8.4 lbs.
METRIC HEIGHT: 0.3 m
METRIC WEIGHT: 3.8 kg
GENDER: ♂ ♀
ABILITIES: Gluttony, Hustle
WEAKNESSES: Fairy, Bug, Fighting

ALOLAN RATTATA   ALOLAN RATICATE

RAYQUAZA
Sky High Pokémon

#0384

TYPE: DRAGON-FLYING

Rayquaza is said to have lived for hundreds of millions of years. Legends remain of how it put to rest the clash between Kyogre and Groudon.

It flies forever through the ozone layer, consuming meteoroids for sustenance. The many meteoroids in its body provide the energy it needs to Mega Evolve.

HOW TO SAY IT: ray-KWAY-zuh
IMPERIAL HEIGHT: 23'00"
IMPERIAL WEIGHT: 455.3 lbs.
METRIC HEIGHT: 7.0 m
METRIC WEIGHT: 206.5 kg
GENDER: Unknown
ABILITIES: Air Lock
WEAKNESSES: Fairy, Dragon, Ice, Rock

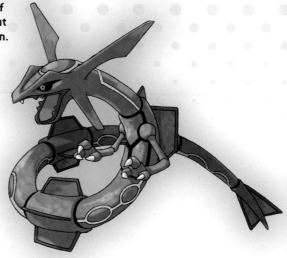

MEGA RAYQUAZA

TYPE: DRAGON-FLYING

IMPERIAL HEIGHT: 35'05"
IMPERIAL WEIGHT: 864.2 lbs.
METRIC HEIGHT: 10.8 m
METRIC WEIGHT: 392.0 kg

RAYQUAZA → **MEGA RAYQUAZA**

#0378

REGICE
Iceberg Pokémon

TYPE: ICE

With cold air that can reach temperatures as low as −328 degrees Fahrenheit, Regice instantly freezes any creature that approaches it.

This Pokémon's body is made of solid ice. It's said that Regice was born beneath thick ice in the ice age.

HOW TO SAY IT: REDGE-ice
IMPERIAL HEIGHT: 5'11"
IMPERIAL WEIGHT: 385.8 lbs.
METRIC HEIGHT: 1.8 m
METRIC WEIGHT: 175.0 kg
GENDER: Unknown
ABILITIES: Clear Body
WEAKNESSES: Fire, Steel, Fighting, Rock

DOES NOT EVOLVE

#0895

REGIDRAGO
Dragon Orb Pokémon

TYPE: DRAGON

An academic theory proposes that Regidrago's arms were once the head of an ancient dragon Pokémon. The theory remains unproven.

Its body is composed of crystallized dragon energy. Regidrago is said to have the powers of every dragon Pokémon.

HOW TO SAY IT: REH-jee-dray-go
IMPERIAL HEIGHT: 6'11"
IMPERIAL WEIGHT: 440.9 lbs.
METRIC HEIGHT: 2.1 m
METRIC WEIGHT: 200.0 kg
GENDER: Unknown
ABILITIES: Dragon's Maw
WEAKNESSES: Fairy, Ice, Dragon

DOES NOT EVOLVE

REGIELEKI
Electron Pokémon

TYPE: ELECTRIC

This Pokémon is a cluster of electrical energy. It's said that removing the rings on Regieleki's body will unleash the Pokémon's latent power.

Its entire body is made up of a single organ that generates electrical energy. Regieleki is capable of creating all Galar's electricity.

HOW TO SAY IT: REH-jee-uh-leh-kee
IMPERIAL HEIGHT: 3'11"
IMPERIAL WEIGHT: 319.7 lbs.
METRIC HEIGHT: 1.2 m
METRIC WEIGHT: 145.0 kg
GENDER: Unknown
ABILITIES: Transistor
WEAKNESSES: Ground

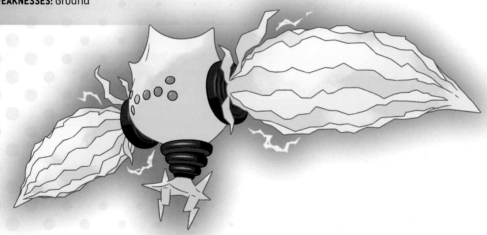

DOES NOT EVOLVE

REGIGIGAS
Colossal Pokémon

TYPE: NORMAL

It is said to have made Pokémon that look like itself from a special ice mountain, rocks, and magma.

There is an enduring legend that states this Pokémon towed continents with ropes.

HOW TO SAY IT: rej-jee-GIG-us
IMPERIAL HEIGHT: 12'02"
IMPERIAL WEIGHT: 925.9 lbs.
METRIC HEIGHT: 3.7 m
METRIC WEIGHT: 420.0 kg
GENDER: Unknown
ABILITIES: Slow Start
WEAKNESSES: Fighting

DOES NOT EVOLVE

REGIROCK
Rock Peak Pokémon

TYPE: ROCK

Every bit of Regirock's body is made of stone. As parts of its body erode, this Pokémon sticks rocks to itself to repair what's been lost.

Cutting-edge technology was used to study the internals of this Pokémon's rock body, but nothing was found—not even a brain or a heart.

HOW TO SAY IT: REDGE-ee-rock
IMPERIAL HEIGHT: 5'07"
IMPERIAL WEIGHT: 507.1 lbs.
METRIC HEIGHT: 1.7 m
METRIC WEIGHT: 230.0 kg
GENDER: Unknown
ABILITIES: Clear Body
WEAKNESSES: Water, Steel, Grass, Fighting, Ground

DOES NOT EVOLVE

#0379

REGISTEEL
Iron Pokémon

TYPE: STEEL

Registeel's body is made of a strange material that is flexible enough to stretch and shrink but also more durable than any metal.

It's rumored that this Pokémon was born deep underground in the planet's mantle and that it emerged onto the surface 10,000 years ago.

HOW TO SAY IT: REDGE-ee-steel
IMPERIAL HEIGHT: 6'03"
IMPERIAL WEIGHT: 451.9 lbs.
METRIC HEIGHT: 1.9 m
METRIC WEIGHT: 205.0 kg
GENDER: Unknown
ABILITIES: Clear Body
WEAKNESSES: Fire, Fighting, Ground

DOES NOT EVOLVE

#0369

RELICANTH
Longevity Pokémon

TYPE: WATER-ROCK

Rock-hard scales and oil-filled swim bladders allow this Pokémon to survive the intense water pressure of the deep sea.

This Pokémon was discovered during deep-sea exploration. Its appearance hasn't changed in 100,000,000 years, so it's called a living fossil.

HOW TO SAY IT: REL-uh-canth
IMPERIAL HEIGHT: 3'03"
IMPERIAL WEIGHT: 51.6 lbs.
METRIC HEIGHT: 1.0 m
METRIC WEIGHT: 23.4 kg
GENDER: ♂ ♀
ABILITIES: Swift Swim, Rock Head
WEAKNESSES: Grass, Electric, Fighting, Ground

DOES NOT EVOLVE

RELLOR

Rolling Pokémon

#0953

TYPE: BUG

This Pokémon creates a mud ball by mixing sand and dirt with psychic energy. It treasures its mud ball more than its own life.

It rolls its mud ball around while the energy it needs for evolution matures. Eventually the time comes for it to evolve.

HOW TO SAY IT: RELL-lor
IMPERIAL HEIGHT: 0'08"
IMPERIAL WEIGHT: 2.2 lbs.
METRIC HEIGHT: 0.2 m
METRIC WEIGHT: 1.0 kg
GENDER: ♂ ♀
ABILITIES: Compound Eyes
WEAKNESSES: Fire, Flying, Rock

RELLOR → RABSCA

REMORAID

Jet Pokémon

#0223

TYPE: WATER

The water they shoot from their mouths can hit moving prey from more than 300 feet away.

Using its dorsal fin as a suction pad, it clings to a Mantine's underside to scavenge for leftovers.

HOW TO SAY IT: REM-oh-raid
IMPERIAL HEIGHT: 2'00"
IMPERIAL WEIGHT: 26.5 lbs.
METRIC HEIGHT: 0.6 m
METRIC WEIGHT: 12.0 kg
GENDER: ♂ ♀
ABILITIES: Hustle, Sniper
WEAKNESSES: Grass, Electric

REMORAID → OCTILLERY

LEGENDARY POKÉMON

#0643

RESHIRAM
Vast White Pokémon

TYPE: DRAGON-FIRE

This legendary Pokémon can scorch the world with fire. It helps those who want to build a world of truth.

When Reshiram's tail flares, the heat energy moves the atmosphere and changes the world's weather.

HOW TO SAY IT: RESH-i-ram
IMPERIAL HEIGHT: 10'06"
IMPERIAL WEIGHT: 727.5 lbs.
METRIC HEIGHT: 3.2 m
METRIC WEIGHT: 330.0 kg
GENDER: Unknown
ABILITIES: Turboblaze
WEAKNESSES: Ground, Rock, Dragon

OVERDRIVE MODE

DOES NOT EVOLVE

REUNICLUS
Multiplying Pokémon

TYPE: PSYCHIC

While it could use its psychic abilities in battle, this Pokémon prefers to swing its powerful arms around to beat opponents into submission.

It's said that drinking the liquid surrounding Reuniclus grants wisdom. Problem is, the liquid is highly toxic to anything besides Reuniclus itself.

SOLOSIS → **DUOSION** → **REUNICLUS**

HOW TO SAY IT: ree-yoo-NIH-klus
IMPERIAL HEIGHT: 3'03"
IMPERIAL WEIGHT: 44.3 lbs.
METRIC HEIGHT: 1.0 m
METRIC WEIGHT: 20.1 kg
GENDER: ♂ ♀
ABILITIES: Overcoat, Magic Guard
WEAKNESSES: Ghost, Dark, Bug

#0966

REVAVROOM
Multi-Cyl Pokémon

TYPE: STEEL-POISON

It creates a gas out of poison and minerals from rocks. It then detonates the gas in its cylinders—now numbering eight—to generate energy.

Revavroom viciously threatens others with the sound of its exhaust. It sticks its tongue out from its cylindrical mouth and sprays toxic fluids.

VAROOM   **REVAVROOM**

HOW TO SAY IT: REV-uh-VROOM
IMPERIAL HEIGHT: 5'11"
IMPERIAL WEIGHT: 264.6 lbs.
METRIC HEIGHT: 1.8 m
METRIC WEIGHT: 120.0 kg
GENDER: ♂ ♀
ABILITIES: Overcoat
WEAKNESSES: Fire, Ground

RHYDON

Drill Pokémon

#0112

TYPE: GROUND-ROCK

It begins walking on its hind legs after Evolution. It can punch holes through boulders with its horn.

Protected by an armor-like hide, it is capable of living in molten lava of 3,600 degrees Fahrenheit.

HOW TO SAY IT: RYE-don
IMPERIAL HEIGHT: 6'03"
IMPERIAL WEIGHT: 264.6 lbs.
METRIC HEIGHT: 1.9 m
METRIC WEIGHT: 120.0 kg
GENDER: ♂ ♀
ABILITIES: Lightning Rod, Rock Head
WEAKNESSES: Steel, Ice, Water, Fighting, Grass, Ground

RHYHORN **RHYDON** **RHYPERIOR**

RHYHORN

Spikes Pokémon

#0111

TYPE: GROUND-ROCK

Strong, but not too bright, this Pokémon can shatter even a skyscraper with its charging tackles.

It can remember only one thing at a time. Once it starts rushing, it forgets why it started.

HOW TO SAY IT: RYE-horn
IMPERIAL HEIGHT: 3'03"
IMPERIAL WEIGHT: 253.3 lbs.
METRIC HEIGHT: 1.0 m
METRIC WEIGHT: 115.0 kg
GENDER: ♂ ♀
ABILITIES: Lightning Rod, Rock Head
WEAKNESSES: Steel, Ice, Water, Fighting, Grass, Ground

RHYHORN **RHYDON** **RHYPERIOR**

#0464 RHYPERIOR

Drill Pokémon

TYPE: GROUND-ROCK

It can load up to three projectiles per arm into the holes in its hands. What launches out of those holes could be either rocks or Roggenrola.

It relies on its carapace to deflect incoming attacks and throw its enemy off balance. As soon as that happens, it drives its drill into the foe.

HOW TO SAY IT: rye-PEER-ee-or
IMPERIAL HEIGHT: 7'10"
IMPERIAL WEIGHT: 623.5 lbs.
GENDER: ♂ ♀
METRIC HEIGHT: 2.4 m
METRIC WEIGHT: 282.8 kg
ABILITIES: Lightning Rod, Solid Rock
WEAKNESSES: Steel, Ice, Water, Fighting, Grass, Ground

RHYHORN → RHYDON → RHYPERIOR

#0743 RIBOMBEE

Bee Fly Pokémon

TYPE: BUG-FAIRY

It makes pollen puffs from pollen and nectar. The puffs' effects depend on the type of ingredients and how much of each one is used.

Ribombee absolutely hate getting wet or rained on. In the cloudy Galar region, they are very seldom seen.

HOW TO SAY IT: rih-BOMB-bee
IMPERIAL HEIGHT: 0'08"
IMPERIAL WEIGHT: 1.1 lbs.
METRIC HEIGHT: 0.2 m
METRIC WEIGHT: 0.5 kg
GENDER: ♂ ♀
ABILITIES: Honey Gather, Shield Dust
WEAKNESSES: Fire, Steel, Flying, Poison, Rock

CUTIEFLY → RIBOMBEE

RILLABOOM

Drumming Pokémon

#0812

TYPE: GRASS

By drumming, it taps into the power of its special tree stump. The roots of the stump follow its direction in battle.

The one with the best drumming techniques becomes the boss of the troop. It has a gentle disposition and values harmony among its group.

HOW TO SAY IT: RIL-uh-boom
IMPERIAL HEIGHT: 6'11"
IMPERIAL WEIGHT: 198.4 lbs.
METRIC HEIGHT: 2.1 m
METRIC WEIGHT: 90.0 kg
GENDER: ♂ ♀
ABILITIES: Overgrow
WEAKNESSES: Fire, Flying, Ice, Poison, Bug

GROOKEY   THWACKEY   RILLABOOM

GIGANTAMAX RILLABOOM

Gigantamax energy has caused Rillaboom's stump to grow into a drum set that resembles a forest.

Rillaboom has become one with its forest of drums and continues to lay down beats that shake all of Galar.

IMPERIAL HEIGHT: 91'10"+
IMPERIAL WEIGHT: ????.? lbs.
METRIC HEIGHT: 28.0+ m
METRIC WEIGHT: ???.? kg

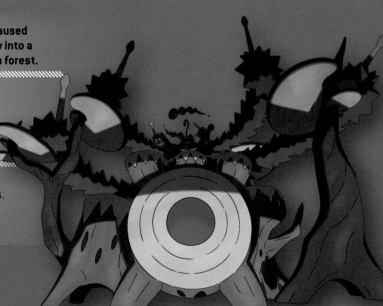

RIOLU
Emanation Pokémon

TYPE: FIGHTING

They communicate with one another using their auras. They are able to run all through the night.

It has the peculiar power of being able to see emotions, such as joy and rage, in the form of waves.

HOW TO SAY IT: ree-OH-loo
IMPERIAL HEIGHT: 2'04"
IMPERIAL WEIGHT: 44.5 lbs.
METRIC HEIGHT: 0.7 m
METRIC WEIGHT: 20.2 kg
GENDER: ♂ ♀
ABILITIES: Steadfast, Inner Focus
WEAKNESSES: Flying, Psychic, Fairy

RIOLU   **LUCARIO**   **MEGA LUCARIO**

PARADOX POKÉMON   #1005

ROARING MOON
Paradox Pokémon

TYPE: DRAGON-DARK

It is possible that this is the creature listed as Roaring Moon in an expedition journal that still holds many mysteries.

According to an article in a dubious magazine, this Pokémon has some connection to a phenomenon that occurs in a certain region.

HOW TO SAY IT: ROAR-ing moon
IMPERIAL HEIGHT: 6'07"
IMPERIAL WEIGHT: 837.8 lbs.
METRIC HEIGHT: 2.0 m
METRIC WEIGHT: 380.0 kg
GENDER: Unknown
ABILITIES: Protosynthesis
WEAKNESSES: Fairy, Ice, Bug, Fighting, Dragon

DOES NOT EVOLVE

 # 0744

ROCKRUFF
Puppy Pokémon

TYPE: ROCK

This Pokémon is very friendly when it's young. Its disposition becomes vicious once it matures, but it never forgets the kindness of its master.

This Pokémon travels in a pack with others until it grows up. When its mood turns sour, it starts striking the ground with the rocks on its neck.

HOW TO SAY IT: ROCK-ruff
IMPERIAL HEIGHT: 1'08"
IMPERIAL WEIGHT: 20.3 lbs.
METRIC HEIGHT: 0.5 m
METRIC WEIGHT: 9.2 kg
GENDER: ♂ ♀
ABILITIES: Keen Eye, Vital Spirit
WEAKNESSES: Water, Steel, Grass, Fighting, Ground

**LYCANROC
(DUSK FORM)**

**LYCANROC
(MIDDAY FORM)**

ROCKRUFF

**LYCANROC
(MIDNIGHT FORM)**

ROGGENROLA
Mantle Pokémon
 # 0524

TYPE: ROCK

It's as hard as steel, but apparently a long soak in water will cause it to soften a bit.

When it detects a noise, it starts to move. The energy core inside it makes this Pokémon slightly warm to the touch.

HOW TO SAY IT: rah-gen-ROH-lah
IMPERIAL HEIGHT: 1'04"
IMPERIAL WEIGHT: 39.7 lbs.
METRIC HEIGHT: 0.4 m
METRIC WEIGHT: 18.0 kg
GENDER: ♂ ♀
ABILITIES: Sturdy, Weak Armor
WEAKNESSES: Water, Steel, Grass, Fighting, Ground

ROGGENROLA

BOLDORE

GIGALITH

ROLYCOLY
Coal Pokémon
#0837

TYPE: ROCK

On sunny days, Rolycoly will come out onto grassy plains and roll around. Then it will eat the grass that gets tangled in its wheel-like leg.

Chunks of the surface of this Pokémon's body that have grown old and flaked off have long been used for fuel as an alternative to coal.

HOW TO SAY IT: ROH-lee-KOH-lee
IMPERIAL HEIGHT: 1'00"
IMPERIAL WEIGHT: 26.5 lbs.
METRIC HEIGHT: 0.3 m
METRIC WEIGHT: 12.0 kg
GENDER: ♂ ♀
ABILITIES: Steam Engine, Heatproof
WEAKNESSES: Water, Steel, Grass, Fighting, Ground

ROLYCOLY   **CARKOL**   **COALOSSAL**

#0821
ROOKIDEE
Tiny Bird Pokémon

TYPE: FLYING

This Pokémon is brave and reckless. The white markings around a Rookidee's eyes intimidate fainthearted Pokémon.

The females are fussier than the males. If another creature dirties a female Rookidee's wings, it'll peck the offender relentlessly in a burning rage.

HOW TO SAY IT: ROOK-ih-dee
IMPERIAL HEIGHT: 0'08"
IMPERIAL WEIGHT: 4.0 lbs.
METRIC HEIGHT: 0.2 m
METRIC WEIGHT: 1.8 kg
GENDER: ♂ ♀
ABILITIES: Keen Eye, Unnerve
WEAKNESSES: Electric, Ice, Rock

ROOKIDEE   **CORVISQUIRE**   **CORVIKNIGHT**

ROSELIA
Thorn Pokémon
#0315

TYPE: GRASS-POISON

Its flowers give off a relaxing fragrance. The stronger its aroma, the healthier the Roselia is.

It uses the different poisons in each hand separately when it attacks. The stronger its aroma, the healthier the Roselia is.

HOW TO SAY IT: roh-ZEH-lee-uh
IMPERIAL HEIGHT: 1'00"
IMPERIAL WEIGHT: 4.4 lbs.
METRIC HEIGHT: 0.3 m
METRIC WEIGHT: 2.0 kg
GENDER: ♂ ♀
ABILITIES: Natural Cure, Poison Point
WEAKNESSES: Fire, Psychic, Flying, Ice

BUDEW   ROSELIA   ROSERADE

ROSERADE
Bouquet Pokémon
#0407

TYPE: GRASS-POISON

After captivating opponents with its sweet scent, it lashes them with its thorny whips.

The poison in its right hand is quick acting. The poison in its left hand is slow acting. Both are life threatening.

HOW TO SAY IT: ROSE-raid
IMPERIAL HEIGHT: 2'11"
IMPERIAL WEIGHT: 32.0 lbs.
METRIC HEIGHT: 0.9 m
METRIC WEIGHT: 14.5 kg
GENDER: ♂ ♀
ABILITIES: Natural Cure, Poison Point
WEAKNESSES: Fire, Psychic, Flying, Ice

BUDEW   ROSELIA   ROSERADE

TYPE: ELECTRIC-GHOST

ROTOM
Plasma Pokémon

Its electricity-like body can enter some kinds of machines and take control in order to make mischief.

Research continues on this Pokémon, which could be the power source of a unique motor.

HOW TO SAY IT: ROH-tom
IMPERIAL HEIGHT: 1'00"
IMPERIAL WEIGHT: 0.7 lbs.
METRIC HEIGHT: 0.3 m
METRIC WEIGHT: 0.3 kg
GENDER: Unknown
ABILITIES: Levitate
WEAKNESSES: Ghost, Dark, Ground

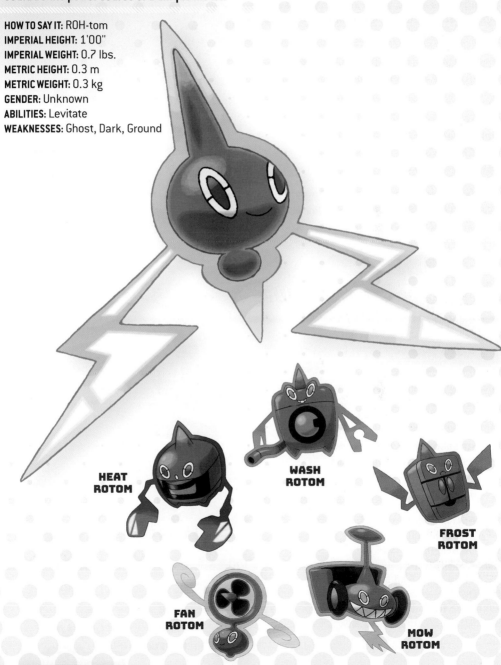

HEAT
ROTOM

WASH
ROTOM

FROST
ROTOM

FAN
ROTOM

MOW
ROTOM

DOES NOT EVOLVE

ROWLET #0722

Grass Quill Pokémon

TYPE: GRASS-FLYING

It sends its feathers, which are as sharp as blades, flying in attack. Its legs are strong, so its kicks are also formidable.

It feels relaxed in tight, dark places and has been known to use its Trainer's pocket or bag as a nest.

HOW TO SAY IT: ROW-let
IMPERIAL HEIGHT: 1'00"
IMPERIAL WEIGHT: 3.3 lbs.
METRIC HEIGHT: 0.3 m
METRIC WEIGHT: 1.5 kg
GENDER: ♂ ♀
ABILITIES: Overgrow
WEAKNESSES: Fire, Flying, Ice, Poison, Rock

ROWLET → DARTRIX →

DECIDUEYE

HISUIAN DECIDUEYE

RUFFLET #0627

Eaglet Pokémon

TYPE: NORMAL-FLYING

They pick fights indiscriminately. They grow stronger and more powerful each time they faint or are injured.

With its sharp claws, this Pokémon pierces its prey, and then it pecks at them. Although it also consumes berries, it's a carnivore at heart.

HOW TO SAY IT: RUF-lit
IMPERIAL HEIGHT: 1'08"
IMPERIAL WEIGHT: 23.1 lbs.
METRIC HEIGHT: 0.5 m
METRIC WEIGHT: 10.5 kg
GENDER: ♂
ABILITIES: Keen Eye, Sheer Force
WEAKNESSES: Electric, Ice, Rock

RUFFLET

BRAVIARY

HISUIAN BRAVIARY

RUNERIGUS
Grudge Pokémon

TYPE: GROUND-GHOST

A powerful curse was woven into an ancient painting. After absorbing the spirit of a Yamask, the painting began to move.

Never touch its shadowlike body, or you'll be shown the horrific memories behind the picture carved into it.

HOW TO SAY IT: ROON-uh-REE-gus
IMPERIAL HEIGHT: 5'03"
METRIC HEIGHT: 1.6 m
IMPERIAL WEIGHT: 146.8 lbs.
METRIC WEIGHT: 66.6 kg
GENDER: ♂ ♀
ABILITIES: Wandering Spirit
WEAKNESSES: Water, Ghost, Grass, Dark, Ice

**GALARIAN
YAMASK**

RUNERIGUS

SABLEYE

Darkness Pokémon

#0302

DARK-GHOST

It dwells in the darkness of caves. It uses its sharp claws to dig up gems to nourish itself.

Materials from gems it has eaten float to the surface of its body and can form an infinite number of patterns among individuals.

HOW TO SAY IT: SAY-bull-eye
IMPERIAL HEIGHT: 1'08"
IMPERIAL WEIGHT: 24.3 lbs.
METRIC HEIGHT: 0.5 m
METRIC WEIGHT: 11.0 kg
GENDER: ♂ ♀
ABILITIES: Keen Eye, Stall
WEAKNESSES: Fairy

MEGA SABLEYE

TYPE: DARK-GHOST

Bathed in the energy of Mega Evolution, the gemstone on its chest expands, rips through its skin, and falls out.

It blocks any and all attacks with its giant-sized gemstone. However, the stone's a heavy burden, and it limits Mega Sableye's movements.

IMPERIAL HEIGHT: 1'08"
IMPERIAL WEIGHT: 354.9 lbs.
METRIC HEIGHT: 0.5 m
METRIC WEIGHT: 161.0 kg

SABLEYE → **MEGA SABLEYE**

TYPE: DRAGON-FLYING

#0373

SALAMENCE
Dragon Pokémon

It flies around on its wings, which have grown in at last. In its happiness, it gushes hot flames, burning up everything it passes over.

It becomes uncontrollable if it is enraged. It destroys everything with shredding claws and fire.

HOW TO SAY IT: SAL-uh-mence
IMPERIAL HEIGHT: 4'11"
IMPERIAL WEIGHT: 226.2 lbs.
METRIC HEIGHT: 1.5 m
METRIC WEIGHT: 102.6 kg
GENDER: ♂ ♀
ABILITIES: Intimidate
WEAKNESSES: Fairy, Dragon, Ice, Rock

MEGA SALAMENCE

TYPE: DRAGON-FLYING

The stress of its two proud wings becoming misshapen and stuck together because of strong energy makes it go on a rampage.

It puts its forelegs inside its shell to streamline itself for flight. Salamence flies at high speeds over all kinds of topographical features.

IMPERIAL HEIGHT: 5'11"
IMPERIAL WEIGHT: 248.2 lbs.
METRIC HEIGHT: 1.8 m
METRIC WEIGHT: 112.6 kg

BAGON   SHELGON   SALAMENCE   MEGA SALAMENCE

SALANDIT

Toxic Lizard Pokémon

#0757

TYPE: POISON-FIRE

It taunts its prey and lures them into narrow, rocky areas where it then sprays them with toxic gas to make them dizzy and take them down.

Only female Salandit can produce gas laden with pheromones. Males entranced by this gas will do whatever the females tell them.

HOW TO SAY IT: suh-LAN-dit
IMPERIAL HEIGHT: 2'00"
IMPERIAL WEIGHT: 10.6 lbs.
METRIC HEIGHT: 0.6 m
METRIC WEIGHT: 4.8 kg
GENDER: ♂ ♀
ABILITIES: Corrosion
WEAKNESSES: Water, Psychic, Ground, Rock

SALANDIT   SALAZZLE

SALAZZLE

Toxic Lizard Pokémon

#0758

TYPE: POISON-FIRE

Salazzle makes its opponents light-headed with poisonous gas, then captivates them with alluring movements to turn them into loyal servants.

When two Salazzle meet, they will use their pheromone gas to fight over the males in each other's group.

HOW TO SAY IT: suh-LAZ-zuhl
IMPERIAL HEIGHT: 3'11"
IMPERIAL WEIGHT: 48.9 lbs.
METRIC HEIGHT: 1.2 m
METRIC WEIGHT: 22.2 kg
GENDER: ♀
ABILITIES: Corrosion
WEAKNESSES: Water, Psychic, Ground, Rock

SALANDIT   SALAZZLE

TYPE: WATER

SAMUROTT
Formidable Pokémon

In the time it takes a foe to blink, it can draw and sheathe the seamitars attached to its front legs.

One swing of the sword incorporated in its armor can fell an opponent. A simple glare from one of them quiets everybody.

HOW TO SAY IT: SAM-uh-raht
IMPERIAL HEIGHT: 4'11"
IMPERIAL WEIGHT: 208.6 lbs.
METRIC HEIGHT: 1.5 m
METRIC WEIGHT: 94.6 kg
GENDER: ♂ ♀
ABILITIES: Torrent
WEAKNESSES: Grass, Electric

OSHAWOTT → DEWOTT → SAMUROTT

#0503

HISUIAN SAMUROTT
Formidable Pokémon

TYPE: WATER-DARK

Hard of heart and deft of blade, this rare form of Samurott is a product of the Pokémon's evolution in the region of Hisui. Its turbulent blows crash into foes like ceaseless pounding waves.

HOW TO SAY IT: SAM-uh-rot
IMPERIAL HEIGHT: 4'11"
IMPERIAL WEIGHT: 128.3 lbs.
METRIC HEIGHT: 1.5 m
METRIC WEIGHT: 58.2 kg
GENDER: ♂ ♀
ABILITIES: N/A
WEAKNESSES: Fairy, Grass, Electric, Fighting, Bug

OSHAWOTT → DEWOTT → HISUIAN SAMUROTT

SANDACONDA

Sand Snake Pokémon

TYPE: GROUND

It will expand its body as much as it can and then contract itself, blasting out sand with enough force to wash away a dump truck.

The sand it spews contains sharp, pointy gravel, which is actually just sand that Sandaconda's saliva has hardened into irregular shapes.

HOW TO SAY IT: san-duh-KAHN-duh
IMPERIAL HEIGHT: 12'06"
IMPERIAL WEIGHT: 144.4 lbs.
METRIC HEIGHT: 3.8 m
METRIC WEIGHT: 65.5 kg
GENDER: ♂ ♀
ABILITIES: Sand Spit, Shed Skin
WEAKNESSES: Water, Grass, Ice

SILICOBRA → SANDACONDA

GIGANTAMAX SANDACONDA

Its sand pouch has grown to tremendous proportions. More than 1,000,000 tons of sand now swirl around its body.

Sand swirls around its body with such speed and power that it could pulverize a skyscraper.

IMPERIAL HEIGHT: 72'02"+
IMPERIAL WEIGHT: ????.? lbs.
METRIC HEIGHT: 22.0+ m
METRIC WEIGHT: ???.? kg

TYPE: GROUND-DARK

It submerges itself in sand and moves as if swimming. This wise behavior keeps its enemies from finding it and maintains its temperature.

They live hidden under hot desert sands in order to keep their body temperature from dropping.

HOW TO SAY IT: SAN-dyle
IMPERIAL HEIGHT: 2'04"
IMPERIAL WEIGHT: 33.5 lbs.
METRIC HEIGHT: 0.7 m
METRIC WEIGHT: 15.2 kg
GENDER: ♂ ♀
ABILITIES: Intimidate, Moxie
WEAKNESSES: Ice, Water, Fighting, Fairy, Grass, Bug

#0551

SANDILE
Desert Croc Pokémon

SANDILE

KROKOROK

KROOKODILE

SANDSHREW

Mouse Pokémon

#0027

TYPE: GROUND

It loves to bathe in the grit of dry, sandy areas. By sand bathing, the Pokémon rids itself of dirt and moisture clinging to its body.

It burrows into the ground to create its nest. If hard stones impede its tunneling, it uses its sharp claws to shatter them and then carries on digging.

HOW TO SAY IT: SAND-shroo
IMPERIAL HEIGHT: 2'00"
IMPERIAL WEIGHT: 26.5 lbs.
METRIC HEIGHT: 0.6 m
METRIC WEIGHT: 12.0 kg
GENDER: ♂ ♀
ABILITIES: Sand Veil
WEAKNESSES: Water, Grass, Ice

SANDSHREW   SANDSLASH

ALOLAN SANDSHREW

Mouse Pokémon

#0027

TYPE: ICE-STEEL

Life on mountains covered with deep snow has granted this Pokémon a body of ice that's as hard as steel.

It lives in snowy mountains on southern islands. When a blizzard rolls in, this Pokémon hunkers down in the snow to avoid getting blown away.

HOW TO SAY IT: SAND-shroo
IMPERIAL HEIGHT: 2'04"
IMPERIAL WEIGHT: 88.2 lbs.
METRIC HEIGHT: 0.7 m
METRIC WEIGHT: 40.0 kg
GENDER: ♂ ♀
ABILITIES: Snow Cloak
WEAKNESSES: Fire, Fighting, Ground

ALOLAN SANDSHREW   ALOLAN SANDSLASH

#0028 SANDSLASH
Mouse Pokémon

TYPE: GROUND

The drier the area Sandslash lives in, the harder and smoother the Pokémon's spikes will feel when touched.

It climbs trees by hooking on with its sharp claws. Sandslash shares the berries it gathers, dropping them down to Sandshrew waiting below the tree.

HOW TO SAY IT: SAND-slash
IMPERIAL HEIGHT: 3'03"
IMPERIAL WEIGHT: 65.0 lbs.
METRIC HEIGHT: 1.0 m
METRIC WEIGHT: 29.5 kg
GENDER: ♂ ♀
ABILITIES: Sand Veil
WEAKNESSES: Water, Grass, Ice

SANDSHREW ➡ SANDSLASH

#0028 ALOLAN SANDSLASH
Mouse Pokémon

TYPE: ICE-STEEL

It uses large, hooked claws to cut a path through deep snow as it runs. On snowy mountains, this Sandslash is faster than any other Pokémon.

Many people climb snowy mountains, hoping to see the icy spikes of these Pokémon glistening in the light of dawn.

HOW TO SAY IT: SAND-slash
IMPERIAL HEIGHT: 3'11"
IMPERIAL WEIGHT: 121.3 lbs.
METRIC HEIGHT: 1.2 m
METRIC WEIGHT: 55.0 kg
GENDER: ♂ ♀
ABILITIES: Snow Cloak
WEAKNESSES: Fire, Fighting, Ground

ALOLAN SANDSHREW ➡ ALOLAN SANDSLASH

SANDY SHOCKS

Paradox Pokémon

#0989

PARADOX POKÉMON

TYPE: ELECTRIC-GROUND

No records exist of this Pokémon being caught. Data is lacking, but the Pokémon's traits match up with a creature shown in an expedition journal.

It slightly resembles a Magneton that lived for 10,000 years and was featured in an article in a paranormal magazine.

HOW TO SAY IT: SAN-dee shox
IMPERIAL HEIGHT: 7'07"
IMPERIAL WEIGHT: 132.3 lbs.
METRIC HEIGHT: 2.3 m
METRIC WEIGHT: 60.0 kg
GENDER: Unknown
ABILITIES: Protosynthesis
WEAKNESSES: Water, Grass, Ice, Ground

DOES NOT EVOLVE

SANDYGAST

Sand Heap Pokémon

#0769

TYPE: GHOST-GROUND

If it loses its shovel, it will stick something else—like a branch—in its head to make do until it finds another shovel.

It flings sand into the eyes of its prey and tries to close in on them while they're blinded, but since Sandygast is so slow, the prey tends to escape.

HOW TO SAY IT: SAN-dee-GAST
IMPERIAL HEIGHT: 1'08"
IMPERIAL WEIGHT: 154.3 lbs.
METRIC HEIGHT: 0.5 m
METRIC WEIGHT: 70.0 kg
GENDER: ♂ ♀
ABILITIES: Water Compaction
WEAKNESSES: Ghost, Dark, Grass, Water, Ice

SANDYGAST

PALOSSAND

SAWK

Karate Pokémon

#0539

TYPE: FIGHTING

If you see a Sawk training in the mountains in its single-minded pursuit of strength, it's best to quietly pass by.

The karate chops of a Sawk that's trained itself to the limit can cleave the ocean itself.

HOW TO SAY IT: SAWK
IMPERIAL HEIGHT: 4'07"
IMPERIAL WEIGHT: 112.4 lbs.
METRIC HEIGHT: 1.4 m
METRIC WEIGHT: 51.0 kg
GENDER: ♂
ABILITIES: Sturdy, Inner Focus
WEAKNESSES: Psychic, Flying, Fairy

DOES NOT EVOLVE

SAWSBUCK

Season Pokémon

#0586

TYPE: NORMAL-GRASS

It seems that a Sawsbuck with many flowers on its antlers will grow at a slightly slower pace because the flowers absorb the Pokémon's nutrients.

There are many Sawsbuck enthusiasts. The paler the pink flowers that bloom on its antlers, the more beautiful the Sawsbuck is considered to be.

HOW TO SAY IT: SAWZ-buk
IMPERIAL HEIGHT: 6'03"
IMPERIAL WEIGHT: 203.9 lbs.
METRIC HEIGHT: 1.9 m
METRIC WEIGHT: 92.5 kg
GENDER: ♂ ♀
ABILITIES: Chlorophyll, Sap Sipper
WEAKNESSES: Fire, Flying, Fighting, Ice, Poison, Bug

SPRING FORM

SUMMER FORM

AUTUMN FORM

WINTER FORM

DEERLING **SAWSBUCK**

SCATTERBUG
Scatterdust Pokémon

#0664

TYPE: BUG

Any poison this Pokémon takes in is converted into a black powder and secreted. That's why Scatterbug can eat poisonous leaves and roots.

This Pokémon scatters poisonous powder to repel enemies. It will eat different plants depending on where it lives.

HOW TO SAY IT: SCAT-ter-BUG
IMPERIAL HEIGHT: 1'00"
IMPERIAL WEIGHT: 5.5 lbs.
METRIC HEIGHT: 0.3 m
METRIC WEIGHT: 2.5 kg
GENDER: ♂ ♀
ABILITIES: Shield Dust, Compound Eyes
WEAKNESSES: Fire, Fighting, Rock

SCATTERBUG   SPEWPA

VIVILLON

TYPE: GRASS

The leaves growing on Sceptile's body are very sharp edged. This Pokémon is very agile—it leaps all over the branches of trees and jumps on its foe from above or behind.

Sceptile has seeds growing on its back. They are said to be bursting with nutrients that revitalize trees. This Pokémon raises the trees in a forest with loving care.

HOW TO SAY IT: SEP-tile
IMPERIAL HEIGHT: 5'07"
IMPERIAL WEIGHT: 115.1 lbs.
METRIC HEIGHT: 1.7 m
METRIC WEIGHT: 52.2 kg
GENDER: ♂ ♀
ABILITIES: Overgrow
WEAKNESSES: Fire, Flying, Ice, Poison, Bug

#0254

SCEPTILE
Forest Pokémon

MEGA SCEPTILE

TYPE: GRASS-DRAGON

IMPERIAL HEIGHT: 6'03"
IMPERIAL WEIGHT: 121.7 lbs.
METRIC HEIGHT: 1.9 m
METRIC WEIGHT: 55.2 kg

TREECKO   GROVYLE   SCEPTILE   MEGA SCEPTILE

SCIZOR
Pincer Pokémon

TYPE: BUG-STEEL

This Pokémon's pincers, which contain steel, can crush any hard object they get ahold of into bits.

It swings its eye-patterned pincers up to scare its foes. This makes it look like it has three heads.

HOW TO SAY IT: SIH-zor
IMPERIAL HEIGHT: 5'11"
IMPERIAL WEIGHT: 260.1 lbs.
METRIC HEIGHT: 1.8 m
METRIC WEIGHT: 118.0 kg
GENDER: ♂ ♀
ABILITIES: Swarm, Technician
WEAKNESSES: Fire

MEGA SCIZOR

TYPE: BUG-STEEL

It stores the excess energy from Mega Evolution, so after a long time passes, its body starts to melt.

It's better at beating things than grasping them. When it battles for a long time, the weight of its pincers becomes too much to bear.

IMPERIAL HEIGHT: 6'07"
IMPERIAL WEIGHT: 275.6 lbs.
METRIC HEIGHT: 2.0 m
METRIC WEIGHT: 125.0 kg

SCYTHER

SCIZOR

MEGA SCIZOR

#0545 SCOLIPEDE
Megapede Pokémon

TYPE: BUG-POISON

Scolipede latches on to its prey with the claws on its neck before slamming them into the ground and jabbing them with its claws' toxic spikes.

Scolipede engage in fierce territorial battles with Centiskorch. At the end of one of these battles, the victor makes a meal of the loser.

HOW TO SAY IT: SKOH-lih-peed
IMPERIAL HEIGHT: 8'02"
IMPERIAL WEIGHT: 442.0 lbs.
METRIC HEIGHT: 2.5 m
METRIC WEIGHT: 200.5 kg
GENDER: ♂ ♀
ABILITIES: Poison Point, Swarm
WEAKNESSES: Fire, Psychic, Flying, Rock

VENIPEDE

WHIRLIPEDE

SCOLIPEDE

SCORBUNNY
Rabbit Pokémon
#0813

TYPE: FIRE

A warm-up of running around gets fire energy coursing through this Pokémon's body. Once that happens, it's ready to fight at full power.

It has special pads on the backs of its feet, and one on its nose. Once it's raring to fight, these pads radiate tremendous heat.

HOW TO SAY IT: SKOHR-buh-nee
IMPERIAL HEIGHT: 1'00"
IMPERIAL WEIGHT: 9.9 lbs.
METRIC HEIGHT: 0.3 m
METRIC WEIGHT: 4.5 kg
GENDER: ♂ ♀
ABILITIES: Blaze
WEAKNESSES: Water, Ground, Rock

SCORBUNNY

RABOOT

CINDERACE

SCOVILLAIN

Spicy Pepper Pokémon

#0952

TYPE: GRASS-FIRE

The red head converts spicy chemicals into fire energy and blasts the surrounding area with a super spicy stream of flame.

The green head has turned vicious due to the spicy chemicals stimulating its brain. Once it goes on a rampage, there is no stopping it.

HOW TO SAY IT: SKOH-vil-lun
IMPERIAL HEIGHT: 2'11"
IMPERIAL WEIGHT: 33.1 lbs.
METRIC HEIGHT: 0.9 m
METRIC WEIGHT: 15.0 kg
GENDER: ♂ ♀
ABILITIES: Chlorophyll, Insomnia
WEAKNESSES: Flying, Poison, Rock

CAPSAKID   **SCOVILLAIN**

SCRAFTY

Hoodlum Pokémon

#0560

TYPE: DARK-FIGHTING

As half-hearted as this Pokémon's kicks may seem, they pack enough power to shatter Conkeldurr's concrete pillars.

While mostly known for having the temperament of an aggressive ruffian, this Pokémon takes very good care of its family, friends, and territory.

HOW TO SAY IT: SKRAF-tee
IMPERIAL HEIGHT: 3'07"
IMPERIAL WEIGHT: 66.1 lbs.
METRIC HEIGHT: 1.1 m
METRIC WEIGHT: 30.0 kg
GENDER: ♂ ♀
ABILITIES: Shed Skin, Moxie
WEAKNESSES: Fairy, Flying, Fighting

SCRAGGY   **SCRAFTY**

SCRAGGY
Shedding Pokémon

TYPE: DARK-FIGHTING

If it locks eyes with you, watch out! Nothing and no one is safe from the reckless headbutts of this troublesome Pokémon.

It protects itself with its durable skin. It's thought that this Pokémon will evolve once its skin has completely stretched out.

HOW TO SAY IT: SKRAG-ee
IMPERIAL HEIGHT: 2'00"
IMPERIAL WEIGHT: 26.0 lbs.
METRIC HEIGHT: 0.6 m
METRIC WEIGHT: 11.8 kg
GENDER: ♂ ♀
ABILITIES: Shed Skin, Moxie
WEAKNESSES: Fairy, Flying, Fighting

SCRAGGY → SCRAFTY

PARADOX POKÉMON

#0985

SCREAM TAIL
Paradox Pokémon

TYPE: FAIRY-PSYCHIC

There has been only one reported sighting of this Pokémon. It resembles a mysterious creature depicted in an old expedition journal.

It resembles a mysterious Pokémon described in a paranormal magazine as a Jigglypuff from one billion years ago.

HOW TO SAY IT: SCREAM tail
IMPERIAL HEIGHT: 3'11"
IMPERIAL WEIGHT: 17.6 lbs.
METRIC HEIGHT: 1.2 m
METRIC WEIGHT: 8.0 kg
GENDER: Unknown
ABILITIES: Protosynthesis
WEAKNESSES: Steel, Ghost, Poison

DOES NOT EVOLVE

SCYTHER

Mantis Pokémon

#0123

TYPE: BUG-FLYING

It slashes through grass with its sharp scythes, moving too fast for the human eye to track.

The sharp scythes on its forearms become increasingly sharp by cutting through hard objects.

HOW TO SAY IT: SY-thur
IMPERIAL HEIGHT: 4'11"
IMPERIAL WEIGHT: 123.5 lbs.
METRIC HEIGHT: 1.5 m
METRIC WEIGHT: 56.0 kg
GENDER: ♂ ♀
ABILITIES: Swarm, Technician
WEAKNESSES: Fire, Flying, Electric, Ice, Rock

SCYTHER

SCIZOR

MEGA SCIZOR

KLEAVOR

SEADRA

Dragon Pokémon

#0117

TYPE: WATER

It's the males that raise the offspring. While Seadra are raising young, the spines on their backs secrete thicker and stronger poison.

Seadra's mouth is slender, but its suction power is strong. In an instant, Seadra can suck in food that's larger than the opening of its mouth.

HOW TO SAY IT: SEE-dra
IMPERIAL HEIGHT: 3'11"
IMPERIAL WEIGHT: 55.1 lbs.
METRIC HEIGHT: 1.2 m
METRIC WEIGHT: 25.0 kg
GENDER: ♂ ♀
ABILITIES: Poison Point, Sniper
WEAKNESSES: Grass, Electric

HORSEA

SEADRA

KINGDRA

#0119

SEAKING
Goldfish Pokémon

TYPE: WATER

In autumn, its body becomes more fatty in preparing to propose to a mate. It takes on beautiful colors.

Using its horn, it bores holes in riverbed boulders, making nests to prevent its eggs from washing away.

HOW TO SAY IT: SEE-king
IMPERIAL HEIGHT: 4'03"
IMPERIAL WEIGHT: 86.0 lbs.
METRIC HEIGHT: 1.3 m
METRIC WEIGHT: 39.0 kg
GENDER: ♂ ♀
ABILITIES: Swift Swim, Water Veil
WEAKNESSES: Grass, Electric

GOLDEEN **SEAKING**

#0364

SEALEO
Ball Roll Pokémon

TYPE: ICE-WATER

Sealeo live on top of drift ice. They go swimming when they're on the hunt, seeking out their prey by scent.

This Pokémon has a habit of spinning round things on its nose, whether those things are Poké Balls or Spheal.

HOW TO SAY IT: SEEL-ee-oh
IMPERIAL HEIGHT: 3'07"
IMPERIAL WEIGHT: 193.1 lbs.
METRIC HEIGHT: 1.1 m
METRIC WEIGHT: 87.6 kg
GENDER: ♂ ♀
ABILITIES: Thick Fat, Ice Body
WEAKNESSES: Grass, Electric, Fighting, Rock

SPHEAL **SEALEO** **WALREIN**

SEEDOT

Acorn Pokémon

#0273

TYPE: GRASS

If it remains still, it looks just like a real nut. It delights in surprising foraging Pokémon.

It attaches itself to a tree branch using the top of its head. Strong winds can sometimes make it fall.

HOW TO SAY IT: SEE-dot
IMPERIAL HEIGHT: 1'08"
IMPERIAL WEIGHT: 8.8 lbs.
METRIC HEIGHT: 0.5 m
METRIC WEIGHT: 4.0 kg
GENDER: ♂ ♀
ABILITIES: Chlorophyll, Early Bird
WEAKNESSES: Fire, Flying, Ice, Poison, Bug

SEEDOT **NUZLEAF** **SHIFTRY**

SEEL

Seal Lion Pokémon

#0086

TYPE: WATER

Loves freezing-cold conditions. Relishes swimming in a frigid climate of around 14 degrees Fahrenheit.

HOW TO SAY IT: SEEL
IMPERIAL HEIGHT: 3'07"
IMPERIAL WEIGHT: 198.4 lbs.
METRIC HEIGHT: 1.1 m
METRIC WEIGHT: 90.0 kg
GENDER: ♂ ♀
ABILITIES: Thick Fat, Hydration
WEAKNESSES: Grass, Electric

SEEL **DEWGONG**

#0537 SEISMITOAD
Vibration Pokémon

TYPE: WATER-GROUND

The vibrating of the bumps all over its body causes earthquake-like tremors. Seismitoad and Croagunk are similar species.

This Pokémon is popular among the elderly, who say the vibrations of its lumps are great for massages.

HOW TO SAY IT: SYZ-mih-tohd
IMPERIAL HEIGHT: 4'11"
IMPERIAL WEIGHT: 136.7 lbs.
METRIC HEIGHT: 1.5 m
METRIC WEIGHT: 62.0 kg
GENDER: ♂ ♀
ABILITIES: Swift Swim, Poison Touch
WEAKNESSES: Grass

TYMPOLE   PALPITOAD   SEISMITOAD

#0161 SENTRET
Scout Pokémon

TYPE: NORMAL

When Sentret sleeps, it does so while another stands guard. The sentry wakes the others at the first sign of danger. When this Pokémon becomes separated from its pack, it becomes incapable of sleep due to fear.

HOW TO SAY IT: SEN-tret
IMPERIAL HEIGHT: 2'07"
IMPERIAL WEIGHT: 13.2 lbs.
METRIC HEIGHT: 0.8 m
METRIC WEIGHT: 6.0 kg
GENDER: ♂ ♀
ABILITIES: Run Away, Keen Eye
WEAKNESSES: Fighting

SENTRET   FURRET

SERPERIOR

Regal Pokémon

#0497

TYPE: GRASS

It only gives its all against strong opponents who are not fazed by the glare from Serperior's noble eyes.

It can stop its opponents' movements with just a glare. It takes in solar energy and boosts it internally.

HOW TO SAY IT: sur-PEER-ee-ur
IMPERIAL HEIGHT: 10'10"
IMPERIAL WEIGHT: 138.9 lbs.
METRIC HEIGHT: 3.3 m
METRIC WEIGHT: 63.0 kg
GENDER: ♂ ♀
ABILITIES: Overgrow
WEAKNESSES: Fire, Flying, Ice, Poison, Bug

SNIVY   SERVINE   SERPERIOR

SERVINE

Grass Snake Pokémon

#0496

TYPE: GRASS

It moves along the ground as if sliding. Its swift movements befuddle its foes, and it then attacks with a vine whip.

When it gets dirty, its leaves can't be used in photosynthesis, so it always keeps itself clean.

HOW TO SAY IT: SUR-vine
IMPERIAL HEIGHT: 2'07"
IMPERIAL WEIGHT: 35.3 lbs.
METRIC HEIGHT: 0.8 m
METRIC WEIGHT: 16.0 kg
GENDER: ♂ ♀
ABILITIES: Overgrow
WEAKNESSES: Fire, Flying, Ice, Poison, Bug

SNIVY   SERVINE   SERPERIOR

#0336 SEVIPER
Fang Snake Pokémon

TYPE: POISON

It sharpens its swordlike tail on hard rocks. It hides in tall grass and strikes unwary prey with venomous fangs.

Constant polishing makes the edge of the blade on its tail extremely sharp. It's Zangoose's archrival.

HOW TO SAY IT: seh-VY-per
IMPERIAL HEIGHT: 8'10"
IMPERIAL WEIGHT: 115.7 lbs.
METRIC HEIGHT: 2.7 m
METRIC WEIGHT: 52.5 kg
GENDER: ♂ ♀
ABILITIES: Shed Skin
WEAKNESSES: Psychic, Ground

DOES NOT EVOLVE

#0540 SEWADDLE
Sewing Pokémon

TYPE: BUG-GRASS

This Pokémon makes clothes for itself. It chews up leaves and sews them with sticky thread extruded from its mouth.

Since this Pokémon makes its own clothes out of leaves, it is a popular mascot for fashion designers.

HOW TO SAY IT: seh-WAH-dul
IMPERIAL HEIGHT: 1'00"
IMPERIAL WEIGHT: 5.5 lbs.
METRIC HEIGHT: 0.3 m
METRIC WEIGHT: 2.5 kg
GENDER: ♂ ♀
ABILITIES: Swarm, Chlorophyll
WEAKNESSES: Fire, Flying, Ice, Poison, Rock, Bug

SEWADDLE **SWADLOON** **LEAVANNY**

SHARPEDO

Brutal Pokémon

#0319

TYPE: WATER-DARK

As soon as it catches the scent of prey, Sharpedo will jet seawater from its backside, hurtling toward the target to attack at 75 mph.

This Pokémon is known as the Bully of the Sea. Any ship entering the waters Sharpedo calls home will be attacked—no exceptions.

HOW TO SAY IT: shar-PEE-do
IMPERIAL HEIGHT: 5'11"
IMPERIAL WEIGHT: 195.8 lbs.
METRIC HEIGHT: 1.8 m
METRIC WEIGHT: 88.8 kg
GENDER: ♂ ♀
ABILITIES: Rough Skin
WEAKNESSES: Fairy, Grass, Electric, Fighting, Bug

MEGA SHARPEDO

TYPE: WATER-DARK

The yellow patterns it bears are old scars. The energy from Mega Evolution runs through them, causing it sharp pain and suffering.

The moment it charges into its opponent, sharp spikes pop out of Sharpedo's head, leaving its opponent with deep wounds.

IMPERIAL HEIGHT: 8'02"
IMPERIAL WEIGHT: 287.3 lbs.
METRIC HEIGHT: 2.5 m
METRIC WEIGHT: 130.3 kg

 CARVANHA **SHARPEDO** **MEGA SHARPEDO**

#0492

SHAYMIN LAND FORME
Gratitude Pokémon

TYPE: GRASS

It can dissolve toxins in the air to instantly transform ruined land into a lush field of flowers.

The blooming of Gracidea flowers confers the power of flight upon it. Feelings of gratitude are the message it delivers.

HOW TO SAY IT: SHAY-min
IMPERIAL HEIGHT: 0'08"
IMPERIAL WEIGHT: 4.6 lbs.
METRIC HEIGHT: 0.2 m
METRIC WEIGHT: 2.1 kg
GENDER: Unknown
ABILITIES: Natural Cure
WEAKNESSES: Fire, Flying, Ice, Poison, Bug

SHAYMIN SKY FORME
Gratitude Pokémon

TYPE: GRASS-FLYING

IMPERIAL HEIGHT: 1'04"
IMPERIAL WEIGHT: 11.5 lbs.
METRIC HEIGHT: 0.4 m
METRIC WEIGHT: 5.2 kg
GENDER: Unknown
ABILITIES: Serene Grace
WEAKNESSES: Fire, Flying, Ice, Poison, Rock

DOES NOT EVOLVE

SHEDINJA

Shed Pokémon

#0292

TYPE: BUG-GHOST

A most peculiar Pokémon that somehow appears in a Poké Ball when a Nincada evolves.

A strange Pokémon—it flies without moving its wings, has a hollow shell for a body, and does not breathe.

HOW TO SAY IT: sheh-DIN-ja
IMPERIAL HEIGHT: 2'07"
IMPERIAL WEIGHT: 2.6 lbs.
METRIC HEIGHT: 0.8 m
METRIC WEIGHT: 1.2 kg
GENDER: Unknown
ABILITIES: Wonder Guard
WEAKNESSES: Fire, Ghost, Flying, Dark, Rock

NINCADA **SHEDINJA**

SHELGON

Endurance Pokémon

#0372

TYPE: DRAGON

The cells within its shell transform with explosive speed, preparing it for evolution.

Its armored body makes all attacks bounce off. The armor is too tough, however, making it heavy and somewhat sluggish.

HOW TO SAY IT: SHELL-gon
IMPERIAL HEIGHT: 3'07"
IMPERIAL WEIGHT: 243.6 lbs.
METRIC HEIGHT: 1.1 m
METRIC WEIGHT: 110.5 kg
GENDER: ♂ ♀
ABILITIES: Rock Head
WEAKNESSES: Fairy, Ice, Dragon

BAGON **SHELGON** **SALAMENCE** **MEGA SALAMENCE**

TYPE: WATER

It is encased in a shell that is harder than diamond. Inside, however, it is surprisingly tender.

Clamping on to an opponent reveals its vulnerable parts, so it uses this move only as a last resort.

HOW TO SAY IT: SHELL-der
IMPERIAL HEIGHT: 1'00"
IMPERIAL WEIGHT: 8.8 lbs.
METRIC HEIGHT: 0.3 m
METRIC WEIGHT: 4.0 kg
GENDER: ♂ ♀
ABILITIES: Shell Armor, Skill Link
WEAKNESSES: Electric, Grass

#0090

SHELLDER
Bivalve Pokémon

SHELLDER ➡ **CLOYSTER**

#0422

SHELLOS
Sea Slug Pokémon

WEST SEA

EAST SEA

TYPE: WATER

It used to have a shell on its back long ago. This species is closely related to Pokémon like Shellder.

It oozes a purple fluid to deter enemies. Apparently, there are more West Sea Shellos now than there were in the past.

HOW TO SAY IT: SHELL-loss
IMPERIAL HEIGHT: 1'00"
IMPERIAL WEIGHT: 13.9 lbs.
METRIC HEIGHT: 0.3 m
METRIC WEIGHT: 6.3 kg
GENDER: ♂ ♀
ABILITIES: Sticky Hold, Storm Drain
WEAKNESSES: Grass, Electric

SHELLOS **GASTRODON**

SHELMET

Snail Pokémon

#0616

TYPE: BUG

When attacked, it tightly shuts the lid of its shell. This reaction fails to protect it from Karrablast, however, because they can still get into the shell.

It has a strange physiology that responds to electricity. When together with Karrablast, Shelmet evolves for some reason.

HOW TO SAY IT: SHELL-meht
IMPERIAL HEIGHT: 1'04"
IMPERIAL WEIGHT: 17.0 lbs.
METRIC HEIGHT: 0.4 m
METRIC WEIGHT: 7.7 kg
GENDER: ♂ ♀
ABILITIES: Hydration, Shell Armor
WEAKNESSES: Fire, Flying, Rock

SHELMET   ACCELGOR

TYPE: ROCK-STEEL

SHIELDON

Shield Pokémon

#0410

A mild-mannered, herbivorous Pokémon, it used its face to dig up tree roots to eat. The skin on its face was plenty tough.

Although its fossils can be found in layers of primeval rock, nothing but its face has ever been discovered.

HOW TO SAY IT: SHEEL-don
IMPERIAL HEIGHT: 1'08"
IMPERIAL WEIGHT: 125.7 lbs.
METRIC HEIGHT: 0.5 m
METRIC WEIGHT: 57.0 kg
GENDER: ♂ ♀
ABILITIES: Sturdy
WEAKNESSES: Water, Fighting, Ground

SHIELDON   BASTIODON

SHIFTRY

Wicked Pokémon

TYPE: GRASS-DARK

A Pokémon that was feared as a forest guardian. It can read the foe's mind and take preemptive action.

It lives quietly in the deep forest. It is said to create chilly winter winds with the fans it holds.

HOW TO SAY IT: SHIFF-tree
IMPERIAL HEIGHT: 4'03"
IMPERIAL WEIGHT: 131.4 lbs.
METRIC HEIGHT: 1.3 m
METRIC WEIGHT: 59.6 kg
GENDER: ♂ ♀
ABILITIES: Chlorophyll, Early Bird
WEAKNESSES: Ice, Fire, Flying, Poison, Fighting, Fairy, Bug

SEEDOT → **NUZLEAF** → **SHIFTRY**

SHIINOTIC

Illuminating Pokémon

TYPE: GRASS-FAIRY

Its flickering spores lure in prey and put them to sleep. Once this Pokémon has its prey snoozing, it drains their vitality with its fingertips.

If you see a light deep in a forest at night, don't go near. Shiinotic will make you fall fast asleep.

HOW TO SAY IT: shee-NAH-tick
IMPERIAL HEIGHT: 3'03"
IMPERIAL WEIGHT: 25.4 lbs.
METRIC HEIGHT: 1.0 m
METRIC WEIGHT: 11.5 kg
GENDER: ♂ ♀
ABILITIES: Illuminate, Effect Spore
WEAKNESSES: Steel, Fire, Flying, Ice, Poison

MORELULL → **SHIINOTIC**

SHINX
Flash Pokémon
#0403

TYPE: ELECTRIC

The extension and contraction of its muscles generates electricity. It glows when in trouble.

The extension and contraction of its muscles generates electricity. Its fur glows when it's in trouble.

HOW TO SAY IT: SHINKS
IMPERIAL HEIGHT: 1'08"
IMPERIAL WEIGHT: 20.9 lbs.
METRIC HEIGHT: 0.5 m
METRIC WEIGHT: 9.5 kg
GENDER: ♂ ♀
ABILITIES: Rivalry, Intimidate
WEAKNESSES: Ground

SHINX **LUXIO** **LUXRAY**

#0944
SHROODLE
Toxic Mouse Pokémon

TYPE: POISON-NORMAL

Though usually a mellow Pokémon, it will sink its sharp, poison-soaked front teeth into any that angers it, causing paralysis in the object of its ire.

To keep enemies away from its territory, it paints markings around its nest using a poisonous liquid that has an acrid odor.

HOW TO SAY IT: SHROO-dul
IMPERIAL HEIGHT: 0'08"
IMPERIAL WEIGHT: 1.5 lbs.
METRIC HEIGHT: 0.2 m
METRIC WEIGHT: 0.7 kg
GENDER: ♂ ♀
ABILITIES: Unburden, Pickpocket
WEAKNESSES: Psychic, Ground

SHROODLE **GRAFAIAI**

#0285 SHROOMISH
Mushroom Pokémon

TYPE: GRASS

It prefers damp places. By day it remains still in the forest shade. It releases toxic powder from its head.

If it senses danger, it scatters spores from the top of its head to protect itself.

HOW TO SAY IT: SHROOM-ish
IMPERIAL HEIGHT: 1'04"
IMPERIAL WEIGHT: 9.9 lbs.
METRIC HEIGHT: 0.4 m
METRIC WEIGHT: 4.5 kg
GENDER: ♂ ♀
ABILITIES: Effect Spore, Poison Heal
WEAKNESSES: Fire, Flying, Ice, Poison, Bug

SHROOMISH   BRELOOM

#0213 SHUCKLE
Mold Pokémon

TYPE: BUG-ROCK

It stores berries inside its shell. To avoid attacks, it hides beneath rocks and remains completely still.

The berries stored in its vaselike shell eventually become a thick, pulpy juice.

HOW TO SAY IT: SHUCK-kull
IMPERIAL HEIGHT: 2'00"
IMPERIAL WEIGHT: 45.2 lbs.
METRIC HEIGHT: 0.6 m
METRIC WEIGHT: 20.5 kg
GENDER: ♂ ♀
ABILITIES: Sturdy, Gluttony
WEAKESSES: Steel, Water, Rock

DOES NOT EVOLVE

SHUPPET

Puppet Pokémon

#0353

TYPE: GHOST

It loves to feed on feelings like envy and malice. Its upright horn catches the emotions of people.

It feeds on the dark emotions of sadness and hatred, which make it grow steadily stronger.

HOW TO SAY IT: SHUP-pett
IMPERIAL HEIGHT: 2'00"
IMPERIAL WEIGHT: 5.1 lbs.
METRIC HEIGHT: 0.6 m
METRIC WEIGHT: 2.3 kg
GENDER: ♂ ♀
ABILITIES: Insomnia, Frisk
WEAKNESSES: Ghost, Dark

SHUPPET   **BANETTE**   **MEGA BANETTE**

SIGILYPH

Avianoid Pokémon

#0561

TYPE: PSYCHIC-FLYING

Psychic power allows these Pokémon to fly. Some say they were the guardians of an ancient city. Others say they were the guardians' emissaries.

A discovery was made in the desert where Sigilyph fly. The ruins of what may have been an ancient city were found beneath the sands.

HOW TO SAY IT: SIH-jih-liff
IMPERIAL HEIGHT: 4'07"
IMPERIAL WEIGHT: 30.9 lbs.
METRIC HEIGHT: 1.4 m
METRIC WEIGHT: 14.0 kg
GENDER: ♂ ♀
ABILITIES: Wonder Skin, Magic Guard
WEAKNESSES: Ghost, Dark, Electric, Ice, Rock

DOES NOT EVOLVE

SILCOON
Cocoon Pokémon

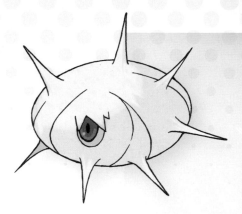

TYPE: BUG

Silcoon tethers itself to a tree branch using silk to keep from falling. There, this Pokémon hangs quietly while it awaits Evolution. It peers out of the silk cocoon through a small hole.

Silcoon was thought to endure hunger and not consume anything before its Evolution. However, it is now thought that this Pokémon slakes its thirst by drinking rainwater that collects on its silk.

HOW TO SAY IT: sill-COON
IMPERIAL HEIGHT: 2'00"
IMPERIAL WEIGHT: 22.0 lbs.
METRIC HEIGHT: 0.6 m
METRIC WEIGHT: 10.0 kg
GENDER: ♂ ♀
ABILITIES: Shed Skin
WEAKNESSES: Fire, Flying, Rock

WURMPLE ➡ SILCOON ➡ BEAUTIFLY

#0843

SILICOBRA
Sand Snake Pokémon

TYPE: GROUND

Silicobra's neck pouch, which can inflate and deflate like a balloon, gets more elastic each time Silicobra sheds its skin.

Silicobra's large nostrils are specialized for spraying sand, so this Pokémon is not very good at telling apart different smells.

HOW TO SAY IT: sih-lih-KOH-bruh
IMPERIAL HEIGHT: 7'03"
IMPERIAL WEIGHT: 16.8 lbs.
METRIC HEIGHT: 2.2 m
METRIC WEIGHT: 7.6 kg
GENDER: ♂ ♀
ABILITIES: Sand Spit, Shed Skin
WEAKNESSES: Water, Grass, Ice

SILICOBRA   SANDACONDA

TYPE: NORMAL

A solid bond of trust between this Pokémon and its Trainer awakened the strength hidden within Silvally. It can change its type at will.

The final factor needed to release this Pokémon's true power was a strong bond with a Trainer it trusts.

HOW TO SAY IT: sill-VAL-lie
IMPERIAL HEIGHT: 7'07"
IMPERIAL WEIGHT: 221.6 lbs.
METRIC HEIGHT: 2.3 m
METRIC WEIGHT: 100.5 kg
GENDER: Unknown
ABILITIES: RKS System
WEAKNESSES: Fighting

TYPE: NULL SILVALLY

SIMIPOUR

Geyser Pokémon

#0516

TYPE: WATER

The high-pressure water expelled from its tail is so powerful, it can destroy a concrete wall.

It prefers places with clean water. When its tuft runs low, it replenishes it by siphoning up water with its tail.

HOW TO SAY IT: SIH-mee-por
IMPERIAL HEIGHT: 3'03"
IMPERIAL WEIGHT: 63.9 lbs.
METRIC HEIGHT: 1.0 m
METRIC WEIGHT: 29.0 kg
GENDER: ♂ ♀
ABILITIES: Gluttony
WEAKNESSES: Grass, Electric

PANPOUR ➡ SIMIPOUR

TYPE: GRASS

It attacks enemies with strikes of its thorn-covered tail. This Pokémon is wild tempered.

Ill-tempered, it fights by swinging its barbed tail around wildly. The leaf growing on its head is very bitter.

HOW TO SAY IT: SIH-mee-sayj
IMPERIAL HEIGHT: 3'07"
IMPERIAL WEIGHT: 67.2 lbs.
METRIC HEIGHT: 1.1 m
METRIC WEIGHT: 30.5 kg
GENDER: ♂ ♀
ABILITIES: Gluttony
WEAKNESSES: Fire, Flying, Ice, Poison, Bug

#0512

SIMISAGE

Thorn Monkey Pokémon

PANSAGE ➡ SIMISAGE

SIMISEAR

Ember Pokémon

#0514

TYPE: FIRE

A flame burns inside its body. It scatters embers from its head and tail to sear its opponents.

When it gets excited, embers rise from its head and tail and it gets hot. For some reason, it loves sweets.

HOW TO SAY IT: SIH-mee-seer
IMPERIAL HEIGHT: 3'03"
IMPERIAL WEIGHT: 61.7 lbs.
METRIC HEIGHT: 1.0 m
METRIC WEIGHT: 28.0 kg
GENDER: ♂ ♀
ABILITIES: Gluttony
WEAKNESSES: Water, Ground, Rock

PANSEAR **SIMISEAR**

SINISTEA

Black Tea Pokémon

#0854

TYPE: GHOST

The soul of someone who died alone possessed some leftover tea. This Pokémon appears in hotels and houses.

Sinistea gets into your body when you drink it, and then it steals your vitality from within. It also tastes awful.

HOW TO SAY IT: SIH-nis-tee
IMPERIAL HEIGHT: 0'04"
IMPERIAL WEIGHT: 0.4 lbs.
METRIC HEIGHT: 0.1 m
METRIC WEIGHT: 0.2 kg
GENDER: Unknown
ABILITIES: Weak Armor
WEAKNESSES: Ghost, Dark

SINISTEA **POLTEAGEIST**

SIRFETCH'D
Wild Duck Pokémon

TYPE: FIGHTING

Only Farfetch'd that have survived many battles can attain this Evolution. When this Pokémon's leek withers, it will retire from combat.

After deflecting attacks with its hard leaf shield, it strikes back with its sharp leek stalk. The leek stalk is both weapon and food.

HOW TO SAY IT: sir-fehcht
IMPERIAL HEIGHT: 2'07"
IMPERIAL WEIGHT: 257.9 lbs.
METRIC HEIGHT: 0.8 m
METRIC WEIGHT: 117.0 kg
GENDER: ♂ ♀
ABILITIES: Steadfast
WEAKNESSES: Psychic, Flying, Fairy

GALARIAN FARFETCH'D **SIRFETCH'D**

SIZZLIPEDE

Radiator Pokémon

#0850

TYPE: FIRE-BUG

It stores flammable gas in its body and uses it to generate heat. The yellow sections on its belly get particularly hot.

It wraps prey up with its heated body, cooking them in its coils. Once they're well-done, it will voraciously nibble them down to the last morsel.

HOW TO SAY IT: SIZ-lih-peed
IMPERIAL HEIGHT: 2'04"
IMPERIAL WEIGHT: 2.2 lbs.
METRIC HEIGHT: 0.7 m
METRIC WEIGHT: 1.0 kg
GENDER: ♂ ♀
ABILITIES: Flash Fire, White Smoke
WEAKNESSES: Water, Flying, Rock

SIZZLIPEDE   CENTISKORCH

#0227

SKARMORY

Armor Bird Pokémon

TYPE: STEEL-FLYING

The pointed feathers of these Pokémon are sharper than swords. Skarmory and Corviknight fight viciously over territory.

People fashion swords from Skarmory's shed feathers, so this Pokémon is a popular element in heraldic designs.

HOW TO SAY IT: SKAR-more-ree
IMPERIAL HEIGHT: 5'07"
IMPERIAL WEIGHT: 111.3 lbs.
METRIC HEIGHT: 1.7 m
METRIC WEIGHT: 50.5 kg
GENDER: ♂ ♀
ABILITIES: Keen Eye, Sturdy
WEAKNESSES: Fire, Electric

DOES NOT EVOLVE

#0911 SKELEDIRGE
Singer Pokémon

TYPE: FIRE-GHOST

The fiery bird changes shape when Skeledirge sings. Rumor has it that the bird was born when the fireball on Skeledirge's head gained a soul.

Skeledirge's gentle singing soothes the souls of all that hear it. It burns its enemies to a crisp with flames of over 5,400 degrees Fahrenheit.

HOW TO SAY IT: SKEL-uh-durj
IMPERIAL HEIGHT: 5'03"
IMPERIAL WEIGHT: 719.8 lbs.
METRIC HEIGHT: 1.6 m
METRIC WEIGHT: 326.5 kg
GENDER: ♂ ♀
ABILITIES: Blaze
WEAKNESSES: Water, Ghost, Ground, Dark, Rock

FUECOCO → **CROCALOR** → **SKELEDIRGE**

#0672 SKIDDO
Mount Pokémon

TYPE: GRASS

Until recently, people living in the mountains would ride on the backs of these Pokémon to traverse the mountain paths.

As long as it has sunlight and water, Skiddo can make energy with the leaves on its body, allowing it to live on rocky mountains barren of food.

HOW TO SAY IT: skid-OO
IMPERIAL HEIGHT: 2'11"
IMPERIAL WEIGHT: 68.3 lbs.
METRIC HEIGHT: 0.9 m
METRIC WEIGHT: 31.0 kg
GENDER: ♂ ♀
ABILITIES: Sap Sipper
WEAKNESSES: Fire, Flying, Ice, Poison, Bug

SKIDDO → **GOGOAT**

SKIPLOOM

Cottonweed Pokémon

#0188

TYPE: GRASS-FLYING

Skiploom enthusiasts can apparently tell where a Skiploom was born by the scent drifting from the flower on the Pokémon's head.

When the weather grows cold, Skiploom's flower closes and the Pokémon cannot photosynthesize, so it flies away to warmer regions.

HOW TO SAY IT: SKIP-loom
IMPERIAL HEIGHT: 2'00"
IMPERIAL WEIGHT: 2.2 lbs.
METRIC HEIGHT: 0.6 m
METRIC WEIGHT: 1.0 kg
GENDER: ♂ ♀
ABILITIES: Chlorophyll, Leaf Guard
WEAKNESSES: Fire, Flying, Ice, Poison, Rock

HOPPIP **SKIPLOOM** **JUMPLUFF**

#0300

SKITTY

Kitten Pokémon

TYPE: NORMAL

Skitty has the habit of becoming fascinated by moving objects and chasing them around. This Pokémon is known to chase after its own tail and become dizzy.

Skitty is known to chase around playfully after its own tail. In the wild, this Pokémon lives in holes in the trees of forests. It is very popular as a pet because of its adorable looks.

HOW TO SAY IT: SKIT-tee
IMPERIAL HEIGHT: 2'00"
IMPERIAL WEIGHT: 24.3 lbs.
METRIC HEIGHT: 0.6 m
METRIC WEIGHT: 11.0 kg
GENDER: ♂ ♀
ABILITIES: Cute Charm, Normalize
WEAKNESSES: Fighting

SKITTY **DELCATTY**

TYPE: POISON-BUG

#0451

SKORUPI
Scorpion Pokémon

After burrowing into the sand, it waits patiently for prey to come near. This Pokémon and Sizzlipede share common descent.

It attacks using the claws on its tail. Once locked in its grip, its prey is unable to move as this Pokémon's poison seeps in.

HOW TO SAY IT: skor-ROOP-ee
IMPERIAL HEIGHT: 2'07"
IMPERIAL WEIGHT: 26.5 lbs.
METRIC HEIGHT: 0.8 m
METRIC WEIGHT: 12.0 kg
GENDER: ♂ ♀
ABILITIES: Battle Armor, Sniper
WEAKNESSES: Fire, Psychic, Flying, Rock

SKORUPI　　　**DRAPION**

SKRELP
Mock Kelp Pokémon

#0690

TYPE: POISON-WATER

Skrelp evades its enemies by hiding amid drifting seaweed. It eats rotten seaweed to create its poison.

This Pokémon is a poor swimmer. If it's caught in a fierce storm, it will sometimes get washed far away and become unable to return to its home.

HOW TO SAY IT: SKRELP
IMPERIAL HEIGHT: 1'08"
IMPERIAL WEIGHT: 16.1 lbs.
METRIC HEIGHT: 0.5 m
METRIC WEIGHT: 7.3 kg
GENDER: ♂ ♀
ABILITIES: Poison Point, Poison Touch
WEAKNESSES: Poison, Electric, Ground

SKRELP　　　**DRAGALGE**

SKUNTANK
Skunk Pokémon

#0435

TYPE: POISON-DARK

It attacks by spraying a horribly smelly fluid from the tip of its tail. Attacks from above confound it.

It attacks by spraying a repugnant fluid from its tail, but the stench dulls after a few squirts.

HOW TO SAY IT: SKUN-tank
IMPERIAL HEIGHT: 3'03"
IMPERIAL WEIGHT: 83.8 lbs.
METRIC HEIGHT: 1.0 m
METRIC WEIGHT: 38.0 kg
GENDER: ♂ ♀
ABILITIES: Stench, Aftermath
WEAKNESSES: Ground

STUNKY → SKUNTANK

#0819

SKWOVET
Cheeky Pokémon

TYPE: NORMAL

It stores berries in its cheeks. When there are no berries to be found, Skwovet will stuff pebbles into its cheeks to stave off its cravings.

No matter how much it stuffs its belly with food, it is always anxious about getting hungry again. So, it stashes berries in its cheeks and tail.

HOW TO SAY IT: SKWUH-vet
IMPERIAL HEIGHT: 1'00"
IMPERIAL WEIGHT: 5.5 lbs.
METRIC HEIGHT: 0.3 m
METRIC WEIGHT: 2.5 kg
GENDER: ♂ ♀
ABILITIES: Cheek Pouch
WEAKNESSES: Fighting

SKWOVET → GREEDENT

TYPE: NORMAL

It is the world's most slothful Pokémon. However, it can exert horrifying power by releasing pent-up energy all at once.

This Pokémon lives lying on its side. It only rolls over and moves when there is no more grass to eat.

HOW TO SAY IT: SLACK-ing
IMPERIAL HEIGHT: 6'07"
IMPERIAL WEIGHT: 287.7 lbs.
METRIC HEIGHT: 2.0 m
METRIC WEIGHT: 130.5 kg
GENDER: ♂ ♀
ABILITIES: Truant
WEAKNESSES: Fighting

#0289

SLAKING
Lazy Pokémon

SLAKOTH **VIGOROTH** **SLAKING**

SLAKOTH
Slacker Pokémon

#0287

TYPE: NORMAL

It sleeps for 20 hours every day. Making drowsy those that see it is one of its abilities.

The way Slakoth lolls around makes anyone who watches it feel like doing the same.

HOW TO SAY IT: SLACK-oth
IMPERIAL HEIGHT: 2'07"
IMPERIAL WEIGHT: 52.9 lbs.
METRIC HEIGHT: 0.8 m
METRIC WEIGHT: 24.0 kg
GENDER: ♂ ♀
ABILITIES: Truant
WEAKNESSES: Fighting

SLAKOTH **VIGOROTH** **SLAKING**

SLIGGOO

Soft Tissue Pokémon

TYPE: DRAGON

The swirly protrusion on its back is filled with all its vital organs, such as its brain and heart.

When Sliggoo senses danger, the mucus coating its entire body becomes more concentrated—it'll dissolve anything.

HOW TO SAY IT: SLIH-goo
IMPERIAL HEIGHT: 2'07"
IMPERIAL WEIGHT: 38.6 lbs.
METRIC HEIGHT: 0.8 m
METRIC WEIGHT: 17.5 kg
GENDER: ♂ ♀
ABILITIES: Sap Sipper, Hydration
WEAKNESSES: Fairy, Ice, Dragon

GOOMY   SLIGGOO   GOODRA

HISUIAN SLIGGOO

Snail Pokémon

TYPE: STEEL-DRAGON

A creature given to melancholy. I suspect its metallic shell developed as a result of the mucus on its skin reacting with the iron in Hisui's water.

HOW TO SAY IT: SLIH-goo
IMPERIAL HEIGHT: 2'04"
IMPERIAL WEIGHT: 151.0 lbs.
METRIC HEIGHT: 0.7 m
METRIC WEIGHT: 68.5 kg
GENDER: ♂ ♀
ABILITIES: N/A
WEAKNESSES: Fighting, Ground

GOOMY   HISUIAN SLIGGOO   HISUIAN GOODRA

SLITHER WING

Paradox Pokémon

TYPE: BUG-FIGHTING

This mysterious Pokémon has some similarities to a creature that an old book introduced as Slither Wing.

This Pokémon somewhat resembles an ancient form of Volcarona that was introduced in a dubious magazine.

HOW TO SAY IT: SLIH-ther wing
IMPERIAL HEIGHT: 10'06"
IMPERIAL WEIGHT: 202.8 lbs.
METRIC HEIGHT: 3.2 m
METRIC WEIGHT: 92.0 kg
GENDER: Unknown
ABILITIES: Protosynthesis
WEAKNESSES: Fire, Psychic, Flying, Fairy

DOES NOT EVOLVE

SLOWBRO
Hermit Crab Pokémon

TYPE: WATER-PSYCHIC

When a Slowpoke went hunting in the sea, its tail was bitten by a Shellder. That made it evolve into Slowbro.

If the tail-biting Shellder is thrown off in a harsh battle, this Pokémon reverts to being an ordinary Slowpoke.

HOW TO SAY IT: SLOW-bro
IMPERIAL HEIGHT: 5'03"
IMPERIAL WEIGHT: 173.1 lbs.
METRIC HEIGHT: 1.6 m
METRIC WEIGHT: 78.5 kg
GENDER: ♂ ♀
ABILITIES: Oblivious, Own Tempo
WEAKNESSES: Ghost, Dark, Grass, Electric, Bug

MEGA SLOWBRO

TYPE: WATER-PSYCHIC

Under the influence of Shellder's digestive fluids, Slowpoke has awakened, gaining a great deal of power—and a little motivation to boot.

IMPERIAL HEIGHT: 6'07"
IMPERIAL WEIGHT: 264.6 lbs.
METRIC HEIGHT: 2.0 m
METRIC WEIGHT: 120.0 kg

SLOWPOKE   SLOWBRO   MEGA SLOWBRO

GALARIAN SLOWBRO

Hermit Crab Pokémon

TYPE: POISON-PSYCHIC

A Shellder bite set off a chemical reaction with the spices inside Slowbro's body, causing Slowbro to become a Poison-type Pokémon.

If this Pokémon squeezes the tongue of the Shellder biting it, the Shellder will launch a toxic liquid from the tip of its shell.

HOW TO SAY IT: SLOW-bro
IMPERIAL HEIGHT: 5'03"
IMPERIAL WEIGHT: 155.4 lbs.
METRIC HEIGHT: 1.6 m
METRIC WEIGHT: 70.5 kg
GENDER: ♂ ♀
ABILITIES: Quick Draw, Own Tempo
WEAKNESSES: Ghost, Dark, Ground

GALARIAN SLOWPOKE

GALARIAN SLOWBRO

SLOWKING

Royal Pokémon

#0199

TYPE: WATER-PSYCHIC

When its head was bitten, toxins entered Slowpoke's head and unlocked an extraordinary power.

It has incredible intellect and intuition. Whatever the situation, it remains calm and collected.

HOW TO SAY IT: SLOW-king
IMPERIAL HEIGHT: 6'07"
IMPERIAL WEIGHT: 175.3 lbs.
METRIC HEIGHT: 2.0 m
METRIC WEIGHT: 79.5 kg
GENDER: ♂ ♀
ABILITIES: Oblivious, Own Tempo
WEAKNESSES: Ghost, Dark, Grass, Electric, Bug

SLOWPOKE → SLOWKING

GALARIAN SLOWKING

#0199

Hexpert Pokémon

TYPE: POISON-PSYCHIC

A combination of toxins and the shock of evolving has increased Shellder's intelligence to the point that Shellder now controls Slowking.

While chanting strange spells, this Pokémon combines its internal toxins with what it's eaten, creating strange potions.

HOW TO SAY IT: SLOW-king
IMPERIAL HEIGHT: 5'11"
IMPERIAL WEIGHT: 175.3 lbs.
METRIC HEIGHT: 1.8 m
METRIC WEIGHT: 79.5 kg
GENDER: ♂ ♀
ABILITIES: Curious Medicine, Own Tempo
WEAKNESSES: Ghost, Dark, Ground

GALARIAN SLOWPOKE → GALARIAN SLOWKING

SLOWPOKE
Dopey Pokémon

SLOWBRO **MEGA SLOWBRO**

SLOWPOKE

SLOWKING

TYPE: WATER-PSYCHIC

It is incredibly slow and dopey. It takes five seconds for it to feel pain when under attack.

It is always vacantly lost in thought, but no one knows what it is thinking about. It is good at fishing with its tail.

HOW TO SAY IT: SLOW-poke
IMPERIAL HEIGHT: 3'11"
IMPERIAL WEIGHT: 79.4 lbs.
METRIC HEIGHT: 1.2 m
METRIC WEIGHT: 36.0 kg
GENDER: ♂ ♀
ABILITIES: Oblivious, Own Tempo
WEAKNESSES: Ghost, Dark, Grass, Electric, Bug

GALARIAN SLOWPOKE
Dopey Pokémon

GALARIAN SLOWBRO

GALARIAN SLOWPOKE

GALARIAN SLOWKING

TYPE: PSYCHIC

Although this Pokémon is normally zoned out, its expression abruptly sharpens on occasion. The cause for this seems to lie in Slowpoke's diet.

Because Galarian Slowpoke eat the seeds of a plant that grows only in Galar, their tails have developed a spicy flavor.

HOW TO SAY IT: SLOW-poke
IMPERIAL HEIGHT: 3'11"
IMPERIAL WEIGHT: 79.4 lbs.
METRIC HEIGHT: 1.2 m
METRIC WEIGHT: 36.0 kg
GENDER: ♂ ♀
ABILITIES: Gluttony, Own Tempo
WEAKNESSES: Ghost, Dark, Bug

SLUGMA

Lava Pokémon

#0218

TYPE: FIRE

Molten magma courses throughout Slugma's circulatory system. If this Pokémon is chilled, the magma cools and hardens. Its body turns brittle and chunks fall off, reducing its size.

Slugma does not have any blood in its body. Instead, intensely hot magma circulates throughout this Pokémon's body, carrying essential nutrients and oxygen to its organs.

HOW TO SAY IT: SLUG-ma
IMPERIAL HEIGHT: 2'04"
IMPERIAL WEIGHT: 77.2 lbs.
METRIC HEIGHT: 0.7 m
METRIC WEIGHT: 35.0 kg
GENDER: ♂ ♀
ABILITIES: Magma Armor, Flame Body
WEAKNESSES: Water, Ground, Rock

SLUGMA **MAGCARGO**

SLURPUFF

Meringue Pokémon

#0685

TYPE: FAIRY

By taking in a person's scent, it can sniff out their mental and physical condition. It's hoped that this skill will have many medical applications.

Slurpuff's fur contains a lot of air, making it soft to the touch and lighter than it looks.

HOW TO SAY IT: SLUR-puff
IMPERIAL HEIGHT: 2'07"
IMPERIAL WEIGHT: 11.0 lbs.
METRIC HEIGHT: 0.8 m
METRIC WEIGHT: 5.0 kg
GENDER: ♂ ♀
ABILITIES: Sweet Veil
WEAKNESSES: Steel, Poison

SWIRLIX **SLURPUFF**

#0235 SMEARGLE
Painter Pokémon

TYPE: NORMAL

The fluid of Smeargle's tail secretions changes in the intensity of its hue as the Pokémon's emotions change.

It draws symbols with the fluid that oozes from the tip of its tail. Depending on the symbol, Smeargle fanatics will pay big money for them.

HOW TO SAY IT: SMEAR-gull
IMPERIAL HEIGHT: 3'11"
IMPERIAL WEIGHT: 127.9 lbs.
METRIC HEIGHT: 1.2 m
METRIC WEIGHT: 58.0 kg
GENDER: ♂ ♀
ABILITIES: Own Tempo, Technician
WEAKNESSES: Fighting

DOES NOT EVOLVE

#0928 SMOLIV
Olive Pokémon

TYPE: GRASS-NORMAL

It protects itself from enemies by emitting oil from the fruit on its head. This oil is bitter and astringent enough to make someone flinch.

This Pokémon converts nutrients into oil, which it stores in the fruit on its head. It can easily go a whole week without eating or drinking.

HOW TO SAY IT: SMAH-liv
IMPERIAL HEIGHT: 1'00"
IMPERIAL WEIGHT: 14.3 lbs.
METRIC HEIGHT: 0.3 m
METRIC WEIGHT: 6.5 kg
GENDER: ♂ ♀
ABILITIES: Early Bird
WEAKNESSES: Ice, Fire, Flying, Poison, Fighting, Bug

SMOLIV　　DOLLIV　　ARBOLIVA

SMOOCHUM

Kiss Pokémon

TYPE: ICE-PSYCHIC

If its face gets even slightly dirty, Smoochum will bathe immediately. But if its body gets dirty, Smoochum doesn't really seem to care.

This is a very curious Pokémon. Smoochum decides what it likes and dislikes by touching things with its lips.

HOW TO SAY IT: SMOO-chum
IMPERIAL HEIGHT: 1'04"
IMPERIAL WEIGHT: 13.2 lbs.
METRIC HEIGHT: 0.4 m
METRIC WEIGHT: 6.0 kg
GENDER: ♀
ABILITIES: Oblivious, Forewarn
WEAKNESSES: Steel, Ghost, Fire, Dark, Rock, Bug

SMOOCHUM

JYNX

SNEASEL
Sharp Claw Pokémon
#0215

TYPE: DARK-ICE

This cunning Pokémon hides under the cover of darkness, waiting to attack its prey.

This is a smart and sneaky Pokémon. A pair may work together to steal eggs by having one lure the parents away.

HOW TO SAY IT: SNEE-zul
IMPERIAL HEIGHT: 2'11"
IMPERIAL WEIGHT: 61.7 lbs.
METRIC HEIGHT: 0.9 m
METRIC WEIGHT: 28.0 kg
GENDER: ♂ ♀
ABILITIES: Inner Focus, Keen Eye
WEAKNESSES: Fighting, Bug, Fire, Rock, Steel, Fairy

SNEASEL → WEAVILE

HISUIAN SNEASEL
Sharp Claw Pokémon
#0215

TYPE: FIGHTING-POISON

Its sturdy, curved claws are ideal for traversing precipitous cliffs. From the tips of these claws drips a venom that infiltrates the nerves of any prey caught in Sneasel's grasp.

HOW TO SAY IT: SNEE-zul
IMPERIAL HEIGHT: 2'11"
IMPERIAL WEIGHT: 59.5 lbs.
METRIC HEIGHT: 0.9 m
METRIC WEIGHT: 27.0 kg
GENDER: ♂ ♀
ABILITIES: N/A
WEAKNESSES: Psychic, Flying, Ground

HISUIAN SNEASEL → SNEASLER

SNEASLER

Free Climb Pokémon

#0903

TYPE: FIGHTING-POISON

Because of Sneasler's virulent poison and daunting physical prowess, no other species could hope to best it on the frozen highlands. Preferring solitude, this species does not form packs.

HOW TO SAY IT: SNEEZ-lur
IMPERIAL HEIGHT: 4'03"
IMPERIAL WEIGHT: 94.8 lbs.
METRIC HEIGHT: 1.3 m
METRIC WEIGHT: 43.0 kg
GENDER: ♂ ♀
ABILITIES: N/A
WEAKNESSES: Psychic, Flying, Ground

HISUIAN SNEASEL

SNEASLER

#0495

SNIVY
Grass Snake Pokémon

TYPE: GRASS

Being exposed to sunlight makes its movements swifter. It uses vines more adeptly than its hands.

They photosynthesize by bathing their tails in sunlight. When they are not feeling well, their tails droop.

HOW TO SAY IT: SNY-vee
IMPERIAL HEIGHT: 2'00"
IMPERIAL WEIGHT: 17.9 lbs.
METRIC HEIGHT: 0.6 m
METRIC WEIGHT: 8.1 kg
GENDER: ♂ ♀
ABILITIES: Overgrow
WEAKNESSES: Fire, Flying, Ice, Poison, Bug

SNIVY   SERVINE   SERPERIOR

#0872

SNOM
Worm Pokémon

TYPE: ICE-BUG

It eats snow that has accumulated on the ground. It prefers soft, freshly fallen snow, so it will eat its way up a mountain, aiming for the peak.

Within its internal organs, Snom amplifies the frigid air it gets from eating snow and then uses this amplified air to create icicle-like spikes.

HOW TO SAY IT: snahm
IMPERIAL HEIGHT: 1'00"
IMPERIAL WEIGHT: 8.4 lbs.
METRIC HEIGHT: 0.3 m
METRIC WEIGHT: 3.8 kg
GENDER: ♂ ♀
ABILITIES: Shield Dust
WEAKNESSES: Fire, Steel, Flying, Rock

SNOM   FROSMOTH

#0143 SNORLAX
Sleeping Pokémon

TYPE: NORMAL

Its stomach can digest any kind of food, even if it happens to be moldy or rotten.

It stops eating only to sleep. It doesn't feel full unless it eats nearly 900 pounds a day.

HOW TO SAY IT: SNOR-lacks
IMPERIAL HEIGHT: 6'11"
IMPERIAL WEIGHT: 1,014.1 lbs.
METRIC HEIGHT: 2.1 m
METRIC WEIGHT: 460.0 kg
GENDER: ♂ ♀
ABILITIES: Immunity, Thick Fat
WEAKNESSES: Fighting

MUNCHLAX ➡ **SNORLAX**

GIGANTAMAX SNORLAX

Gigantamax energy has affected stray seeds and even pebbles that got stuck to Snorlax, making them grow to a huge size.

Terrifyingly strong, this Pokémon is the size of a mountain—and moves about as much as one as well.

IMPERIAL HEIGHT: 114'10"+
IMPERIAL WEIGHT: ????.? lbs.
METRIC HEIGHT: 35.0 + m
METRIC WEIGHT: ???.? kg

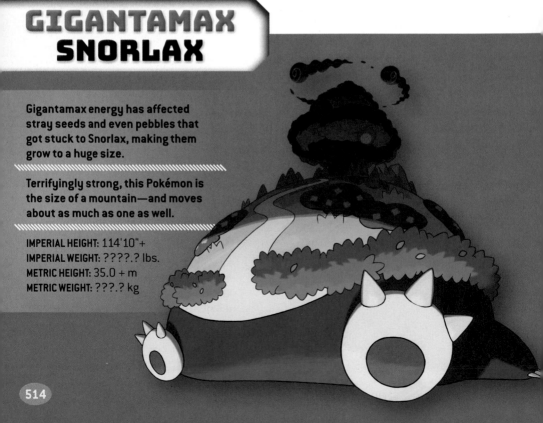

TYPE: ICE

It is said that several Snorunt gather under giant leaves and live together in harmony.

It is said that a home visited by a Snorunt will prosper. It can withstand cold of −150 degrees Fahrenheit.

HOW TO SAY IT: SNOW-runt
IMPERIAL HEIGHT: 2'04"
IMPERIAL WEIGHT: 37.0 lbs.
METRIC HEIGHT: 0.7 m
METRIC WEIGHT: 16.8 kg
GENDER: ♂ ♀
ABILITIES: Inner Focus, Ice Body
WEAKNESSES: Fire, Fighting, Rock, Steel

GLALIE   MEGA GLALIE

SNORUNT

FROSLASS

TYPE: GRASS-ICE

During cold seasons, it migrates to the mountain's lower reaches. It returns to the snow-covered summit in the spring.

Seemingly curious about people, they gather around footsteps they find on snowy mountains.

HOW TO SAY IT: SNOW-vur
IMPERIAL HEIGHT: 3'03"
IMPERIAL WEIGHT: 111.3 lbs.
METRIC HEIGHT: 1.0 m
METRIC WEIGHT: 50.5 kg
GENDER: ♂ ♀
ABILITIES: Snow Warning
WEAKNESSES: Fire, Bug, Fighting, Flying, Poison, Rock, Steel

SNOVER

ABOMASNOW

MEGA ABOMASNOW

#0209 SNUBBULL
Fairy Pokémon

TYPE: FAIRY

It grows close to others easily and is also easily spoiled. The disparity between its face and its actions makes many young people wild about it.

In contrast to its appearance, it's quite timid. When playing with other puppy Pokémon, it sometimes gets bullied.

HOW TO SAY IT: SNUB-bull
IMPERIAL HEIGHT: 2'00"
IMPERIAL WEIGHT: 17.2 lbs.
METRIC HEIGHT: 0.6 m
METRIC WEIGHT: 7.8 kg
GENDER: ♂ ♀
ABILITIES: Intimidate, Run Away
WEAKNESSES: Steel, Poison

SNUBBULL   GRANBULL

#0816 SOBBLE
Water Lizard Pokémon

TYPE: WATER

When scared, this Pokémon cries. Its tears pack the chemical punch of 100 onions, and attackers won't be able to resist weeping.

When it gets wet, its skin changes color, and this Pokémon becomes invisible as if it were camouflaged.

HOW TO SAY IT: SAH-bull
IMPERIAL HEIGHT: 1'00"
IMPERIAL WEIGHT: 8.8 lbs.
METRIC HEIGHT: 0.3 m
METRIC WEIGHT: 4.0 kg
GENDER: ♂ ♀
ABILITIES: Torrent
WEAKNESSES: Grass, Electric

 SOBBLE DRIZZILE  INTELEON

SOLGALEO

Sunne Pokémon

#0791

TYPE: PSYCHIC-STEEL

Sometimes the result of its opening an Ultra Wormhole is that energy and life-forms from other worlds are called here to this world.

In writings from the distant past, it's called by the name "the beast that devours the sun."

HOW TO SAY IT: SOUL-gah-LAY-oh
IMPERIAL HEIGHT: 11'02"
IMPERIAL WEIGHT: 507.1 lbs.
METRIC HEIGHT: 3.4 m
METRIC WEIGHT: 230.0 kg
GENDER: Unknown
ABILITIES: Full Metal Body
WEAKNESSES: Ghost, Fire, Dark, Ground

COSMOG   COSMOEM   SOLGALEO

SOLOSIS

#0577

Cell Pokémon

TYPE: PSYCHIC

It communicates with others telepathically. Its body is encapsulated in liquid, but if it takes a heavy blow, the liquid will leak out.

Many say that the special liquid covering this Pokémon's body would allow it to survive in the vacuum of space.

HOW TO SAY IT: soh-LOH-sis
IMPERIAL HEIGHT: 1'00"
IMPERIAL WEIGHT: 2.2 lbs.
METRIC HEIGHT: 0.3 m
METRIC WEIGHT: 1.0 kg
GENDER: ♂ ♀
ABILITIES: Overcoat, Magic Guard
WEAKNESSES: Ghost, Dark, Bug

SOLOSIS   DUOSION   REUNICLUS

SOLROCK

Meteorite Pokémon

#0338

TYPE: ROCK-PSYCHIC

When it rotates itself, it gives off light similar to the sun, thus blinding its foes.

Solar energy is the source of its power, so it is strong during the daytime. When it spins, its body shines.

HOW TO SAY IT: SOLE-rock
IMPERIAL HEIGHT: 3'11"
IMPERIAL WEIGHT: 339.5 lbs.
METRIC HEIGHT: 1.2 m
METRIC WEIGHT: 154.0 kg
GENDER: Unknown
ABILITIES: Levitate
WEAKNESSES: Steel, Ghost, Water, Dark, Grass, Bug, Ground

DOES NOT EVOLVE

SPEAROW

Tiny Bird Pokémon

#0021

TYPE: NORMAL-FLYING

Inept at flying high. However, it can fly around very fast to protect its territory.

HOW TO SAY IT: SPEER-oh
IMPERIAL HEIGHT: 1'00"
IMPERIAL WEIGHT: 4.4 lbs.
METRIC HEIGHT: 0.3 m
METRIC WEIGHT: 2.0 kg
GENDER: ♂ ♀
ABILITIES: Keen Eye
WEAKNESSES: Electric, Ice, Rock

SPEAROW ➡ FEAROW

SPECTRIER
Swift Horse Pokémon

TYPE: GHOST

It probes its surroundings with all its senses save one—it doesn't use its sense of sight. Spectrier's kicks are said to separate soul from body.

As it dashes through the night, Spectrier absorbs the life force of sleeping creatures. It craves silence and solitude.

HOW TO SAY IT: SPEK-treer
IMPERIAL HEIGHT: 6'07"
IMPERIAL WEIGHT: 98,1 lbs.
METRIC HEIGHT: 2.0 m
METRIC WEIGHT: 44.5 kg
GENDER: Unknown
ABILITIES: Grim Neigh
WEAKNESSES: Ghost, Dark

DOES NOT EVOLVE

SPEWPA
Scatterdust Pokémon

#0665

TYPE: BUG

If Rufflet attacks this Pokémon by pecking at it, it will retaliate with its sharp fur and poisonous black powder.

Spewpa doesn't live in a fixed location. It roams where it pleases across the fields and mountains, building up the energy it needs to evolve.

HOW TO SAY IT: SPEW-puh
IMPERIAL HEIGHT: 1'00"
IMPERIAL WEIGHT: 18.5 lbs.
METRIC HEIGHT: 0.3 m
METRIC WEIGHT: 8.4 kg
GENDER: ♂ ♀
ABILITIES: Shed Skin
WEAKNESSES: Fire, Flying, Rock

SCATTERBUG　　SPEWPA　　VIVILLON

#0363

SPHEAL
Clap Pokémon

TYPE: ICE-WATER

This Pokémon's body is covered in blubber and impressively round. It's faster for Spheal to roll around than walk.

As it drifts among the waves, Spheal probes the sea. As soon as it spots prey, it informs the Walrein in its herd.

HOW TO SAY IT: SFEEL
IMPERIAL HEIGHT: 2'07"
IMPERIAL WEIGHT: 87.1 lbs.
METRIC HEIGHT: 0.8 m
METRIC WEIGHT: 39.5 kg
GENDER: ♂ ♀
ABILITIES: Thick Fat, Ice Body
WEAKNESSES: Grass, Electric, Fighting, Rock

SPHEAL　　SEALEO　　WALREIN

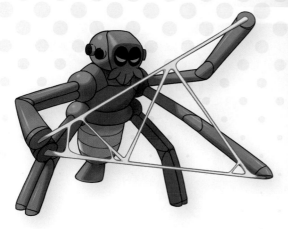

TAROUNTULA → **SPIDOPS**

#0918 SPIDOPS
Trap Pokémon

TYPE: BUG

It clings to branches and ceilings using its threads and moves without a sound. It takes out its prey before the prey even notices it.

Spidops covers its territory in tough, sticky threads to set up traps for intruders.

HOW TO SAY IT: SPY-dops
IMPERIAL HEIGHT: 3'03"
IMPERIAL WEIGHT: 36.4 lbs.
METRIC HEIGHT: 1.0 m
METRIC WEIGHT: 16.5 kg
GENDER: ♂ ♀
ABILITIES: Insomnia
WEAKNESSES: Fire, Flying, Rock

#0167 SPINARAK
String Spit Pokémon

TYPE: BUG-POISON

With threads from its mouth, it fashions sturdy webs that won't break even if you set a rock on them.

Although the poison from its fangs isn't that strong, it's potent enough to weaken prey that gets caught in its web.

HOW TO SAY IT: SPIN-uh-rack
IMPERIAL HEIGHT: 1'08"
IMPERIAL WEIGHT: 18.7 lbs.
METRIC HEIGHT: 0.5 m
METRIC WEIGHT: 8.5 kg
GENDER: ♂ ♀
ABILITIES: Swarm, Insomnia
WEAKNESSES: Fire, Psychic, Flying, Rock

SPINARAK → **ARIADOS**

SPINDA

Spot Panda Pokémon

#0327

TYPE: NORMAL

Its steps are shaky and stumbling. Walking for a long time makes it feel sick.

Each Spinda's spot pattern is different. With its stumbling movements, it evades opponents' attacks brilliantly!

HOW TO SAY IT: SPIN-dah
IMPERIAL HEIGHT: 3'07"
IMPERIAL WEIGHT: 11.0 lbs.
METRIC HEIGHT: 1.1 m
METRIC WEIGHT: 5.0 kg
GENDER: ♂ ♀
ABILITIES: Own Tempo, Tangled Feet
WEAKNESSES: Fighting

DOES NOT EVOLVE

SPIRITOMB

Forbidden Pokémon

#0442

TYPE: GHOST-DARK

Its constant mischief and misdeeds resulted in it being bound to an Odd Keystone by a mysterious spell.

It was formed by uniting 108 spirits. It has been bound to the Odd Keystone to keep it from doing any mischief.

HOW TO SAY IT: SPIR-it-tomb
IMPERIAL HEIGHT: 3'03"
IMPERIAL WEIGHT: 238.1 lbs.
METRIC HEIGHT: 1.0 m
METRIC WEIGHT: 108.0 kg
GENDER: ♂ ♀
ABILITIES: Pressure
WEAKNESSES: Fairy

DOES NOT EVOLVE

SPOINK
Bounce Pokémon

TYPE: PSYCHIC

Spoink will die if it stops bouncing. The pearl on its head amplifies its psychic powers.

Using its tail like a spring, it keeps its heart beating by bouncing constantly. If it stops, it dies.

HOW TO SAY IT: SPOINK
IMPERIAL HEIGHT: 2'04"
IMPERIAL WEIGHT: 67.5 lbs.
METRIC HEIGHT: 0.7 m
METRIC WEIGHT: 30.6 kg
GENDER: ♂ ♀
ABILITIES: Thick Fat, Own Tempo
WEAKNESSES: Ghost, Dark, Bug

SPOINK → **GRUMPIG**

#0906

SPRIGATITO
Grass Cat Pokémon

TYPE: GRASS

Its fluffy fur is similar in composition to plants. This Pokémon frequently washes its face to keep it from drying out.

The sweet scent its body gives off mesmerizes those around it. The scent grows stronger when this Pokémon is in the sun.

HOW TO SAY IT: SPRIG-uh-TEE-toh
IMPERIAL HEIGHT: 1'04"
IMPERIAL WEIGHT: 9.0 lbs.
METRIC HEIGHT: 0.4 m
METRIC WEIGHT: 4.1 kg
GENDER: ♂ ♀
ABILITIES: Overgrow
WEAKNESSES: Fire, Flying, Ice, Poison, Bug

SPRIGATITO **FLORAGATO** **MEOWSCARADA**

SPRITZEE

Perfume Pokémon

#0682

TYPE: FAIRY

A scent pouch within this Pokémon's body allows it to create various scents. A change in its diet will alter the fragrance it produces.

The scent its body gives off enraptures those who smell it. Noble ladies had no shortage of love for Spritzee.

HOW TO SAY IT: SPRIT-zee
IMPERIAL HEIGHT: 0'08"
IMPERIAL WEIGHT: 1.1 lbs.
METRIC HEIGHT: 0.2 m
METRIC WEIGHT: 0.5 kg
GENDER: ♂ ♀
ABILITIES: Healer
WEAKNESSES: Steel, Poison

SPRITZEE → AROMATISSE

SQUAWKABILLY

Parrot Pokémon

#0931

TYPE: NORMAL-FLYING

These Pokémon prefer to live in cities. They form flocks based on the color of their feathers, and they fight over territory.

Green-feathered flocks hold the most sway. When they're out searching for food in the mornings and evenings, it gets very noisy.

HOW TO SAY IT: SKWAHK-uh-BIHL-ee
IMPERIAL HEIGHT: 2'00"
IMPERIAL WEIGHT: 5.3 lbs.
METRIC HEIGHT: 0.6 m
METRIC WEIGHT: 2.4 kg
GENDER: ♂ ♀
ABILITIES: Intimidate, Hustle
WEAKNESSES: Electric, Ice, Rock

DOES NOT EVOLVE

TYPE: WATER

SQUIRTLE
Tiny Turtle Pokémon

#0007

When it retracts its long neck into its shell, it squirts out water with vigorous force.

When it feels threatened, it draws its limbs inside its shell and sprays water from its mouth.

HOW TO SAY IT: SKWIR-tul
IMPERIAL HEIGHT: 1'08"
IMPERIAL WEIGHT: 19.8 lbs.
METRIC HEIGHT: 0.5 m
METRIC WEIGHT: 9.0 kg
GENDER: ♂ ♀
ABILITIES: Torrent
WEAKNESSES: Grass, Electric

| SQUIRTLE | WARTORTLE | BLASTOISE | MEGA BLASTOISE |

STAKATAKA
Rampart Pokémon

#0805

TYPE: ROCK-STEEL

It appeared from an Ultra Wormhole. Each one appears to be made up of many life-forms stacked one on top of each other.

When stone walls started moving and attacking, the brute's true identity was this mysterious life-form, which brings to mind an Ultra Beast.

HOW TO SAY IT: STACK-uh-TACK-uh
IMPERIAL HEIGHT: 18'01"
IMPERIAL WEIGHT: 1,807.8 lbs.
METRIC HEIGHT: 5.5 m
METRIC WEIGHT: 820.0 kg
GENDER: Unknown
ABILITIES: Beast Boost
WEAKNESSES: Water, Fighting, Ground

DOES NOT EVOLVE

STANTLER

#0234

Big Horn Pokémon

TYPE: NORMAL

This Pokémon apparently used to live in much harsher environments, and thus it once had stronger psychic powers than it does now.

It's said that this Pokémon used to be stronger long ago when it had many enemies, and that it was even able to evolve under its own power.

HOW TO SAY IT: STAN-tler
IMPERIAL HEIGHT: 4'07"
IMPERIAL WEIGHT: 157.0 lbs.
METRIC HEIGHT: 1.4 m
METRIC WEIGHT: 71.2 kg
GENDER: ♂ ♀
ABILITIES: Intimidate, Frisk
WEAKNESSES: Fighting

STANTLER **WYRDEER**

TYPE: NORMAL-FLYING

STARAPTOR

#0398

Predator Pokémon

When Staravia evolve into Staraptor, they leave the flock to live alone. They have sturdy wings.

It never stops attacking even if it is injured. It fusses over the shape of its comb.

HOW TO SAY IT: star-RAP-tor
IMPERIAL HEIGHT: 3'11"
IMPERIAL WEIGHT: 54.9 lbs.
METRIC HEIGHT: 1.2 m
METRIC WEIGHT: 24.9 kg
GENDER: ♂ ♀
ABILITIES: Intimidate
WEAKNESSES: Electric, Ice, Rock

STARLY **STARAVIA** **STARAPTOR**

#0397 STARAVIA
Starling Pokémon

TYPE: NORMAL-FLYING

Recognizing their own weakness, they always live in a group. When alone, a Staravia cries noisily.

They maintain huge flocks, although fierce scuffles break out between various flocks.

HOW TO SAY IT: star-EY-vee-a
IMPERIAL HEIGHT: 2'00"
IMPERIAL WEIGHT: 34.2 lbs.
METRIC HEIGHT: 0.6 m
METRIC WEIGHT: 15.5 kg
GENDER: ♂ ♀
ABILITIES: Intimidate
WEAKNESSES: Electric, Ice, Rock

STARLY   STARAVIA   STARAPTOR

STARLY #0396
Starling Pokémon

TYPE: NORMAL-FLYING

They flock around mountains and fields, chasing after bug Pokémon. Their singing is noisy and annoying.

Because they are weak individually, they form groups. However, they bicker if the group grows too big.

HOW TO SAY IT: STAR-lee
IMPERIAL HEIGHT: 1'00"
IMPERIAL WEIGHT: 4.4 lbs.
METRIC HEIGHT: 0.3 m
METRIC WEIGHT: 2.0 kg
GENDER: ♂ ♀
ABILITIES: Keen Eye
WEAKNESSES: Electric, Ice, Rock

STARLY   STARAVIA   STARAPTOR

STARMIE

Mysterious Pokémon

#0121

TYPE: WATER-PSYCHIC

This Pokémon has an organ known as its core. The organ glows in seven colors when Starmie is unleashing its potent psychic powers.

Starmie swims by spinning its body at high speed. As this Pokémon cruises through the ocean, it absorbs tiny plankton.

HOW TO SAY IT: STAR-mee
IMPERIAL HEIGHT: 3'07"
IMPERIAL WEIGHT: 176.4 lbs.
METRIC HEIGHT: 1.1 m
METRIC WEIGHT: 80.0 kg
GENDER: Unknown
ABILITIES: Illuminate, Natural Cure
WEAKNESSES: Ghost, Dark, Grass, Electric, Bug

STARYU   STARMIE

#0121

STARYU

Star Shape Pokémon

TYPE: WATER

If you visit a beach at the end of summer, you'll be able to see groups of Staryu lighting up in a steady rhythm.

Fish Pokémon nibble at it, but Staryu isn't bothered. Its body regenerates quickly, even if part of it is completely torn off.

HOW TO SAY IT: STAR-you
IMPERIAL HEIGHT: 2'07"
IMPERIAL WEIGHT: 76.1 lbs.
METRIC HEIGHT: 0.8 m
METRIC WEIGHT: 34.5 kg
GENDER: Unknown
ABILITIES: Illuminate, Natural Cure
WEAKNESSES: Grass, Electric

STARYU   STARMIE

STEELIX

Iron Snake Pokémon

#0208

TYPE: STEEL-GROUND

It is said that if an Onix lives for over 100 years, its composition changes to become diamond-like.

It is thought its body transformed as a result of iron accumulating internally from swallowing soil.

HOW TO SAY IT: STEE-licks
IMPERIAL HEIGHT: 30'02"
IMPERIAL WEIGHT: 881.8 lbs.
METRIC HEIGHT: 9.2 m
METRIC WEIGHT: 400.0 kg
GENDER: ♂ ♀
ABILITIES: Rock Head, Sturdy
WEAKNESSES: Fire, Water, Fighting, Ground

MEGA STEELIX

TYPE: STEEL-GROUND

Steelix lives even further underground than Onix. This Pokémon is known to dig toward the earth's core. There are records of this Pokémon reaching a depth of over six-tenths of a mile underground.

IMPERIAL HEIGHT: 34'05"
IMPERIAL WEIGHT: 1,631.4 lbs.
METRIC HEIGHT: 10.5 m
METRIC WEIGHT: 740.0 kg

ONIX **STEELIX** **MEGA STEELIX**

STEENEE
Fruit Pokémon

#0762

TYPE: GRASS

Steenee spreads a sweet scent that makes others feel invigorated. This same scent is popular for antiperspirants.

Steenee bounces energetically through forests. If the rind that peels off its body is pulverized, it can be used to treat stomach pains.

HOW TO SAY IT: STEE-nee
IMPERIAL HEIGHT: 2'04"
IMPERIAL WEIGHT: 18.1 lbs.
METRIC HEIGHT: 0.7 m
METRIC WEIGHT: 8.2 kg
GENDER: ♀
ABILITIES: Leaf Guard, Oblivious
WEAKNESSES: Fire, Flying, Ice, Poison, Bug

BOUNSWEET → **STEENEE** → **TSAREENA**

#0874

STONJOURNER
Big Rock Pokémon

TYPE: ROCK

The elemental composition of the rocks that form its body were found to match the bedrock of a land far away from this Pokémon's habitat.

This Pokémon spends its life gazing at the setting sun. It strides leisurely across grassy plains on legs of rock that weigh over 400 pounds each.

HOW TO SAY IT: STONE-jer-ner
IMPERIAL HEIGHT: 8'02"
IMPERIAL WEIGHT: 1146.4 lbs.
METRIC HEIGHT: 2.5 m
METRIC WEIGHT: 520.0 kg
GENDER: ♂ ♀
ABILITIES: Power Spot
WEAKNESSES: Water, Steel, Grass, Fighting, Ground

DOES NOT EVOLVE

#0508 STOUTLAND
Big-Hearted Pokémon

TYPE: NORMAL

These Pokémon seem to enjoy living with humans. Even a Stoutland caught in the wild will warm up to people in about three days.

Stoutland is immensely proud of its impressive mustache. It's said that mustache length is what determines social standing among this species.

HOW TO SAY IT: STOWT-lund
IMPERIAL HEIGHT: 3'11"
IMPERIAL WEIGHT: 134.5 lbs.
METRIC HEIGHT: 1.2 m
METRIC WEIGHT: 61.0 kg
GENDER: ♂ ♀
ABILITIES: Intimidate, Sand Rush
WEAKNESSES: Fighting

LILLIPUP → **HERDIER** → **STOUTLAND**

#0759 STUFFUL
Flailing Pokémon

TYPE: NORMAL-FIGHTING

Its fluffy fur is a delight to pet, but carelessly reaching out to touch this Pokémon could result in painful retaliation.

The way it protects itself by flailing its arms may be an adorable sight, but stay well away. This is flailing that can snap thick tree trunks.

HOW TO SAY IT: STUFF-fuhl
IMPERIAL HEIGHT: 1'08"
IMPERIAL WEIGHT: 15.0 lbs.
METRIC HEIGHT: 0.5 m
METRIC WEIGHT: 6.8 kg
GENDER: ♂ ♀
ABILITIES: Fluffy, Klutz
WEAKNESSES: Psychic, Flying, Fairy, Fighting

STUFFUL → **BEWEAR**

STUNFISK

Trap Pokémon

#0618

TYPE: GROUND-ELECTRIC

Its skin is very hard, so it is unhurt even if stepped on by sumo wrestlers. It smiles when transmitting electricity.

It conceals itself in the mud of the seashore. Then it waits. When prey touch it, it delivers a jolt of electricity.

HOW TO SAY IT: STUN-fisk
IMPERIAL HEIGHT: 2'04"
IMPERIAL WEIGHT: 24.3 lbs.
METRIC HEIGHT: 0.7 m
METRIC WEIGHT: 11.0 kg
GENDER: ♂ ♀
ABILITIES: Static, Limber
WEAKNESSES: Water, Grass, Ice, Ground

DOES NOT EVOLVE

#0618

GALARIAN STUNFISK

Trap Pokémon

TYPE: GROUND-STEEL

Living in mud with a high iron content has given it a strong steel body.

Its conspicuous lips lure prey in as it lies in wait in the mud. When prey gets close, Stunfisk clamps its jagged steel fins down on them.

HOW TO SAY IT: STUN-fisk
IMPERIAL HEIGHT: 2'04"
IMPERIAL WEIGHT: 45.2 lbs.
METRIC HEIGHT: 0.7 m
METRIC WEIGHT: 20.5 kg
GENDER: ♂ ♀
ABILITIES: Mimicry
WEAKNESSES: Fire, Water, Fighting, Ground

DOES NOT EVOLVE

STUNKY
Skunk Pokémon

#0434

TYPE: POISON-DARK

It sprays a foul fluid from its rear. Its stench spreads over a mile radius, driving Pokémon away.

The foul fluid from its rear is so revolting that it can make people feel queasy up to a mile and a quarter away.

HOW TO SAY IT: STUNK-ee
IMPERIAL HEIGHT: 1'04"
IMPERIAL WEIGHT: 42.3 lbs.
METRIC HEIGHT: 0.4 m
METRIC WEIGHT: 19.2 kg
GENDER: ♂ ♀
ABILITIES: Stench, Aftermath
WEAKNESSES: Ground

STUNKY → SKUNTANK

#0185

SUDOWOODO
Imitation Pokémon

TYPE: ROCK

Although it always pretends to be a tree, its composition appears more similar to rock than to vegetation.

To avoid being attacked, it does nothing but mimic a tree. It hates water and flees from rain.

HOW TO SAY IT: SOO-doe-WOO-doe
IMPERIAL HEIGHT: 3'11"
IMPERIAL WEIGHT: 83.8 lbs.
METRIC HEIGHT: 1.2 m
METRIC WEIGHT: 38.0 kg
GENDER: ♂ ♀
ABILITIES: Sturdy, Rock Head
WEAKNESSES: Fighting, Grass, Ground, Steel, Water

BONSLY → SUDOWOODO

SUICUNE

Aurora Pokémon

#0245

TYPE: WATER

Suicune embodies the compassion of a pure spring of water. It runs across the land with gracefulness. This Pokémon has the power to purify dirty water.

HOW TO SAY IT: SWEE-koon
IMPERIAL HEIGHT: 6'07"
IMPERIAL WEIGHT: 412.3 lbs.
METRIC HEIGHT: 2.0 m
METRIC WEIGHT: 187.0 kg
GENDER: Unknown
ABILITIES: Pressure
WEAKNESSES: Grass, Electric

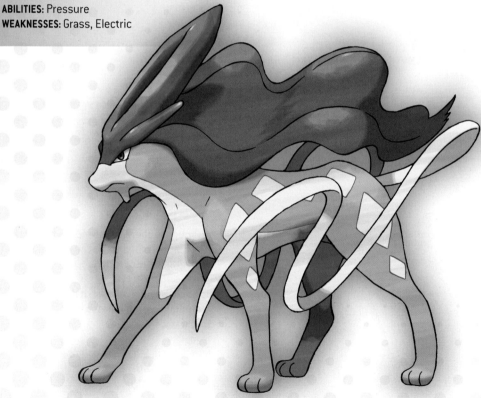

DOES NOT EVOLVE

SUNFLORA

Sun Pokémon

#0192

TYPE: GRASS

In the daytime, it rushes about in a hectic manner, but it comes to a complete stop when the sun sets.

Since it converts sunlight into energy, it is always looking in the direction of the sun.

HOW TO SAY IT: SUN-FLOR-uh
IMPERIAL HEIGHT: 2'07"
IMPERIAL WEIGHT: 18.7 lbs.
METRIC HEIGHT: 0.8 m
METRIC WEIGHT: 8.5 kg
GENDER: ♂ ♀
ABILITIES: Chlorophyll, Solar Power
WEAKNESSES: Fire, Flying, Ice, Poison, Bug

SUNKERN   SUNFLORA

SUNKERN

Seed Pokémon

#0191

TYPE: GRASS

It suddenly falls out of the sky in the morning. Knowing it's weak, It simply feeds until it evolves.

It is very weak. Its only means of defense is to shake its leaves desperately at its attacker.

HOW TO SAY IT: SUN-kurn
IMPERIAL HEIGHT: 1'00"
IMPERIAL WEIGHT: 4.0 lbs.
METRIC HEIGHT: 0.3 m
METRIC WEIGHT: 1.8 kg
GENDER: ♂ ♀
ABILITIES: Chlorophyll, Solar Power
WEAKNESSES: Fire, Flying, Ice, Poison, Bug

SUNKERN   SUNFLORA

TYPE: BUG-WATER

#0283 SURSKIT
Pond Skater Pokémon

They usually live on ponds, but after an evening shower, they may appear on puddles in towns.

It secretes a thick, sweet-scented syrup from the tip of its head. It lives on weed-choked ponds.

HOW TO SAY IT: SUR-skit
IMPERIAL HEIGHT: 1'08"
IMPERIAL WEIGHT: 3.7 lbs.
METRIC HEIGHT: 0.5 m
METRIC WEIGHT: 1.7 kg
GENDER: ♂ ♀
ABILITIES: Swift Swim
WEAKNESSES: Flying, Electric, Rock

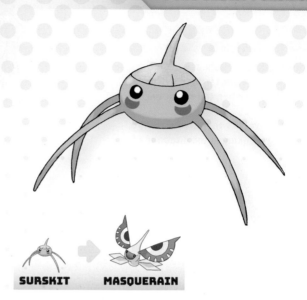

SURSKIT → MASQUERAIN

TYPE: NORMAL-FLYING

#0333 SWABLU
Cotton Bird Pokémon

It constantly grooms its cotton-like wings. It takes a shower to clean itself if it becomes dirty.

It can't relax if it or its surroundings are not clean. It wipes off dirt with its wings.

HOW TO SAY IT: swah-BLUE
IMPERIAL HEIGHT: 1'04"
IMPERIAL WEIGHT: 2.6 lbs.
METRIC HEIGHT: 0.4 m
METRIC WEIGHT: 1.2 kg
GENDER: ♂ ♀
ABILITIES: Natural Cure
WEAKNESSES: Electric, Ice, Rock

SWABLU → ALTARIA → MEGA ALTARIA

SWADLOON

Leaf-Wrapped Pokémon

TYPE: BUG-GRASS

Forests where Swadloon live have superb foliage because the nutrients they make from fallen leaves nourish the plant life.

It protects itself from the cold by wrapping up in leaves. It stays on the move, eating leaves in forests.

HOW TO SAY IT: swahd-LOON
IMPERIAL HEIGHT: 1'08"
IMPERIAL WEIGHT: 16.1 lbs.
METRIC HEIGHT: 0.5 m
METRIC WEIGHT: 7.3 kg
GENDER: ♂ ♀
ABILITIES: Leaf Guard, Chlorophyll
WEAKNESSES: Fire, Flying, Ice, Poison, Rock, Bug

SEWADDLE → **SWADLOON** → **LEAVANNY**

#0317

SWALOT

Poison Bag Pokémon

TYPE: POISON

It gulps anything that fits in its mouth. Its special enzymes can dissolve anything.

It can swallow a tire whole in one gulp. It secretes a horribly toxic fluid from the pores on its body.

HOW TO SAY IT: SWAH-lot
IMPERIAL HEIGHT: 5'07"
IMPERIAL WEIGHT: 176.4 lbs.
METRIC HEIGHT: 1.7 m
METRIC WEIGHT: 80.0 kg
GENDER: ♂ ♀
ABILITIES: Liquid Ooze, Sticky Hold
WEAKNESSES: Psychic, Ground

GULPIN → **SWALOT**

TYPE: WATER-GROUND

Swampert is very strong. It has enough power to easily drag a boulder weighing more than a ton. This Pokémon also has powerful vision that lets it see even in murky water.

Swampert predicts storms by sensing subtle differences in the sounds of waves and tidal winds with its fins. If a storm is approaching, it piles up boulders to protect itself.

HOW TO SAY IT: SWAM-pert
IMPERIAL HEIGHT: 4'11"
IMPERIAL WEIGHT: 180.6 lbs.
METRIC HEIGHT: 1.5 m
METRIC WEIGHT: 81.9 kg
GENDER: ♂ ♀
ABILITIES: Torrent
WEAKNESSES: Grass

#0260 SWAMPERT
Mud Fish Pokémon

MEGA SWAMPERT

TYPE: WATER-GROUND

IMPERIAL HEIGHT: 6'03"
IMPERIAL WEIGHT: 224.9 lbs.
METRIC HEIGHT: 1.9 m
METRIC WEIGHT: 102.0 kg

MUDKIP

MARSHTOMP

SWAMPERT

MEGA SWAMPERT

SWANNA

White Bird Pokémon

#0581

TYPE: WATER-FLYING

Despite their elegant appearance, they can flap their wings strongly and fly for thousands of miles.

Swanna start to dance at dusk. The one dancing in the middle is the leader of the flock.

HOW TO SAY IT: SWAH-nuh
IMPERIAL HEIGHT: 4'03"
IMPERIAL WEIGHT: 53.4 lbs.
METRIC HEIGHT: 1.3 m
METRIC WEIGHT: 24.2 kg
GENDER: ♂ ♀
ABILITIES: Keen Eye, Big Pecks
WEAKNESSES: Electric, Rock

DUCKLETT　　**SWANNA**

SWELLOW

Swallow Pokémon

#0277

TYPE: NORMAL-FLYING

Swellow flies high above our heads, making graceful arcs in the sky. This Pokémon dives at a steep angle as soon as it spots its prey. The hapless prey is tightly grasped by Swellow's clawed feet, preventing escape.

Swellow is very conscientious about the upkeep of its glossy wings. Once two Swellow are gathered, they diligently take care of cleaning each other's wings.

HOW TO SAY IT: SWELL-low
IMPERIAL HEIGHT: 2'04"
IMPERIAL WEIGHT: 43.7 lbs.
METRIC HEIGHT: 0.7 m
METRIC WEIGHT: 19.8 kg
GENDER: ♂ ♀
ABILITIES: Guts
WEAKNESSES: Electric Ice, Rock

TAILLOW　　**SWELLOW**

TYPE: ICE-GROUND

It rubs its snout on the ground to find and dig up food. It sometimes discovers hot springs.

If it smells something enticing, it dashes off headlong to find the source of the aroma.

HOW TO SAY IT: SWY-nub
IMPERIAL HEIGHT: 1'04"
IMPERIAL WEIGHT: 14.3 lbs.
METRIC HEIGHT: 0.4 m
METRIC WEIGHT: 6.5 kg
GENDER: ♂ ♀
ABILITIES: Oblivious, Snow Cloak
WEAKNESSES: Steel, Fire, Grass, Water, Fighting

#0220

SWINUB
Pig Pokémon

SWINUB **PILOSWINE** **MAMOSWINE**

#0684

SWIRLIX
Cotton Candy Pokémon

TYPE: FAIRY

It eats its own weight in sugar every day. If it doesn't get enough sugar, it becomes incredibly grumpy.

The sweet smell of cotton candy perfumes Swirlix's fluffy fur. This Pokémon spits out sticky string to tangle up its enemies.

HOW TO SAY IT: SWUR-licks
IMPERIAL HEIGHT: 1'04"
IMPERIAL WEIGHT: 7.7 lbs.
METRIC HEIGHT: 0.4 m
METRIC WEIGHT: 3.5 kg
GENDER: ♂ ♀
ABILITIES: Sweet Veil
WEAKNESSES: Steel, Poison

SWIRLIX **SLURPUFF**

SWOOBAT
#0528
Courting Pokémon

TYPE: PSYCHIC-FLYING

Emitting powerful sound waves tires it out. Afterward, it won't be able to fly for a little while.

The auspicious shape of this Pokémon's nose apparently led some regions to consider Swoobat a symbol of good luck.

HOW TO SAY IT: SWOO-bat
IMPERIAL HEIGHT: 2'11"
IMPERIAL WEIGHT: 23.1 lbs.
METRIC HEIGHT: 0.9 m
METRIC WEIGHT: 10.5 kg
GENDER: ♂ ♀
ABILITIES: Unaware, Klutz
WEAKNESSES: Ghost, Dark, Electric, Ice, Rock

WOOBAT → SWOOBAT

SYLVEON
#0700
Intertwining Pokémon

TYPE: FAIRY

This Pokémon uses its ribbonlike feelers to send a soothing aura into its opponents, erasing their hostility.

Sylveon cuts an elegant figure as it dances lightly around, feelers fluttering, but its piercing moves aim straight for its opponents' weak spots.

HOW TO SAY IT: SIL-vee-on
IMPERIAL HEIGHT: 3'03"
IMPERIAL WEIGHT: 51.8 lbs.
METRIC HEIGHT: 1.0 m
METRIC WEIGHT: 23.5 kg
GENDER: ♂ ♀
ABILITIES: Cute Charm
WEAKNESSES: Steel, Poison

EEVEE → SYLVEON

TADBULB

EleTadpole Pokémon

#0938

TYPE: ELECTRIC

Tadbulb shakes its tail to generate electricity. If it senses danger, it will make its head blink on and off to alert its allies.

It floats using the electricity stored in its body. When thunderclouds are around, Tadbulb will float higher off the ground.

HOW TO SAY IT: TAD-bulb
IMPERIAL HEIGHT: 1'00"
IMPERIAL WEIGHT: 0.9 lbs.
METRIC HEIGHT: 0.3 m
METRIC WEIGHT: 0.4 kg
GENDER: ♂ ♀
ABILITIES: Own Tempo, Static
WEAKNESSES: Ground

TADBULB   BELLIBOLT

TYPE: NORMAL-FLYING

#0276

TAILLOW

Tiny Swallow Pokémon

Taillow courageously stands its ground against foes, however strong they may be. This gutsy Pokémon will remain defiant even after a loss. On the other hand, it cries loudly if it becomes hungry.

Taillow is young—it has only just left its nest. As a result, it sometimes becomes lonesome and cries at night. This Pokémon feeds on Wurmple that live in forests.

HOW TO SAY IT: TAY-low
IMPERIAL HEIGHT: 1'00"
IMPERIAL WEIGHT: 5.1 lbs.
METRIC HEIGHT: 0.3 m
METRIC WEIGHT: 2.3 kg
GENDER: ♂ ♀
ABILITIES: Guts
WEAKNESSES: Electric, Ice, Rock

TAILLOW   SWELLOW

TYPE: FIRE-FLYING

It has top-notch flying capabilities. It flies around easily, even while carrying prey that weighs more than 220 lbs.

When it gets excited, it vents sparks from the gaps between its feathers. These unburnable feathers are used as a fireproof material.

HOW TO SAY IT: TAL-un-flame
IMPERIAL HEIGHT: 3'11"
IMPERIAL WEIGHT: 54.0 lbs.
METRIC HEIGHT: 1.2 m
METRIC WEIGHT: 24.5 kg
GENDER: ♂ ♀
ABILITIES: Flame Body
WEAKNESSES: Water, Elcctric, Rock

TALONFLAME
Scorching Pokémon

#0663

FLETCHLING → **FLETCHINDER** → **TALONFLAME**

#0924

TANDEMAUS
Couple Pokémon

TYPE: NORMAL

Exhibiting great teamwork, they use their incisors to cut pieces out of any material that might be useful for a nest, then make off with them.

The pair sticks together no matter what. They split any food they find exactly in half and then eat it together.

HOW TO SAY IT: TAN-duh-mouse
IMPERIAL HEIGHT: 1'00"
IMPERIAL WEIGHT: 4.0 lbs.
METRIC HEIGHT: 0.3 m
METRIC WEIGHT: 1.8 kg
GENDER: Unknown
ABILITIES: Run Away, Pickup
WEAKNESSES: Fighting

 TANDEMAUS → **MAUSHOLD**

TANGELA

Vine Pokémon

#0114

TYPE: GRASS

Hidden beneath a tangle of vines that grows nonstop even if the vines are torn off, this Pokémon's true appearance remains a mystery.

The vines of a Tangela have a distinct scent. In some parts of Galar, Tangela vines are used as herbs.

HOW TO SAY IT: TANG-ghel-a
IMPERIAL HEIGHT: 3'03"
IMPERIAL WEIGHT: 77.2 lbs.
METRIC HEIGHT: 1.0 m
METRIC WEIGHT: 35.0 kg
GENDER: ♂ ♀
ABILITIES: Chlorophyll, Leaf Guard
WEAKNESSES: Fire, Flying, Ice, Poison, Bug

TANGELA → TANGROWTH

TANGROWTH

Vine Pokémon

#0465

TYPE: GRASS

Tangrowth has two arms that it can extend as it pleases. Recent research has shown that these arms are, in fact, bundles of vines.

Vine growth is accelerated for Tangrowth living in warm climates. If the vines grow long, Tangrowth shortens them by tearing parts of them off.

HOW TO SAY IT: TANG-growth
IMPERIAL HEIGHT: 6'07"
IMPERIAL WEIGHT: 283.5 lbs.
METRIC HEIGHT: 2.0 m
METRIC WEIGHT: 128.6 kg
GENDER: ♂ ♀
ABILITIES: Chlorophyll, Leaf Guard
WEAKNESSES: Fire, Flying, Ice, Poison, Bug

TANGELA → TANGROWTH

TAPU BULU
Land Spirit Pokémon

TYPE: GRASS-FAIRY

Although it's called a guardian deity, it's violent enough to crush anyone it sees as an enemy.

It makes ringing sounds with its tail to let others know where it is, avoiding unneeded conflicts. This guardian deity of Ula'ula controls plants.

HOW TO SAY IT: TAH-poo BOO-loo
IMPERIAL HEIGHT: 6'03"
IMPERIAL WEIGHT: 100.3 lbs.
METRIC HEIGHT: 1.9 m
METRIC WEIGHT: 45.5 kg
GENDER: Unknown
ABILITIES: Grassy Surge
WEAKNESSES: Steel, Fire, Flying, Ice, Poison

DOES NOT EVOLVE

LEGENDARY POKÉMON

#0788

TAPU FINI
Land Spirit Pokémon

TYPE: WATER-FAIRY

This guardian deity of Poni Island manipulates water. Because it lives deep within a thick fog, it came to be both feared and revered.

Although it's called a guardian deity, terrible calamities sometimes befall those who recklessly approach Tapu Fini.

HOW TO SAY IT: TAH-poo FEE-nee
IMPERIAL HEIGHT: 4'03"
IMPERIAL WEIGHT: 46.7 lbs.
METRIC HEIGHT: 1.3 m
METRIC WEIGHT: 21.2 kg
GENDER: Unknown
ABILITIES: Misty Surge
WEAKNESSES: Grass, Electric, Poison

DOES NOT EVOLVE

TAPU KOKO

Land Spirit Pokémon

#0785

TYPE: ELECTRIC-FAIRY

Although it's called a guardian deity, if a person or Pokémon puts it in a bad mood, it will become a malevolent deity and attack.

The lightning-wielding guardian deity of Melemele, Tapu Koko is brimming with curiosity and appears before people from time to time.

HOW TO SAY IT: TAH-poo KO-ko
IMPERIAL HEIGHT: 5'11"
IMPERIAL WEIGHT: 45.2 lbs.
METRIC HEIGHT: 1.8 m
METRIC WEIGHT: 20.5 kg
GENDER: Unknown
ABILITIES: Electric Surge
WEAKNESSES: Poison, Ground

DOES NOT EVOLVE

#0786

TAPU LELE

Land Spirit Pokémon

TYPE: PSYCHIC-FAIRY

It heals the wounds of people and Pokémon by sprinkling them with its sparkling scales. This guardian deity is worshiped on Akala.

Although called a guardian deity, Tapu Lele is devoid of guilt about its cruel disposition and can be described as nature incarnate.

HOW TO SAY IT: TAH-poo LEH-leh
IMPERIAL HEIGHT: 3'11"
IMPERIAL WEIGHT: 41.0 lbs.
METRIC HEIGHT: 1.2 m
METRIC WEIGHT: 18.6 kg
GENDER: Unknown
ABILITIES: Psychic Surge
WEAKNESSES: Ghost, Steel, Poison

DOES NOT EVOLVE

#0917 TAROUNTULA
String Ball Pokémon

TYPE: BUG

The ball of threads wrapped around its body is elastic enough to deflect the scythes of Scyther, this Pokémon's natural enemy.

The thread it secretes from its rear is as strong as wire. The secret behind the thread's strength is the topic of ongoing research.

HOW TO SAY IT: tuh-ROWN-chuh-luh
IMPERIAL HEIGHT: 1'00"
IMPERIAL WEIGHT: 8.8 lbs.
METRIC WEIGHT: 4.0 kg
METRIC HEIGHT: 0.3 m
GENDER: ♂ ♀
ABILITIES: Insomnia
WEAKNESSES: Fire, Flying, Rock

TAROUNTULA   SPIDOPS

CURLY FORM

#0978 TATSUGIRI
Mimicry Pokémon

TYPE: DRAGON-WATER

This is a small dragon Pokémon. It lives inside the mouth of Dondozo to protect itself from enemies on the outside.

Tatsugiri is an extremely cunning Pokémon. It feigns weakness to lure in prey, then orders its partner to attack.

HOW TO SAY IT: TAHT-soo-gee-ree
IMPERIAL HEIGHT: 1'00"
IMPERIAL WEIGHT: 17.6 lbs.
METRIC HEIGHT: 0.3 m
METRIC WEIGHT: 8.0 kg
GENDER: ♂ ♀
ABILITIES: Commander
WEAKNESSES: Fairy, Dragon

DROOPY FORM

STRETCHY FORM

DOES NOT EVOLVE

TAUROS
Wild Bull Pokémon

#0128

TYPE: NORMAL

Once it takes aim at its prey, it makes a headlong charge. It is famous for its violent nature.

HOW TO SAY IT: TORE-ros
IMPERIAL HEIGHT: 4'07"
IMPERIAL WEIGHT: 194.9 lbs.
METRIC HEIGHT: 1.4 m
METRIC WEIGHT: 88.4 kg
GENDER: ♂
ABILITIES: Intimidate, Anger Point
WEAKNESSES: Fighting

DOES NOT EVOLVE

PALDEAN TAUROS
AQUA BREED
Wild Bull Pokémon

#0128

TYPE: FIGHTING-WATER

This Pokémon blasts water from holes on the tips of its horns—the high-pressure jets pierce right through Tauros's enemies.

It swims by jetting water from its horns. The most notable characteristic of the Aqua Breed is its high body fat, which allows it to float easily.

HOW TO SAY IT: TORE-ros
IMPERIAL HEIGHT: 4'07"
IMPERIAL WEIGHT: 242.5 lbs.
METRIC HEIGHT: 1.4 m
METRIC WEIGHT: 110.0 kg
GENDER: ♂
ABILITIES: Intimidate, Anger Point
WEAKNESSES: Psychic, Flying, Grass, Fairy, Electric

DOES NOT EVOLVE

PALDEAN TAUROS
BLAZE BREED
Wild Bull Pokémon

DOES NOT EVOLVE

TYPE: FIGHTING-FIRE

When heated by fire energy, its horns can get hotter than 1,800 degrees Fahrenheit. Those gored by them will suffer both wounds and burns.

People call this kind of Tauros the Blaze Breed due to the hot air it snorts from its nostrils. Its three tails are intertwined.

HOW TO SAY IT: TORE-ros
IMPERIAL HEIGHT: 4'07"
IMPERIAL WEIGHT: 187.4 lbs.
METRIC HEIGHT: 1.4 m
METRIC WEIGHT: 85.0 kg
GENDER: ♂
ABILITIES: Intimidate, Anger Point
WEAKNESSES: Water, Psychic, Flying, Ground

#0128

PALDEAN TAUROS
COMBAT BREED
Wild Bull Pokémon

TYPE: FIGHTING

This Pokémon has a muscular body and excels at close-quarters combat. It uses its short horns to strike the opponent's weak spots.

This kind of Tauros, known as the Combat Breed, is distinguished by its thick, powerful muscles and its fierce disposition.

HOW TO SAY IT: TORE-ros
IMPERIAL HEIGHT: 4'07"
IMPERIAL WEIGHT: 253.5 lbs.
METRIC HEIGHT: 1.4 m
METRIC WEIGHT: 115.0 kg
GENDER: ♂
ABILITIES: Intimidate, Anger Point
WEAKNESSES: Psychic, Flying, Fairy

DOES NOT EVOLVE

TEDDIURSA

Little Bear Pokémon

#0216

TYPE: NORMAL

This Pokémon discreetly follows Combee to find their hive. It scoops up big dollops of honey in its palms to eat.

Its paws are soaked in oodles of honey. When nervous, Teddiursa will lick its paws and soon have a smile back on its face. blending fruits and pollen collected by Beedrill.

HOW TO SAY IT: TED-dee-UR-sa
IMPERIAL HEIGHT: 2'00"
IMPERIAL WEIGHT: 19.4 lbs.
METRIC HEIGHT: 0.6 m
METRIC WEIGHT: 8.8 kg
GENDER: ♂♀
ABILITIES: Pickup, Quick Feet
WEAKNESSES: Fighting

TEDDIURSA   **URSARING**   **URSALUNA**

TENTACOOL

Jellyfish Pokémon

#0072

TYPE: WATER-POISON

Tentacool is not a particularly strong swimmer. It drifts across the surface of shallow seas as it searches for prey.

This Pokémon is mostly made of water. A Tentacool out in the ocean is very hard to spot, because its body blends in with the sea.

HOW TO SAY IT: TEN-ta-cool
IMPERIAL HEIGHT: 2'11"
IMPERIAL WEIGHT: 100.3 lbs.
METRIC HEIGHT: 0.9 m
METRIC WEIGHT: 45.5 kg
GENDER: ♂ ♀
ABILITIES: Clear Body, Liquid Ooze
WEAKNESSES: Psychic, Electric, Ground

TENTACOOL   **TENTACRUEL**

#0073 TENTACRUEL
Jellyfish Pokémon

TYPE: WATER-POISON

When the red orbs on Tentacruel's head glow brightly, watch out. The Pokémon is about to fire off a burst of ultrasonic waves.

Its 80 tentacles can stretch and shrink freely. Tentacruel ensnares prey in a net of spread-out tentacles, delivering venomous stings to its catch.

HOW TO SAY IT: TEN-ta-crool
IMPERIAL HEIGHT: 5'03"
IMPERIAL WEIGHT: 121.3 lbs.
METRIC HEIGHT: 1.6 m
METRIC WEIGHT: 55.0 kg
GENDER: ♂ ♀
ABILITIES: Clear Body, Liquid Ooze
WEAKNESSES: Psychic, Electric, Ground

TENTACOOL

TENTACRUEL

TYPE: FIRE

#0498

TEPIG
Fire Pig Pokémon

It can deftly dodge its foe's attacks while shooting fireballs from its nose. It roasts berries before it eats them.

It loves to eat roasted berries, but sometimes it gets too excited and burns them to a crisp.

HOW TO SAY IT: TEH-pig
IMPERIAL HEIGHT: 1'08"
IMPERIAL WEIGHT: 21.8 lbs.
METRIC HEIGHT: 0.5 m
METRIC WEIGHT: 9.9 kg
GENDER: ♂ ♀
ABILITIES: Blaze
WEAKNESSES: Water, Ground, Rock

TEPIG

PIGNITE

EMBOAR

TERRAKION
Cavern Pokémon

#0639

LEGENDARY POKÉMON

TYPE: ROCK-FIGHTING

It has phenomenal power. It will mercilessly crush anyone or anything that bullies small Pokémon.

In Unovan legend, Terrakion battled against humans in an effort to protect other Pokémon.

HOW TO SAY IT: tur-RAK-ee-un
IMPERIAL HEIGHT: 6'03"
IMPERIAL WEIGHT: 573.2 lbs.
METRIC HEIGHT: 1.9 m
METRIC WEIGHT: 260.0 kg
GENDER: Unknown
ABILITIES: Justified
WEAKNESSES: Steel, Psychic, Fighting, Water, Fairy, Grass, Ground

DOES NOT EVOLVE

#0828 THIEVUL
Fox Pokémon

TYPE: DARK

It secretly marks potential targets with a scent. By following the scent, it stalks its targets and steals from them when they least expect it.

With a lithe body and sharp claws, it goes around stealing food and eggs. Boltund is its natural enemy.

HOW TO SAY IT: THEEV-ull
IMPERIAL HEIGHT: 3'11"
IMPERIAL WEIGHT: 43.9 lbs.
METRIC HEIGHT: 1.2 m
METRIC WEIGHT: 19.9 kg
GENDER: ♂ ♀
ABILITIES: Run Away, Unburden
WEAKNESSES: Fairy, Bug, Fighting

NICKIT → THIEVUL

THROH #0538
Judo Pokémon

TYPE: FIGHTING

It performs throwing moves with first-rate skill. Over the course of many battles, Throh's belt grows darker as it absorbs its wearer's sweat.

They train in groups of five. Any member that can't keep up will discard its belt and leave the group.

HOW TO SAY IT: THROH
IMPERIAL HEIGHT: 4'03"
IMPERIAL WEIGHT: 122.4 lbs.
METRIC HEIGHT: 1.3 m
METRIC WEIGHT: 55.5 kg
GENDER: ♂
ABILITIES: Guts, Inner Focus
WEAKNESSES: Psychic, Flying, Fairy

DOES NOT EVOLVE

THUNDURUS
Bolt Strike Pokémon

TYPE: ELECTRIC-FLYING

The spikes on its tail discharge immense bolts of lightning. It flies around the Unova region firing off lightning bolts.

As it flies around, it shoots lightning all over the place and causes forest fires. It is therefore disliked.

HOW TO SAY IT: THUN-duh-rus
IMPERIAL HEIGHT: Incarnate Forme: 4'11" /
Therian Forme: 9'10"
IMPERIAL WEIGHT: 134.5 lbs.
METRIC HEIGHT: Incarnate Forme: 1.5 m /
Therian Forme: 3.0 m
METRIC WEIGHT: 61.0 kg
GENDER: ♂
ABILITIES: Incarnate Forme: Prankster /
Therian Forme: Volt Absorb
WEAKNESSES: Ice, Rock

INCARNATE FORME

THERIAN FORME

DOES NOT EVOLVE

THWACKEY

Beat Pokémon

#0811

TYPE: GRASS

The faster a Thwackey can beat out a rhythm with its two sticks, the more respect it wins from its peers.

When it's drumming out rapid beats in battle, it gets so caught up in the rhythm that it won't even notice that it's already knocked out its opponent.

HOW TO SAY IT: THWAK-ee
IMPERIAL HEIGHT: 2'04"
IMPERIAL WEIGHT: 30.9 lbs.
METRIC HEIGHT: 0.7 m
METRIC WEIGHT: 14.0 kg
GENDER: ♂ ♀
ABILITIES: Overgrow
WEAKNESSES: Fire, Flying, Ice, Poison, Bug

GROOKEY **THWACKEY** **RILLABOOM**

#0532

TIMBURR

Muscular Pokémon

TYPE: FIGHTING

It loves helping out with construction projects. It loves it so much that if rain causes work to halt, it swings its log around and throws a tantrum.

Timburr that have started carrying logs that are about three times their size are nearly ready to evolve.

HOW TO SAY IT: TIM-bur
IMPERIAL HEIGHT: 2'00"
IMPERIAL WEIGHT: 27.6 lbs.
METRIC HEIGHT: 0.6 m
METRIC WEIGHT: 12.5 kg
GENDER: ♂ ♀
ABILITIES: Guts, Sheer Force
WEAKNESSES: Psychic, Flying, Fairy

TIMBURR **GURDURR** **CONKELDURR**

TING-LU

Ruinous Pokémon

#1003

LEGENDARY POKÉMON

TYPE: DARK-GROUND

The fear poured into an ancient ritual vessel has clad itself in rocks and dirt to become a Pokémon.

It slowly brings its exceedingly heavy head down upon the ground, splitting the earth open with huge fissures that run over 160 feet deep.

HOW TO SAY IT: TIHNG-loo
IMPERIAL HEIGHT: 8'10"
IMPERIAL WEIGHT: 1,542.6 lbs.
METRIC HEIGHT: 2.7 m
METRIC WEIGHT: 699.7 kg
GENDER: Unknown
ABILITIES: Vessel of Ruin
WEAKNESSES: Fighting, Water, Ice, Fairy, Grass, Bug

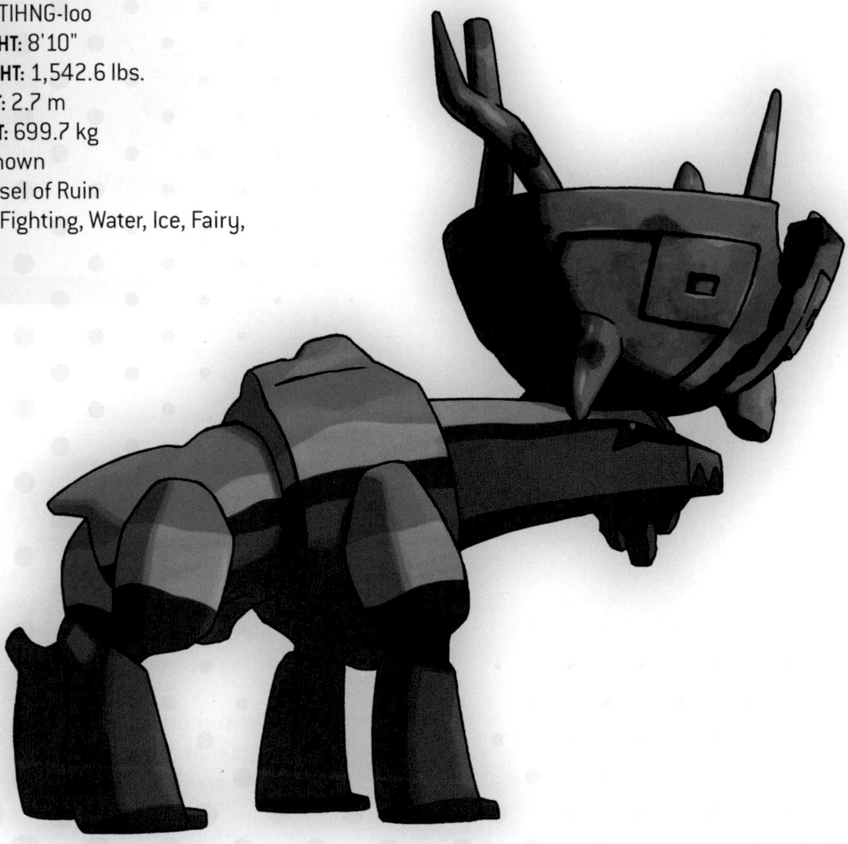

DOES NOT EVOLVE

TINKATINK

Metalsmith Pokémon

TYPE: FAIRY-STEEL

It swings its handmade hammer around to protect itself, but the hammer is often stolen by Pokémon that eat metal.

This Pokémon pounds iron scraps together to make a hammer. It will remake the hammer again and again until it's satisfied with the result.

HOW TO SAY IT: TIHNK-uh-tihnk
IMPERIAL HEIGHT: 1'04"
IMPERIAL WEIGHT: 19.6 lbs.
METRIC HEIGHT: 0.4 m
METRIC WEIGHT: 8.9 kg
GENDER: ♀
ABILITIES: Mold Breaker, Own Tempo
WEAKNESSES: Fire, Ground

TINKATINK

TINKATUFF

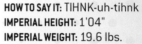

TINKATON

#0959

TINKATON

Hammer Pokémon

TYPE: FAIRY-STEEL

This intelligent Pokémon has a very daring disposition. It knocks rocks into the sky with its hammer, aiming for flying Corviknight.

The hammer tops 220 pounds, yet it gets swung around easily by Tinkaton as it steals whatever it pleases and carries its plunder back home.

HOW TO SAY IT: TIHNK-uh-tuhn
IMPERIAL HEIGHT: 2'04"
IMPERIAL WEIGHT: 248.7 lbs.
METRIC HEIGHT: 0.7 m
METRIC WEIGHT: 112.8 kg
GENDER: ♀
ABILITIES: Mold Breaker, Own Tempo
WEAKNESSES: Fire, Ground

TINKATINK

TINKATUFF

TINKATON

TINKATUFF

Hammer Pokémon

#0958

TYPE: FAIRY-STEEL

This Pokémon will attack groups of Pawniard and Bisharp, gathering metal from them in order to create a large and sturdy hammer.

These Pokémon make their homes in piles of scrap metal. They test the strength of each other's hammers by smashing them together.

HOW TO SAY IT: TIHNK-uh-tuhf
IMPERIAL HEIGHT: 2'04"
IMPERIAL WEIGHT: 130.3 lbs.
METRIC HEIGHT: 0.7 m
METRIC WEIGHT: 59.1 kg
GENDER: ♀
ABILITIES: Mold Breaker, Own Tempo
WEAKNESSES: Fire, Ground

TINKATINK → TINKATUFF → TINKATON

TIRTOUGA

Prototurtle Pokémon

#0564

TYPE: WATER-ROCK

This Pokémon inhabited ancient seas. Although it can only crawl, it still comes up onto land in search of prey.

Tirtouga is considered to be the ancestor of many turtle Pokémon. It was restored to life from a fossil.

HOW TO SAY IT: teer-TOO-gah
IMPERIAL HEIGHT: 2'04"
IMPERIAL WEIGHT: 36.4 lbs.
METRIC HEIGHT: 0.7 m
METRIC WEIGHT: 16.5 kg
GENDER: ♂ ♀
ABILITIES: Solid Rock, Sturdy
WEAKNESSES: Grass, Electric, Fighting, Ground

TIRTOUGA   CARRACOSTA

TOEDSCOOL
#0948
Woodear Pokémon

TYPE: GROUND-GRASS

Toedscool lives in muggy forests. The flaps that fall from its body are chewy and very delicious.

Though it looks like Tentacool, Toedscool is a completely different species. Its legs may be thin, but it can run at a speed of 30 mph.

HOW TO SAY IT: TOHDS-cool
IMPERIAL HEIGHT: 2'11"
IMPERIAL WEIGHT: 72.8 lbs.
METRIC HEIGHT: 0.9 m
METRIC WEIGHT: 33.0 kg
GENDER: ♂ ♀
ABILITIES: Mycelium Might
WEAKNESSES: Fire, Flying, Bug, Ice

TOEDSCOOL → TOEDSCRUEL

TOEDSCRUEL
#0949
Woodear Pokémon

TYPE: GROUND-GRASS

These Pokémon gather into groups and form colonies deep within forests. They absolutely hate it when strangers approach.

It coils its ten tentacles around prey and sucks out their nutrients, causing the prey pain. The folds along the rim of its head are a popular delicacy.

HOW TO SAY IT: TOHDS-croo-ull
IMPERIAL HEIGHT: 6'03"
IMPERIAL WEIGHT: 127.9 lbs.
METRIC HEIGHT: 1.9 m
METRIC WEIGHT: 58.0 kg
GENDER: ♂ ♀
ABILITIES: Mycelium Might
WEAKNESSES: Fire, Flying, Bug, Ice

TOEDSCOOL TOEDSCRUEL

TOGEDEMARU #0777

Roly-Poly Pokémon

TYPE: ELECTRIC-STEEL

With the long hairs on its back, this Pokémon takes in electricity from other electric Pokémon. It stores what it absorbs in an electric sac.

When it's in trouble, it curls up into a ball, makes its fur spikes stand on end, and then discharges electricity indiscriminately.

HOW TO SAY IT: TOH-geh-deh-MAH-roo
IMPERIAL HEIGHT: 1'00"
IMPERIAL WEIGHT: 7.3 lbs.
METRIC HEIGHT: 0.3 m
METRIC WEIGHT: 3.3 kg
GENDER: ♂ ♀
ABILITIES: Iron Barbs, Lightning Rod
WEAKNESSES: Fire, Fighting, Ground

DOES NOT EVOLVE

TOGEKISS #0468

Jubilee Pokémon

TYPE: FAIRY-FLYING

These Pokémon are never seen anywhere near conflict or turmoil. In recent times, they've hardly been seen at all.

Known as a bringer of blessings, it's been depicted on good-luck charms since ancient times.

HOW TO SAY IT: TOE-geh-kiss
IMPERIAL HEIGHT: 4'11"
IMPERIAL WEIGHT: 83.8 lbs.
METRIC HEIGHT: 1.5 m
METRIC WEIGHT: 38.0 kg
GENDER: ♂ ♀
ABILITIES: Hustle, Serene Grace
WEAKNESSES: Steel, Poison, Electric, Ice, Rock

TOGEPI

TOGETIC

TOGEKISS

#0175 TOGEPI
Spike Ball Pokémon

TYPE: FAIRY

The shell seems to be filled with joy.
It is said that it will share good luck
when treated kindly.

It is considered to be a symbol of
good luck. Its shell is said to be filled
with happiness.

HOW TO SAY IT: TOE-ghep-pee
IMPERIAL HEIGHT: 1'00"
IMPERIAL WEIGHT: 3.3 lbs.
METRIC HEIGHT: 0.3 m
METRIC WEIGHT: 1.5 kg
GENDER: ♂ ♀
ABILITIES: Hustle, Serene Grace
WEAKNESSES: Steel, Poison

TOGEPI   **TOGETIC**   **TOGEKISS**

#0176 TOGETIC
Happiness Pokémon

TYPE: FAIRY-FLYING

They say that it will appear before kindhearted,
caring people and shower them with happiness.

It grows dispirited if it is not with kind people. It
can float in midair without moving its wings.

HOW TO SAY IT: TOE-ghet-tic
IMPERIAL HEIGHT: 2'00"
IMPERIAL WEIGHT: 7.1 lbs.
METRIC HEIGHT: 0.6 m
METRIC WEIGHT: 3.2 kg
GENDER: ♂ ♀
ABILITIES: Hustle, Serene Grace
WEAKNESSES: Steel, Poison, Electric, Ice, Rock

TOGEPI   **TOGETIC**   **TOGEKISS**

TORCHIC
Chick Pokémon

#0255

TYPE: FIRE

Torchic sticks with its Trainer, following behind with unsteady steps. This Pokémon breathes fire of over 1,800 degrees Fahrenheit, including fireballs that leave the foe scorched black.

Torchic has a place inside its body where it keeps its flame. Give it a hug—it will be glowing with warmth. This Pokémon is covered all over by a fluffy coat of down.

HOW TO SAY IT: TOR-chick
IMPERIAL HEIGHT: 1'04"
IMPERIAL WEIGHT: 5.5 lbs.
METRIC HEIGHT: 0.4 m
METRIC WEIGHT: 2.5 kg
GENDER: ♂ ♀
ABILITIES: Blaze
WEAKNESSES: Water, Ground, Rock

TORCHIC **COMBUSKEN** **BLAZIKEN** **MEGA BLAZIKEN**

TORKOAL
Coal Pokémon

#0324

TYPE: FIRE

It burns coal inside its shell for energy. It blows out black soot if it is endangered.

Coal is the source of Torkoal's energy. Large amounts of coal can be found in the mountains where they live.

HOW TO SAY IT: TOR-coal
IMPERIAL HEIGHT: 1'08"
IMPERIAL WEIGHT: 177.3 lbs.
METRIC HEIGHT: 0.5 m
METRIC WEIGHT: 80.4 kg
GENDER: ♂ ♀
ABILITIES: White Smoke, Drought
WEAKNESSES: Water, Ground, Rock

DOES NOT EVOLVE

TORNADUS
Cyclone Pokémon

INCARNATE FORME

TYPE: FLYING

The lower half of its body is wrapped in a cloud of energy. It zooms through the sky at 200 mph.

Tornadus expels massive energy from its tail, causing severe storms. Its power is great enough to blow houses away.

HOW TO SAY IT: tohr-NAY-dus
IMPERIAL HEIGHT: Incarnate Forme: 4'11"
                 Therian Forme: 4'07"
IMPERIAL WEIGHT: 138.9 lbs.
METRIC HEIGHT: Incarnate Forme: 1.5 m
               Therian Forme: 1.4 m
METRIC WEIGHT: 63.0 kg
GENDER: ♂ ♀
ABILITIES: Incarnate Forme: Prankster
             Therian Forme: Regenerator
WEAKNESSES: Electric, Ice, Rock

THERIAN FORME

TORRACAT

Fire Cat Pokémon

#0726

TYPE: FIRE

It can act spoiled if it grows close to its Trainer. A powerful Pokémon, its sharp claws can leave its Trainer's whole body covered in scratches.

When its mane is standing on end, you can tell it's feeling good. When it isn't feeling well, its fur will lie down flat.

HOW TO SAY IT: TOR-ruh-cat
IMPERIAL HEIGHT: 2'04"
IMPERIAL WEIGHT: 55.1 lbs.
METRIC HEIGHT: 0.7 m
METRIC WEIGHT: 25.0 kg
GENDER: ♂ ♀
ABILITIES: Blaze
WEAKNESSES: Water, Ground, Rock

LITTEN   TORRACAT   INCINEROAR

TORTERRA

Continent Pokémon

#0389

TYPE: GRASS-GROUND

Ancient people imagined that beneath the ground, a gigantic Torterra dwelled.

Small Pokémon occasionally gather on its unmoving back to begin building their nests.

HOW TO SAY IT: tor-TER-ra
IMPERIAL HEIGHT: 7'03"
IMPERIAL WEIGHT: 683.4 lbs.
METRIC HEIGHT: 2.2 m
METRIC WEIGHT: 310.0 kg
GENDER: ♂ ♀
ABILITIES: Overgrow
WEAKNESSES: Fire, Flying, Bug, Ice

TURTWIG   GROTLE   TORTERRA

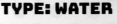

TOTODILE
Big Jaw Pokémon

#0158

TYPE: WATER

Despite the smallness of its body, Totodile's jaws are very powerful. While the Pokémon may think it is just playfully nipping, its bite has enough power to cause serious injury.

HOW TO SAY IT: TOE-toe-dyle
IMPERIAL HEIGHT: 2'00"
IMPERIAL WEIGHT: 20.9 lbs.
METRIC HEIGHT: 0.6 m
METRIC WEIGHT: 9.5 kg
GENDER: ♂ ♀
ABILITIES: Torrent
WEAKNESSES: Grass, Electric

TOTODILE **CROCONAW** **FERALIGATR**

TOUCANNON
Cannon Pokémon

#0733

TYPE: NORMAL-FLYING

They smack beaks with others of their kind to communicate. The strength and number of hits tell each other how they feel.

Known for forming harmonious couples, this Pokémon is brought to wedding ceremonies as a good-luck charm.

HOW TO SAY IT: too-CAN-nun
IMPERIAL HEIGHT: 3'07"
IMPERIAL WEIGHT: 57.3 lbs.
METRIC HEIGHT: 1.1 m
METRIC WEIGHT: 26.0 kg
GENDER: ♂ ♀
ABILITIES: Keen Eye, Skill Link
WEAKNESSES: Electric, Ice, Rock

PIKIPEK **TRUMBEAK** **TOUCANNON**

TOXAPEX #0748

Brutal Star Pokémon

TYPE: POISON-WATER

This Pokémon lives within a dome made by its own legs. Toxapex monitors its surroundings by sensing the flow of the tide through its spikes.

Toxapex gets into fierce battles with Bruxish over areas where warm ocean currents flow, but the odds are always against it.

HOW TO SAY IT: TOX-uh-pex
IMPERIAL HEIGHT: 2'04"
IMPERIAL WEIGHT: 32.0 lbs.
METRIC HEIGHT: 0.7 m
METRIC WEIGHT: 14.5 kg
GENDER: ♂ ♀
ABILITIES: Merciless, Limber
WEAKNESSES: Psychic, Electric, Ground

MAREANIE ➡ TOXAPEX

TOXEL #0848

Baby Pokémon

TYPE: ELECTRIC-POISON

It has no problem drinking dirty water. An organ inside Toxel's body filters such water into a poisonous liquid that is harmless to Toxel.

This selfish, attention-seeking Pokémon stores poison and electricity in two different sacs inside its body.

HOW TO SAY IT: TAHKS-ull
IMPERIAL HEIGHT: 1'04"
IMPERIAL WEIGHT: 24.3 lbs.
METRIC HEIGHT: 0.4 m
METRIC WEIGHT: 11.0 kg
GENDER: ♂ ♀
ABILITIES: Rattled, Static
WEAKNESSES: Psychic, Ground

TOXEL ➡ TOXTRICITY

TOXICROAK
Toxic Mouth Pokémon

TYPE: POISON-FIGHTING

Swaying and dodging the attacks of its foes, it weaves its flexible body in close, then lunges out with its poisonous claws.

It has a poison sac at its throat. When it croaks, the stored poison is churned for greater potency.

HOW TO SAY IT: TOX-uh-croak
IMPERIAL HEIGHT: 4'03"
IMPERIAL WEIGHT: 97.9 lbs.
METRIC HEIGHT: 1.3 m
METRIC WEIGHT: 44.4 kg
GENDER: ♂ ♀
ABILITIES: Anticipation, Dry Skin
WEAKNESSES: Psychic, Flying, Ground

CROAGUNK   TOXICROAK

TOXTRICITY

Punk Pokémon

#0849

LOW KEY FORM

TYPE: ELECTRIC-POISON

Many youths admire the way this Pokémon listlessly picks fights and keeps its cool no matter what opponent it faces.

As it gulps down stagnant water and generates electricity in its body, a sound like a rhythm played by a bass guitar reverberates all around.

HOW TO SAY IT: tahks-TRIS-ih-tee
IMPERIAL HEIGHT: 5'03"
IMPERIAL WEIGHT: 88.2 lbs.
METRIC HEIGHT: 1.6 m
METRIC WEIGHT: 40.0 kg
GENDER: ♂ ♀
ABILITIES: Punk Rock, Minus
WEAKNESSES: Psychic, Ground

AMPED FORM

TOXEL   **TOXTRICITY**

GIGANTAMAX TOXTRICITY

Its excessive electric energy is its weapon. This Pokémon can build up more electricity than any thundercloud.

Out of control after its own poison penetrated its brain, it tears across the land in a rampage, contaminating the earth with toxic sweat.

IMPERIAL HEIGHT: 78'09"+
IMPERIAL WEIGHT: ????.? lbs.
METRIC HEIGHT: 24.0+ m
METRIC WEIGHT: ???.? kg

#0520 TRANQUILL
Wild Pigeon Pokémon

TYPE: NORMAL-FLYING

It can fly moderately quickly. No matter how far it travels, it can always find its way back to its master and its nest.

These bright Pokémon have acute memories. Apparently delivery workers often choose them as their partners.

HOW TO SAY IT: TRAN-kwil
IMPERIAL HEIGHT: 2'00"
IMPERIAL WEIGHT: 33.1 lbs.
METRIC HEIGHT: 0.6 m
METRIC WEIGHT: 15.0 kg
GENDER: ♂ ♀
ABILITIES: Big Pecks, Super Luck
WEAKNESSES: Electric, Ice, Rock

PIDOVE **TRANQUILL** **UNFEZANT**

#0328 TRAPINCH
Ant Pit Pokémon

TYPE: GROUND

Its nest is a sloped, bowl-like pit in the desert. Once something has fallen in, there is no escape.

It makes an inescapable conical pit and lies in wait at the bottom for prey to come tumbling down.

HOW TO SAY IT: TRAP-inch
IMPERIAL HEIGHT: 2'04"
IMPERIAL WEIGHT: 33.1 lbs.
METRIC HEIGHT: 0.7 m
METRIC WEIGHT: 15.0 kg
GENDER: ♂ ♀
ABILITIES: Hyper Cutter, Arena Trap
WEAKNESSES: Water, Grass, Ice

TRAPINCH **VIBRAVA** **FLYGON**

TREECKO
Wood Gecko Pokémon

#0252

TYPE: GRASS

Treecko has small hooks on the bottom of its feet that enable it to scale vertical walls. This Pokémon attacks by slamming foes with its thick tail.

Treecko is cool, calm, and collected—it never panics under any situation. If a bigger foe were to glare at this Pokémon, it would glare right back without conceding an inch of ground.

HOW TO SAY IT: TREE-ko
IMPERIAL HEIGHT: 1'08"
IMPERIAL WEIGHT: 11.0 lbs.
METRIC HEIGHT: 0.5 m
METRIC WEIGHT: 5.0 kg
GENDER: ♂ ♀
ABILITIES: Overgrow
WEAKNESSES: Fire, Flying, Ice, Poison, Bug

TREECKO   **GROVYLE**   **SCEPTILE**   **MEGA SCEPTILE**

TREVENANT
Elder Tree Pokémon

#0709

TYPE: GHOST-GRASS

People fear it due to a belief that it devours any who try to cut down trees in its forest, but to the Pokémon it shares its woods with, it's kind.

Small roots that extend from the tips of this Pokémon's feet can tie into the trees of the forest and give Trevenant control over them.

HOW TO SAY IT: TREV-uh-nunt
IMPERIAL HEIGHT: 4'11"
IMPERIAL WEIGHT: 156.5 lbs.
METRIC HEIGHT: 1.5 m
METRIC WEIGHT: 71.0 kg
GENDER: ♂ ♀
ABILITIES: Natural Cure, Frisk
WEAKNESSES: Ghost, Fire, Flying, Dark, Ice

PHANTUMP   **TREVENANT**

#0357 TROPIUS
Fruit Pokémon

TYPE: GRASS-FLYING

It lives in tropical jungles. The bunch of fruit around its neck is delicious. The fruit grows twice a year.

Delicious fruits grew out from around its neck because it always ate the same kind of fruit.

HOW TO SAY IT: TROP-ee-us
IMPERIAL HEIGHT: 6'07"
IMPERIAL WEIGHT: 220.5 lbs.
METRIC HEIGHT: 2.0 m
METRIC WEIGHT: 100.0 kg
GENDER: ♂ ♀
ABILITIES: Chlorophyll, Solar Power
WEAKNESSES: Fire, Flying, Ice, Poison, Rock

DOES NOT EVOLVE

#0568 TRUBBISH
Trash Bag Pokémon

TYPE: POISON

Its favorite places are unsanitary ones. If you leave trash lying around, you could even find one of these Pokémon living in your room.

This Pokémon was born from a bag stuffed with trash. Galarian Weezing relish the fumes belched by Trubbish.

HOW TO SAY IT: TRUB-bish
IMPERIAL HEIGHT: 2'00"
IMPERIAL WEIGHT: 68.3 lbs.
METRIC HEIGHT: 0.6 m
METRIC WEIGHT: 31.0 kg
GENDER: ♂ ♀
ABILITIES: Stench, Sticky Hold
WEAKNESSES: Psychic, Ground

TRUBBISH → GARBODOR

TRUMBEAK
Bugle Beak Pokémon

#0732

TYPE: NORMAL-FLYING

It can bend the tip of its beak to produce over a hundred different cries at will.

From its mouth, it fires the seeds of berries it has eaten. The scattered seeds give rise to new plants.

HOW TO SAY IT: TRUM-beak
IMPERIAL HEIGHT: 2'00"
IMPERIAL WEIGHT: 32.6 lbs.
METRIC HEIGHT: 0.6 m
METRIC WEIGHT: 14.8 kg
GENDER: ♂ ♀
ABILITIES: Keen Eye, Skill Link
WEAKNESSES: Electric, Ice, Rock

PIKIPEK

TRUMBEAK

TOUCANNON

TSAREENA
Fruit Pokémon

#0763

TYPE: GRASS

This Pokémon is proud and aggressive. However, it is said that a Tsareena will instantly become calm if someone touches the crown on its calyx.

This Pokémon launches fierce yet elegant kicks with its long, slender legs. It views Quaquaval as its rival.

HOW TO SAY IT: zar-EE-nuh
IMPERIAL HEIGHT: 3'11"
IMPERIAL WEIGHT: 47.2 lbs.
METRIC HEIGHT: 1.2 m
METRIC WEIGHT: 21.4 kg
GENDER: ♀
ABILITIES: Leaf Guard, Queenly Majesty
WEAKNESSES: Fire, Flying, Ice, Poison, Bug

BOUNSWEET

STEENEE

TSAREENA

TURTONATOR
Blast Turtle Pokémon

TYPE: FIRE-DRAGON

Explosive substances coat the shell on its back. Enemies that dare attack it will be blown away by an immense detonation.

Eating sulfur in its volcanic habitat is what causes explosive compounds to develop in its shell. Its droppings are also dangerously explosive.

HOW TO SAY IT: TURT-nay-ter
IMPERIAL HEIGHT: 6'07"
IMPERIAL WEIGHT: 467.4 lbs.
METRIC HEIGHT: 2.0 m
METRIC WEIGHT: 212.0 kg
GENDER: ♂ ♀
ABILITIES: Shell Armor
WEAKNESSES: Ground, Rock, Dragon

DOES NOT EVOLVE

#0387

TURTWIG
Tiny Leaf Pokémon

TYPE: GRASS

Photosynthesis occurs across its body under the sun. The shell on its back is actually hardened soil.

It undertakes photosynthesis with its body, making oxygen. The leaf on its head wilts if it is thirsty.

HOW TO SAY IT: TUR-twig
IMPERIAL HEIGHT: 1'04"
IMPERIAL WEIGHT: 22.5 lbs.
METRIC HEIGHT: 0.4 m
METRIC WEIGHT: 10.2 kg
GENDER: ♂ ♀
ABILITIES: Overgrow
WEAKNESSES: Fire, Flying, Ice, Poison, Bug

TURTWIG   **GROTLE**   **TORTERRA**

TYMPOLE

Tadpole Pokémon

#0535

TYPE: WATER

Graceful ripples running across the water's surface are a sure sign that Tympole are singing in high-pitched voices below.

It uses sound waves to communicate with others of its kind. People and other Pokémon species can't hear its cries of warning.

HOW TO SAY IT: TIM-pohl
IMPERIAL HEIGHT: 1'08"
IMPERIAL WEIGHT: 9.9 lbs.
METRIC HEIGHT: 0.5 m
METRIC WEIGHT: 4.5 kg
GENDER: ♂ ♀
ABILITIES: Swift Swim, Hydration
WEAKNESSES: Grass, Electric

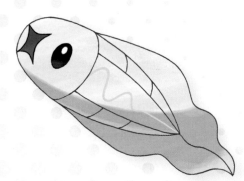

TYMPOLE   PALPITOAD   SEISMITOAD

TYNAMO

EleFish Pokémon

#0602

TYPE: ELECTRIC

While one alone doesn't have much power, a chain of many Tynamo can be as powerful as lightning.

These Pokémon move in schools. They have an electricity-generating organ, so they discharge electricity if in danger.

HOW TO SAY IT: TY-nuh-moh
IMPERIAL HEIGHT: 0'08"
IMPERIAL WEIGHT: 0.7 lbs.
METRIC HEIGHT: 0.2 m
METRIC WEIGHT: 0.3 kg
GENDER: ♂ ♀
ABILITIES: Levitate
WEAKNESSES: Ground

TYNAMO   EELEKTRIK   EELEKTROSS

TYPE: NULL
Synthetic Pokémon

TYPE: NORMAL

Rumor has it that the theft of top-secret research notes led to a new instance of this Pokémon being created in the Galar region.

It was modeled after a mighty Pokémon of myth. The mask placed upon it limits its power in order to keep it under control.

HOW TO SAY IT: TYPE NULL
IMPERIAL HEIGHT: 6'03"
IMPERIAL WEIGHT: 265.7 lbs.
METRIC HEIGHT: 1.9 m
METRIC WEIGHT: 120.5 kg
GENDER: Unknown
ABILITIES: Battle Armor
WEAKNESSES: Fighting

TYPE: NULL   SILVALLY

TYPHLOSION
Volcano Pokémon

TYPE: FIRE

It attacks using blasts of fire. It creates heat shimmers with intense fire to hide itself.

HOW TO SAY IT: tie-FLOW-zhun
IMPERIAL HEIGHT: 5'07"
IMPERIAL WEIGHT: 175.3 lbs.
METRIC HEIGHT: 1.7 m
METRIC WEIGHT: 79.5 kg
GENDER: ♂ ♀
ABILITIES: Blaze
WEAKNESSES: Water, Ground, Rock

CYNDAQUIL ➡ QUILAVA ➡ TYPHLOSION

HISUIAN TYPHLOSION
Ghost Flame Pokémon

TYPE: FIRE-GHOST

Said to purify lost, forsaken souls with its flames and guide them to the afterlife. I believe its form has been influenced by the energy of the sacred mountain towering at Hisui's center.

HOW TO SAY IT: tie-FLOW-zhun
IMPERIAL HEIGHT: 5'03"
IMPERIAL WEIGHT: 153.9 lbs.
METRIC HEIGHT: 1.6 m
METRIC WEIGHT: 69.8 kg
GENDER: ♂ ♀
ABILITIES: N/A
WEAKNESSES: Water, Ghost, Ground, Dark, Rock

CYNDAQUIL QUILAVA HISUIAN TYPHLOSION

TYRANITAR

Armor Pokémon

#0248

TYPE: ROCK-DARK

Extremely strong, it can change the landscape. It is so insolent that it doesn't care about others.

In just one of its mighty hands, it has the power to make the ground shake and mountains crumble.

HOW TO SAY IT: tie-RAN-uh-tar
IMPERIAL HEIGHT: 6'07"
IMPERIAL WEIGHT: 445.3 lbs.
METRIC HEIGHT: 2.0 m
METRIC WEIGHT: 202.0 kg
GENDER: ♂ ♀
ABILITIES: Sand Stream
WEAKNESSES: Steel, Fighting, Water, Fairy, Grass, Bug, Ground

MEGA TYRANITAR

TYPE: ROCK-DARK

Due to the colossal power poured into it, this Pokémon's back split right open. Its destructive instincts are the only thing keeping it moving.

The effects of Mega Evolution make it more ferocious than ever. It's unclear whether it can even hear its Trainer's orders.

IMPERIAL HEIGHT: 8'02"
IMPERIAL WEIGHT: 562.2 lbs.
METRIC HEIGHT: 2.5 m
METRIC WEIGHT: 255.0 kg

LARVITAR → **PUPITAR** → **TYRANITAR** → **MEGA TYRANITAR**

TYRANTRUM

Despot Pokémon

#0697

TYPE: ROCK-DRAGON

This Pokémon is from about 1000236years ago. It has the presence of a king, vicious but magnificent.

A single bite of Tyrantrum's massive jaws will demolish a car. This Pokémon was the king of the ancient world.

HOW TO SAY IT: tie-RAN-trum
IMPERIAL HEIGHT: 8'02"
IMPERIAL WEIGHT: 595.2 lbs.
METRIC HEIGHT: 2.5 m
METRIC WEIGHT: 270.0 kg
GENDER: ♂ ♀
ABILITIES: Strong Jaw
WEAKNESSES: Steel, Fighting, Dragon, Ice, Fairy, Ground

TYRUNT   TYRANTRUM

TYROGUE

Scuffle Pokémon

#0236

TYPE: FIGHTING

It is always bursting with energy. To make itself stronger, it keeps on fighting even if it loses.

Even though it is small, it can't be ignored because it will slug any handy target without warning.

HOW TO SAY IT: tie-ROHG
IMPERIAL HEIGHT: 2'04"
IMPERIAL WEIGHT: 46.3 lbs.
METRIC HEIGHT: 0.7 m
METRIC WEIGHT: 21.0 kg
GENDER: ♂
ABILITIES: Guts, Steadfast
WEAKNESSES: Psychic, Flying, Fairy

TYROGUE

HITMONLEE

HITMONCHAN

HITMONTOP

TYRUNT #0696
Royal Heir Pokémon

TYPE: ROCK-DRAGON

This is an ancient Pokémon, revived in modern times. It has a violent disposition, and it'll tear apart anything it gets between its hefty jaws.

This Pokémon is selfish and likes to be pampered. It can also inflict grievous wounds on its Trainer just by playing around.

HOW TO SAY IT: TIE-runt
IMPERIAL HEIGHT: 2'07"
IMPERIAL WEIGHT: 57.3 lbs.
METRIC HEIGHT: 0.8 m
METRIC WEIGHT: 26.0 kg
GENDER: ♂ ♀
ABILITIES: Strong Jaw
WEAKNESSES: Steel, Fighting, Dragon, Ice, Fairy, Ground

TYRUNT   TYRANTRUM

TYPE: DARK

UMBREON #0197
Moonlight Pokémon

When exposed to the moon's aura, the rings on its body glow faintly and it gains a mysterious power.

When darkness falls, the rings on the body begin to glow, striking fear in the hearts of anyone nearby.

HOW TO SAY IT: UM-bree-on
IMPERIAL HEIGHT: 3'03"
IMPERIAL WEIGHT: 59.5 lbs.
METRIC HEIGHT: 1.0 m
METRIC WEIGHT: 27.0 kg
GENDER: ♂ ♀
ABILITIES: Synchronize
WEAKNESSES: Fairy, Bug, Fighting

EEVEE   UMBREON

MALE FORM

FEMALE FORM

PIDOVE → TRANQUILL → UNFEZANT

UNFEZANT
Proud Pokémon

#0521

TYPE: NORMAL-FLYING

Unfezant are exceptional fliers. The females are known for their stamina, while the males outclass them in terms of speed.

This Pokémon is intelligent and intensely proud. People will sit up and take notice if you become the Trainer of one.

HOW TO SAY IT: un-FEZ-ent
IMPERIAL HEIGHT: 3'11"
IMPERIAL WEIGHT: 63.9 lbs.
METRIC HEIGHT: 1.2 m
METRIC WEIGHT: 29.0 kg
GENDER: ♂ ♀
ABILITIES: Big Pecks, Super Luck
WEAKNESSES: Electric, Ice, Rock

UNOWN
Symbol Pokémon

#0201

TYPE: PSYCHIC

This Pokémon is shaped like ancient writing. It is a mystery as to which came first, the ancient writings or the various Unown. Research into this topic is ongoing but nothing is known.

HOW TO SAY IT: un-KNOWN
IMPERIAL HEIGHT: 1'08"
IMPERIAL WEIGHT: 11.0 lbs.
METRIC HEIGHT: 0.5 m
METRIC WEIGHT: 5.0 kg
GENDER: Unknown
ABILITIES: Levitate
WEAKNESSES: Ghost, Dark, Bug

DOES NOT EVOLVE

#0901 URSALUNA
Peat Pokémon

TYPE: GROUND-NORMAL

I believe it was Hisui's swampy terrain that gave Ursaluna its burly physique and newfound capacity to manipulate peat at will.

This Pokémon is intelligent and intensely proud. People will sit up and take notice if you become the Trainer of one.

HOW TO SAY IT: UR-sa-LOO-nuh
IMPERIAL HEIGHT: 7'10"
IMPERIAL WEIGHT: 639.3 lbs.
METRIC HEIGHT: 2.4 m
METRIC WEIGHT: 290.0 kg
GENDER: ♂ ♀
ABILITIES: N/A
WEAKNESSES: Water, Grass, Ice, Fighting

TEDDIURSA **URSARING** **URSALUNA**

URSARING #0217
Hibernator Pokémon

TYPE: NORMAL

It usually wears a hardened expression, but when it's licking up honey—which it loves—the joy it feels will cause it to break into a wide grin.

It is quite skilled at climbing trees. If it comes across a Primeape while searching for berries in the treetops, trouble will surely ensue.

HOW TO SAY IT: UR-sa-ring
IMPERIAL HEIGHT: 5'11"
IMPERIAL WEIGHT: 277.3 lbs.
METRIC HEIGHT: 1.8 m
METRIC WEIGHT: 125.8 kg
GENDER: ♂ ♀
ABILITIES: Guts, Quick Feet
WEAKNESSES: Fighting

TEDDIURSA **URSARING** **URSALUNA**

URSHIFU
RAPID STRIKE STYLE
Wushu Pokémon

#0892

TYPE: FIGHTING-WATER

It's believed that this Pokémon modeled its fighting style on the flow of a river—sometimes rapid, sometimes calm.

This form of Urshifu is a strong believer in defeating foes by raining many blows down on them. Its strikes are nonstop, flowing like a river.

HOW TO SAY IT: UR-shee-foo
IMPERIAL HEIGHT: 6'03"
IMPERIAL WEIGHT: 231.5 lbs.
METRIC HEIGHT: 1.9 m
METRIC WEIGHT: 105.0 kg
GENDER: ♂ ♀
ABILITIES: Unseen Fist
WEAKNESSES: Psychic, Flying, Grass, Fairy, Electric

KUBFU   ➡   URSHIFU

GIGANTAMAX
URSHIFU
RAPID STRIKE STYLE

As it waits for the right moment to unleash its Gigantamax power, this Pokémon maintains a perfect one-legged stance. It won't even twitch.

All it takes is a glare from this Pokémon to take the lives of those with evil in their hearts—or so they say.

IMPERIAL HEIGHT: 84'04"+
IMPERIAL WEIGHT: ????.? lbs.
METRIC HEIGHT: 26.0+ m
METRIC WEIGHT: ???.? kg

URSHIFU
SINGLE STRIKE STYLE
Wushu Pokémon

#0892

TYPE: FIGHTING-DARK

This form of Urshifu is a strong believer in the one-hit KO. Its strategy is to leap in close to foes and land a devastating blow with a hardened fist.

Inhabiting the mountains of a distant region, this Pokémon races across sheer cliffs, training its legs and refining its moves.

HOW TO SAY IT: UR-shee-foo
IMPERIAL HEIGHT: 6'03"
IMPERIAL WEIGHT: 231.5 lbs.
METRIC HEIGHT: 1.9 m
METRIC WEIGHT: 105.0 kg
GENDER: ♂ ♀
ABILITIES: Unseen Fist
WEAKNESSES: Fairy, Flying, Fighting

KUBFU   **URSHIFU**

GIGANTAMAX
URSHIFU
SINGLE STRIKE STYLE

People call it the embodiment of rage. It's said that this Pokémon's terrifying expression and shout will rid the world of malevolence.

The energy released by this Pokémon's fists forms shock waves that can blow away Dynamax Pokémon in just one hit.

IMPERIAL HEIGHT: 95'02"+
IMPERIAL WEIGHT: ????.? lbs.
METRIC HEIGHT: 29.0+ m
METRIC WEIGHT: ???.? kg

LEGENDARY POKÉMON

#0480

UXIE
Knowledge Pokémon

DOES NOT EVOLVE

TYPE: PSYCHIC

Known as "The Being of Knowledge." It is said that it can wipe out the memory of those who see its eyes.

It is said that its emergence gave humans the intelligence to improve their quality of life.

HOW TO SAY IT: YOOK-zee
IMPERIAL HEIGHT: 1'00"
IMPERIAL WEIGHT: 0.7 lbs.
METRIC HEIGHT: 0.3 m
METRIC WEIGHT: 0.3 kg
GENDER: Unknown
ABILITIES: Levitate
WEAKNESSES: Ghost, Dark, Bug

VANILLISH
Icy Snow Pokémon

#0583

TYPE: ICE

By drinking pure water, it grows its icy body. This Pokémon can be hard to find on days with warm, sunny weather.

It blasts enemies with cold air reaching −148 degrees Fahrenheit, freezing them solid. But it spares their lives afterward—it's a kind Pokémon.

HOW TO SAY IT: vuh-NIHL-lish
IMPERIAL HEIGHT: 3'07"
IMPERIAL WEIGHT: 90.4 lbs.
METRIC HEIGHT: 1.1 m
METRIC WEIGHT: 41.0 kg
GENDER: ♂ ♀
ABILITIES: Ice Body, Snow Cloak
WEAKNESSES: Fire, Steel, Fighting, Rock

VANILLITE   **VANILLISH**   **VANILLUXE**

VANILLITE
Fresh Snow Pokémon

#0582

TYPE: ICE

Unable to survive in hot areas, it makes itself comfortable by breathing out air cold enough to cause snow. It burrows into the snow to sleep.

Supposedly, this Pokémon was born from an icicle. It spews out freezing air at −58 degrees Fahrenheit to make itself more comfortable.

HOW TO SAY IT: vuh-NIHL-lyte
IMPERIAL HEIGHT: 1'04"
IMPERIAL WEIGHT: 12.6 lbs.
METRIC HEIGHT: 0.4 m
METRIC WEIGHT: 5.7 kg
GENDER: ♂ ♀
ABILITIES: Ice Body, Snow Cloak
WEAKNESSES: Fire, Steel, Fighting, Rock

VANILLITE   VANILLISH   VANILLUXE

#0584

VANILLUXE
Snowstorm Pokémon

TYPE: ICE

When its anger reaches a breaking point, this Pokémon unleashes a fierce blizzard that freezes every creature around it, be they friend or foe.

People believe this Pokémon formed when two Vanillish stuck together. Its body temperature is roughly 21 degrees Fahrenheit.

HOW TO SAY IT: vuh-NIHL-lux
IMPERIAL HEIGHT: 4'03"
IMPERIAL WEIGHT: 126.8 lbs.
METRIC HEIGHT: 1.3 m
METRIC WEIGHT: 57.5 kg
GENDER: ♂ ♀
ABILITIES: Ice Body, Snow Warning
WEAKNESSES: Fire, Steel, Fighting, Rock

VANILLITE   VANILLISH   VANILLUXE

VAPOREON #0134

Bubble Jet Pokémon

TYPE: WATER

It lives close to water. Its long tail is ridged with a fin, which is often mistaken for a mermaid's.

Its cell composition is similar to water molecules. As a result, it can't be seen when it melts away into water.

HOW TO SAY IT: vay-POUR-ree-on
IMPERIAL HEIGHT: 3'03"
IMPERIAL WEIGHT: 63.9 lbs.
METRIC HEIGHT: 1.0 m
METRIC WEIGHT: 29.0 kg
GENDER: ♂ ♀
ABILITIES: Water Absorb
WEAKNESSES: Grass, Electric

EEVEE   **VAPOREON**

VAROOM #0965

Single-Cyl Pokémon

TYPE: STEEL-POISON

It is said that this Pokémon was born when an Unknown poison Pokémon entered and inspirited an engine left at a scrap-processing factory.

The steel section is Varoom's actual body. This Pokémon clings to rocks and converts the minerals within into energy to fuel its activities.

HOW TO SAY IT: vuh-ROOM
IMPERIAL HEIGHT: 3'03"
IMPERIAL WEIGHT: 77.2 lbs.
METRIC HEIGHT: 1.0 m
METRIC WEIGHT: 35.0 kg
GENDER: ♂ ♀
ABILITIES: Overcoat
WEAKNESSES: Fire, Ground

VAROOM   **REVAVROOM**

#0976

VELUZA
Jettison Pokémon

TYPE: WATER-PSYCHIC

When Veluza discards unnecessary flesh, its mind becomes honed and its psychic power increases. The spare flesh has a mild but delicious flavor.

Veluza has excellent regenerative capabilities. It sheds spare flesh from its body to boost its agility, then charges at its prey.

HOW TO SAY IT: veh-LOOZ-uh
IMPERIAL HEIGHT: 8'02"
IMPERIAL WEIGHT: 198.4 lbs.
METRIC HEIGHT: 2.5 m
METRIC WEIGHT: 90.0 kg
GENDER: ♂ ♀
ABILITIES: Mold Breaker
WEAKNESSES: Ghost, Dark, Grass, Electric, Bug

DOES NOT EVOLVE

#0543

VENIPEDE
Centipede Pokémon

TYPE: BUG-POISON

Venipede and Sizzlipede are similar species, but when the two meet, a huge fight ensues.

Its fangs are highly venomous. If this Pokémon finds prey it thinks it can eat, it leaps for them without any thought of how things might turn out.

HOW TO SAY IT: VEHN-ih-peed
IMPERIAL HEIGHT: 1'04"
IMPERIAL WEIGHT: 11.7 lbs.
METRIC HEIGHT: 0.4 m
METRIC WEIGHT: 5.3 kg
GENDER: ♂ ♀
ABILITIES: Poison Point, Swarm
WEAKNESSES: Fire, Psychic, Flying, Rock

VENIPEDE   **WHIRLIPEDE**   **SCOLIPEDE**

TYPE: BUG-POISON

The wings are covered with dustlike scales. Every time it flaps its wings, it looses highly toxic dust.

When it attacks, it flaps its large wings violently to scatter its poisonous powder all around.

HOW TO SAY IT: VEH-no-moth
IMPERIAL HEIGHT: 4'11"
IMPERIAL WEIGHT: 27.6 lbs.
METRIC HEIGHT: 1.5 m
METRIC WEIGHT: 12.5 kg
GENDER: ♂ ♀
ABILITIES: Shield Dust, Tinted Lens
WEAKNESSES: Fire, Psychic, Flying, Rock

#0049

VENOMOTH
Poison Moth Pokémon

VENONAT → VENOMOTH

#0048

VENONAT
Insect Pokémon

TYPE: BUG-POISON

Poison oozes from all over its body. It catches small bug Pokémon at night that are attracted by light.

Its eyes act as radar, enabling it to be active in darkness. The eyes can also shoot powerful beams.

HOW TO SAY IT: VEH-no-nat
IMPERIAL HEIGHT: 3'03"
IMPERIAL WEIGHT: 66.1 lbs.
METRIC HEIGHT: 1.0 m
METRIC WEIGHT: 30.0 kg
GENDER: ♂ ♀
ABILITIES: Compound Eyes, Tinted Lens
WEAKNESSES: Fire, Psychic, Flying, Rock

VENONAT VENOMOTH

VENUSAUR

Seed Pokémon

#0003

TYPE: GRASS-POISON

Its plant blooms when it is absorbing solar energy. It stays on the move to seek sunlight.

A bewitching aroma wafts from its flower. The fragrance becalms those engaged in a battle.

HOW TO SAY IT: VEE-nuh-sore
IMPERIAL HEIGHT: 6'07"
IMPERIAL WEIGHT: 220.5 lbs.
METRIC HEIGHT: 2.0 m
METRIC WEIGHT: 100.0 kg
GENDER: ♂ ♀
ABILITIES: Overgrow
WEAKNESSES: Fire, Psychic, Flying, Ice

MEGA VENUSAUR

TYPE: GRASS-POISON

In order to support its flower, which has grown larger due to Mega Evolution, its back and legs have become stronger.

IMPERIAL HEIGHT: 7'10"
IMPERIAL WEIGHT: 342.8 lbs.
METRIC HEIGHT: 2.4 m
METRIC WEIGHT: 155.5 kg

BULBASAUR → **IVYSAUR** → **VENUSAUR** → **MEGA VENUSAUR**

GIGANTAMAX
VENUSAUR

In battle, this Pokémon swings around two thick vines. If these vines slammed into a 10-story building, they could easily topple it.

Huge amounts of pollen burst from it with the force of a volcanic eruption. Breathing in too much of the pollen can cause fainting.

IMPERIAL HEIGHT: 78'09"+
IMPERIAL WEIGHT: ????.? lbs.
METRIC HEIGHT: 24.0+ m
METRIC WEIGHT: ???.? kg

VESPIQUEN

Beehive Pokémon

#0416

TYPE: BUG-FLYING

It houses its colony in cells in its body and releases various pheromones to make those grubs do its bidding.

It raises grubs in the holes in its body. It secretes pheromones to control Combee.

HOW TO SAY IT: VES-pih-kwen
IMPERIAL HEIGHT: 3'11"
IMPERIAL WEIGHT: 84.9 lbs.
METRIC HEIGHT: 1.2 m
METRIC WEIGHT: 38.5 kg
GENDER: ♀
ABILITIES: Pressure
WEAKNESSES: Fire, Flying, Electric, Ice, Rock

COMBEE   VESPIQUEN

VIBRAVA

Vibration Pokémon

#0329

TYPE: GROUND-DRAGON

The ultrasonic waves it generates by rubbing its two wings together cause severe headaches.

To help make its wings grow, it dissolves quantities of prey in its digestive juices and guzzles them down every day.

HOW TO SAY IT: VY-BRAH-va
IMPERIAL HEIGHT: 3'07"
IMPERIAL WEIGHT: 33.7 lbs.
METRIC HEIGHT: 1.1 m
METRIC WEIGHT: 15.3 kg
GENDER: ♂ ♀
ABILITIES: Levitate
WEAKNESSES: Fairy, Ice, Dragon

TRAPINCH

VIBRAVA

FLYGON

#0494

VICTINI
Victory Pokémon

TYPE: PSYCHIC-FIRE

This Pokémon brings victory. It is said that Trainers with Victini always win, regardless of the type of encounter.

When it shares the infinite energy it creates, that being's entire body will be overflowing with power.

HOW TO SAY IT: vik-TEE-nee
IMPERIAL HEIGHT: 1'04"
IMPERIAL WEIGHT: 8.8 lbs.
METRIC HEIGHT: 0.4 m
METRIC WEIGHT: 4.0 kg
GENDER: Unknown
ABILITIES: Victory Star
WEAKNESSES: Ghost, Water, Ground, Dark, Rock

DOES NOT EVOLVE

#0071

VICTREEBEL
Flycatcher Pokémon

TYPE: GRASS-POISON

Lures prey with the sweet aroma of honey. Swallowed whole, the prey is dissolved in a day, bones and all.

HOW TO SAY IT: VICK-tree-bell
IMPERIAL HEIGHT: 5'07"
IMPERIAL WEIGHT: 34.2 lbs.
METRIC HEIGHT: 1.7 m
METRIC WEIGHT: 15.5 kg
GENDER: ♂ ♀
ABILITIES: Chlorophyll
WEAKNESSES: Fire, Psychic, Flying, Ice

BELLSPROUT   **WEEPINBELL**   **VICTREEBEL**

#0288

VIGOROTH
Wild Monkey Pokémon

TYPE: NORMAL

Its stress level rises if it cannot keep moving constantly. Too much stress makes it feel sick.

It is always hungry because it won't stop rampaging. Even while it is eating, it can't keep still.

HOW TO SAY IT: VIG-er-roth
IMPERIAL HEIGHT: 4'07"
IMPERIAL WEIGHT: 102.5 lbs.
METRIC HEIGHT: 1.4 m
METRIC WEIGHT: 46.5 kg
GENDER: ♂ ♀
ABILITIES: Vital Spirit
WEAKNESSES: Fighting

SLAKOTH → VIGOROTH → SLAKING

#0738

VIKAVOLT
Stag Beetle Pokémon

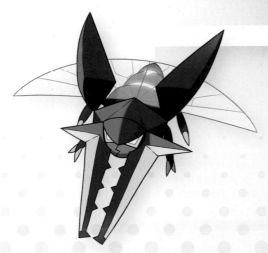

TYPE: BUG-ELECTRIC

It builds up electricity in its abdomen, focuses it through its jaws, and then fires the electricity off in concentrated beams.

If it carries a Charjabug to use as a spare battery, a flying Vikavolt can rapidly fire high-powered beams of electricity.

HOW TO SAY IT: VIE-kuh-volt
IMPERIAL HEIGHT: 4'11"
IMPERIAL WEIGHT: 99.2 lbs.
METRIC HEIGHT: 1.5 m
METRIC WEIGHT: 45.0 kg
GENDER: ♂ ♀
ABILITIES: Levitate
WEAKNESSES: Fire, Rock

GRUBBIN → CHARJABUG → VIKAVOLT

TYPE: GRASS-POISON

It has the world's largest petals. With every step, the petals shake out heavy clouds of toxic pollen.

The larger its petals, the more toxic pollen it contains. Its big head is heavy and hard to hold up.

HOW TO SAY IT: VILE-ploom
IMPERIAL HEIGHT: 3'11"
IMPERIAL WEIGHT: 41.0 lbs.
METRIC HEIGHT: 1.2 m
METRIC WEIGHT: 18.6 kg
GENDER: ♂ ♀
ABILITIES: Chlorophyll
WEAKNESSES: Fire, Psychic, Flying, Ice

VILEPLUME
Flower Pokémon

ODDISH ➡ **GLOOM** ➡ **VILEPLUME**

LEGENDARY POKÉMON

#0640

VIRIZION
Grassland Pokémon

TYPE: GRASS-FIGHTING

A legend tells of this Pokémon working together with Cobalion and Terrakion to protect the Pokémon of the Unova region.

It darts around opponents with a flurry of quick movements, slicing them up with its horns.

HOW TO SAY IT: vih-RY-zee-un
IMPERIAL HEIGHT: 6'07"
IMPERIAL WEIGHT: 440.9 lbs.
METRIC HEIGHT: 2.0 m
METRIC WEIGHT: 200.0 kg
GENDER: Unknown
ABILITIES: Justified
WEAKNESSES: Fire, Psychic, Flying, Ice, Poison, Fairy

DOES NOT EVOLVE

#0666

VIVILLON
Scale Pokémon

TYPE: BUG-FLYING

The patterns on this Pokémon depend on the climate and topography of the land it was born in. This form is from a mysterious land.

This Pokémon was born in a mysterious land. It scatters colorful, toxic scales from its wings during battle.

HOW TO SAY IT: VIH-vee-yon
IMPERIAL HEIGHT: 3'11"
IMPERIAL WEIGHT: 37.5 lbs.
METRIC HEIGHT: 1.2 m
METRIC WEIGHT: 17.0 kg
GENDER: ♂ ♀
ABILITIES: Shield Dust
WEAKNESSES: Fire, Flying, Electric, Ice, Rock

SCATTERBUG   **SPEWPA**   **VIVILLON**

#0313

VOLBEAT
Firefly Pokémon

TYPE: BUG

With the arrival of night, Volbeat emits light from its tail. It communicates with others by adjusting the intensity and flashing of its light. This Pokémon is attracted by the sweet aroma of Illumise.

Volbeat's tail glows like a light bulb. With other Volbeat, it uses its tail to draw geometric shapes in the night sky. This Pokémon loves the sweet aroma given off by Illumise.

HOW TO SAY IT: VOLL-beat
IMPERIAL HEIGHT: 2'04"
IMPERIAL WEIGHT: 39.0 lbs.
METRIC HEIGHT: 0.7 m
METRIC WEIGHT: 17.7 kg
GENDER: ♂
ABILITIES: Illuminate, Swarm
WEAKNESSES: Fire, Flying, Rock

DOES NOT EVOLVE

#0721

VOLCANION
Steam Pokémon

TYPE: FIRE-WATER

It lets out billows of steam and disappears into the dense fog. It's said to live in mountains where humans do not tread.

It expels its internal steam from the arms on its back. It has enough power to blow away a mountain.

HOW TO SAY IT: vol-KAY-nee-un
IMPERIAL HEIGHT: 5'07"
IMPERIAL WEIGHT: 429.9 lbs.
METRIC HEIGHT: 1.7 m
METRIC WEIGHT: 195.0 kg
GENDER: Unknown
ABILITIES: Water Absorb
WEAKNESSES: Ground, Electric, Rock

DOES NOT EVOLVE

#0637

VOLCARONA
Sun Pokémon

TYPE: BUG-FIRE

Its burning body causes it to be unpopular in hot parts of the world, but in cold ones, Volcarona is revered as an embodiment of the sun.

This Pokémon scatters burning scales. Most of the danger of these scales is not in their heat—it's in the way they rob the surrounding air of oxygen.

HOW TO SAY IT: vol-kah-ROH-nah
IMPERIAL HEIGHT: 5'03"
IMPERIAL WEIGHT: 101.4 lbs.
METRIC HEIGHT: 1.6 m
METRIC WEIGHT: 46.0 kg
GENDER: ♂ ♀
ABILITIES: Flame Body
WEAKNESSES: Water, Flying, Rock

LARVESTA

VOLCARONA

#0100 VOLTORB
Ball Pokémon

TYPE: ELECTRIC

It rolls to move. If the ground is uneven, a sudden jolt from hitting a bump can cause it to explode.

It's usually found in power plants. Easily mistaken for a Poké Ball, it has zapped many people.

HOW TO SAY IT: VOLT-orb
IMPERIAL HEIGHT: 1'08"
IMPERIAL WEIGHT: 22.9 lbs.
METRIC HEIGHT: 0.5 m
METRIC WEIGHT: 10.4 kg
GENDER: Unknown
ABILITIES: Soundproof, Static
WEAKNESSES: Ground

VOLTORB　　**ELECTRODE**

#0100 HISUIAN VOLTORB
Sphere Pokémon

TYPE: ELECTRIC-GRASS

An enigmatic Pokémon that happens to bear a resemblance to a Poké Ball. When excited, it discharges the electric current it has stored in its belly, then lets out a great, uproarious laugh.

HOW TO SAY IT: VOLT-orb
IMPERIAL HEIGHT: 1'08"
IMPERIAL WEIGHT: 28.7 lbs.
METRIC HEIGHT: 0.5 m
METRIC WEIGHT: 13.0 kg
GENDER: Unknown
ABILITIES: N/A
WEAKNESSES: Fire, Ice, Poison, Bug

HISUIAN　　**HISUIAN**
VOLTORB　　**ELECTRODE**

VULLABY

Diapered Pokémon

TYPE: DARK-FLYING

It wears a bone to protect its rear. It often squabbles with others of its kind over particularly comfy bones.

Vullaby grow quickly. Bones that have gotten too small for older Vullaby to wear often get passed down to younger ones in the nest.

HOW TO SAY IT: VUL-luh-bye
IMPERIAL HEIGHT: 1'08"
IMPERIAL WEIGHT: 19.8 lbs.
METRIC HEIGHT: 0.5 m
METRIC WEIGHT: 9.0 kg
GENDER: ♀
ABILITIES: Big Pecks, Overcoat
WEAKNESSES: Fairy, Electric, Ice, Rock

VULLABY → MANDIBUZZ

TYPE: FIRE

While young, it has six gorgeous tails. When it grows, several new tails are sprouted.

As each tail grows, its fur becomes more lustrous. When held, it feels slightly warm.

HOW TO SAY IT: VULL-picks
IMPERIAL HEIGHT: 2'00"
IMPERIAL WEIGHT: 21.8 lbs.
METRIC HEIGHT: 0.6 m
METRIC WEIGHT: 9.9 kg
GENDER: ♂ ♀
ABILITIES: Flash Fire
WEAKNESSES: Water, Ground, Rock

VULPIX

Fox Pokémon

VULPIX → **NINETALES**

ALOLAN VULPIX

Fox Pokémon

TYPE: ICE

After long years in the ever-snowcapped mountains of Alola, this Vulpix has gained power over ice.

If you observe its curly hairs through a microscope, you'll see small ice particles springing up.

HOW TO SAY IT: VULL-picks
IMPERIAL HEIGHT: 2'00"
IMPERIAL WEIGHT: 21.8 lbs.
METRIC HEIGHT: 0.6 m
METRIC WEIGHT: 9.9 kg
GENDER: ♂ ♀
ABILITIES: Snow Cloak
WEAKNESSES: Fire, Steel, Fighting, Rock

ALOLAN VULPIX   **ALOLAN NINETALES**

WAILMER

Ball Whale Pokémon

#0320

TYPE: WATER

It shows off by spraying jets of seawater from the nostrils above its eyes. It eats a solid ton of Wishiwashi every day.

When it sucks in a large volume of seawater, it becomes like a big, bouncy ball. It eats a ton of food daily.

HOW TO SAY IT: WAIL-murr
IMPERIAL HEIGHT: 6'07"
IMPERIAL WEIGHT: 286.6 lbs.
METRIC HEIGHT: 2.0 m
METRIC WEIGHT: 130.0 kg
GENDER: ♂ ♀
ABILITIES: Water Veil, Oblivious
WEAKNESSES: Grass, Electric

WAILMER → WAILORD

WAILORD

Float Whale Pokémon

#0321

TYPE: WATER

It can sometimes knock out opponents with the shock created by breaching and crashing its big body onto the water.

Its immense size is the reason for its popularity. Wailord watching is a favorite sightseeing activity in various parts of the world.

HOW TO SAY IT: WAIL-ord
IMPERIAL HEIGHT: 47'07"
IMPERIAL WEIGHT: 877.4 lbs.
METRIC HEIGHT: 14.5 m
METRIC WEIGHT: 398.0 kg
GENDER: ♂ ♀
ABILITIES: Water Veil, Oblivious
WEAKNESSES: Grass, ELectric

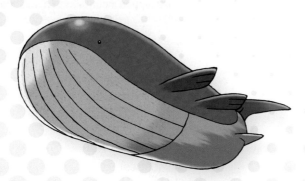

WAILMER → WAILORD

TYPE: ICE-WATER

Walrein form herds of 20 to 30 individuals. When a threat appears, the herd's leader will protect the group with its life.

Walrein's tusks keep growing throughout its life. Tusks broken in battle will grow back to their usual impressive size in a year.

HOW TO SAY IT: WAL-rain
IMPERIAL HEIGHT: 4'07"
IMPERIAL WEIGHT: 332.0 lbs.
METRIC HEIGHT: 1.4 m
METRIC WEIGHT: 150.6 kg
GENDER: ♂ ♀
ABILITIES: Thick Fat, Ice Body
WEAKNESSES: Grass, Electric, Fighting, Rock

#0365 WALREIN
Ice Break Pokémon

SPHEAL SEALEO WALREIN

TYPE: WATER

It is recognized as a symbol of longevity. If its shell has algae on it, that Wartortle is very old.

It cleverly controls its furry ears and tail to maintain its balance while swimming.

HOW TO SAY IT: WOR-TORE-tul
IMPERIAL HEIGHT: 3'03"
IMPERIAL WEIGHT: 49.6 lbs.
METRIC HEIGHT: 1.0 m
METRIC WEIGHT: 22.5 kg
GENDER: ♂ ♀
ABILITIES: Torrent
WEAKNESSES: Grass, Electric

#0008 WARTORTLE
Turtle Pokémon

SQUIRTLE WARTORTLE BLASTOISE MEGA BLASTOISE

WATCHOG

Lookout Pokémon

#0505

TYPE: NORMAL

Using luminescent matter, it makes its eyes and body glow and stuns attacking opponents.

When they see an enemy, their tails stand high, and they spit the seeds of berries stored in their cheek pouches.

HOW TO SAY IT: WAH-chawg
IMPERIAL HEIGHT: 3'07"
IMPERIAL WEIGHT: 59.5 lbs.
METRIC HEIGHT: 1.1 m
METRIC WEIGHT: 27.0 kg
GENDER: ♂ ♀
ABILITIES: Illuminate, Keen Eye
WEAKNESSES: Fighting

PATRAT   WATCHOG

WATTREL

Storm Petrel Pokémon

#0940

TYPE: ELECTRIC-FLYING

When its wings catch the wind, the bones within produce electricity. This Pokémon dives into the ocean, catching prey by electrocuting them.

These Pokémon make their nests on coastal cliffs. The nests have a strange, crackling texture, and they're a popular delicacy.

HOW TO SAY IT: WAHT-rel
IMPERIAL HEIGHT: 1'04"
IMPERIAL WEIGHT: 7.9 lbs.
METRIC HEIGHT: 0.4 m
METRIC WEIGHT: 3.6 kg
GENDER: ♂ ♀
ABILITIES: Wind Power, Volt Absorb
WEAKNESSES: Ice, Rock

WATTREL   KILOWATTREL

TYPE: DARK-ICE

WEAVILE
Sharp Claw Pokémon

Evolution made it even more devious. It communicates by clawing signs in boulders.

They travel in groups of four or five, leaving signs for one another on trees and rocks. They bring down their prey with coordinated attacks.

HOW TO SAY IT: WEE-vile
IMPERIAL HEIGHT: 3'07"
IMPERIAL WEIGHT: 75.0 lbs.
METRIC HEIGHT: 1.1 m
METRIC WEIGHT: 34.0 kg
GENDER: ♂ ♀
ABILITIES: Pressure
WEAKNESSES: Steel, Fire, Fighting, Rock, Fairy, Bug

SNEASEL   **WEAVILE**

WEEDLE
Hairy Bug Pokémon

TYPE: BUG-POISON

Beware of the sharp stinger on its head. It hides in grass and bushes where it eats leaves.

HOW TO SAY IT: WEE-dull
IMPERIAL HEIGHT: 1'00"
IMPERIAL WEIGHT: 7.1 lbs.
METRIC HEIGHT: 0.3 m
METRIC WEIGHT: 3.2 kg
GENDER: ♂ ♀
ABILITIES: Shield Dust
WEAKNESSES: Fire, Psychic, Flying, Rock

WEEDLE **KAKUNA** **BEEDRILL** **MEGA BEEDRILL**

#0070

WEEPINBELL
Flycatcher Pokémon

TYPE: GRASS-POISON

When hungry, it swallows anything that moves. Its hapless prey is dissolved by strong acids.

HOW TO SAY IT: WEE-pin-bell
IMPERIAL HEIGHT: 3'03"
IMPERIAL WEIGHT: 14.1 lbs.
METRIC HEIGHT: 1.0 m
METRIC WEIGHT: 6.4 kg
GENDER: ♂ ♀
ABILITIES: Chlorophyll
WEAKNESSES: Fire, Psychic, Flying, Ice

 BELLSPROUT **WEEPINBELL** **VICTREEBEL**

WEEZING
Poison Gas Pokémon

TYPE: POISON

It grows by feeding on gases released by garbage. Though very rare, triplets have been found.

HOW TO SAY IT: WEEZ-ing
IMPERIAL HEIGHT: 3'11"
IMPERIAL WEIGHT: 20.9 lbs.
METRIC HEIGHT: 1.2 m
METRIC WEIGHT: 9.5 kg
GENDER: ♂ ♀
ABILITIES: Levitate, Neutralizing Gas
WEAKNESSES: Psychic, Ground

KOFFING → WEEZING

GALARIAN WEEZING
Poison Gas Pokémon

#0110

TYPE: POISON-FAIRY

This Pokémon consumes particles that contaminate the air. Instead of leaving droppings, it expels clean air.

Long ago, during a time when droves of factories fouled the air with pollution, Weezing changed into this form for some reason.

HOW TO SAY IT: WEEZ-ing
IMPERIAL HEIGHT: 9'10"
IMPERIAL WEIGHT: 35.3 lbs.
METRIC HEIGHT: 3.0 m
METRIC WEIGHT: 16.0 kg
GENDER: ♂ ♀
ABILITIES: Levitate, Neutralizing Gas
WEAKNESSES: Steel, Psychic, Ground

KOFFING → GALARIAN WEEZING

WHIMSICOTT

Windveiled Pokémon

TYPE: GRASS-FAIRY

It scatters cotton all over the place as a prank. If it gets wet, it'll become too heavy to move and have no choice but to answer for its mischief.

As long as this Pokémon bathes in sunlight, its cotton keeps growing. If too much cotton fluff builds up, Whimsicott tears it off and scatters it.

HOW TO SAY IT: WHIM-zih-kaht
IMPERIAL HEIGHT: 2'04"
IMPERIAL WEIGHT: 14.6 lbs.
METRIC HEIGHT: 0.7 m
METRIC WEIGHT: 6.6 kg
GENDER: ♂ ♀
ABILITIES: Prankster, Infiltrator
WEAKNESSES: Steel, Fire, Flying, Ice, Poison

COTTONEE   WHIMSICOTT

WHIRLIPEDE

Curlipede Pokémon

TYPE: BUG-POISON

This Pokémon spins itself rapidly and charges into its opponents. Its top speed is just over 60 mph.

Whirlipede protects itself with a sturdy shell and poisonous spikes while it stores up the energy it'll need for Evolution.

HOW TO SAY IT: WHIR-lih-peed
IMPERIAL HEIGHT: 3'11"
IMPERIAL WEIGHT: 129.0 lbs.
METRIC HEIGHT: 1.2 m
METRIC WEIGHT: 58.5 kg
GENDER: ♂ ♀
ABILITIES: Poison Point, Swarm
WEAKNESSES: Fire, Psychic, Flying, Rock

VENIPEDE   WHIRLIPEDE   SCOLIPEDE

WHISCASH

Whiskers Pokémon

#0340

TYPE: WATER-GROUND

It is extremely protective of its territory. If any foe approaches, it attacks using vicious tremors.

Sighting Whiscash leaping from the water is believed to herald an earthquake.

HOW TO SAY IT: WISS-cash
IMPERIAL HEIGHT: 2'11"
IMPERIAL WEIGHT: 52.0 lbs.
METRIC HEIGHT: 0.9 m
METRIC WEIGHT: 23.6 kg
GENDER: ♂ ♀
ABILITIES: Oblivious, Anticipation
WEAKNESSES: Grass

BARBOACH   WHISCASH

WHISMUR

Whisper Pokémon

#0293

TYPE: NORMAL

The cry of a Whismur is over 100 decibels. If you're close to a Whismur when it lets out a cry, you'll be stuck with an all-day headache.

When Whismur cries, the sound of its own voice startles it, making the Pokémon cry even louder. It cries until it's exhausted, and then it falls asleep.

HOW TO SAY IT: WHIS-mur
IMPERIAL HEIGHT: 2'00"
IMPERIAL WEIGHT: 35.9 lbs.
METRIC HEIGHT: 0.6 m
METRIC WEIGHT: 16.3 kg
GENDER: ♂ ♀
ABILITIES: Soundproof
WEAKNESSES: Fighting

WHISMUR   LOUDRED   EXPLOUD

#0040 WIGGLYTUFF
Balloon Pokémon

TYPE: NORMAL-FAIRY

It has a very fine fur. Take care not to make it angry, or it may inflate steadily and hit with a body slam.

The rich, fluffy fur that covers its body feels so good that anyone who feels it can't stop touching it.

HOW TO SAY IT: WIG-lee-tuff
IMPERIAL HEIGHT: 3'03"
IMPERIAL WEIGHT: 26.5 lbs.
METRIC HEIGHT: 1.0 m
METRIC WEIGHT: 12.0 kg
GENDER: ♂ ♀
ABILITIES: Cute Charm, Competitive
WEAKNESSES: Steel, Poison

| IGGLYBUFF | JIGGLYPUFF | WIGGLYTUFF |

WIGLETT #0960
Garden Eel Pokémon

TYPE: WATER

This Pokémon can pick up the scent of a Veluza just over 65 feet away and will hide itself in the sand.

Though it looks like Diglett, Wiglett is an entirely different species. The resemblance seems to be a coincidental result of environmental adaptation.

HOW TO SAY IT: WIG-let
IMPERIAL HEIGHT: 3'11"
IMPERIAL WEIGHT: 4.0 lbs.
METRIC HEIGHT: 1.2 m
METRIC WEIGHT: 1.8 kg
GENDER: ♂ ♀
ABILITIES: Gooey, Rattled
WEAKNESSES: Grass, Electric

WIGLETT   WUGTRIO

#0767 WIMPOD
Turn Tail Pokémon

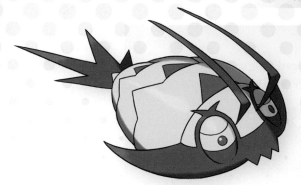

TYPE: BUG-WATER

It's nature's cleaner—it eats anything and everything, including garbage and rotten things. The ground near its nest is always clean.

Wimpod gather in swarms, constantly on the lookout for danger. They scatter the moment they detect an enemy's presence.

HOW TO SAY IT: WIM-pod
IMPERIAL HEIGHT: 1'08"
IMPERIAL WEIGHT: 26.5 lbs.
METRIC HEIGHT: 0.5 m
METRIC WEIGHT: 12.0 kg
GENDER: ♂ ♀
ABILITIES: Wimp Out
WEAKNESSES: Flying, Electric, Rock

WIMPOD **GOLISOPOD**

WINGULL #0278
Seagull Pokémon

TYPE: WATER-FLYING

It soars high in the sky, riding on updrafts like a glider. It carries food tucked in its bill.

It rides upon ocean winds as if it were a glider. In the winter, it hides food around its nest.

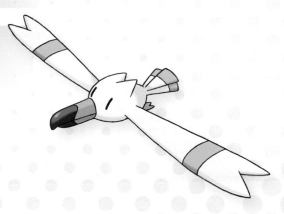

HOW TO SAY IT: WING-gull
IMPERIAL HEIGHT: 2'00"
IMPERIAL WEIGHT: 20.9 lbs.
METRIC HEIGHT: 0.6 m
METRIC WEIGHT: 9.5 kg
GENDER: ♂ ♀
ABILITIES: Keen Eye, Hydration
WEAKNESSES: Electric, Rock

WINGULL **PELIPPER**

WISHIWASHI

Small Fry Pokémon

TYPE: WATER

Individually, they're incredibly weak. It's by gathering up into schools that they're able to confront opponents.

When it senses danger, its eyes tear up. The sparkle of its tears signals other Wishiwashi to gather.

HOW TO SAY IT: WISH-ee-WASH-ee
IMPERIAL HEIGHT: Solo Form: 0'08" / School Form: 26'11"
IMPERIAL WEIGHT: Solo Form: 0.7 lbs. /
School Form: 173.3 lbs.
METRIC HEIGHT: Solo Form: 0.2 m / School Form: 8.2 m
METRIC WEIGHT: Solo Form: 0.3 kg /
School Form: 78.6 kg
GENDER: ♂ ♀
ABILITIES: Schooling
WEAKNESSES: Grass, Electric

SOLO FORM

SCHOOL FORM

DOES NOT EVOLVE

WO-CHIEN
Ruinous Pokémon

TYPE: DARK-GRASS

The grudge of a person punished for writing the king's evil deeds upon wooden tablets has clad itself in dead leaves to become a Pokémon.

It drains the life force from vegetation, causing nearby forests to instantly wither and fields to turn barren.

HOW TO SAY IT: WOH-chyehn
IMPERIAL HEIGHT: 4'11"
IMPERIAL WEIGHT: 163.6 lbs.
METRIC HEIGHT: 1.5 m
METRIC WEIGHT: 74.2 kg
GENDER: Unknown
ABILITIES: Tablets of Ruin
WEAKNESSES: Fire, Flying, Fighting, Ice, Poison, Fairy, Bug

DOES NOT EVOLVE

TYPE: PSYCHIC

It hates light and shock. If attacked, it inflates its body to pump up its counterstrike.

To keep its pitch-black tail hidden, it lives quietly in the darkness. It is never first to attack.

HOW TO SAY IT: WAH-buf-fett
IMPERIAL HEIGHT: 4'03"
IMPERIAL WEIGHT: 62.8 lbs.
METRIC HEIGHT: 1.3 m
METRIC WEIGHT: 28.5 kg
GENDER: ♂ ♀
ABILITIES: Shadow Tag
WEAKNESSES: Ghost, Dark, Bug

#0202

WOBBUFFET
Patient Pokémon

WYNAUT → **WOBBUFFET**

WOOBAT
Bat Pokémon

TYPE: PSYCHIC-FLYING

While inside a cave, if you look up and see lots of heart-shaped marks lining the walls, it's evidence that Woobat live there.

It emits ultrasonic waves as it flutters about, searching for its prey—bug Pokémon.

HOW TO SAY IT: WOO-bat
IMPERIAL HEIGHT: 1'04"
IMPERIAL WEIGHT: 4.6 lbs.
METRIC HEIGHT: 0.4 m
METRIC WEIGHT: 2.1 kg
GENDER: ♂ ♀
ABILITIES: Unaware, Klutz
WEAKNESSES: Ghost, Dark, Electric, Ice, Rock

WOOBAT   **SWOOBAT**

WOOLOO
Sheep Pokémon

#0831

TYPE: NORMAL

Its curly fleece is such an effective cushion that this Pokémon could fall off a cliff and stand right back up at the bottom, unharmed.

If its fleece grows too long, Wooloo won't be able to move. Cloth made with the wool of this Pokémon is surprisingly strong.

HOW TO SAY IT: WOO-loo
IMPERIAL HEIGHT: 2'00"
IMPERIAL WEIGHT: 13.2 lbs.
METRIC HEIGHT: 0.6 m
METRIC WEIGHT: 6.0 kg
GENDER: ♂ ♀
ABILITIES: Fluffy, Run Away
WEAKNESSES: Fighting

WOOLOO   **DUBWOOL**

WOOPER
#0194
Water Fish Pokémon

TYPE: WATER-GROUND

This Pokémon lives in cold water. It will leave the water to search for food when it gets cold outside.

When walking on land, it covers its body with a poisonous film that keeps its skin from dehydrating.

HOW TO SAY IT: WOOP-pur
IMPERIAL HEIGHT: 1'04"
IMPERIAL WEIGHT: 18.7 lbs.
METRIC HEIGHT: 0.4 m
METRIC WEIGHT: 8.5 kg
GENDER: ♂ ♀
ABILITIES: Damp, Water Absorb
WEAKNESSES: Grass

WOOPER **QUAGSIRE**

PALDEAN WOOPER
#0194
Poison Fish Pokémon

TYPE: POISON-GROUND

After losing a territorial struggle, Wooper began living on land. The Pokémon changed over time, developing a poisonous film to protect its body. It's dangerous for Wooper to travel alone.

They line up in groups of three or four and help each other as they walk around the wetlands.

HOW TO SAY IT: WOOP-pur
IMPERIAL HEIGHT: 1'04"
IMPERIAL WEIGHT: 24.3 lbs.
METRIC HEIGHT: 0.4 m
METRIC WEIGHT: 11.0 kg
GENDER: ♂ ♀
ABILITIES: Poison Point, Water Absorb
WEAKNESSES: Water, Psychic, Ice, Ground

PALDEAN WOOPER **CLODSIRE**

WORMADAM

Bagworm Pokémon

#0413

PLANT CLOAK TYPE: **BUG-GRASS**
SANDY CLOAK TYPE: **BUG-GROUND**
TRASH CLOAK TYPE: **BUG-STEEL**

Its appearance changes depending on where it evolved. The materials on hand become a part of its body.

When Burmy evolved, its cloak became a part of this Pokémon's body. The cloak is never shed.

HOW TO SAY IT: WUR-muh-dam
IMPERIAL HEIGHT: 1'08"
IMPERIAL WEIGHT: 14.3 lbs.
METRIC HEIGHT: 0.5 m
METRIC WEIGHT: 6.5 kg
GENDER: ♀
ABILITIES: Anticipation
WEAKNESSES: Plant Cloak: Fire, Flying, Ice, Poison, Rock, Bug
Sandy Cloak: Fire, Water, Flying, Ice
Trash Cloak: Fire

PLANT CLOAK

SANDY CLOAK

TRASH CLOAK

BURMY

WORMADAM

WUGTRIO
Garden Eel Pokémon

TYPE: WATER

It has a vicious temperament, contrary to what its appearance may suggest. It wraps its long bodies around prey, then drags the prey into its den.

A variety of fish Pokémon, Wugtrio was once considered to be a regional form of Dugtrio.

HOW TO SAY IT: WUHG-TREE-oh
IMPERIAL HEIGHT: 3'11"
IMPERIAL WEIGHT: 11.9 lbs.
METRIC HEIGHT: 1.2 m
METRIC WEIGHT: 5.4 kg
GENDER: ♂ ♀
ABILITIES: Gooey, Rattled
WEAKNESSES: Grass, Electric

WIGLETT → **WUGTRIO**

WURMPLE
Worm Pokémon

TYPE: BUG

Using the spikes on its rear end, Wurmple peels the bark off trees and feeds on the sap that oozes out. This Pokémon's feet are tipped with suction pads that allow it to cling to glass without slipping.

Wurmple is targeted by Swellow as prey. This Pokémon will try to resist by pointing the spikes on its rear at the attacking predator. It will weaken the foe by leaking poison from the spikes.

HOW TO SAY IT: WERM-pull
IMPERIAL HEIGHT: 1'00"
IMPERIAL WEIGHT: 7.9 lbs.
METRIC HEIGHT: 0.3 m
METRIC WEIGHT: 3.6 kg
GENDER: ♂ ♀
ABILITIES: Shield Dust
WEAKNESSES: Fire, Flying, Rock

SILCOON → **BEAUTIFLY**

WURMPLE

CASCOON → **DUSTOX**

WYNAUT

Bright Pokémon

#0360

TYPE: PSYCHIC

It tends to move in a pack. Individuals squash against one another to toughen their spirits.

It tends to move in a pack with others. They cluster in a tight group to sleep in a cave.

HOW TO SAY IT: WHY-not
IMPERIAL HEIGHT: 2'00"
IMPERIAL WEIGHT: 30.9 lbs.
METRIC HEIGHT: 0.6 m
METRIC WEIGHT: 14.0 kg
GENDER: ♂ ♀
ABILITIES: Shadow Tag
WEAKNESSES: Ghost, Dark, Bug

WYNAUT   WOBBUFFET

WYRDEER

Big Horn Pokémon

#0899

TYPE: NORMAL-PSYCHIC

The black orbs shine with an uncanny light when the Pokémon is erecting invisible barriers. The fur shed from its beard retains heat well and is a highly useful material for winter clothing.

HOW TO SAY IT: WEER-DEER
IMPERIAL HEIGHT: 5'11"
IMPERIAL WEIGHT: 209.7 lbs.
METRIC HEIGHT: 1.8 m
METRIC WEIGHT: 95.1 kg
GENDER: ♂ ♀
ABILITIES: N/A
WEAKNESSES: Dark, Bug

STANTLER   WYRDEER

XATU
Mystic Pokémon

TYPE: PSYCHIC-FLYING

They say that it stays still and quiet because it is seeing both the past and future at the same time.

This odd Pokémon can see both the past and the future. It eyes the sun's movement all day.

HOW TO SAY IT: ZAH-too
IMPERIAL HEIGHT: 4'11"
IMPERIAL WEIGHT: 33.1 lbs.
METRIC HEIGHT: 1.5 m
METRIC WEIGHT: 15.0 kg
GENDER: ♂ ♀
ABILITIES: Synchronize, Early Bird
WEAKNESSES: Ghost, Dark, Electric, Ice, Rock

NATU → XATU

LEGENDARY POKÉMON

#0716

XERNEAS
Life Pokémon

TYPE: FAIRY

Legends say it can share eternal life. It slept for a thousand years in the form of a tree before its revival.

When the horns on its head shine in seven colors, it is said to be sharing everlasting life.

HOW TO SAY IT: ZURR-nee-us
IMPERIAL HEIGHT: 9'10"
IMPERIAL WEIGHT: 474.0 lbs.
METRIC HEIGHT: 3.0 m
METRIC WEIGHT: 215.0 kg
GENDER: Unknown
ABILITIES: Fairy Aura
WEAKNESSES: Steel, Poison

DOES NOT EVOLVE

XURKITREE

Glowing Pokémon

#0796

TYPE: ELECTRIC

Although it's alien to this world and a danger here, it's apparently a common organism in the world where it normally lives.

They've been dubbed Ultra Beasts. Some of them stand unmoving, like trees, with their arms and legs stuck into the ground.

HOW TO SAY IT: ZURK-ih-tree
IMPERIAL HEIGHT: 12'06"
IMPERIAL WEIGHT: 220.5 lbs.
METRIC HEIGHT: 3.8 m
METRIC WEIGHT: 100.0 kg
GENDER: Unknown
ABILITIES: Beast Boost
WEAKNESSES: Ground

DOES NOT EVOLVE

#0562 YAMASK
Spirit Pokémon

TYPE: GHOST

It wanders through ruins by night, carrying a mask that's said to have been the face it had when it was still human.

The spirit of a person from a bygone age became this Pokémon. It rambles through ruins, searching for someone who knows its face.

HOW TO SAY IT: YAH-mask
IMPERIAL HEIGHT: 1'08"
IMPERIAL WEIGHT: 3.3 lbs.
METRIC HEIGHT: 0.5 m
METRIC WEIGHT: 1.5 kg
GENDER: ♂ ♀
ABILITIES: Mummy
WEAKNESSES: Ghost, Dark

YAMASK → COFAGRIGUS

#0562 GALARIAN YAMASK
Spirit Pokémon

TYPE: GROUND-GHOST

A clay slab with cursed engravings took possession of a Yamask. The slab is said to be absorbing the Yamask's dark power.

It's said that this Pokémon was formed when an ancient clay tablet was drawn to a vengeful spirit.

HOW TO SAY IT: YAH-mask
IMPERIAL HEIGHT: 1'08"
IMPERIAL WEIGHT: 3.3 lbs.
METRIC HEIGHT: 0.5 m
METRIC WEIGHT: 15. kg
GENDER: ♂ ♀
ABILITIES: Wandering Spirit
WEAKNESSES: Water, Ghost, Grass, Dark, Ice

GALARIAN YAMASK → RUNERIGUS

YAMPER

Puppy Pokémon

#0835

TYPE: ELECTRIC

This Pokémon is very popular as a herding dog in the Galar region. As it runs, it generates electricity from the base of its tail.

This gluttonous Pokémon only assists people with their work because it wants treats. As it runs, it crackles with electricity.

HOW TO SAY IT: YAM-per
IMPERIAL HEIGHT: 1'00"
IMPERIAL WEIGHT: 29.8 lbs.
METRIC HEIGHT: 0.3 m
METRIC WEIGHT: 13.5 kg
GENDER: ♂ ♀
ABILITIES: Ball Fetch
WEAKNESSES: Ground

YAMPER → **BOLTUND**

YANMA

Clear Wing Pokémon

#0193

TYPE: BUG-FLYING

Yanma is capable of seeing 360 degrees without having to move its eyes. It is a great flier that is adept at making sudden stops and turning midair. This Pokémon uses its flying ability to quickly chase down targeted prey.

HOW TO SAY IT: YAN-ma
IMPERIAL HEIGHT: 3'11"
IMPERIAL WEIGHT: 83.8 lbs.
METRIC HEIGHT: 1.2 m
METRIC WEIGHT: 38.0 kg
GENDER: ♂ ♀
ABILITIES: Speed Boost, Compound Eyes
WEAKNESSES: Fire, Flying, Electric, Ice, Rock

YANMA → **YANMEGA**

#0469

YANMEGA
Ogre Darner Pokémon

TYPE: BUG-FLYING

It prefers to battle by biting apart foes' heads instantly while flying by at high speed.

This six-legged Pokémon is easily capable of transporting an adult in flight. The wings on its tail help it stay balanced.

HOW TO SAY IT: yan-MEG-ah
IMPERIAL HEIGHT: 6'03"
IMPERIAL WEIGHT: 113.5 lbs.
METRIC HEIGHT: 1.9 m
METRIC WEIGHT: 51.5 kg
GENDER: ♂ ♀
ABILITIES: Speed Boost, Tinted Lens
WEAKNESSES: Fire, Flying, Electric, Ice, Rock

YANMA ➡ **YANMEGA**

TYPE: NORMAL

Its stomach fills most of its torso. It wanders the same path every day, searching for fresh food.

It spends its waking hours searching endlessly for food. When Yungoos is hungry, its ferocity gains a certain edge.

#0734

YUNGOOS
Loitering Pokémon

HOW TO SAY IT: YUNG-goose
IMPERIAL HEIGHT: 1'04"
IMPERIAL WEIGHT: 13.2 lbs.
METRIC HEIGHT: 0.4 m
METRIC WEIGHT: 6.0 kg
GENDER: ♂ ♀
ABILITIES: Stakeout, Strong Jaw
WEAKNESSES: Fighting

YUNGOOS ➡ **GUMSHOOS**

YVELTAL

Destruction Pokémon

#0717

TYPE: DARK-FLYING

When this legendary Pokémon's wings and tail feathers spread wide and glow red, it absorbs the life force of living creatures.

When its life comes to an end, it absorbs the life energy of every living thing and turns into a cocoon once more.

HOW TO SAY IT: ee-VELL-tall
IMPERIAL HEIGHT: 19'00" **METRIC HEIGHT:** 5.8 m
IMPERIAL WEIGHT: 447.5 lbs. **METRIC WEIGHT:** 203.0 kg
GENDER: Unknown
ABILITIES: Dark Aura
WEAKNESSES: Fairy, Electric, Ice, Rock

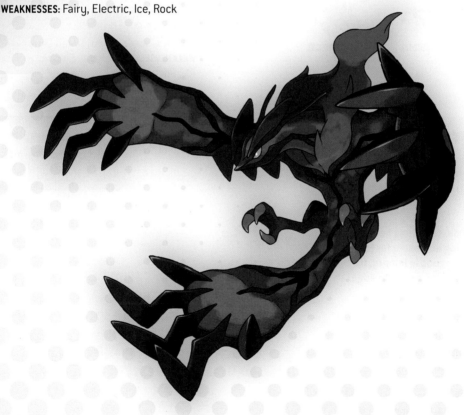

DOES NOT EVOLVE

ZACIAN
HERO OF MANY BATTLES
Warrior Pokémon

TYPE: FAIRY

Known as a legendary hero, this Pokémon absorbs metal particles, transforming them into a weapon it uses to battle.

This Pokémon has slumbered for many years. Some say it's Zamazenta's elder sister—others say the two Pokémon are rivals.

HOW TO SAY IT: ZAH-shee-uhn
IMPERIAL HEIGHT: 9'02"
IMPERIAL WEIGHT: 242.5 lbs.
METRIC HEIGHT: 2.8 m
METRIC WEIGHT: 110.0 kg
GENDER: Unknown
ABILITIES: Intrepid Sword
WEAKNESSES: Steel, Poison

ZACIAN
CROWNED SWORD
Warrior Pokémon

TYPE: FAIRY-STEEL

Now armed with a weapon it used in ancient times, this Pokémon needs only a single strike to fell even Gigantamax Pokémon.

Able to cut down anything with a single strike, it became known as the Fairy King's Sword, and it inspired awe in friend and foe alike.

IMPERIAL HEIGHT: 9'02"
IMPERIAL WEIGHT: 782.6 lbs.
METRIC HEIGHT: 2.8 m
METRIC WEIGHT: 355.0 kg
GENDER: Unknown
ABILITIES: Intrepid Sword
WEAKNESSES: Fire, Ground

DOES NOT EVOLVE

ZAMAZENTA
HERO OF MANY BATTLES
Warrior Pokémon

#0889

TYPE: FIGHTING

In times past, it worked together with a king of the people to save the Galar region. It absorbs metal that it then uses in battle.

This Pokémon slept for aeons while in the form of a statue. It was asleep for so long, people forgot that it ever existed.

HOW TO SAY IT: ZAH-mah-ZEN-tuh
IMPERIAL HEIGHT: 9'06"
IMPERIAL WEIGHT: 463.0 lbs.
METRIC HEIGHT: 2.9 m
METRIC WEIGHT: 210.0 kg
GENDER: Unknown
ABILITIES: Dauntless Shield
WEAKNESSES: Psychic, Flying, Fairy

ZAMAZENTA
CROWNED SHIELD
Warrior Pokémon

TYPE: FIGHTING-STEEL

Its ability to deflect any attack led to it being known as the Fighting Master's Shield. It was feared and respected by all.

Now that it's equipped with its shield, it can shrug off impressive blows, including the attacks of Dynamax Pokémon.

IMPERIAL HEIGHT: 9'06"
IMPERIAL WEIGHT: 1,730.6 lbs.
METRIC HEIGHT: 2.9 m
METRIC WEIGHT: 785.0 kg
GENDER: Unknown
ABILITIES: Dauntless Shield
WEAKNESSES: Fire, Fighting, Ground

DOES NOT EVOLVE

ZANGOOSE

Cat Ferret Pokémon

TYPE: NORMAL

It's Seviper's archrival. To threaten those it encounters, it fans out the claws on its front paws.

If it comes across a Seviper, its fur bristles and it assumes its battle pose. Its sharp claws are its best weapon.

HOW TO SAY IT: ZANG-goose
IMPERIAL HEIGHT: 4'03"
IMPERIAL WEIGHT: 88.8 lbs.
METRIC HEIGHT: 1.3 m
METRIC WEIGHT: 40.3 kg
GENDER: ♂ ♀
ABILITIES: Immunity
WEAKNESSES: Fighting

DOES NOT EVOLVE

ZAPDOS
Electric Pokémon

#0145

TYPE: ELECTRIC-FLYING

This legendary Pokémon is said to live in thunderclouds. It freely controls lightning bolts.

HOW TO SAY IT: ZAP-dose
IMPERIAL HEIGHT: 5'03"
IMPERIAL WEIGHT: 116.0 lbs.
METRIC HEIGHT: 1.6 m
METRIC WEIGHT: 52.6 kg
GENDER: Unknown
ABILITIES: Pressure
WEAKNESSES: Ice, Rock

DOES NOT EVOLVE

GALARIAN ZAPDOS
Strong Legs Pokémon

#0145

TYPE: FIGHTING-FLYING

When its feathers rub together, they produce a crackling sound like the zapping of electricity. That's why this Pokémon is called Zapdos.

One kick from its powerful legs will pulverize a dump truck. Supposedly, this Pokémon runs through the mountains at over 180 mph.

HOW TO SAY IT: ZAP-dose
IMPERIAL HEIGHT: 5'03"
IMPERIAL WEIGHT: 128.3 lbs.
METRIC HEIGHT: 1.6 m
METRIC WEIGHT: 58.2 kg
GENDER: Unknown
ABILITIES: Defiant
WEAKNESSES: Psychic, Flying, Fairy, Electric, Ice

DOES NOT EVOLVE

#0893

ZARUDE
Rogue Monkey Pokémon

TYPE: DARK-GRASS

Within dense forests, this Pokémon lives in a pack with others of its kind. It's incredibly aggressive, and the other Pokémon of the forest fear it

Once the vines on Zarude's body tear off, they become nutrients in the soil. This helps the plants of the forest grow.

HOW TO SAY IT: zuh-ROOD
IMPERIAL HEIGHT: 5'11"
IMPERIAL WEIGHT: 154.3 lbs.
METRIC HEIGHT: 1.8 m
METRIC WEIGHT: 70.0 kg
GENDER: Unknown
ABILITIES: Leaf Guard
WEAKNESSES: Fire, Flying, Fighting, Ice, Poison, Fairy, Bug

DOES NOT EVOLVE

#0523

ZEBSTRIKA
Thunderbolt Pokémon

TYPE: ELECTRIC

When this ill-tempered Pokémon runs wild, it shoots lightning from its mane in all directions.

They have lightning-like movements. When Zebstrika run at full speed, the sound of thunder reverberates.

HOW TO SAY IT: zehb-STRY-kuh
IMPERIAL HEIGHT: 5'03"
IMPERIAL WEIGHT: 175.3 lbs.
METRIC HEIGHT: 1.6 m
METRIC WEIGHT: 79.5 kg
GENDER: ♂ ♀
ABILITIES: Lightning Rod, Motor Drive
WEAKNESSES: Ground

BLITZLE → **ZEBSTRIKA**

ZEKROM

Deep Black Pokémon

#0644

TYPE: DRAGON-ELECTRIC

This legendary Pokémon can scorch the world with lightning. It assists those who want to build an ideal world.

Concealing itself in lightning clouds, it flies throughout the Unova region. It creates electricity in its tail.

HOW TO SAY IT: ZECK-rahm
IMPERIAL HEIGHT: 9'06"
IMPERIAL WEIGHT: 760.6 lbs.
METRIC HEIGHT: 2.9 m
METRIC WEIGHT: 345.0 kg
GENDER: Unknown
ABILITIES: Teravolt
WEAKNESSES: Fairy, Dragon, Ice, Ground

OVERDRIVE FORM

628

DOES NOT EVOLVE

ZERAORA
Thunderclap Pokémon

#0807

TYPE: ELECTRIC

It electrifies its claws and tears its opponents apart with them. Even if they dodge its attack, they'll be electrocuted by the flying sparks.

It approaches its enemies at the speed of lightning, then tears them limb from limb with its sharp claws.

HOW TO SAY IT: ZEH-rah-OH-rah
IMPERIAL HEIGHT: 4'11"
IMPERIAL WEIGHT: 98.1 lbs.
METRIC HEIGHT: 1.5 m
METRIC WEIGHT: 44.5 kg
GENDER: Unknown
ABILITIES: Volt Absorb
WEAKNESSES: Ground

DOES NOT EVOLVE

ZIGZAGOON

Tiny Raccoon Pokémon

#0263

TYPE: NORMAL

It walks in zigzag fashion. It's good at finding items in the grass and even in the ground.

HOW TO SAY IT: ZIG-zag-GOON
IMPERIAL HEIGHT: 1'04"
IMPERIAL WEIGHT: 38.6 lbs.
METRIC HEIGHT: 0.4 m
METRIC WEIGHT: 17.5 kg
GENDER: ♂ ♀
ABILITIES: Pickup, Gluttony
WEAKNESSES: Fighting

ZIGZAGOON → LINOONE

#0263

GALARIAN ZIGZAGOON

Tiny Raccoon Pokémon

TYPE: DARK-NORMAL

Its restlessness has it constantly running around. If it sees another Pokémon, it will purposely run into them in order to start a fight.

Thought to be the oldest form of Zigzagoon, it moves in zigzags and wreaks havoc upon its surroundings.

HOW TO SAY IT: ZIG-zag-GOON
IMPERIAL HEIGHT: 1'04"
IMPERIAL WEIGHT: 38.6 lbs.
METRIC HEIGHT: 0.4 m
METRIC WEIGHT: 17.5 kg
GENDER: ♂ ♀
ABILITIES: Pickup, Gluttony
WEAKNESSES: Fairy, Bug, Fighting

GALARIAN ZIGZAGOON → GALARIAN LINOONE → OBSTAGOON

ZOROARK

Illusion Fox Pokémon

#0571

TYPE: DARK

Stories say those who tried to catch Zoroark were trapped in an illusion and punished.

Each has the ability to fool a large group of people simultaneously. They protect their lair with illusory scenery.

HOW TO SAY IT: ZORE-oh-ark
IMPERIAL HEIGHT: 5'03"
IMPERIAL WEIGHT: 178.8 lbs.
METRIC HEIGHT: 1.6 m
METRIC WEIGHT: 81.1 kg
GENDER: ♂ ♀
ABILITIES: Illusion
WEAKNESSES: Fairy, Bug, Fighting

ZORUA → **ZOROARK**

#0571

HISUIAN ZOROARK

Baneful Fox Pokémon

TYPE: NORMAL-GHOST

With its disheveled white fur, it looks like an embodiment of death. Heedless of its own safety, Zoroark attacks its nemeses with a bitter energy so intense, it lacerates Zoroark's own body.

HOW TO SAY IT: ZORE-oh-ark
IMPERIAL HEIGHT: 5'03"
IMPERIAL WEIGHT: 160.9 lbs.
METRIC HEIGHT: 1.6 m
METRIC WEIGHT: 73.0 kg
GENDER: ♂ ♀
ABILITIES: N/A
WEAKNESSES: Dark

HISUIAN ZORUA →

HISUIAN ZOROARK

ZORUA #0570

Tricky Fox Pokémon

TYPE: DARK

It changes into the forms of others to surprise them. Apparently, it often transforms into a silent child.

To protect themselves from danger, they hide their true identities by transforming into people and Pokémon.

HOW TO SAY IT: ZORE-oo-ah
IMPERIAL HEIGHT: 2'04"
IMPERIAL WEIGHT: 27.6 lbs.
METRIC HEIGHT: 0.7 m
METRIC WEIGHT: 12.5 kg
GENDER: ♂ ♀
ABILITIES: Illusion
WEAKNESSES: Fairy, Bug, Fighting

ZORUA   ZOROARK

HISUIAN ZORUA #0570

Spiteful Fox Pokémon

TYPE: NORMAL-GHOST

A once-departed soul, returned to life in Hisui. Derives power from resentment, which rises as energy atop its head and takes on the forms of foes. In this way, Zorua vents lingering malice.

HOW TO SAY IT: ZORE-oo-ah
IMPERIAL HEIGHT: 2'04"
IMPERIAL WEIGHT: 27.6 lbs.
METRIC HEIGHT: 0.7 m
METRIC WEIGHT: 12.5 kg
GENDER: ♂ ♀
ABILITIES: N/A
WEAKNESSES: Dark

HISUIAN ZORUA   HISUIAN ZOROARK

ZUBAT
Bat Pokémon

TYPE: POISON-FLYING

It emits ultrasonic waves from its mouth to check its surroundings. Even in tight caves, Zubat flies around with skill.

Zubat live in caves, down where the sun's light won't reach. In the morning, they gather together to keep each other warm as they sleep.

HOW TO SAY IT: ZOO-bat
IMPERIAL HEIGHT: 2'07"
IMPERIAL WEIGHT: 16.5 lbs.
METRIC HEIGHT: 0.8 m
METRIC WEIGHT: 7.5 kg
GENDER: ♂ ♀
ABILITIES: Inner Focus
WEAKNESSES: Psychic, Electric, Ice, Rock

ZUBAT **GOLBAT** **CROBAT**

#0634

ZWEILOUS
Hostile Pokémon

TYPE: DARK-DRAGON

The two heads do not get along at all. If you don't give each head the same amount of attention, they'll begin fighting out of jealousy.

The two heads have different likes and dislikes. Because the heads fight with each other, Zweilous gets stronger without needing to rely on others.

HOW TO SAY IT: ZVY-lus
IMPERIAL HEIGHT: 4'07"
IMPERIAL WEIGHT: 110.2 lbs.
METRIC HEIGHT: 1.4 m
METRIC WEIGHT: 50.0 kg
GENDER: ♂ ♀
ABILITIES: Hustle
WEAKNESSES: Fairy, Fighting, Bug, Ice, Dragon

DEINO **ZWEILOUS** **HYDREIGON**

ZYGARDE

Order Pokémon

#0718

TYPE: DRAGON-GROUND

HOW TO SAY IT: ZY-gard
GENDER: Unknown
ABILITIES: Aura Break, Power Construct
WEAKNESSES: Fairy, Ice, Dragon

ZYGARDE CORE

ZYGARDE 10%

This is Zygarde when about 10% of its pieces have been assembled. It leaps at its opponent's chest and sinks its sharp fangs into them.

Born when around 10% of Zygarde's cells have been gathered from all over, this form is skilled in close-range combat.

IMPERIAL HEIGHT: 3'11"
IMPERIAL WEIGHT: 73.9 lbs.
METRIC HEIGHT: 1.2 m
METRIC WEIGHT: 33.5 kg

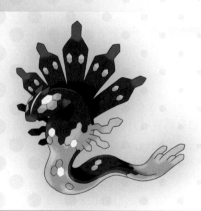

ZYGARDE 50%

This is Zygarde's form when about half of its pieces have been assembled. It plays the role of monitoring the ecosystem.

Some say it can change to an even more powerful form when battling those who threaten the ecosystem.

IMPERIAL HEIGHT: 16'05"
IMPERIAL WEIGHT: 672.4 lbs.
METRIC HEIGHT: 5.0 m
METRIC WEIGHT: 305.0 kg

ZYGARDE COMPLETE

This is Zygarde's perfected form. From the orifice on its chest, it radiates high-powered energy that eliminates everything.

Born when all of Zygarde's cells have been gathered together, it uses force to neutralize those who harm the ecosystem.

IMPERIAL HEIGHT: 14'09"
IMPERIAL WEIGHT: 1,344.8 lbs.
METRIC HEIGHT: 4.5 m
METRIC WEIGHT: 610.0 kg

DOES NOT EVOLVE

INDEX

POKÉMON LISTED BY NATIONAL POKÉDEX NUMBER

0154	Meganium	0211	Qwilfish	0268	Cascoon
0155	Cyndaquil	0212	Scizor	0269	Dustox
0156	Quilava	0213	Shuckle	0270	Lotad
0157	Typhlosion	0214	Heracross	0271	Lombre
0158	Totodile	0215	Sneasel	0272	Ludicolo
0159	Croconaw	0216	Teddiursa	0273	Seedot
0160	Feraligatr	0217	Ursaring	0274	Nuzleaf
0161	Sentret	0218	Slugma	0275	Shiftry
0162	Furret	0219	Magcargo	0276	Taillow
0163	Hoothoot	0220	Swinub	0277	Swellow
0164	Noctowl	0221	Piloswine	0278	Wingull
0165	Ledyba	0222	Corsola	0279	Pelipper
0166	Ledian	0223	Remoraid	0280	Ralts
0167	Spinarak	0224	Octillery	0281	Kirlia
0168	Ariados	0225	Delibird	0282	Gardevoir
0169	Crobat	0226	Mantine	0283	Surskit
0170	Chinchou	0227	Skarmory	0284	Masquerain
0171	Lanturn	0228	Houndour	0285	Shroomish
0172	Pichu	0229	Houndoom	0286	Breloom
0173	Cleffa	0230	Kingdra	0287	Slakoth
0174	Igglybuff	0231	Phanpy	0288	Vigoroth
0175	Togepi	0232	Donphan	0289	Slaking
0176	Togetic	0233	Porygon2	0290	Nincada
0177	Natu	0234	Stantler	0291	Ninjask
0178	Xatu	0235	Smeargle	0292	Shedinja
0179	Mareep	0236	Tyrogue	0293	Whismur
0180	Flaaffy	0237	Hitmontop	0294	Loudred
0181	Ampharos	0238	Smoochum	0295	Exploud
0182	Bellossom	0239	Elekid	0296	Makuhita
0183	Marill	0240	Magby	0297	Hariyama
0184	Azumarill	0241	Miltank	0298	Azurill
0185	Sudowoodo	0242	Blissey	0299	Nosepass
0186	Politoed	0243	Raikou	0300	Skitty
0187	Hoppip	0244	Entei	0301	Delcatty
0188	Skiploom	0245	Suicune	0302	Sableye
0189	Jumpluff	0246	Larvitar	0303	Mawile
0190	Aipom	0247	Pupitar	0304	Aron
0191	Sunkern	0248	Tyranitar	0305	Lairon
0192	Sunflora	0249	Lugia	0306	Aggron
0193	Yanma	0250	Ho-Oh	0307	Meditite
0194	Wooper	0251	Celebi	0308	Medicham
0195	Quagsire	0252	Treecko	0309	Electrike
0196	Espeon	0253	Grovyle	0310	Manectric
0197	Umbreon	0254	Sceptile	0311	Plusle
0198	Murkrow	0255	Torchic	0312	Minun
0199	Slowking	0256	Combusken	0313	Volbeat
0200	Misdreavus	0257	Blaziken	0314	Illumise
0201	Unown	0258	Mudkip	0315	Roselia
0202	Wobbuffet	0259	Marshtomp	0316	Gulpin
0203	Girafarig	0260	Swampert	0317	Swalot
0204	Pineco	0261	Poochyena	0318	Carvanha
0205	Forretress	0262	Mightyena	0319	Sharpedo
0206	Dunsparce	0263	Zigzagoon	0320	Wailmer
0207	Gligar	0264	Linoone	0321	Wailord
0208	Steelix	0265	Wurmple	0322	Numel
0209	Snubbull	0266	Silcoon	0323	Camerupt
0210	Granbull	0267	Beautifly	0324	Torkoal

0325	Spoink	0382	Kyogre	0439	Mime Jr.
0326	Grumpig	0383	Groudon	0440	Happiny
0327	Spinda	0384	Rayquaza	0441	Chatot
0328	Trapinch	0385	Jirachi	0442	Spiritomb
0329	Vibrava	0386	Deoxys	0443	Gible
0330	Flygon	0387	Turtwig	0444	Gabite
0331	Cacnea	0388	Grotle	0445	Garchomp
0332	Cacturne	0389	Torterra	0446	Munchlax
0333	Swablu	0390	Chimchar	0447	Riolu
0334	Altaria	0391	Monferno	0448	Lucario
0335	Zangoose	0392	Infernape	0449	Hippopotas
0336	Seviper	0393	Piplup	0450	Hippowdon
0337	Lunatone	0394	Prinplup	0451	Skorupi
0338	Solrock	0395	Empoleon	0452	Drapion
0339	Barboach	0396	Starly	0453	Croagunk
0340	Whiscash	0397	Staravia	0454	Toxicroak
0341	Corphish	0398	Staraptor	0455	Carnivine
0342	Crawdaunt	0399	Bidoof	0456	Finneon
0343	Baltoy	0400	Bibarel	0457	Lumineon
0344	Claydol	0401	Kricketot	0458	Mantyke
0345	Lileep	0402	Kricketune	0459	Snover
0346	Cradily	0403	Shinx	0460	Abomasnow
0347	Anorith	0404	Luxio	0461	Weavile
0348	Armaldo	0405	Luxray	0462	Magnezone
0349	Feebas	0406	Budew	0463	Lickilicky
0350	Milotic	0407	Roserade	0464	Rhyperior
0351	Castform	0408	Cranidos	0465	Tangrowth
0352	Kecleon	0409	Rampardos	0466	Electivire
0353	Shuppet	0410	Shieldon	0467	Magmortar
0354	Banette	0411	Bastiodon	0468	Togekiss
0355	Duskull	0412	Burmy	0469	Yanmega
0356	Dusclops	0413	Wormadam	0470	Leafeon
0357	Tropius	0414	Mothim	0471	Glaceon
0358	Chimecho	0415	Combee	0472	Gliscor
0359	Absol	0416	Vespiquen	0473	Mamoswine
0360	Wynaut	0417	Pachirisu	0474	Porygon-Z
0361	Snorunt	0418	Buizel	0475	Gallade
0362	Glalie	0419	Floatzel	0476	Probopass
0363	Spheal	0420	Cherubi	0477	Dusknoir
0364	Sealeo	0421	Cherrim	0478	Froslass
0365	Walrein	0422	Shellos	0479	Rotom
0366	Clamperl	0423	Gastrodon	0480	Uxie
0367	Huntail	0424	Ambipom	0481	Mesprit
0368	Gorebyss	0425	Drifloon	0482	Azelf
0369	Relicanth	0426	Drifblim	0483	Dialga
0370	Luvdisc	0427	Buneary	0484	Palkia
0371	Bagon	0428	Lopunny	0485	Heatran
0372	Shelgon	0429	Mismagius	0486	Regigigas
0373	Salamence	0430	Honchkrow	0487	Giratina
0374	Beldum	0431	Glameow	0488	Cresselia
0375	Metang	0432	Purugly	0489	Phione
0376	Metagross	0433	Chingling	0490	Manaphy
0377	Regirock	0434	Stunky	0491	Darkrai
0378	Regice	0435	Skuntank	0492	Shaymin
0379	Registeel	0436	Bronzor	0493	Arceus
0380	Latias	0437	Bronzong	0494	Victini
0381	Latios	0438	Bonsly	0495	Snivy

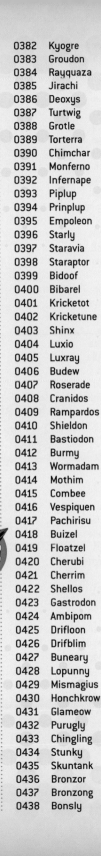

0496	Servine	0553	Krookodile	0610	Axew
0497	Serperior	0554	Darumaka	0611	Fraxure
0498	Tepig	0555	Darmanitan	0612	Haxorus
0499	Pignite	0556	Maractus	0613	Cubchoo
0500	Emboar	0557	Dwebble	0614	Beartic
0501	Oshawott	0558	Crustle	0615	Cryogonal
0502	Dewott	0559	Scraggy	0616	Shelmet
0503	Samurott	0560	Scrafty	0617	Accelgor
0504	Patrat	0561	Sigilyph	0618	Stunfisk
0505	Watchog	0562	Yamask	0619	Mienfoo
0506	Lillipup	0563	Cofagrigus	0620	Mienshao
0507	Herdier	0564	Tirtouga	0621	Druddigon
0508	Stoutland	0565	Carracosta	0622	Golett
0509	Purrloin	0566	Archen	0623	Golurk
0510	Liepard	0567	Archeops	0624	Pawniard
0511	Pansage	0568	Trubbish	0625	Bisharp
0512	Simisage	0569	Garbodor	0626	Bouffalant
0513	Pansear	0570	Zorua	0627	Rufflet
0514	Simisear	0571	Zoroark	0628	Braviary
0515	Panpour	0572	Minccino	0629	Vullaby
0516	Simipour	0573	Cinccino	0630	Mandibuzz
0517	Munna	0574	Gothita	0631	Heatmor
0518	Musharna	0575	Gothorita	0632	Durant
0519	Pidove	0576	Gothitelle	0633	Deino
0520	Tranquill	0577	Solosis	0634	Zweilous
0521	Unfezant	0578	Duosion	0635	Hydreigon
0522	Blitzle	0579	Reuniclus	0636	Larvesta
0523	Zebstrika	0580	Ducklett	0637	Volcarona
0524	Roggenrola	0581	Swanna	0638	Cobalion
0525	Boldore	0582	Vanillite	0639	Terrakion
0526	Gigalith	0583	Vanillish	0640	Virizion
0527	Woobat	0584	Vanilluxe	0641	Tornadus
0528	Swoobat	0585	Deerling	0642	Thundurus
0529	Drilbur	0586	Sawsbuck	0643	Reshiram
0530	Excadrill	0587	Emolga	0644	Zekrom
0531	Audino	0588	Karrablast	0645	Landorus
0532	Timburr	0589	Escavalier	0646	Kyurem
0533	Gurdurr	0590	Foongus	0647	Keldeo
0534	Conkeldurr	0591	Amoonguss	0648	Meloetta
0535	Tympole	0592	Frillish	0649	Genesect
0536	Palpitoad	0593	Jellicent	0650	Chespin
0537	Seismitoad	0594	Alomomola	0651	Quilladin
0538	Throh	0595	Joltik	0652	Chesnaught
0539	Sawk	0596	Galvantula	0653	Fennekin
0540	Sewaddle	0597	Ferroseed	0654	Braixen
0541	Swadloon	0598	Ferrothorn	0655	Delphox
0542	Leavanny	0599	Klink	0656	Froakie
0543	Venipede	0600	Klang	0657	Frogadier
0544	Whirlipede	0601	Klinklang	0658	Greninja
0545	Scolipede	0602	Tynamo	0659	Bunnelby
0546	Cottonee	0603	Eelektrik	0660	Diggersby
0547	Whimsicott	0604	Eelektross	0661	Fletchling
0548	Petilil	0605	Elgyem	0662	Fletchinder
0549	Lilligant	0606	Beheeyem	0663	Talonflame
0550	Basculin	0607	Litwick	0664	Scatterbug
0551	Sandile	0608	Lampent	0665	Spewpa
0552	Krokorok	0609	Chandelure	0666	Vivillon

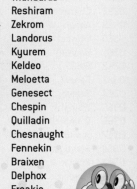

0667 Litleo	0724 Decidueye	0781 Dhelmise
0668 Pyroar	0725 Litten	0782 Jangmo-o
0669 Flabébé	0726 Torracat	0783 Hakamo-o
0670 Floette	0727 Incineroar	0784 Kommo-o
0671 Florges	0728 Popplio	0785 Tapu Koko
0672 Skiddo	0729 Brionne	0786 Tapu Lele
0673 Gogoat	0730 Primarina	0787 Tapu Bulu
0674 Pancham	0731 Pikipek	0788 Tapu Fini
0675 Pangoro	0732 Trumbeak	0789 Cosmog
0676 Furfrou	0733 Toucannon	0790 Cosmoem
0677 Espurr	0734 Yungoos	0791 Solgaleo
0678 Meowstic	0735 Gumshoos	0792 Lunala
0679 Honedge	0736 Grubbin	0793 Nihilego
0680 Doublade	0737 Charjabug	0794 Buzzwole
0681 Aegislash	0738 Vikavolt	0795 Pheromosa
0682 Spritzee	0739 Crabrawler	0796 Xurkitree
0683 Aromatisse	0740 Crabominable	0797 Celesteela
0684 Swirlix	0741 Oricorio	0798 Kartana
0685 Slurpuff	0742 Cutiefly	0799 Guzzlord
0686 Inkay	0743 Ribombee	0800 Necrozma
0687 Malamar	0744 Rockruff	0801 Magearna
0688 Binacle	0745 Lycanroc	0802 Marshadow
0689 Barbaracle	0746 Wishiwashi	0803 Poipole
0690 Skrelp	0747 Mareanie	0804 Naganadel
0691 Dragalge	0748 Toxapex	0805 Stakataka
0692 Clauncher	0749 Mudbray	0806 Blacephalon
0693 Clawitzer	0750 Mudsdale	0807 Zeraora
0694 Helioptile	0751 Dewpider	0808 Meltan
0695 Heliolisk	0752 Araquanid	0809 Melmetal
0696 Tyrunt	0753 Fomantis	0810 Grookey
0697 Tyrantrum	0754 Lurantis	0811 Thwackey
0698 Amaura	0755 Morelull	0812 Rillaboom
0699 Aurorus	0756 Shiinotic	0813 Scorbunny
0700 Sylveon	0757 Salandit	0814 Raboot
0701 Hawlucha	0758 Salazzle	0815 Cinderace
0702 Dedenne	0759 Stufful	0816 Sobble
0703 Carbink	0760 Bewear	0817 Drizzile
0704 Goomy	0761 Bounsweet	0818 Inteleon
0705 Sliggoo	0762 Steenee	0819 Skwovet
0706 Goodra	0763 Tsareena	0820 Greedent
0707 Klefki	0764 Comfey	0821 Rookidee
0708 Phantump	0765 Oranguru	0822 Corvisquire
0709 Trevenant	0766 Passimian	0823 Corviknight
0710 Pumpkaboo	0767 Wimpod	0824 Blipbug
0711 Gourgeist	0768 Golisopod	0825 Dottler
0712 Bergmite	0769 Sandygast	0826 Orbeetle
0713 Avalugg	0770 Palossand	0827 Nickit
0714 Noibat	0771 Pyukumuku	0828 Thievul
0715 Noivern	0772 Type: Null	0829 Gossifleur
0716 Xerneas	0773 Silvally	0830 Eldegoss
0717 Yveltal	0774 Minior	0831 Wooloo
0718 Zygarde	0775 Komala	0832 Dubwool
0719 Diancie	0776 Turtonator	0833 Chewtle
0720 Hoopa	0777 Togedemaru	0834 Drednaw
0721 Volcanion	0778 Mimikyu	0835 Yamper
0722 Rowlet	0779 Bruxish	0836 Boltund
0723 Dartrix	0780 Drampa	0837 Rolycoly

0838 Carkol	0895 Regidrago	0952 Scovillain
0839 Coalossal	0896 Glastrier	0953 Rellor
0840 Applin	0897 Spectrier	0954 Rabsca
0841 Flapple	0898 Calyrex	0955 Flittle
0842 Appletun	0899 Wyrdeer	0956 Espathra
0843 Silicobra	0900 Kleavor	0957 Tinkatink
0844 Sandaconda	0901 Ursaluna	0958 Tinkatuff
0845 Cramorant	0902 Basculegion	0959 Tinkaton
0846 Arrokuda	0903 Sneasler	0960 Wiglett
0847 Barraskewda	0904 Overqwil	0961 Wugtrio
0848 Toxel	0905 Enamorus	0962 Bombirdier
0849 Toxtricity	0906 Sprigatito	0963 Finizen
0850 Sizzlipede	0907 Floragato	0964 Palafin
0851 Centiskorch	0908 Meowscarada	0965 Varoom
0852 Clobbopus	0909 Fuecoco	0966 Revavroom
0853 Grapploct	0910 Crocalor	0967 Cyclizar
0854 Sinistea	0911 Skeledirge	0968 Orthworm
0855 Polteageist	0912 Quaxly	0969 Glimmet
0856 Hatenna	0913 Quaxwell	0970 Glimmora
0857 Hattrem	0914 Quaquaval	0971 Greavard
0858 Hatterene	0915 Lechonk	0972 Houndstone
0859 Impidimp	0916 Oinkologne	0973 Flamigo
0860 Morgrem	0917 Tarountula	0974 Cetoddle
0861 Grimmsnarl	0918 Spidops	0975 Cetitan
0862 Obstagoon	0919 Nymble	0976 Veluza
0863 Perrserker	0920 Lokix	0977 Dondozo
0864 Cursola	0921 Pawmi	0978 Tatsugiri
0865 Sirfetch'd	0922 Pawmo	0979 Annihilape
0866 Mr. Rime	0923 Pawmot	0980 Clodsire
0867 Runerigus	0924 Tandemaus	0981 Farigiraf
0868 Milcery	0925 Maushold	0982 Dudunsparce
0869 Alcremie	0926 Fidough	0983 Kingambit
0870 Falinks	0927 Dachsbun	0984 Great Tusk
0871 Pincurchin	0928 Smoliv	0985 Scream Tail
0872 Snom	0929 Dolliv	0986 Brute Bonnet
0873 Frosmoth	0930 Arboliva	0987 Flutter Mane
0874 Stonjourner	0931 Squawkabilly	0988 Slither Wing
0875 Eiscue	0932 Nacli	0989 Sandy Shocks
0876 Indeedee	0933 Naclstack	0990 Iron Treads
0877 Morpeko	0934 Garganacl	0991 Iron Bundle
0878 Cufant	0935 Charcadet	0992 Iron Hands
0879 Copperajah	0936 Armarouge	0993 Iron Jugulis
0880 Dracozolt	0937 Ceruledge	0994 Iron Moth
0881 Arctozolt	0938 Tadbulb	0995 Iron Thorns
0882 Dracovish	0939 Bellibolt	0996 Frigibax
0883 Arctovish	0940 Wattrel	0997 Arctibax
0884 Duraludon	0941 Kilowattrel	0998 Baxcalibur
0885 Dreepy	0942 Maschiff	0999 Gimmighoul
0886 Drakloak	0943 Mabosstiff	1000 Gholdengo
0887 Dragapult	0944 Shroodle	1001 Wo-Chien
0888 Zacian	0945 Grafaiai	1002 Chien-Pao
0889 Zamazenta	0946 Bramblin	1003 Ting-Lu
0890 Eternatus	0947 Brambleghast	1004 Chi-Yu
0891 Kubfu	0948 Toedscool	1005 Roaring Moon
0892 Urshifu	0949 Toedscruel	1006 Iron Valiant
0893 Zarude	0950 Klawf	1007 Koraidon
0894 Regieleki	0951 Capsakid	1008 Miraidon